TURKISH PARAMILITARISM IN
NORTHERN KURDISTAN

TURKISH PARAMILITARISM IN NORTHERN KURDISTAN

State Violence in the 1990s

Ayhan Işık

EDINBURGH
University Press

Edinburgh University Press is one of the leading university presses in the UK. We publish academic books and journals in our selected subject areas across the humanities and social sciences, combining cutting-edge scholarship with high editorial and production values to produce academic works of lasting importance. For more information visit our website: edinburghuniversitypress.com

Edinburgh University Press Ltd
13 Infirmary Street
Edinburgh EH1 1LT

First published in hardback by Edinburgh University Press 2024

Typeset in 11/15 EB Garamond by
IDSUK (DataConnection) Ltd

A CIP record for this book is available from the British Library

ISBN 978 1 3995 0598 7 (hardback)
ISBN 978 1 3995 0599 4 (paperback)
ISBN 978 1 3995 0600 7 (webready PDF)
ISBN 978 1 3995 0601 4 (epub)

CONTENTS

ILLUSTRATIONS

ACKNOWLEDGEMENTS

This book is based on my doctoral research. Many people and organisations have made important contributions in different ways, both during my PhD and postdoctoral period and during the preparation of this book. First of all, I would like to express my special thanks to my PhD supervisors Prof. Dr Uğur Ümit Üngör and Prof. Dr Ido de Haan for their support and valuable guidance throughout the research process. Besides, my colleague Dr Iva Vukusic, with whom I worked in the same project, made an important contribution to my work. For this, I am grateful. In addition, I would like to extend my sincere gratitude to Utrecht University, the Department of History, and my colleagues for their support and the wonderful working environment they created during my research. I am also grateful to my friends Assoc. Prof. Joost Jongerden, Dr Ruken Şengül and Dr Onur Günay, who read the whole book and made very important criticisms and contributions to the completion of this study with their suggestions. My sincere thanks also go to my friends Behzat Hıroğlu, Çağrı Kurt, Dr Özlem Has and Dr Adnan Çelik, who always assisted me during my research and gave me access to many sources. I am also thankful to my dear editor Andy Hilton, who read and edited all the text at various intervals, to dear editors of Edinburgh University Press and referees for their guidance through the review process.

I would also like to express my sincere thanks to my colleagues Prof. Dr Pieter Lagrou, Dr Mazyar Khoojinian and Ararat Apaligan from the

Department of Modern and Contemporary Worlds (MMC), Université Libre de Bruxelles, who made it possible for me to prepare this book during my postdoctoral research. I would also like to express my sincere thanks to the staff of the International Institute of Social Studies (ISS), Erasmus University Rotterdam, where I was a visiting researcher during the same period, and especially to my colleagues and friends Dr Jeff Handmaker and Dr Zeynep Kaşlı.

I would like to thank the Dutch Research Council (*Nederlandse Organisatie voor Wetenschappelijk Onderzoek*, NWO), which provides funds for the realisation of the Paramilitarism, the State and Organised Crime project of which I was part. My thanks also go to several institutions – the Human Rights Association (Diyarbakır and Istanbul Branches), Truth Justice Memory Center/*Hafıza Merkezi*, GÖÇ-DER (Migrants' Association for Social Solidarity and Culture), İsmail Beşikci Vakfı Research Library, NIOD Institute for War, Holocaust and Genocide Studies, Research School Political History and International Institute of Social Studies – for providing access to their archives and use of their library facilities and allowing me to attend their conferences during my research. I would like to give special thanks to all of the members of *Toplum ve Kuram* journal and Zan Institute, who have supported my research in different ways from the beginning.

I conducted forty-one interviews during my research in six countries and more than ten cities. I would like to express my sincere thanks to all of the interviewees for accepting to be interviewed. Theirs has been a vital contribution to this work.

I owe my most sincere gratitude to my family for their motivation, patience, continuous moral support and love.

PRINCIPAL ABBREVIATIONS

AKP	*Adalet ve Kalkınma Partisi* (Justice and Development Party)
ANAP	*Anavatan Partisi* (Motherland Party)
ASALA	Armenian Secret Army for the Liberation of Armenia
CHP	*Cumhuriyet Halk Partisi* (Republican People's Party)
CKMP	*Cumhuriyetçi Köylü Millet Partisi* (Republican Villagers Nation Party)
CUP	*İttihat ve Terakki Cemiyeti* (Committee of Union and Progress)
DDKO	*Devrimci Doğu Kültür Ocakları* (Revolutionary Cultural Hearts of the East)
DEP	*Demokrasi Partisi* (Democracy Party)
DYP	*Doğru Yol Partisi* (True Path Party)
GÖÇ-DER	*Göç Edenler Sosyal Yardımlaşma ve Kültür Derneği* (Migrants' Association for Social Solidarity and Culture)
HRW	Human Rights Watch
İHD	*İnsan Hakları Derneği* (Human Rights Association)
JİTEM	*Jandarma İstihbarat ve Terörle Mücadele* (Gendarmerie Intelligence and Counter-Terrorism Organisation)
LIC	low-intensity conflict
MAH	*Milli Emniyet Hizmeti* (National Security Service)
MBK	*Milli Birlik Komitesi* (National Unity Committee)
MGK	*Milli Güvenlik Kurulu* (National Security Council)

MHP   *Milliyetçi Hareket Partisi* (Nationalist Movement Party)
MİT   *Milli İstihbarat Teşkilatı* (National Intelligence Organisation)
MSP   *Millî Selâmet Partisi* (National Salvation Party)
MTTB   *Milli Türk Talebe Birliği* (National Turkish Students Union)
NATO   North Atlantic Treaty Organisation
NGO   Non-governmental organisation
OHAL   *Olağanüstü Hal* (State of Emergency)
ÖHD   *Özel Harp Dairesi* (Special Warfare Department)
PGM   Pro-government militias
PKK   *Partiya Karkerên Kurdistan* (Kurdistan Workers' Party)
RP   *Refah Partisi* (Welfare Party)
STK   *Seferberlik Tetkik Kurulu* (Mobilisation Research Council)
TBMM   *Türkiye Büyük Millet Meclisi* (Grand National Assembly of Turkey)
TİHV   *Türkiye İnsan Hakları Vakfı* (Human Rights Foundation of Turkey)
TİP   *Türkiye İşçi Partisi* (Workers Party of Turkey)
TKMD   *Türkiye Komünizmle Mücadele Dernekleri* (Associations of Struggle Against Communism)
TMT   *Türk Mukavemet Teşkilatı* (Turkish Resistance Organisation)

INTRODUCTION

There have been armed conflicts of varying lengths of time and levels of intensity between Kurdish political movements and the Turkish state regarding the rights of Kurds and territorial sovereignty over northern Kurdistan (south-east Turkey) for almost a century. The longest and most severe of these conflicts has been that involving the Kurdistan Workers' Party (*Partiya Karkerên Kurdistan*, PKK), which has been ongoing for more than forty years now at a cost of tens of thousands of lives. The PKK launched its armed struggle against the Turkish state in August 1984. As the conflict developed into a full-blown guerrilla or asymmetric war, the state responded by establishing various new institutions, some of which had a paramilitary character. This book investigates the ways in which these paramilitary organisations emerged, functioned and were deactivated. The focus is placed on the most violent decade of the war, the notorious 1990s, the most intensely violent period in the hundred-year history of violence in northern Kurdistan.[1]

---

[1] Serhat Bozkurt and Alişan Akpınar (eds), *Osmanlı Kürdistanı*, 1. baskı (Istanbul: bgst Yayınları, 2011), 20–1. The name 'northern Kurdistan' (Kurdish: *Bakurê Kurdistanê*, North Kurdistan) is used here to denote a historically, demographically, culturally and politically specified territory situated in the (south-)eastern part of Turkey (i.e. for the Turkish part of a geography named 'Kurdistan' divided between the countries of Iraq, Iran, Syria and Turkey); also used, both popularly and in the academic literature, are 'Turkish Kurdistan', and 'the East' and 'South-East' (i.e. of Turkey).

It was in the middle of the decade, in 1996, when a Mercedes car carrying four people crashed into a truck near the township of Susurluk in western Turkey, triggering a public scandal. Three of the four occupants of the car died instantly: Abdullah Çatlı, Gonca Us (his girlfriend) and Hüseyin Kocadağ. Çatlı was a mafia leader and well-known radical right-wing militant wanted by Interpol for his involvement in assassinations, while Kocadağ was a director of the Istanbul School of Police. The other passenger was Sedat Bucak MP, head of a prominent Kurdish tribe (*aşiret*) that was regarded as the most significant part of the state-established Village Guards (*Köy Korucuları*), the largest paramilitary organisation in Turkey. The car was also full of sophisticated, unlicensed weapons.[2]

The 'Susurluk incident' exposed the network of relationships between criminal and paramilitary organisations operating in northern Kurdistan, on the one hand, and state institutions and government authorities, on the other. These organisations ranged between the clandestine (such as local mafia gangs) and the legally enshrined (like the Village Guards). The MP in the car, Sedat Bucak, was known to be close to the then Turkish prime minister, Tansu Çiller, who stated her government's approach to the conflict with the PKK in blunt terms: 'Those who shoot bullets and those who are the targets of bullets in the name of the state are both honourable . . . they are heroes'.[3]

The shady relations within the state were not revealed for the first or the last time by the Susurluk scandal, however. Notably, a report prepared by the National Intelligence Organization (*Millî İstihbarat Teşkilatı*, MİT) showing the relationship between the mafia, bureaucracy and state institutions had been leaked to the press a decade previously, in 1987. Similarly, twenty-five years after the Susurluk scandal, the confessions of the ultranationalist, pan-Turkist, mafia-leader Sedat Peker have recently made waves in Turkey.

---

[2] Hamit Bozarslan, *Network-Building, Ethnicity and Violence in Turkey* (Abu Dhabi: ECSSR, 1999); Elise Massicard, '"Gangs in Uniform" in Turkey: Politics at the Articulation between Security Institutions and the Criminal World', in *Organized Crime and States: The Hidden Face of Politics*, ed. Jean-Louis Briquet (Basingstoke: Palgrave Macmillan, 2010), 41–71.

[3] Mehtap Söyler, *The Turkish Deep State: State Consolidation, Civil–Military Relations and Democracy* (Abingdon: Routledge, 2015), 147.

Peker has enjoyed relations with politicians, bureaucrats, the military and intelligence officials and allegedly participated in the war against the PKK and many Kurdish civilians who support it since the 1990s. In 2020, he released a series of ten videos making claims and confessions that once again shook Turkey's politics.[4] Peker made statements in these videos targeting both the former and current interior ministers (Mehmet Ağar and Süleyman Soylu), along with other politicians, former intelligence officers, high-ranking army and police officials, business people and journalists. Finally, in mid-2021, he took aim at President Erdoğan. Indeed, the history of modern Turkey expresses an anti-democratic political regime in which dark relations have repeatedly emerged.

The Susurluk incident and the reactions it triggered were particularly significant in terms of the evolution of relations between the state and para-military organisations. In the wake of the public outcry and media coverage, parliament installed a commission to investigate these relations. The report prepared by the Susurluk Research Commission revealed an illegal organised crime network and detailed extensive relationships between members of paramilitary groups, right-wing parties, mafia leaders, MPs and military and administrative personnel.[5] According to the report, members of this network had committed many crimes against civilians, especially against Kurdish businessmen blacklisted by the state and were involved in narcotics trafficking and the underground economy generally.[6] Thus, the Susurluk incident prompted a new debate around the origins and functions of the paramilitary organisations in Turkey, particularly regarding their role in the ongoing war against the PKK, while the various links among the legal and non-legal groups led to many discussions about the nature and structure of the Turkish state.

The origins and history of paramilitary groups in Turkey can be traced in three different episodes, thus: influences from the late Ottoman Empire,[7]

[4] See https://www.youtube.com/c/sedatpekerreis/videos.
[5] Kutlu Savaş, *Susurluk Raporu*, 1997, https://tr.wikisource.org/wiki/Susurluk_Raporu_(Kutlu_Sava%C5%9F).
[6] Massicard, 'Gangs in Uniform'.
[7] Şemsa Özar, Nesrin Uçarlar and Osman Aytar, *From Past to Present a Paramilitary Organization in Turkey: Village Guard System* (Diyarbakır: Disa Yayınları, 2013), http://disa.org.tr/pdf_media/SONKORUCULUKKTAPNG.pdf.

NATO's anti-communist secret agencies in the 1950s and '80s,[8] and the conflict between the Turkish state and the PKK. Regarding the latter, underground paramilitary organisations had been used against Turkish and Kurdish leftist movements prior to the 1980 *coup d'état*.[9] After the coup, the PKK, which had located its base outside the country, in Iraq, remained the only effective opposition against the Turkish state. Subsequently, as it enjoyed success in its armed struggle, paramilitary forces emerged as a vital part of the state response and one of the most important actors in the conflict. Because, as will be discussed in the following pages, the Turkish army was an unwieldy organisation, organised according to conventional warfare, cold war and NATO rules. It was not organised for irregular guerrilla warfare. Paramilitary groups, on the other hand, became mobile, more familiar with local areas, legally irresponsible and therefore very useful apparatus for conflicts.

During the harshest years of the war, various semi-formal and informal forces emerged within the formal structure of the state. In addition to the formally established and legally enshrined security forces – the intelligence service (MİT) and the Village Guards as well as the military (army, etc.) and rural-based military police (*Jandarma*) – these included the Special Warfare Department (*Özel Harp Dairesi*, ÖHD), the Gendarmerie Intelligence and Counter-Terrorism (*Jandarma İstihbarat ve Terörle Mücadele*, JİTEM) and the Special Operations Department (*Özel Harekat Dairesi Başkanlığı*). The relations of all these forces and their hierarchical structure within the state institutions and right-wing parties were quite complex.[10]

The war between the Turkish state and the PKK had devastating consequences. In 2013, The Human Rights Investigation Commission of the Grand National Assembly of Turkey published a report stating that between 1984 and 2013, a period of 'terror and violence', 35,576 people died; 7,918 of them were public servants (police, soldiers and members of paramilitary forces) and

---

[8] Mehtap Söyler, 'Informal Institutions, Forms of State and Democracy: The Turkish Deep State', *Democratization* 20, no. 2 (2013): 316.

[9] Ergun Aydınoğlu, *Türkiye Solu, 1960–1980: Bir Amneziğin Anıları* (Istanbul: Versus Kitap, 2007).

[10] Söyler, 'Informal Institutions, Forms of State and Democracy'; Massicard, 'Gangs in Uniform'.

the remainder mainly guerrillas and Kurdish civilians.[11] Paramilitary organisations were found to have had a significant responsibility in the violation of the most basic human rights and the deaths of civilians. The war saw thousands of extrajudicial executions,[12] unsolved murders[13] and enforced disappearances[14] (these three concepts, which are often emphasised when referring to human rights violations, are different from each other). It also saw military evacuations of more than 4,000 villages and towns, leading to the forced migration of an estimated 2.5 million people.[15]

This book focuses on how paramilitary groups emerged, developed, functioned and disappeared in the context of the war in Turkey in the 1990s. It describes and examines the foundations and the development of the paramilitary organisations, as well as their relations with the state. Also, in order to examine the functioning of paramilitary organisations in more detail, it focuses

[11] TBMM İnsan Haklarını İnceleme Komisyonu, *Terör ve Şiddet Olayları Kapsamında Yaşam Hakkı İhlallerini İnceleme Raporu* (Ankara: TBMM, 2013).

[12] 'Extrajudicial Killings', *OMCT*, accessed 24 January 2023, https://www.omct.org/en/what-we-do/extrajudicial-killings. 'Extrajudicial killings, or extrajudicial executions, happen when someone in an official position deliberately kills a person without any legal process. Such arbitrary deprivations of life, which can also be carried out by militias, death squads or other non-State actors, often target political opponents, activists, or marginalized groups.'

[13] TBMM, *Ülkemizin Çeşitli Yörelerinde İşlenmiş Faili Meçhul Siyasal Cinayetler Konusunda Meclis Araştırma Komisyonu* (Ankara: TBMM, 1995), 12. '"Unsolved political murder" means a person who has been the victim of an act of murder because of his/her political opinion or used to describe the situation where the perpetrators of politically motivated murder remain unknown.'

[14] Özgür Sevgi Göral, Ayhan Işık and Özlem Kaya, *The Unspoken Truth: Enforced Disappearances* (Istanbul: Truth Justice Memory Center, 2013), 11. 'Enforced disappearance or enforced or involuntary disappearance in international literature, is generally referred to in Turkey as "*kayıp*" (lit. "missing") or "*gözaltında kayıp*" (lit. "missing under custody") . . . Enforced disappearance, on the other hand, is a much more appropriate term for this deed for a number of reasons: it refers to the use of force; it makes it clear that the enforced disappearance does not only happen by being taken officially into custody; and because it differentiates this phenomenon from other forms of disappearance.'

[15] Namık Kemal Dinç, ed., *Stories of Migration 'One Who's Seen Pain Doesn't Inflict Pain Upon Others'*, trans. Kolektif Atölye (Istanbul: Göç-Der Yayınları, 2008), http://www.gocder.com/sites/default/files/proje-photo/goc-hikayeleri-en.pdf; Dilek Kurban *et al.*, *Zorunlu Göç Ile Yüzleşmek: Türkiye'de Yerinden Edilme Sonrası Vatandaşlığın İnşası* (Istanbul: TESEV, 2006).

on two areas where intense violence occurred: the province of Batman and the city-district of Cizre (in the province of Şırnak).

Definition of Paramilitarism

There is more than one definition of paramilitarism, but the term is mostly used for pro-state armed groups operating in some way outside of the official state institutions of the army and police.[16] The term 'paramilitarism' typically refers to the state's deployment of and reliance on (pro-state) semi-formal or informal armed groups as a form of security enforcement. This certainly applies to Turkey in the 1990s. As discussed below, the primary characteristics of paramilitarism include links with states, hierarchical structures, legal and formal positions, extra-legal actions and violence, plausible deniability and economic expectations and relations.

In terms of their relations with the dominant force of the state, paramilitary groups may be considered as the opposite to 'terrorists' (where, because of the inequivalent opposition, it is the latter that are presented as problematic, highlighted in standard media outlets, etc.). Names for these pro-state armed groups include 'vigilantes', '(pro-government) militia' and 'death squads' as well as 'paramilitaries'. Against opposition armed forces, the terms 'counter-terrorist' and 'contra-guerrilla' can also cover paramilitary forces and their activities.[17]

---

[16] Uğur Ümit Üngör, *Paramilitarism: Mass Violence in the Shadow of the State* (Oxford: Oxford University Press, 2019), 6.

[17] Alex Alvarez, 'Militias and Genocide', *War Crimes, Genocide, & Crimes Against Humanity* 2 (2006): 1–33; Bruce B. Campbell, 'Death Squads: Definition, Problems and Historical Context', in *Death Squads in Global Perspective: Murder with Deniability*, eds Arthur D. Brenner and Bruce B. Campbell (Basingstoke: Palgrave Macmillan, 2002), 1–26; David Kowalewski, 'Counterinsurgent Vigilantism and Public Response: A Philippine Case Study', *Sociological Perspectives* 34, no. 2 (1991): 127–44; T. David Mason and Dale A. Krane, 'The Political Economy of Death Squads: Toward a Theory of the Impact of State-Sanctioned Terror', *International Studies Quarterly* 33, no. 2 (1989): 175–98; Kay B. Warren, 'Death Squads and Wider Complicities: Dilemmas for the Anthropology of Violence', in *Death Squad: The Anthropology of State Terror*, ed. Jeffrey A. Sluka (Philadelphia: University of Pennsylvania Press, 2000); Julie Mazzei, *Death Squads or Self-Defense Forces?: How Paramilitary Groups Emerge and Challenge Democracy in Latin America* (Chapel Hill: University of North Carolina Press, 2009); Adam Jones, 'Parainstitutional Violence in Latin America', *Latin American Politics and Society* 46, no. 4 (1 December 2004): 127–48;

Alvarez defines paramilitary groups by contrasting them with official military units of the state:

> First, modern military organisations tend to be rigidly organized along regimental lines while paramilitaries are usually less formally organized with a looser structure . . . Second, militaries are composed of professionals whereas paramilitaries are made up of amateurs . . . Third, the military also clearly and overtly acts on the authority of the state, while the connection between paramilitaries and the government tends to be much more obscured . . . Fourth and last, paramilitary groups often act for personal gain and profit, while members of the military and police do not generally profit personally from their activities.[18]

Although mostly affiliated with governments, paramilitary groups are distinct from the army in Turkey (which deals with the external security of the country), the gendarmerie (a rural, militarised police force) and the police (responsible for internal security in urban areas). According to the above definitions, there are structural, professional, economic and hierarchical differences between paramilitary forces and the official military institutions of the state.

Another way of defining 'paramilitaries' is to follow Bruce Campbell's description of death squads:

> Death squads are clandestine and usually irregular organisations, often paramilitary in nature, which carry out extrajudicial executions and other violent acts (torture, rape, arson, bombing, etc.) against clearly defined individuals or groups of people. Murder is their primary or even sole activity . . . Death squads may be a part of a government strategy of state terrorism . . . Moreover,

Javier Auyero, *Routine Politics and Violence in Argentina: The Gray Zone of State Power* (Cambridge: Cambridge University Press, 2007); Stathis N. Kalyvas, *The Logic of Violence in Civil War* (Cambridge: Cambridge University Press, 2006); Michael Mann, *The Dark Side of Democracy: Explaining Ethnic Cleansing* (Cambridge: Cambridge University Press, 2005); Ariel I. Ahram, 'Pro-Government Militias and the Repertoires of Illicit State Violence', *Studies in Conflict & Terrorism* 39, no. 3 (3 March 2016): 207–26; Sabine C. Carey and Neil J. Mitchell, 'Progovernment Militias', *Annual Review of Political Science* 20, no. 1 (2017): 127–47.

[18] Alvarez, 'Militias and Genocide', 5–6.

death squads exist to act outside of the law: by definition, their 'job' is to commit extrajudicial murder.[19]

Death squads are probably the most violent examples of paramilitary formations. They generally target specific individuals and groups. According to Mason and Krane,

> The term 'death squad' denotes those military, paramilitary, and irregular units that engage in violent acts against a population in order to deter them from lending support to opposition groups ... They may consist of secret police, special counterinsurgency units, or regular units of the armed forces engaged in various forms of institutionalised violence. They may also consist of armed units structured along military lines but organisationally autonomous from state security forces, at least in a formal and legal sense.[20]

Pro-government militias (PGMs) also have paramilitary characteristics. Carey and Mitchell argue that such militias have various forms and functions:

> Some PGMs act as the president's personal guard. Others represent the armed wing of a ruling party or are organized and controlled by the military. Some groups boast hundreds of thousands of members. Elsewhere, fewer than a hundred people constitute a PGM.[21]

According to Carey and Mitchell, such units mainly emerge in 'third world' or in 'weak states', but they are also deployed elsewhere, for instance by the United States in Iraq and Afghanistan.[22] Jentzsch, Kalyvas and Schubiger argue that PGMs have 'emerged in all kinds of civil wars, including irregular civil wars in which states seek high-quality local information ..., ethnic or separatist insurgencies ..., wars against foreign occupiers ... as well as conventional and symmetric nonconventional civil wars ...'[23] They also

---

[19] Campbell, 'Death Squads', 1–6.

[20] Mason and Krane, 'The Political Economy of Death Squads', 178.

[21] Carey and Mitchell, 'Progovernment Militias', 130.

[22] Ibid., 129.

[23] Corinna Jentzsch, Stathis N. Kalyvas and Livia Isabella Schubiger, 'Militias in Civil Wars', *Journal of Conflict Resolution* 59, no. 5 (1 August 2015): 757.

explain that the groups vary in terms of their size, operations, tasks, organisations and membership.

Vigilantism can be seen as another form of paramilitarism. This notion characterises a larger social group that is organised in a time of unrest as an auxiliary paramilitary force and used by the state as part of its counterinsurgency policy against dissidents or insurgents. Kowalewski argues that vigilantes arise for two reasons: first, they 'arise out of a generalised public unease about disruption' resulting from minority challenges to the political order, and second, they grow out of the 'need of regimes to mobilise auxiliary forces to counter growing dissident threats to their power'. Kowalewski analyses both models for vigilantes in the Philippines and argues that the second model seems superior. The second model, of social formations used by regimes as auxiliary forces, also has similarities to paramilitary groups.[24] A little differently from the case of the Philippines (as discussed below), the pro-state vigilante groups in Turkey were very actively used against both religious minorities and ethnically non-Turk dissident 'threats' at different times, especially from the 1930s to the 1990s.

Paramilitary groups are driven by a variety of motives. One important motive is economic gain.[25] Thus, paramilitary groups may function in a nebulous area between military and mercenary activities:[26]

> In many ways, militias can be seen as a type of mercenary organisation. Historically, mercenary groups have been perceived as military forces that operate solely for pay rather than out of loyalty or affiliation to a specific cause. Paramilitary groups seem to operate in a nebulous area between the two extremes of pure military and pure mercenary.[27]

[24] Kowalewski, 'Counterinsurgent Vigilantism and Public Response', 127–44.

[25] Alvarez, 'Militias and Genocide'; Mason and Krane, 'The Political Economy of Death Squads'; Ryan Gingeras, *Heroin, Organized Crime, and the Making of Modern Turkey* (Oxford: Oxford University Press, 2014); Frank Bovenkerk and Yücel Yeşilgöz, 'The Turkish Mafia and the State', in *Organised Crime in Europe: Concepts, Patterns and Control Policies in the European Union and Beyond*, eds C. Fijnaut and L. Paoli (Dordrecht: Springer Netherlands, 2004), 585–602.

[26] Alvarez, 'Militias and Genocide'.

[27] Ibid., 6.

Yet, paramilitary organisations differ from mercenaries in that the latter use weapons mainly for economic gain, while paramilitaries are mobilised for many other motives (ideology, politics, ethnic identities, religious beliefs, etc.). Paramilitaries also differ from mercenaries in terms of scope, and they bear arms and fight not only for private reasons but also for a host of political reasons. Paramilitaries often pursue power in a consistent attempt to influence the distribution of power within the state.

The characteristic features of these PGMs are also related to their organisational forms, as emphasised in Üngör's recent study:

> Paramilitarism can then be conceived of as an umbrella concept that covers a broad continuum, distinguished by levels of state involvement. At the left end of this spectrum, there are spontaneous, bottom-up initiatives such as local vigilantes, lynch mobs, and self-defence groups, and on the other end of the continuum stand the much more organized, top-down, professional paramilitary units of the state.[28]

Therefore, paramilitarism is understood in terms of irregular armed groups and defined according to the following features. First, they are used as pro-state semi-formal or informal forces, mainly against ethnic insurgencies or political opponents during internal violent conflicts in which a state faces an armed threat (here, the PKK). Second, they are part of the state's military and political strategy (used sometimes in conjunction with but nevertheless separately from the standard security forces). Third, they are hierarchically flexible (so their structure is different from the states' official security forces). Fourth, the state denies the existence of or its responsibility for these groups (and, therefore, also the acts of violence they commit). Fifth, structurally, they can be organised by bottom-up initiatives and top-down by the state.

Additionally, the semi-formal and informal aspects can be defined in the case of Turkey. First, the Village Guards and special police teams can be evaluated in the semi-formal category. Both of these groups were formed according to Turkish law. However, the recruitment of members of special police teams was not transparent and they wereoften chosen from among members of

---

[28] Üngör, *Paramilitarism*, 7.

ultranationalist parties. The Village Guard were uniformed and legally attached to the gendarmerie but did not serve full time, some of them also continuing their work as farmers or artisans. Their recruitment was determined either by force or by pro-government tribes and families, and they acted in conjunction with other units of the army, special police teams and other informal paramilitary groups. Thus, semi-formal paramilitary groups had a status that was partly state controlled and partly local and in which a variety of dynamics were in play. Second, the informal category of paramilitary group can be used for JİTEM, which is very clearly denied by government agencies, as a paramilitary group that everyone knew about, but was neither formally established nor officially declared.

Paramilitarism in the Turkish Context

All of the types of paramilitary organisations discussed above are represented here. The most well-known is the Gendarmerie Intelligence and Counter-Terrorism Organisation (*Jandarma İstihbarat ve Terörle Mücadele*, JİTEM), a paramilitary group active in the 1990s that can be best labelled as an organisation of death squads.[29] JİTEM units were employed as a tool for murder due to their invisibility and because they did not fall under any official jurisdiction. Thus, the government could always claim they had no control over these units.[30] As mentioned above, the Village Guard was the largest paramilitary organisation. Previously a semi-legal structure (institutionally enabled but not much organised), this was formally established on 28 March 1985 as a 'temporary Village Guard system'.[31] A third paramilitary organisation, the Police Special Operations Department (or Special Police

---

[29] Martin van Bruinessen, 'Turkey's Death Squads', *Middle East Report*, no. 199 (1996): 20–3. http://www.merip.org/mer/mer199/turkeys-death-squads.

[30] 'Modern states have a habit of subcontracting. In certain crisis situations (and here the literature on state violence in general is still very useful), this subcontracting can occur even at the risk of diminishing the states' legitimacy by violating the law, or by compromising its monopoly on the use of violence.' Campbell, 'Death Squads', 17.

[31] 'During the 1990s when the clashes were at their peak, the number of this armed force was over 90 thousand. The village guards were under the command of the village headman administratively and the Commander of the Gendarmerie Squad in professional matters'. Özar *et al.*, *From Past to Present*, 9.

Teams, *Özel Harekat Timleri*), was reorganised mostly due to the growth of the conflict in 1993.[32] A fourth, Hizbullah, emerged in the early 1980s as an Islamic illegally armed organisation that fought against the PKK, pro-PKK Kurdish civilians and rival Islamic communities.[33] There were some other groups besides these, whose role in the war is still unclear but which committed extra-legal violence throughout their existence and in various ways affected the state's monopoly of violence.

Regarding the study of these organisations, there is an emerging body of literature on the Turkish paramilitary forces during the war waged between the Turkish state and the PKK. Most studies, however, still focus on the two main actors of the conflict, the Turkish state and the PKK, disregarding the paramilitary forces and their roles (discussions on paramilitarism can mostly be found in the details of these studies). Two important PhD dissertations related to this field have been written in recent years. Özlem Has discusses the structures and motivation of paramilitary perpetrators and their ties with the law through the paramilitary group JİTEM;[34] Yeşim Yaprak Yıldız focuses on the confessions of perpetrators, their rhetorical and performative strategies and relations with state institutions during the conflicts in northern Kurdistan.[35] In contrast to the limited academic literature, journalists and NGOs have made many investigations and contributed significantly to galvanising a public debate as well as academic discussions.

Two main lessons are to be drawn from this literature. First, the history of the paramilitary organisations active in the 1990s was rooted in the three episodes in the development of the Turkish state listed above (the late Ottoman Empire, the influence of NATO between the 1950s and '90s, and the battle against leftist and Kurdish movements during the 1970s). Second, paramilitary organisations emerged as a key element in the state

---

[32] Söyler, *The Turkish Deep State*, 143–55.

[33] Ruşen Çakır, *Derin Hizbullah: İslamcı Şiddetin Geleceği*, 2. baskı (Istanbul: Metis Yayınları, 2011); Mehmet Kurt, *Din, Şiddet ve Aidiyet: Türkiye'de Hizbullah* (Istanbul: İletişim Yayıncılık, 2015).

[34] Özlem Has, 'Structured Agencies of Paramilitaries in the Kurdish-Turkish Conflict: The JİTEM Case' (PhD diss., University of Copenhagen, 2021).

[35] Yeşim Yaprak Yıldız, '(Dis)Avowal of State Violence: Public Confessions of Perpetrators of State Violence Against Kurds in Turkey' (PhD diss., University of Cambridge, 2018).

doctrine of *low-intensity conflict* formulated in the early 1990s in response to the success of the PKK.

Recent studies have argued that the paramilitary forces in Turkey are the product of a longer-term development of these institutions since the late Ottoman Empire.[36] Ayşegül Aydın and Cem Emrence discussed the counter-insurgency policy of the Turkish state in a chapter of their work on the conflict between the PKK and the Turkish state. They argue that the state's counterinsurgency policy in the 1990s originated in the late Ottoman Empire.[37]

Several authors have explored the development of the paramilitary forces or informal institutions in the late Ottoman Empire and the Republic of Turkey.[38] They frame these continuities in terms of threat to national security, undeveloped democracy and gang activity. The late Ottoman Empire utilised diverse paramilitary groups and organisations during the Armenian genocide, against the political dissent among the Greeks in western Anatolia, and in the deportation, resettlement and persecution of Muslim populations (mainly Kurds). The nationalist activities of the non-Muslim groups (especially Armenians and Greeks) constituted an important threat to the *İttihat ve Terakki Cemiyeti* (Committee of Union and Progress, CUP) government, while paramilitaries were also used against Assyrians during World War I.[39] Thus, the

---

[36] Ayşegül Aydın and Cem Emrence, *Zones of Rebellion: Kurdish Insurgents and the Turkish State* (New York: Cornell University Press, 2015); Özar *et al.*, *From Past to Present*; Söyler, *The Turkish Deep State*; H. Akın Ünver, 'Turkey's "Deep-State" and the Ergenekon Conundrum', *Middle East Institute*, 2009, http://www.mei.edu/content/turkeys-deep-state-and-ergenekon-conundrum; Mann, *The Dark Side of Democracy*.

[37] Aydin and Emrence, *Zones of Rebellion*, 73–134.

[38] Özar *et al.*, *From Past to Present*; Ünver, 'Turkey's "Deep-State" and the Ergenekon Conundrum'; Söyler, 'Informal Institutions, Forms of State and Democracy'; Fuat Dündar, *İttihat ve Terakki'nin Müslümanları İskan Politikası (1913–1918)*, 1. baskı (Istanbul: İletişim, 2001); Ümit Cizre Sakallıoğlu, 'The Anatomy of the Turkish Military's Political Autonomy', *Comparative Politics* 29, no. 2 (1997): 151–66; Suavi Aydın and Yüksel Taşkın, *1960'tan Günümüze Türkiye Tarihi* (Istanbul: İletişim, 2014); Gingeras, *Heroin, Organized Crime, and the Making of Modern Turkey*; Bovenkerk and Yeşilgöz, 'The Turkish Mafia and the State', 585–602; Massicard, 'Gangs in Uniform'.

[39] David Gaunt, Jan Bet-Şawoce and Racho Donef, *Massacres, Resistance, Protectors: Muslim-Christian Relations in Eastern Anatolia during World War I*, 1st Gorgias Press edn (Piscataway, NJ: Gorgias Press, 2006).

traditions of establishing paramilitaries of different forms and characteristics have been preserved throughout the Republic.[40]

Focusing on the Village Guards, Şemsa Özar, Nesrin Uçarlar and Osman Aytar[41] have argued that since the establishment of the (mainly pro-state Kurdish) Hamidiye Cavalry Regiments (*Hamidiye Süvari Alayları*) during the late Ottoman Empire, the state has armed the civilian population and turned groups into paramilitary forces to be deployed against political dissenters. Similarly, Akın Ünver claims that the '"deep-state" (*derin devlet*) tradition in Turkish politics started with the revolution of 1908, during which the CUP indirectly took over the rule of Sultan Abdulhamid II, rendering subsequent sultans and governments subservient to the young Ottoman military officers.'[42] This tradition of autonomous power acting within and for a part of the state, the deep state, is an indispensable element in all discussions of the genesis of the Turkish paramilitaries.[43]

According to Mehtap Söyler's book on Turkey's deep state, paramilitarism is primarily a consequence of this structure. She agrees with Ünver that the members of the CUP created deep state institutions in the 1908 revolution and the following decade. Paramilitary groups, such as the intelligence and propaganda service of the Committee (the Special Organisation, *Teşkilat-I Mahsusa*) and the Hamidiye Regiments (now known as the Tribal Light Cavalry Regiments – *Aşiret Hafif Süvari Alayları* – as they were renamed in 1909), carried out mass deportations and massacres targeting Ottoman Armenians and facilitated the deportation of fully one third of the population by the CUP.[44]

Similarly, Özar, Ünver and Söyler point to the similarities and connections between the late Ottoman Empire and the Turkish Republic in terms of activities of paramilitary forces.[45] Instead of offering a comprehensive study

---

[40] Özar *et al.*, *From Past to Present*; Ünver, 'Turkey's "Deep-State" and the Ergenekon Conundrum'; Dündar, *İttihat ve Terakki'nin Müslümanları İskan Politikası*.

[41] Özar *et al.*, *From Past to Present*.

[42] Ünver, 'Turkey's "Deep-State" and the Ergenekon Conundrum', 3–4.

[43] Kerem Öktem, *Angry Nation: Turkey Since 1989* (London: Zed Books, 2011).

[44] Söyler, *The Turkish Deep State*, 72–8.

[45] Özar *et al.*, *From Past to Present*; Ünver, 'Turkey's "Deep-State"'; Söyler, *The Turkish Deep State*.

of these continuities, they focus on the similarities of forces with paramilitary features since the late Ottoman era. Especially, the organisation of the Village Guards as a paramilitary group has a lot of resemblances to the regiments from the late Ottoman period. Janet Klein, arguing that 'it is important to bring this connection to light and to understand the tradition out of which the contemporary organisation has grown', also highlights the continuity between the late Ottoman period and the 1990s.[46]

The ideological legitimation of paramilitary groups also emerged during the late Ottoman Empire and the period of the early Republic. At the time, political elites wanted to create a new homogeneous nation.[47] They redesigned society on the basis of a new Turkish nationalism in which all the other identities (Kurds, Alevis and non-Muslim groups) were excluded from the nation. Paramilitary groups were important instruments in the suppression of groups that were seen as a threat to a homogeneous Turkish identity.

In 1952, Turkey joined the anti-Soviet bloc of the West, NATO. As a result, the perception of the threat to the state shifted from an ethnic rivalry to a fear of communism. Several studies argue that after 1945, during the multi-party period of Turkey (previously there had been single-party rule), paramilitaries in the Republic were the product of a conspiracy of NATO, or some of the powerful NATO members.[48] For Söyler, a significant role was played by Western intelligence services (primarily, the US Central Intelligence Agency – CIA – and the British Secret Intelligence Service) and NATO in the formation of the deep state in Turkey.[49] Daniele Ganser explains that

[46] Janet Klein, 'Power in the Periphery: Hamidiye Light Cavalry and the Struggle Over Ottoman Kurdistan, 1890–1914' (PhD diss., Princeton University, 2002), 22–3.

[47] Uğur Ümit Üngör, *The Making of Modern Turkey: Nation and State in Eastern Anatolia, 1913–1950* (Oxford: Oxford University Press, 2011); Ümit Cizre, 'Ideology, Context and Interest: The Turkish Military', in *The Cambridge History of Turkey, vol. 4: Turkey in the Modern World*, ed. Reşat Kasaba (Cambridge: Cambridge University Press, 2008), 301–22; Fuat Dündar, *Modern Türkiye'nin Şifresi: İttihat ve Terakki'nin Etnisite Mühendisliği, 1913–1918*, 3. baskı (Istanbul: İletişim, 2008).

[48] Söyler, 'Informal Institutions, Forms of State and Democracy'; Daniele Ganser, *NATO's Secret Armies: Operation GLADIO and Terrorism in Western Europe* (Abingdon: Routledge, 2005); Ecevit Kılıç, *Özel Harp Dairesi* (Istanbul: Timaş Yayınları, 2010).

[49] Söyler, 'Informal Institutions, Forms of State and Democracy', 316.

NATO established secret anti-communist armies in fourteen countries (the members of NATO including Turkey). According to Ganser, 'in each country the military secret service operated as the anti-Communist army within the state in close collaboration with the CIA or the MI6 unknown to parliaments and populations'.[50] Gingeras also argues that Turkey became part of the NATO initiative to create a so-called 'stay-behind' counter espionage/ counter-insurgency programme.[51] Kemal Yamak, a former Turkish general, wrote in his memoirs that the Special Warfare Department (*Özel Harp Dairesi*, ÖHD) was established in accordance with NATO's covert operations strategy with the support of the Americans.[52]

According to several researchers, the ÖHD and MİT contributed to one of the most violent periods in recent Turkish history, the bloody 1970s.[53] In this period, right-wing extremist militias were organised by the state as paramilitary forces against the radical student movements, against the Turkish left, and against nationalist and socialist Kurdish movements. These militias were organised initially (in the mid-1960s) under the umbrella organisation of the Associations of Struggle Against Communism (*Türkiye Komünizmle Mücadele Dernekleri*, TKMD). They began their military training in commando camps in 1968 as paramilitary forces against dissenters.[54] In 1969, the Nationalist Movement Party (*Milliyetçi Hareket Partisi*, MHP) was established, within which the Idealist Youth (*Ülkücü Gençlik*) was created as its youth movement. Already before that time, in 1958, a Turkish Resistance Organisation (*Türk Mukavemet Teşkilatı*, TMT) had been established under the command and control of the ÖHD. There is convincing evidence that during the Turkish annexation of northern Cyprus in 1974, the TMT carried out massacres of Greek (and some Turkish) civilians, and that it was also involved in the confiscation of Greek property.[55] It can be argued that

---

[50] Ganser, *NATO's Secret Armies*, 1.

[51] Gingeras, *Heroin, Organized Crime, and the Making of Modern Turkey*, 228.

[52] Kılıç, *Özel Harp Dairesi*.

[53] Ünver, 'Turkey's "Deep-State" and the Ergenekon Conundrum'; Söyler, 'Informal Institutions, Forms of State and Democracy'.

[54] Aydın and Taşkın, *1960'tan Günümüze Türkiye Tarihi*, 158–9.

[55] Kılıç, *Özel Harp Dairesi*; European Court of Human Rights, *Case of Loizidou V. Turkey (Application No. 15318/89)*. Strasbourg, 18 December 1996, file:///Users/ayhanisik/Downloads/001-58007%20(2).pdf.

Cyprus offered an area of training for the ÖHD and other Turkish nationalist militias to cut their teeth in combat.[56]

Scholars like Massicard and Bozarslan trace the relations of the members of right-wing parties to informal networks within the state institutions. They explore the ways in which the right-wing extremist militias who came from Idealist Youth were used by the state during the four decades between 1960s and 1990s. High-ranking members of the Idealist Youth, including Abdullah Çatlı who died in the Susurluk accident, were reportedly used by an 'informal network' in the state against various political opposition movements from the 1970s to the 1990s.[57]

After the beginning of the war between the state and the PKK in 1984, the state both redesigned the existing paramilitary groups (like the ÖHD and right extremist militias) and also established new paramilitary groups, including the Village Guard system (1985), JİTEM and the Special Police Teams.[58] Other groups with a paramilitary character – such as the repentants (*itirafçılar*),[59] former members of the PKK,[60] and Hizbullah[61] – also became involved in the war against the Kurdish guerrillas in the 1990s. Finally, the Turkish National Security Council (*Milli Güvenlik Kurulu*, MGK), established with the 1961 constitution, had its aims redefined to coordinate and connect the government and the military bureaucracy, and from 1993 onwards started to deploy the radical right-wing militants to eliminate pro-PKK business people.[62]

Scholars and journalists alike have argued that these paramilitary organisations were the product of the development of a low-intensity conflict in the

[56] Niyazi Kızılyürek, 'Rauf Denktaş ve Kıbrıs Türk Milliyetçiliği', in *Modern Türkiye'de Siyasi Düşünce 4: Milliyetçilik*, by Kolektif (Istanbul: İletişim Yayınevi, 2008), 335–44; Söyler, 'Informal Institutions, Forms of State and Democracy'; Kemal Yamak, *Gölgede Kalan İzler ve Gölgeleşen Bizler* (Istanbul: Doğan Kitap, 2009).
[57] Bozarslan, *Network-Building, Ethnicity and Violence in Turkey*; Massicard, 'Gangs in Uniform'.
[58] Ünver, 'Turkey's "Deep-State" and the Ergenekon Conundrum'.
[59] The repentants are former PKK militants. They are those who left the organisation and collaborated with the military institutions of the state with their confessions, and some of them became hitmen in state-affiliated death squads.
[60] Zerrin Özlem Biner, 'From Terrorist to Repentant: Who Is the Victim?', *History and Anthropology* 17, no. 4 (2006): 339–53.
[61] Kurt, *Din, Şiddet ve Aidiyet*; Çakır, *Derin Hizbullah*.
[62] Bozarslan, *Network-Building, Ethnicity and Violence in Turkey*; Söyler, *The Turkish Deep State*.

early 1990s.[63] Low-intensity conflict (LIC) is a central term in theory about warfare in which irregular troops play a pivotal role.[64] Mary Kaldor describes the historical background of this term: 'In most of the literature, the new wars[65] are described as internal or civil wars[66]or else as "low-intensity conflicts"', the term 'low intensity conflict' having been 'coined during the Cold War period by the US military to describe guerrilla warfare or terrorism'.[67] This also applies to Turkey.

After the outburst of the conflict and the imminence of an 'internal threat', the Turkish state restructured its security policies. This comprised a major shift in the design of its military forces towards irregular warfare in which paramilitary forces, such as the JİTEM and the Village Guards, were assigned an important role.[68]According to Joost Jongerden, this 'new' war between the Turkish state and the PKK was characterised by 'a harsh resettlement prac-tice, with forcible, wholesale evictions accompanied by summary executions, the slaughter of livestock and the burning of villages'.[69] Thus, the control of the zone of warfare in the rurality of northern Kurdistan became regarded as one of the most significant objectives of the new war.

---

[63] Evren Balta Paker, 'Dış Tehditten İç Tehdide: Türkiye'de Doksanlarda Ulusal Güvenliğin Yeniden İnşaası', in *Türkiye'de Ordu, Devlet Ve Güvenlik Siyaseti*, by Evren Balta Paker and İsmet Akça (Istanbul: İstanbul Bilgi Üniversitesi, 2010), 407–32; Joost Jongerden, *The Settlement Issue in Turkey and the Kurds: An Analysis of Spatial Policies, Modernity and War* (Leiden: Brill, 2007); Mehmet Ali Kışlalı, *Güneydoğu: Düşük Yoğunluklu Çatışma* (Ümit Yayıncılık, 1996).

[64] Kışlalı, *Güneydoğu*, 26, 162.

[65] Mary Kaldor, *New and Old Wars: Organized Violence in a Global Era*, 3rd edn (Stanford: Stanford University Press, 2012), vi. 'New wars involve networks of state and non-state actors and most violence is directed against civilians . . . new wars in which the difference between internal and external is blurred; they are both global and local and they are different both from classic inter-state wars and classic civil wars.'

[66] For a more detailed explanation of the Kurdish-Turkish conflict as a civil war, see Mehmet Gurses' book. Mehmet Gurses, *Anatomy of a Civil War: Sociopolitical Impacts of the Kurdish Conflict in Turkey*, illustrated edn (Ann Arbor: University of Michigan Press, 2018).

[67] Kaldor, *New and Old Wars*, 2.

[68] Balta Paker, 'Dış Tehditten İç Tehdide', 2010.

[69] Jongerden, *The Settlement Issue in Turkey and the Kurds*, 43.

Mehmet Ali Kışlalı describes how, although the Turkish military institutions engaged in conventional warfare against the PKK between 1984 and 1990, the PKK had become a huge political movement during this era. As a result, in the early 1990s, Turkish military institutions developed the notion of LIC as the starting point of a new conception of warfare. The concept of LIC was first used by Doğan Güreş, a commander in the Turkish army between 1990 and 1994, and the doctrine refers both to a military conflict and a political one. The expressed aim of this doctrine was to control the conflicts by the regular and irregular military institutions in the contested territory. This required the military and paramilitary institutions to have strong intelligence services that could be mobilised against the PKK.

The LIC doctrine also led to the conversion of state institutions. Both military and political institutions were transformed and radicalised within the framework of this strategy. Hamit Bozarslan describes this radicalisation as the 'paramilitarisation of the state',[70] which can be considered as the relations established by the military and administrative bureaucracy and politicians with the paramilitary groups; the spread of paramilitary relations to the institutions of the state through these individuals, groups and networks; and the determination of the security strategy implemented by the state through these relations.

Another strand of the academic literature explores organised crime.[71] In a major study of the phenomenon, Gingeras argues that organised crime and heroin trafficking during the twentieth century cannot be seen as isolated criminal issues. The origins of the mafia lay in urban gangs (*Kabadayı*), bandits (*eşkiya*) and rural bands (*çete*) in the late Ottoman Empire, the Young Turk/Kemalist era (1908–38); yet the Turkish mafia itself was established in the

---

[70] Bozarslan, *Network-Building, Ethnicity and Violence in Turkey*; Hamit Bozarslan, 'The Turkey of the 2010's: Conflict, Pluralism, and Spaces of Life in a Modern Anti-Democracy', Keynote lecture presented at the *Societal Conflict and Cohabitation in Turkey and Beyond, CEST Conference 2018, Stockholm University, 29 November 2018*; Hamit Bozarslan, *Akp'nin Artık Legalite Diye Bir Derdi Yok*, interview by İrfan Aktan, 13 April 2019, https://www.gazeteduvar.com.tr/yazarlar/2019/04/13/hamit-bozarslan-akpnin-artik-legalite-diye-bir-derdi-yok/.

[71] Gingeras, *Heroin, Organized Crime, and the Making of Modern Turkey*; Bovenkerk and Yeşilgöz, 'The Turkish Mafia and the State'.

1960s, during the reign of Adnan Menderes and the years surrounding the rise of the Justice Party (1950–70), when smugglers, politicians, policemen, thugs, spies, diplomats and hitmen combined to construct the world of drug trafficking and organised crime in Turkey. Soon the mafia also developed relations with right-wing parties and state institutions. In the violent decade preceding Kenan Evren's 1980 coup (1970–80), members of Turkish mafia were used against Kurdish businessmen regarded as a threat to national security.[72]

Similarly, Bovenkerk and Yeşilgöz argue thus:

> The state gangs are helpful in fighting the Kurdish separatists and donate funds to the secret national treasury to pay for a war that was never actually declared. And it is unique that the discovery of these state gangs does not lead to the perpetrators being brought to court and punished; it leads instead to a veneration of heroism on behalf of the state ideology.[73]

According to this interpretation, these gangs threatened the two major state monopolies: the right to levy taxes and the right to use violence.[74] This ties in with Massicard's findings, that organised crime in Turkey during the second half of the twentieth century became enmeshed in the 'deep state', becoming a 'vast network of corruption that links the crime industry, the highest levels of government, and the death squads of the radical right'.[75] The deep state discussion in Turkey has been a topic of debate not only in terms of the formation and use of paramilitary groups but also in terms of the relationship of state institutions, and military and administrative bureaucracy to organised crime. As is discussed in the following chapters, the deep state was conceived as a secret network that determined and coordinated the relations between all these groups. In fact, adoption of the term more widely for such linkages and hidden, directive power, used now especially in the USA and

---

[72] See also Bovenkerk and Yeşilgöz, 'The Turkish Mafia and the State'; Bozarslan, *Network-Building, Ethnicity and Violence in Turkey*; Massicard, 'Gangs in Uniform'.

[73] Bovenkerk and Yeşilgöz, 'The Turkish Mafia and the State', 593. Also, the concept of gangs was used by authors particularly for right-wing extremist militants in connection with the state institutions and bureaucracy about organised crime.

[74] Ibid., 593.

[75] Massicard, 'Gangs in Uniform', 45.

fuelling 'conspiracy theories', has its roots in the Turkish case. The term itself is a direct translation of the Turkish language original ('*derin devlet*') – but in the (original) Turkish form, violent usage of paramilitaries was a major, even defining component.

Summarising, therefore, the study of paramilitary groups of the 1990s in this book involves the following discussions. First, the Ottoman and Turkish state's paramilitary policy and tradition is discussed since the late Ottoman period in order to better understand the paramilitary legacy that was introduced into the 1990s. This historical background is discussed through the concept of continuity and focused on three periods (late Ottoman, early Republic and multi-party). This continuity is illustrated through ideology, institutions and cadres. I discuss the reasons and circumstances in which paramilitary groups emerged and how they transformed during the intense conflict period. The emergence of these groups is discussed through ideas about national security, threats to the state, the lack of state's irregular warfare capacity and deniability. The transformation and reorganisation of paramilitary groups is interpreted with the doctrine of LIC. I examine the relations of paramilitary groups with state institutions and local allies, especially in northern Kurdistan, through two examples (Cizre and Batman). Finally, In the concluding part of the book, I also briefly discuss the paramilitary groups used by the state authorities during the conflicts in 2015–16. In the light of these discussions, this study aims to make a contribution to the paramilitarism literature as discussed above.

Challenges of Studying Paramilitarism in Turkey

Paramilitarism is a complex phenomenon, involving historical and contemporary concerns, which require an eclectic combination of research methods. Moreover, it is intrinsically difficult to investigate, due to its secretive and criminal nature (where criminality may be determined by international as well as national law across a range of varying contexts and interpretations). Furthermore, the situation in Turkey remains sensitive and unresolved, further complicating research. Although possibilities for research widened with the opening up of the past due to progress towards peace and Turkey's own political process during the early 2000s, these became restricted again as the situation worsened and effectively ended in 2015. In general, this is a difficult research domain in Turkey, which in itself presents an opportunity to contribute to the relatively thin body of research on the subject.[76]

In terms of location and timing for the focus of study, the research presented here is guided by the question of where paramilitary groups were the most violent. From the more than twenty Kurdish-inhabited provinces in Turkey, I decided to focus on Batman and Cizre (in Şırnak). Batman was an important area in terms of understanding the relationship between the state's administrative bureaucracy and paramilitary groups and especially the role of the shadowy radical Sunni-Islamist group Hizbullah (not to be confused with the Lebanese Shi'ite militant group Hezbollah). Cizre was the most important area in terms of the Kurdish uprising against the state during the 1990s and a centre for the most intense paramilitary violence. Therefore, it is presented for a case study of paramilitary violence, particularly in terms of the role of JİTEM.

Although Batman and Cizre are analysed partly from a comparative perspective, they are mostly interpreted as two separate areas in terms of the role of influential paramilitary groups and their relationships with government agencies. Thus, this study focuses on fifteen years of the war (between 1984 and 1999), but particularly the 1990s as the most intense period of the conflict and violence between the PKK and the Turkish state military and paramilitary forces. During this time the paramilitary forces were used most intensively, and Batman and Cizre were particularly notorious for suffering the brunt of paramilitary violence.

This work approaches paramilitarism through the historical methods of primary source study and oral history interviews, but augmented with approaches from political science, law, criminology and sociology. Content analysis is applied to newspapers of different ideologies in the 1990s, combined

---

[76] For example, in the secondary literature phase of preparatory research, I looked at the Databases of the National Thesis Center of the Council of Higher Education of Turkey for Masters and PhD theses related to the four main paramilitary forces operative in northern Kurdistan in the 1990s. This search gave thirteen results from my search for 'village guard' (köy koruculuğu); for 'Hizbullah', there were twenty-four theses related to Hizbullah in Turkey (there were many others on Hizbullah, but mainly about Hizbullah in Lebanon); there was only one Master's thesis on 'Police Special Operation' (Polis Özel Harekat) and not a single thesis was shown in the search for 'JİTEM'. At https://tez.yok.gov.tr/UlusalTezMerkezi/giris.jsp.

with a qualitative analysis of in-depth interviews[77] with relatives of victims, with former soldiers who served during the 1990s in northern Kurdistan, and with human rights activists and lawyers who worked during the war. Use is also made of archival research and analysis of court proceedings and parliament documents (especially reports) about the paramilitary forces and conflict during the 1990s. Also, three different methods were employed for gathering the sources, as related to (1) newspapers/journalism, (2) interviews/ testimonies and (3) criminal prosecutions of national and local cases.

Newspapers/Journalism

This study has gathered systematic data about incidents during the war that included the paramilitary forces. Analysing newspapers that followed different ideological strands and editorial policies was a necessary exercise, because only journalists had close and sustained contact with the actors in the conflict. Nevertheless, since state-censored mainstream newspapers and pro-Kurdish media (*Gündem* newspaper) can both be assumed to be biased, I made sure to cross-check data with the pro-government, *Milliyet* newspaper (from 1950), and pro-Kemalist (secular, modernising and Turkish nationalist) *Cumhuriyet* newspaper (from 1930), to facilitate a best attempt at corroborating events, individuals and interpretations.[78] The archives of these three newspapers were very rich and offered unique glimpses of daily life under the war as well as articles and examinations of particular events germane to paramilitarism.

Interviews/Testimonies

In order to delineate the ways through which paramilitaries operate, I conducted in-depth interviews with a range of individuals.[79] In total, I have conducted thirty-eight interviews with forty-one different people (two interviews with more than one person) in ten cities across five countries (Belgium, France, Germany and the Netherlands in addition to Turkey, including

---

[77] Paul Thompson, *Voice of the Past: Oral History* (Oxford: Oxford University Press, 2000).

[78] The pro-Islamic Zaman newspaper, which had an online archive, was also to be investigated but was closed by the Turkish government in 2016, before I was able to make a search.

[79] Antonius C. G. M. Robben and Jeffrey A. Sluka, eds, *Ethnographic Fieldwork: An Anthropological Reader*, 2nd edn (Chichester: Wiley-Blackwell, 2012).

northern Kurdistan). The interviews were archived as audio recordings, and I also kept notes while the interviews were being conducted. I reached out to interviewers through people they could trust and assured them that I would not use their names. Some interviewees said I could use their names, while others said it would be better not to. For the safety of the interviewees, I have safeguarded their anonymity by numbering the interviewees.

Some interview requests with former members of the paramilitary groups (including Village Guards, a former member of a special team and a few repentants) were rejected at the last moment, even though accepted beforehand. Among those who had served during the conflicts in the 1990s and accepted and then pulled out of the interviews were a former Village Guard leader, a soldier and a former member of a Special Police Team. In the end, it was determined to be too dangerous to insist on interviews with former paramilitary members, especially as the war flared up again, and these people might have some reasons not to want to talk about the 1990s and state-sponsored violence. However, some Village Guards, repentants and Special Team members did write memoirs or give interviews. These were useful sources because they offered a unique personal perspective.

Because of the paucity of first-hand accounts available from members of paramilitary organisations, two other types or groups of interlocutors were used to provide information and insights and fill this gap. First, I conducted interviews with a few soldiers who did their military service in northern Kurdistan in the 1990s, which shed light on the relations between paramilitary and formal military organisations. Second, the relatives of the victims and witnesses of the crimes committed by paramilitaries also provided their perspectives. Through their testimony during trials as well as from the interviews conducted here, killings, disappearances, the burning of villages and forced migrations carried out by paramilitary groups were revealed.

Additionally, two more groups of interviews were conducted (making four interviewee groups in total). These were a group comprising lawyers, academic researchers and members of non-governmental organisations (NGOs), such as the Human Rights Association (*İnsan Hakları Derneği*, İHD) branches of Istanbul and Diyarbakır and the Human Rights Foundation of Turkey in Diyarbakır, which collected testimonies of the victims, their relatives and witnesses to the crimes committed against them. These interviews offer relevant information and details on the kinds of court cases that were opened against members of paramilitary groups. A final group of interviewees consisted of journalists who had investigated the paramilitary groups and Kurdish politicians who were members of parliament in the 1990s. These people were also very helpful because of their privileged (i.e. first-person) accounts of the period and particular events. The journalists I interviewed were also threatened by members of the paramilitary groups because they were investigating their violence.

I interviewed the victims' relatives, lawyers and journalists for two reasons. The first was to understand the ways, locations and times of the actions, with the latter being important for an understanding of how Turkish paramilitarism did not only commit illegitimate violence but also prevented that violence from being dealt with through restorative justice. The other reason was a negative one, the lack of interviews with the members of paramilitary organisations. In general, only the victims' relatives, lawyers and journalists are accessible and talkative actors in respect to the paramilitarism (and on whose lives this has left indelible and unforgettable traces). Witness accounts kept by NGOs, journalists and human rights organisations were also helpful in this regard.

My questions were distinguished according to interviewee groups. For instance, questions with the victims' relatives focused on the acts carried out by paramilitary forces and on following the legal process. Questions for lawyers and members of NGOs, meanwhile, focused on the legal process after the incidents and methods used by paramilitary forces (the types of violence and weapons, time and place of acts and characteristic features of the paramilitary forces). Questions for journalists mostly concerned the relations between paramilitary forces and state institutions, parties in the parliament and the members of paramilitary forces' economic motivations. Finally, and importantly, the Truth Justice Memory Center (*Hakikat Adalet Hafıza Merkezi*) is the main NGO in Turkey to have recorded enforced disappearances. It has collected a vast and unique archive, and its staff has conducted interviews with the relatives of the victims (for a while, I participated in that project and am therefore very familiar with its collections).

Criminal Prosecutions

Court proceedings have been an important source of information for this work. After all, journalistic accounts rarely provide information on relations between state institutions and the ways paramilitary forces operate. The court proceedings provide, through the case records, in-depth portrayals of the perpetrators and their relations with formal and informal state institutions. Therefore, these documents play an important role for discussion on impunity, if used prudently – bearing in mind, that is, that the strategies followed by the prosecutors are employed to make a case stick rather than necessarily get at an objective truth and present an overview of the nature of paramilitarism in Turkey. However, some prosecutors were keenly aware of the pernicious and insidious influence of paramilitary networks in Turkish state agencies, which they did attempt to expose in these trials. The relatives of the people who were the subjects of enforced disappearances and unsolved political murders could not bring suits against the state military and paramilitary institutions because they were terrified of the consequences. For this reason, many of the cases against the perpetrators started to be opened only in the 2000s. As deniability and impunity were key elements of paramilitarism in Turkey, the fact that the court proceedings contributed to an understanding of these two issues was crucially important for this work.

Organisation of the Book

The book consists of five chapters together with the introduction and a conclusion. The first chapter focuses on the historical background of the Turkish state's paramilitary policy. It looks at the historical heritage, origins and continuity of paramilitary groups – with different features in different periods – up to the 1990s, analysing the formation of such organisations during the late Ottoman Empire and the Republic. The relationships among the secret military networks, military institutions and Turkish parliament are discussed, along with relations between NATO and the Turkish state in relation to the concept of Gladio and the position of the right-wing parties and their paramilitary organisation relations, which were important after the multiparty period (from 1950). In short, this chapter considers the origin of paramilitary forces in Turkey and the background to the secret relations with state institutions.

The second chapter studies the establishment of the paramilitary forces during the conflict with the PKK and the beginning of the usage of paramilitary organisations by the state, particularly in the 1980s. What was the historical background of these forces? What was their relationship with the state? This chapter discusses the formation and scope of paramilitaries (JİTEM, Village Guards, Special Police Teams and Hizbullah). It further investigates the paramilitaries' training and the ideological backgrounds of these groups.

The third chapter focuses on the transformation and the acts of the paramilitary forces in the early 1990s. Between 1991 and 1996 the Turkish security forces sought to improve their irregular warfare capacity by implementing the LIC doctrine. While the PKK had declared a unilateral ceasefire in March 1993 and some Turkish authorities were making steps toward a democratic solution of the Kurdish question, the leadership of the Turkish army remained convinced that this issue could only be settled by military means. Furthermore, it was convinced that a military solution to the conflict required a transformed military organisation and development of paramilitary forces. This chapter also presents the state's political and military strategy as the *paramilitarisation of the state.*

The fourth chapter discusses Batman, a Kurdish province where paramilitary violence was intense during the conflict between the PKK and the state. In order to better understand the relationships of paramilitary formations to one another and to state institutions, the local level perspective of Batman affords one of the best examples, for the following reasons. There were certain constants in this local region: Batman was made a province on 16 May 1990, purely for military reasons of combating the PKK. The role of the local administrative bureaucracy and provincial governor in terms of their relationship with the paramilitary groups was key.

The fifth chapter presents a close examination of Cizre, perhaps the most significant Kurdish area for paramilitary activities and massacres. Paramilitary organisations, especially JİTEM, along with other military institutions of the state, were involved in the extrajudicial executions, murders by unknown assailant, enforced disappearances, burning of villages and forced migrations. Cizre is a critical place for an understanding of the interrelations of the different paramilitary groups (JİTEM, Village Guards and pro-government Kurdish tribes, the Special Police Teams and Hizbullah). I argue that the *aim* of paramilitary violence in Cizre was to target civilians; it was committed by a death squad constructed from different paramilitary formations, with two government officers (gendarmerie commander and mayor) ruling the group which played a major role in carrying out the enforced disappearances and unsolved murders in Cizre.

I present in the concluding chapter a general summary of the research and discussion of the main arguments in the book, including continuity of the state paramilitary politics and paramilitarisation of the state. I also indicate why these groups have been reduced or partly deactivated since the late 1990s, and it highlights a comparison between the 1990s and 2015 with the differences between the paramilitary groups and the policies implemented by the state in these years. The reason for the special emphasis on 2015 is that I also briefly discuss the intensified conflicts between the Turkish state and the PKK following the failed peace negotiations that began in 2013 and ended in 2015, and the state authorities' use of reorganised paramilitary formations in these conflicts.

1

ORIGIN, LEGACY AND CONTINUITY OF TURKISH PARAMILITARY FORMATIONS

Introduction

The historical background of Turkish paramilitarism can be divided into three distinct periods: the Hamidian and CUP periods during the late Ottoman Empire (1890–1918), the Republic (or Kemalist) period (1923–50) and the multi-party period (1950s–90s). Manifestly, there was a long tradition and continuity in terms of the emergence and mobilisation of paramilitary forces from the late Ottoman Empire to 1990s Turkey. Thus, this chapter addresses the question of how the Turkish state performed and transformed paramilitary policies before the 1990s, and how this transformation and legacy influenced the formation of paramilitary organisations in the 1990s.

The usage of paramilitary forces varied according to their origins and functions during these periods. In the late Ottoman Empire, the paramilitary forces were used by the state as death squads and as auxiliary forces to the regular army, mainly to prevent the rise of nationalist movements, which were considered a threat in the Balkans and the eastern part of the Empire. During the Kemalist, or single-party dictatorship period, paramilitary forces were again used as death squads (particularly in the early Republic) and as auxiliary forces (including pro-government Kurdish tribes and informers). They were particularly used to eliminate opposition (to the Republic or to Mustafa Kemal). Then, during the multi-party period, the state used paramilitary forces as death squads, auxiliary forces and vigilantes against non-Muslim communities, the left-wing opposition, Kurdish leftist and nationalist movements, and against Alevi civilians. The main purpose of paramilitary forces during this period was to prevent the rise of Communist movements and Kurdish organisations.

Consequently, I argue that although the Turkish state was governed by different regimes (the period of the late Ottoman Empire with the sultanate, the Kemalist or single-party period with a dictatorship and the multi-party democratic period with a premiership), there was a continuity in the nature and function of Turkish paramilitarism across these periods. I discuss paramilitary groups during these periods, particularly in the context of the political parties, organised crime, tribes and the ethno-religious minority policies of the state. In addition, I emphasise the examples of the Kurdish provinces, to understand if and how the effects of these organisations continued into the 1990s.

Paramilitary Organisations during the Late Ottoman Empire (1890–1918)

In terms of the origin of paramilitary forces, the late Ottoman Empire can be divided into two distinct periods. The first comprises the reign of Abdulhamid II (1876–1908), when the best-known paramilitary group was the Hamidiye Regiments.[1] The second began in 1914, during the CUP period (1908–18), when the well-known paramilitary group *Teşkilât-ı Mahsusa* was founded.[2] Other Ottoman paramilitary youth organisations that had connections with *Teşkilat-ı Mahsusa* also existed at that time.[3] In addition, there were other local armed paramilitary forces that also had links with the *Teşkilât-ı Mahsusa*, including Al-Khamsin,[4] Bejik[5] and some other bandits based in the Diyarbakır

---

[1] Janet Klein, *The Margins of Empire: Kurdish Militias in the Ottoman Tribal Zone* (Stanford: Stanford University Press, 2011).

[2] Arif Cemil Denker, *I. Dünya Savaşı'nda Teşkilat-ı Mahsusa* (Istanbul: Arba, 1997); Erik Jan Zürcher, *Turkey: A Modern History*, 3rd edn (London: I. B. Tauris, 2004).

[3] Sanem Yamak, 'II. Meşrutiyet Döneminde Paramiliter Gençlik Örgütleri' (PhD diss., Istanbul Üniversitesi, 2009); Sadık Sarısaman, 'Birinci Dünya Savaşı Sırasında Ihtiyat Kuvveti Olarak Kurulan Osmanlı Genç Dernekleri', *OTAM (Ankara Üniversitesi Osmanlı Tarihi Araştırma ve Uygulama Merkezi Dergisi)*, no. 11 (2000): 439–501.

[4] Gaunt, Beṯ-Şawoce and Donef, *Massacres, Resistance, Protectors*, 314.

[5] Adnan Çelik and Namık Kemal Dinç, *Yüzyıllık Ah: Toplumsal Hafızanın İzinde 1915 Diyarbakır* (Istanbul: İsmail Beşikci Vakfı Yayınları, 2015).

province. These two armed paramilitary forces were established by Abdulhamid II and the CUP.

Hamidiye/Tribal Light Cavalry Regiments

Why did the Ottoman Empire establish the Hamidiye Regiments as an auxiliary or paramilitary force in 1891? The late nineteenth century was a period of dramatic decline for the Ottoman Empire. With the Treaty of Berlin in 1878 concluding a disastrous war with Russia, the Empire lost a large part of its Balkan territory (and a predominantly non-Muslim population). Hence, the Empire took new measures to prevent the loss of further land. According to Abdulhamid II, the eastern part of the Empire was threatened by Armenian and Kurdish nationalism. Armenian nationalist movements demanded reforms (including self-rule) in the six eastern provinces of the Empire after the Treaty of Berlin.[6] Thus, it was in order to prevent the rise of nationalism in the eastern part of the Empire that the Hamidiye Regiments were established as a paramilitary force.

The Hamidiye Regiments comprised a new armed force alongside the official military powers of the state to deal with internal and external 'enemies' and conflicts in the eastern provinces of the Empire. They were established by Zeki Pasha for two specific reasons: most importantly, to engage in internal struggles (particularly against Armenian and Kurdish nationalism),[7] and secondly, to counter the interference of foreign states in the east (primarily, Russia and Iran).[8] Abdulhamid II trusted Zeki Pasha because he was 'a bright and promising young officer of Circassian origin who was connected to the sultan through marriage (the pasha's sister was in the sultan's "harem")'.[9]

There are a number of competing academic arguments about the reasons for the establishment of the Hamidiye Regiments. Bayram Kodaman argues that several reasons motivated the establishment of the Regiments: (1) to establish a

---

[6] Reşat Kasaba, ed., *Turkey in the Modern World*, The Cambridge History of Turkey, vol. 4 (Cambridge: Cambridge University Press, 2008).

[7] Özar *et al.*, *From Past to Present*; Ayhan Işık, 'Kurdish and Armenian Relations in the Ottoman Kurdish Press (1898–1914)' (MA Thesis, Istanbul Bilgi University, 2014).

[8] Klein, 'Power in the Periphery: Hamidiye Light Cavalry and the Struggle over Ottoman Kurdistan, 1890–1914'.

[9] Ibid., 42.

central authority, (2) to establish a new socio-political balance in the east, (3) to benefit from the military power of the tribes, (4) to prevent Armenian activity and establish a new power balance between Muslims and non-Muslims, (5) to protect eastern Anatolia from Russian attacks and British policies, and (6) to conduct the pan-Islamism policy.[10] Janet Klein, who focuses on the Regiments in the late Empire, argues that they played important local roles in many of the massacres in the eastern part of the Empire. Hence, it can be deduced that the main goal of the establishment of the Regiments was to control two communities, the Armenians and Kurds, and to protect the eastern borders.[11]

Another discussion about the formation of the Hamidiye Regiments involves the suggestion that they were intended to forestall the development of a national unity among Kurds during the rise of nationalism. The Regiments consisted almost entirely of Kurdish tribes, and according to Martin van Bruinessen, many of the tribes who joined did not have a strong standing among the Kurdish tribes in general; thus, the aim was to counter-balance the powerful Kurdish tribes through the Regiment policy.[12] In other words, the Empire supported weak Kurdish tribes against strong ones and manoeuvred them into a pro-state position with a politics of divide-and-rule.[13] Therefore, the divide-and-rule policy against the Kurds seems to be another important reason for the formation of the Regiment.

François Georgeon also argues that, even though the Empire was in conflict with Kurds throughout the nineteenth century, Sultan Abdulhamid chose Kurds and not Armenians to execute his pan-Islamist policies, because the majority of Kurds were Sunni Muslim.[14] Of the sixty-four or sixty-five Hamidiye Regiments, only a few were made up of Arab and Karapapak tribes,[15] and among the Kurds there were very few Alawites. Another important factor was that a power vacuum had emerged after the most important

[10] Bayram Kodaman, *Sultan II. Abdülhamid Devri Doğu Anadolu Politikası* (Ankara: Türk Kültürünü Araştırma Enstitüsü, 1987).

[11] Klein, 'Power in the Periphery.

[12] Martin van Bruinessen, *Ağa, Şeyh ve Devlet: Agha, Shaikh and State the Social and Political Structures of Kurdistan*, 5. baskı (Istanbul: İletişim Yayınları, 2008), 287.

[13] Osman Aytar, *Hamidiye Alaylarından Köy Koruculuğuna* (Istanbul: Medya Güneşi, 1992).

[14] François Georgeon, *Sultan Abdülhamid* (Istanbul: Homer, 2006), 310.

[15] Klein, 'Power in the Periphery', 82.

local authority, the Kurdish Emirates, was eliminated in the context of the early nineteenth century centralisation of the Ottoman Empire. Seen from this perspective, the main role of the Regiments was to consolidate the power of the central authority by co-opting tribes and thus preventing both the unity of the Kurds and the development of rival, dissident proto-nationalist movements on a pan-Islamist basis.

The Hamidiye Regiments were modelled after the Russian Cossack militias.[16] The structure and hierarchy of the regiments themselves was similar to that of the semi-regular army. The fighting units were created by the central Ottoman authority from more than sixty Sunni-Islam Kurdish tribes. The most senior commander was from the regular army, while other commanders were tribal leaders. Thus, there was a hierarchy between state military institutions and local militia forces. The leader of each tribe became leader of his own regiments, which comprised men coming from his own tribe. The aim of the state was to recruit 50,000 warriors, but the actual number of regiment members was much less.[17] Consequently, these paramilitary regiments were organised by the state as paramilitary tribe forces providing support for the regular army and other military institutions.

By placing the Kurdish tribal leaders in the bureaucracy and awarding them military titles through regiments, Abdulhamid II pulled the tribal leaders into a pro-state position. The state gave the rank of 'pasha' to the leaders of the Kurdish tribes that were members of the Hamidiye Regiments, taking them under control and then effectively eliminating them as a threat.[18] As the need for these tribal forces diminished, their influence and the importance of their leaders was similarly reduced. For example, the fate of Milli İbrahim Pasha, leader of the Milli tribe and another four regiments of the Hamidiye, was to

---

[16] Ibid., 32.

[17] Ibid., 41–56.

[18] This policy of the state was not new for the Empire. According to Karen Barkey, the imperial authority had used it for the riots in the early seventeenth century against bandits/rebels. In 1606, one of the leaders of the rebellion, Canboladoğlu Ali, was made a *beylerbeyi* (a feudal title with territorial land-labour rights) in exchange for stopping the rebellion; the main leader of the rebellion, however, was invited to the capital, Istanbul. The sultan then exiled him and had him strangled. Karen Barkey, *Eşkiyalar ve Devlet: Osmanlı Tarzı Devlet Merkezileşmesi*, trans. Zeynep Altok (Istanbul: Tarih Vakfı Yurt Yayınları, 1999), 195–217.

end in this way.[19] The state gave out titles to the leader of the tribes as a symbol of political prestige and with accompanying economic interests. This unofficial contract between the state and the paramilitary forces worked for both sides, albeit with a limited duration, enabling economic security for the tribes and control of the territory for the state. Consequently, three of the most important ways in which the Kurdish tribes involved in the Hamidiye/Tribal Regiment paramilitary related to the state were through bureaucracy, rank and economic interest.

The Hamidiye Regiments were used by the Empire against Armenian nationalists and socialist movements active among and alongside Kurdish villagers. They are known to have collaborated with the regular troops in pogroms and massacres against members of Armenian movements and Armenian peasants in the eastern regions of the Empire, especially in 1894–6.[20] According to several sources, 100,000 to 300,000 Armenians were killed in these massacres, in which the role of the Regiments, along with the regular army, was crucial.[21] Next to the killings, this tribal paramilitary organisation was used to forcibly seize property, especially the land of the non-Muslim communities. Armenian lands were simply taken and claimed by the leaders of the Hamidiye Regiments for their own people (tribes). In other words, these tribes gained economic as well as political and military power from their arrangement with the central state (Ottoman pashas and Abdulhamid II). Klein argues that a particularly important economic motivation for the usurpation of land was its increased value with the development of agrarian capitalism.[22] She even argues that the paramilitary regiments in this respect took the initiative: 'Although the government did not initiate the process whereby large tracts of land were

---

[19] Klein, 'Power in the Periphery'.

[20] 'There are conflicting reports about Zeki Pasha's role in the massacres; some claim that he attempted to stop them where he could, while others allege that he was the responsible party, giving orders to the Hamidiye and the regular troops he commanded to murder and plunder.' Ibid., 158.

[21] Hans-Lukas Kieser, *Iskalanmış Barış: Doğu Vilayetleri'nde Misyonerlik, Etnik Kimlik ve Devlet 1839–1938 = Verpasste Friede: Mission, Ethnie Und Staat in Den Ostprovinzen Der Türkei 1839–1938*, 2. baskı (Istanbul: İletişim, 2005); Klein, 'Power in the Periphery'; Özar et al., *From Past to Present*; Malmîsanij, *İlk Kürt Gazetesi Kurdıstan'ı Yayımlayan Abdurrahman Bedirhan, 1868–1936* (Istanbul: Vate Yayınevi, 2009).

[22] Klein, 'Power in the Periphery', 270–1.

confiscated by Kurdish chiefs who were often affiliated with the Hamidiye Cavalry, it did support it in order to advance its own projects.'[23]

As a result, it can be stated that the Regiments worked in collaboration with the army and other state agencies as a subcontracted[24] militia force in the eastern part of the Empire. Some of these tribal paramilitary organisations participated in the Armenian genocide, alongside the *Teşkilat-ı Mahsusa* and local paramilitary forces. They threatened Armenians, controlled Kurdish tribes, organised local massacres and cooperated with the Ottoman state, which in its turn regained authority in the region. This alliance with the state changed according to government policies in the region. The interests of the Regiments in general were supported by the state against other Kurdish tribes and Armenians, which found their petitions about the usurpation of the land and about the leaders of this paramilitary force ignored. This confirmed the impunity regarding the acts of the paramilitary force. The Regiments also were a subcontractor compensating for the lack of military and administrative capacity of the state at the local level. These forces were mostly deactivated by the state after the end of the First World War.

The Teşkilat-ı Mahsusa as a Paramilitary Force of the CUP

The CUP came to power in 1908 as the first political party to have been established in the Ottoman Empire (in 1889).[25] In 1914, under the order of Enver Pasha (Minister of War and one of the leaders of the CUP), it established a new

---

[23] Ibid., 259.

[24] According to the Cambridge Dictionary, subcontracting is 'the act of paying an outside person or organization to do work that might normally be done within an organization': https://dictionary.cambridge.org/dictionary/english/subcontracting. In other words, the term subcontractor also means that the subcontractor group exists independently of the employer and has a certain power or potential to perform the task given by the employer. And it can be used for groups that already exist and are converted when needed for certain periods and purposes. The reason for using the concept of subcontractors for Hamidiye Regiments is that the regiments were used to design the Eastern politics of the Ottoman Empire. These groups can be tribes or various mafia groups and radical Islamist groups, as they were in the post-Republican era. When selecting subcontractor groups, the state generally makes sure that they are ideologically (Turkish nationalism and Islamism) close to it.

[25] Tarık Zafer Tunaya, *Türkiyede Siyasi Partiler: 1859–1952*, vol. 1, 2. baskı (Istanbul: Hürriyet Vakfı Yayınları, 1988), 19–37.

paramilitary group, the *Teşkilât-ı Mahsusa*, as secret intelligence organisation of the CUP. The origins and first members of this organisation came from secret fedayis (*fedai*, 'self-sacrificing volunteers') in the early 1900s.[26] Many of these volunteers had been used in secret military and intelligence actions, especially against nationalist movements in the Balkans before the Balkan Wars (in 1912 and '13).[27] They had gained experience of irregular warfare and counterinsurgency tactics during the conflicts in Macedonia and Libya.[28] Between 1908 and 1913, after the last sultan, Abdulhamid II, had been overthrown, the CUP gradually gained control over the state. During this time, the fedayis also carried out several political assassinations, particularly against opposition journalists.[29] Some military leaders of the *Teşkilat-ı Mahsusa* also gained experience in irregular war as Hamidiye Cavalry leaders.[30]

The leading cadres of the *Teşkilat-ı Mahsusa* were generally members of the official army, and they were mostly sent to the eastern provinces. The first chairman of the organisation, Süleyman Askeri, was a major in the regular army.[31] The members of the organisation, officially named the '*Umuru Şarkiye Dairesi*' (Eastern Affairs Office), were sent to all corners of the Empire to prevent the rise of the nationalist movements, but especially in the east.[32] After its defeat in the Balkan Wars, the Ottoman state focused on Anatolia and Kurdistan, as the CUP government was primarily afraid of losing the

---

[26] Üngör, *The Making of Modern Turkey*, 28; M. Şükrü Hanioğlu, *Preparation for a Revolution: The Young Turks, 1902–1908* (Oxford: Oxford University Press, 2001), 217.

[27] Uğur Ümit Üngör, 'Paramilitary Violence in the Collapsing Ottoman Empire', in *War in Peace: Paramilitary Violence in Europe After the Great War*, eds Robert Gerwarth and John Horne (Oxford: Oxford University Press, 2013), 164–83.

[28] Ryan Gingeras, 'Last Rites for a "Pure Bandit": Clandestine Service, Historiography and the Origins of the Turkish "Deep State"', *Past & Present* 206, no. 1 (1 February 2010): 159.

[29] Suat Parlar, *Osmanlı'dan Günümüze Gizli Devlet*, 3. baskı (Istanbul: Mephisto, 2005), 52–3.

[30] İsrafil Kurtcephe and Mustafa Balcıoğlu, 'Birinci Dünya Savaşı Başlarında Romantik Bir Türk-Alman Projesi -Rauf Bey Müfrezesi-', *OTAM (Ankara Üniversitesi Osmanlı Tarihi Araştırma ve Uygulama Merkezi Dergisi)*, no. 3 (1992): 250.

[31] Samih Nafiz Tansu, *Teşkilat-ı Mahsusa İki Devrin Perde Arkası* (Istanbul: Nokta Kitap, 2012), 88.

[32] Kurtcephe and Balcıoğlu, 'Birinci Dünya Savaşı Başlarında Romantik Bir Türk-Alman Projesi'.

eastern territories to the relatively well-developed Armenian and Kurdish nationalists. Thus, the first target of this paramilitary force, like the Hamidiye Cavalry, was the eastern part of the Empire.

There were some other, less effective youth paramilitary groups, particularly at the beginning of World War I.[33] These paramilitary groups were the *Müdafaa-i Milliye Cemiyeti* (Society of National Defense), *Türk Gücü Cemiyeti* (Society of Turkish Power), *Osmanlı Güç Dernekleri* (Association of Ottoman Power) and *Osmanlı Genç Dernekleri* (Association of Ottoman Youth). Established in 1912, *Müdafaa-i Milliye Cemiyeti* was officially responsible for culture and health. The *Türk Gücü Cemiyeti* was created a year later as a scout organisation of the CUP. In 1913, Enver Pasha invited a Belgian military expert to help with the establishment of the *Osmanlı Güç Dernekleri*, which was officially established in 1914.[34] In 1916, *Osmanlı Genç Dernekleri* was renamed *Osmanlı Güç Dernekleri* and replaced them. This was a project suggested to the Minister of War in 1916 by the German general inspector in the Ottoman Empire, Heinrich von Hoff, as a way to train reserve forces for the regular army during the war.[35] The idea of the paramilitary youth groups may have come from the German imperial paramilitary youth organisations *Kaiserlich Deutsche Jugendwehr*.[36] The CUP government organised many paramilitary forces under different names in different parts of the Empire before and during the war. Tarık Zafer Tunaya claims that 706 youth branches of the *Osmanlı Genç Dernekleri* were created in forty-four different provinces and districts (*vilayet* and *sancak*) of the Empire during 1916–17.[37] All of these groups were connected with the *Teşkilat-ı Mahsusa* at the local level. Importantly, these (uniformed) paramilitary youth organisations were intertwined with the formal educational institutions. Moreover, it appears that the CUP

---

[33] Mehmet Beşikçi, 'Militarizm, Topyekün Savaş ve Gençliğin Seferber Edilmesi: Birinci Dünya Savaşı'nda Osmanlı İmparatorluğu'nda Paramiliter Dernekler', *Tarih ve Toplum Yeni Yaklaşımlar* 248, no. 8 (2009): 49–92.

[34] Zafer Toprak, 'İttihat ve Terakki'nin Paramiliter Gençlik Örgütleri', *Boğaziçi Üniversitesi Dergisi: Hümaniter Bilimler* VII (1979): 96.

[35] Tunaya, *Türkiyede Siyasi Partiler*, 1:448–73.

[36] Sarısaman, 'Birinci Dünya Savaşı Sırasında Ihtiyat Kuvveti Olarak Kurulan Osmanlı Genç Dernekleri', 443.

[37] Tunaya, *Türkiyede Siyasi Partiler*, 1:472–3.

was working to impose the paramilitary policy on the whole society through irregular warfare training.

The paramilitary groups affiliated to the CUP were of two kinds: death squads and paramilitary youth organisations. First, some paramilitary forces, such as the *Teşkilat-ı Mahsusa*, were used as death squads in different parts of the Empire, especially during the genocide on non-Muslims in the east and the forced displacement of Greeks (mostly in North and West Anatolia). Second, the paramilitary youth organisations were used as auxiliary forces for the regular army during the war. The Minister of War had profited from the German paramilitary experience in the creation of the Ottoman paramilitary legacy.[38] The training and practical motivations of these groups followed two distinct but interconnected ideological directions: pan-Turkism and pan-Islamism. One of the leaders of the *Teşkilat-ı Mahsusa*, Hüsamettin Ertürk explained the ideological motivation of this paramilitary force in his memoir: 'The aim of this organisation, on the one hand, is to gather all Muslims under one flag and thus reach the ideal of pan-Islamism', he stated, and 'On the other hand, it is to keep the Turkish race in a political union and in this regard realise pan-Turkism.'[39] Physical training was used to prepare the members of the youth paramilitary organisations from the age of twelve for war alongside the official army.[40] Thus, the state began to prepare a reserve power.

The paramilitary forces carried out acts against non-Muslims and non-Turks, including organising the confiscation of the lands and properties of the Greek people in Thrace and western Anatolia, and to replace the population in this area in the same way as the Hamidiye Cavalry did in the east.[41] This transfer of the Greek-owned land and properties in western Anatolia was organised by the *Teşkilat-ı Mahsusa* and other local Caucasian gangs.[42] The paramilitaries of the CUP used local gangs, each with their specific, local characteristics in different parts of the Empire in the murder of Armenians

---

[38] There were many high-ranking German officers in the Ottoman army, and they suggested one of the paramilitary youth organisations during World War I.

[39] Tansu, *Teşkilat-ı Mahsusa İki Devrin Perde Arkası*, 88.

[40] Yamak, 'II. Meşrutiyet Döneminde Paramiliter Gençlik Örgütleri', 91.

[41] Dündar, *Modern Türkiye'nin Şifresi*, 202.

[42] Gingeras, 'Last Rites for a "Pure Bandit"', 160–2.

and other non-Muslims, and in burning and destroying their property.[43] The *Teşkilât-ı Mahsusa* was deployed across the Empire in various ways and staffed by different types of groups. For example, Topal Osman and his gang were actively involved in the genocide by the *Teşkilât-ı Mahsusa* in the Black Sea region.

In 1915, the governor of Diyarbekir province, Dr Mehmed Reşid, and some local leaders (Kurdish notables) organised a local paramilitary force called *Bejik* or *Bejike Kurmanca* (countryside guard, Kurdish militia) to be used for the extermination of the Armenians during the war. By now, Ottoman military defeat had allowed the Russian army, aided by local Armenians, to advance into Anatolia, south and westwards from the Caucasus. South from the Russian controlled area, in northern Kurdistan, the Kurdish militias were active in the Armenian genocide in the province of Diyarbekir.[44] Doctor Mehmed Reşid, a member of the CUP, was one of those responsible.[45] Most Armenians who were gathered in different areas of the Empire were later sent through Diyarbakır to Der el Zor (in today's Syria). Governor Dr Reşid's Circassian troops and local paramilitary forces exterminated almost all the Armenians in the province of Diyarbakır. The Kurdish *Bejik* paramilitary forces were formed quickly, and their salaries were valuable goods looted from Armenians and other non-Muslims (mostly Assyrians).[46] Another local paramilitary force in Diyarbekir province was established by Reşid from the Arabs there. As Gaunt, Beṯ-Şawoce and Donef argue, these units, consisting of fifty men (hence their name in the local Arab dialect of the Al-Khamsin) 'had uniforms and armbands and had leaders holding military rank'. According to Gaunt, Beṯ-Sawoce and Donef, they 'functioned much like the *Einsatz* groups of the Nazis; these would organise mass executions with the collaboration of local people'.[47]

[43] Üngör, *The Making of Modern Turkey*, 71–85; Gaunt *et al.*, *Massacres, Resistance, Protectors*.

[44] Çelik and Dinç, *Yüzyıllık Ah*, 121–37.

[45] Hans-Lukas Kieser, 'Dr Mehmed Reshid (1873–1919): A Political Doctor', in *Der Völkermord an Den Armeniern Und Die Shoah – the Armenian Genocide and the Shoa*, 3. Auflage mit neuem Vorwort. (Zürich: Chronos, 2014), 245–80.

[46] Ugur Ümit Üngör and Mehmet Polatel, *Confiscation and Destruction: The Young Turk Seizure of Armenian Property* (London: Continuum, 2011), 141–2; Hüseyin Demirer, *Ha Wer Delal Emine Perixane'nin Hayatı* (Istanbul: Avesta Yayınları, 2009), 79.

[47] Gaunt *et al.*, *Massacres, Resistance, Protectors*, 159.

Governor Dr Reşid enlisted the help of bandits, such as the brothers Ömer and Mustafa, leaders of the Raman tribe in Diyarbekir province. Two factors mobilised these bandits: economic interests (plunder) and ideology (Islam). These bandit groups were used by the state for specific short-term tasks.[48] The memoir of a member of the Raman tribe mentioned clarified what these tasks entailed.[49] According to this memoir, the governor's agreement with the two brothers was that they would take Armenians on rafts down the Tigris to a quiet area where they would kill them. The bandits would then share the gold and other valuable goods of the Armenians with the governor. Many Armenians were killed in this way. Afterwards, the two brothers, who knew a lot about the role of the Governor and local state institutions during the genocide, were killed on the order of Reşid. Doctor Reşid and the relevant government authorities probably also made also similar agreements with other bandit groups and pro-state tribes in other regions.

Although the Ottoman ruling elite was responsible for the formation of paramilitary units, it denied the violence paramilitaries had perpetrated. Yet even when they had thus tried to create a plausible denial of their involvement, after the First World War, the leaders of CUP were held responsible and tried in Istanbul as perpetrators of the genocide and for massacres perpetrated by the paramilitary forces.[50]

The Hamidiye Regiments were most effective in the 1890s, when they became a source of gangs and organised crime and carried out many massacres and plunders in the east of the Empire. After the overthrow of Abdulhamid II and declaration of the constitutional regime in 1908, the influence of the Regiments decreased and they changed their name to 'Tribal Light Cavalry Regiments', dropping 'Hamidiye' in order to remove the connection to Abdulhamid II.[51] The tribal paramilitary force took part in the Balkan Wars, fought during the First World War, and engaged in the genocide against non-Muslim

[48] Demirer, *Ha Wer Delal Emine Perixane'nin Hayatı*; Üngör, *The Making of Modern Turkey*, 72.

[49] Demirer, *Ha Wer Delal Emine Perixane'nin Hayatı*.

[50] Vahakn N. Dadrian, 'A Summary of the Conditions Surrounding the Trials', in *Judgment at Istanbul: The Armenian Genocide Trials*, eds Vahakn N. Dadrian and Taner Akçam, 1st edn (New York: Berghahn Books, 2011), 154–76.

[51] Ibid., 154–76.

communities alongside the regular army and *Teşkilat-ı Mahsusa* because of its experience in irregular conflict.[52] Towards the end of the war, however, the tribal forces gradually lost their influence,[53] although still continuing to exist and participate in some military operations into the 1920s and the first decade of the Republic.

In total, the Regiments were active as a paramilitary force for nearly thirty years and continued to play a role in armed conflict in the Balkans, especially in the form of small gangs (*çete*) led by the officers of the *Teşkilat-ı Mahsusa*.[54] Both the Regiments and the gangs established in the Balkans were important in terms of the origins of the history of the Turkish paramilitary, primarily because they had more irregular warfare experience than regular military units and also because they had the experience of organising gangs, fugitives, tribes and local gangs with local violence along with weapons experience.

The Republic Period (1923–50)

As Zürcher argued in *Modern Turkey*, 'despite the break-up of the Empire in 1918 and the establishment of the Turkish Republic in 1923, politically, ideologically and economically, there [was] a great deal of continuity'.[55] From the establishment of the Republic to 1950, Mustafa Kemal and then İsmet İnönü, the first two leaders of the new country, governed it through a single-party dictatorship.[56] The paramilitary policy of this single-party dictatorship period under the Republican People's Party (*Cumhuriyet Halk Partisi*, CHP) was a little different from that of the previous period. There were similar paramilitary forces, informers and local collaborations for intelligence purposes (with bandits, gangs and members and leaders of pro-state local tribes). Some of the tribal regiments and paramilitary youth organisations continued to be involved, although replaced in part, one may say, by the introduction of the

---

[52] Robert W. Olson, *The Emergence of Kurdish Nationalism and the Sheikh Said Rebellion, 1880–1925*, 1st edn (Austin: University of Texas Press, 1989), 11; Faik Bulut, *Dersim Raporları*, 2. baskı (Istanbul, 2013), 88.

[53] Özar *et al.*, *From Past to Present*.

[54] Denker, *I. Dünya Savaşı'nda Teşkilat-ı Mahsusa*, 272–388.

[55] Erik Jan Zürcher, *Milli Mücadelede İttihatçılık*, trans. Nüzhet Salihoğlu, 1. baskı (Istanbul: Bağlam, 1987), pp. 3–4

[56] Üngör, *The Making of Modern Turkey*, 253.

Village Guard system. More clearly, I argue here that paramilitaries are one of the founding actors/groups of the modern Turkish state.

The establishment of the Republic of Turkey was directly linked to the paramilitary policies of the late Ottoman period. The ideology, politics and economy of the new Republic had been discussed by the Ottoman intellectuals before and during the CUP reign.[57] The ideology of the state elites after the Balkan Wars transformed dramatically into pan-Turkism, which now began to be expressed very clearly among the CUP elites and Turkish intellectuals and was to become the source of state ideology for the founders of the Republic.[58] The genocide and massacres of non-Muslims between 1913 and 1922 were a direct result of the aim of the authorities of the Empire to create an ethnically homogeneous society, and the paramilitary forces were actively employed to realise this. The transitional government between the Empire and Republic (*Ankara hükümeti*, 1920–3) consisted of former members of the CUP and continued the paramilitary approach and activities it had inherited as a legacy of the Empire. Thus, there were extensive continuities between these periods.

When British forces moved into Istanbul to direct the Porte and thus control the rump Empire in 1918, the CUP abolished itself, which included a formal curtailing of the *Teşkilat-ı Mahsusa*. However, former members of the CUP immediately began organising new paramilitary forces to replace the *Teşkilat-ı Mahsusa*, including the *Karakol Cemiyeti* (Outpost Society) founded in 1918.[59] This paramilitary force was used in different parts of Anatolia during the national resistance movement, particularly between 1918 and 1920. It had some obvious commonalities with the *Teşkilat-ı Mahsusa*. After they were arrested, former leaders of *Teşkilat-ı Mahsusa* Hüsamettin Ertürk and Kuşçubaşı Eşref mentioned there were other secret armed forces, and many members of *Karakol Cemiyeti* also mentioned this

[57] Şerif Mardin, *Jön Türklerin Siyasi Fikirleri, 1895–1908*, 6. baskı (İst: İletişim Yayınları, 1999); M. Şükrü Hanioğlu, *Bir Siyasal Düşünür Olarak Doktor Abdullah Cevdet ve Dönemi* (Istanbul: Üçdal Neşriyat, 1981).

[58] Dündar, *Modern Türkiye'nin Şifresi*, 59–60.

[59] Zürcher, *Turkey A Modern History*, 135; Stanford J. Shaw and Ezel Kural Shaw, *History of the Ottoman Empire and Modern Turkey* (Cambridge: Cambridge University Press, 2002), 340.

in their memoirs.[60] These secret intelligence and paramilitary forces were active during the transition period (1918–1923) and were associated with the Ankara government.[61]

Actions and Crimes of the Gangs and the State

Topal (Lame) Osman was the leader of a notorious local band that operated as an effective paramilitary force during the establishment of the Ankara government. He had fought in the Balkan Wars and later, in the First World War, when, along with his volunteer bandits, he fought as a local paramilitary organisation with the *Teşkilat-ı Mahsusa* in the north-east of the Empire.[62] After the Bolshevik Revolution, the Russian army withdrew, and Osman and his gang perpetrated various massacres. These were aimed against the non-Muslim communities (Greek and Armenian) and some Muslim villages (e.g. in Giresun province and areas around the eastern Black Sea coast). The Ukrainian revolutionary leader, Mikhail Vasilyevich Frunze, mentions the brutality of Topal Osman enacted against Greeks and Kurds in his memoirs related to Turkey.[63] The oppression of Topal Osman and his gang was also directed against Alevi Kurds south of the coastal area, in Sivas province. When Mustafa Kemal began the nationalist fight in May 1919, Topal Osman was wanted as a criminal by the Istanbul authority because of his actions in the Armenian genocide in the Pontus ([Greek] Black Sea) region. In the following days, Mustafa Kemal and Topal Osman had several meetings, following which Osman and his gang became part of the Turkish nationalist struggle.[64]

---

[60] The Müsellah Müdafai Milliye (Armed National Defense), Mim Mim (Müdafai Milliye, National Defense), Hamza, Mücahid (Mujahedin), Muharib (Combatant), Felah (Liberation), Muaveneti Bahriye (Auxiliary Force for Navy) were some of the other secret armed forces. Ahmet Efe, *Kuşçubaşı Eşref* (Istanbul: Bengi Yayınları, 2007), 137; Tansu, *Teşkilat-ı Mahsusa İki Devrin Perde Arkası*.

[61] Erol Ülker, 'İşgal İstanbul'unda Müdafaa-i Milliye'nin Kuruluşu Üzerine Bir Değerlendirme: İttihatçılar, Komünistler, Sosyalistler' [An Assessment on the Establishment of the Committee of National Defense in Istanbul under Occupation: Unionists, Communists, Socialists], *Kebikeç İnsan Bilimleri İçin Kaynak Araştırmaları Dergisi*, no. 41 (January 2016): 67–94.

[62] Cemal Şener, *Topal Osman Olayı*, 10. baskı (Istanbul: Etik Yayınları, 2004), 49.

[63] M. V. Frunze, *Frunze'nin Türkiye Anıları Kasım 1921–Ocak 1922: Ukraynalı Devrimci Lider*, trans. Ahmet Ekeş (İzmir: Cem Yayınevi, 1978), 18.

[64] Bulut, *Dersim Raporları*, 114.

In 1920, the Treaty of Sèvres, which was to divide Anatolia into various zones, was signed by the Porte, but the imperial authority did not implement the conditions of the treaty. In the same year, Mustafa Kemal and other members of the Turkish nationalist movement established the Ankara government. Hence, the period of uprisings following the defeat of the Empire, such as the Koçgiri Kurdish[65] and Pontus (Greek) resistances (1919–21), were initiated variously against both the Istanbul authority and the Ankara government.[66] The former of these was Alevi Kurds in the Kurdish Koçgiri region, or (roughly) Sivas province.[67] The Ankara government sent a force from its Central Army (itself with roots in the Ottoman army), led by Sakallı Nurettin Pasha (who had irregular war experience in the Balkan Wars), assisted by Topal Osman's gang (acting as a voluntary paramilitary), to suppress the revolt. Together, they suppressed the Koçgiri resistance in a bloody and violent way. The main actions of this paramilitary gang consisted of the burning and plundering of villages and the rape of its female inhabitants. The severity and brutality of the acts was discussed in the Ankara parliament, with several members calling for the punishment of Nurettin Pasha.[68]

Topal Osman and his gang played an important role in suppressing the resistance in the east and the north-east of the Empire and modern Turkey, including assassinations. After the Koçgiri resistance, they moved north to suppress the Pontus resistance, again alongside the regular army, taking up a prominent role in the suppression and carrying out similar massacres of non-Muslim, especially Greek civilians in 1921.[69] Basically, Mustafa Kemal used Osman to eliminate opposition groups and individuals to facilitate the establishment of the Republic. Eventually, Topal Osman was to become commander of the Guard Battalion of the Grand National Assembly (*Türkiye Büyük Millet Meclisi*, TBMM) in Ankara. There, the Trabzon deputy Ali

[65] Dilek Kızıldağ Soileau, *Koçgiri İsyanı: Sosyo Tarihsel Bir Analiz* (Istanbul: İletişim Yayınları, 2017).

[66] Stefanos Yerasimos, *Milliyetler ve Sınırlar: Balkanlar, Kafkasya ve Orta-Doğu*, trans. Tekeli Şirin, 6. baskı (Istanbul: İletişim, 2010), 345–417; Ahmet Kahraman, *Kürt Isyanları: Tedip Ve Tenkil* (Istanbul: Evrensel Basım Yayın, 2004), 267–75.

[67] Kahraman, *Kürt Isyanları*, 267–75.

[68] Bulut, *Dersim Raporları*, 99–116.

[69] Yerasimos, *Milliyetler ve Sınırlar*, 345–417.

Şükrü was one of the leaders of an opposition group to Mustafa Kemal that had emerged. He was killed, and Topal Osman was held responsible for the murder.[70] A few days later, Topal Osman was caught and executed, probably because he was not needed anymore.[71]

Topal Osman is a very important figure in making sense of the relation between the state and the paramilitary forces. His gang was a local bandit group and had a prominent role during the Armenian genocide in 1915 and then during the massacres against Kurds and Pontus Greeks, particularly during 1919–22. He rose to a position of some prominence in Ankara, but was then eliminated. Other gang leaders were liquidated like this after being used by the state, although some were tolerated.[72] They became national heroes in Turkish-nation culture, feted in various publications and then in movies and TV series (including at the present time).[73] The development of Topal Osman's gang demonstrates the transformation of gang activity from the criminal position of outlaw or renegade into the military bureaucracy for purposes of furthering the power of the state through secondment and support, that is, as a paramilitary force.

Tribes as Irregular Armed Forces and the State

Another active paramilitary organisation was the Village Guard system, established in 1924 under the Village Law (*Köy Kanunu*). According to this law, every village had to have at least one Village Guard, under the orders of the village headman. The number of Village Guards could increase depending on the size of the village and if threats (banditry, looting, etc.) increased in the village and surrounding areas.[74] It was one of the first laws adopted by the

---

[70] Efe, *Kuşçubaşı Eşref*, 231.

[71] Ayşe Hür, 'Çağımızın Bir (Başka) Kahramanı: Topal Osman', *Birikim*, 31 January 2006, http://www.birikimdergisi.com/guncel-yazilar/70/cagimizin-bir-baska-kahramani-topal-osman#.WB3--dxer_R.

[72] Murat Belge, *Militarist Modernleşme: Almanya, Japonya ve Türkiye*, 2. baskı (Istanbul: İletişim yayınları, 2012), 774.

[73] Berfin Emre Çetin, *The Paramilitary Hero on Turkish Television: A Case Study on* Valley of the Wolves (Newcastle: Cambridge Scholars Publishing, 2015); Riza Nur, *Mangal Yurekli Adam Topal Osman* (Istanbul: Orgun Yayınları, 2010).

[74] 'Köy Kanunu' (TBMM, 1924), http://www.mevzuat.gov.tr/MevzuatMetin/1.3.442.pdf.

Grand National Assembly of Turkey, given such precedence because most of the population at that time lived in the countryside.[75] However, the Village Guards was not an armed force like the army or the police, but rather they were formed as auxiliary forces to the gendarmerie units in the local area. Moreover, they seem likely to have been created for intelligence purposes and thus state control; individuals were used by the state as informers, because they knew both the local threats (for intelligence) and the territory (for military operations). These paramilitaries also depended on the local forces of the official army and the district governors. According to this law, Village Guards were also to join military operations with the army and the gendarmerie, as needed. Kurdish rebellions and resistances in the east of the Republic continued until 1938, and Village Guards were most likely used to suppress rebellions and resistance. The law, which had initially just instituted a temporary system of voluntary protection – for the locals to register as 'security protectors' (*güvenlik korucusu*) in order to carry arms against 'gangsters and bandits' (*çapulcular ve eşkiya*) – was in effect until 1985, when it was amended for the establishment of what became referred to as the 'Village Guards' (*Köy Korucuları*). However, new additions and regulations were made in the law several times from 1924 to 1985. Thus, the permanent arrangement for a temporary force bridged the gap between the Hamidiye/Tribal Regiments and the (indefinitely instituted) Village Guards of the 1990s but had a different role from the Regiments in terms of actions, since, although remaining involved in armed conflicts, the role established in the early Republic for the Village Guards was primarily as information gathering, as part of the intelligence network.

The Tribal Light Cavalry Regiments were deactivated at the end of World War I, but they were not removed as an institution. The Republic of Turkey was different from the Ottoman Empire in terms of the regime type, but the new regime mostly continued the old paramilitary policy in this respect. In fact, various regiments probably continued in active engagements during the period of the early Republic, and, equally, failed to join uprisings – although, as ever, the full situation was complex and the overall picture mixed. Some of the leaders of a tribal regiment, such as Cibranlı Halit Bey, would eventually

---

[75] Evren Balta, Murat Yüksel and Yasemin Acar, *Geçici Köy Koruculuğu Sistemi ve 'Çözüm Süreci'* (Istanbul: SÜREÇ Araştırma Merkezi, 2015), 15.

become involved in organisations against the state. However, Robert Olson argues that the Hamidiye did not help the tribes that participated in the Koçgiri Kurdish rebellion; for example:

> Most of the Hamidiye regiment had been created from tribes that lived further east and south. This deprived the Koçgiri rebellion of much military experience. It took place closer to Ankara than the Sheikh Said rebellion and thus was more accessible, albeit over difficult terrain, to Turkish forces.[76]

Yet, there is an interesting argument in this regard that Kör Hüseyin Pasha (a famous regiment leader) and his tribal cavalry helped Topal Osman and Nurettin Pasha during the Koçgiri resistance against the Alevi Kurds.[77] Other sources mention the structure of the military institutions in 1928, with the Regiments included in the military hierarchy[78] – but they were inactive and sometimes moved against the Turkish state. Cibranlı Halit Bey was a tribal regiment leader (the tribe of Cibran). Despite having been trained at the Imperial Tribal School (*Mekteb-i Aşiret-i Humayun*) in Istanbul,[79] he became leader of the Freedom Organisation (*Azadi Örgütü*) that organised the Sheikh Said Kurdish rebellion in 1925. Similarly, Kör Hüseyin Pasha, leader of another tribal regiment (the tribe of Heyderan), wanted to participate in the Sheikh Said rebellion, and although he could not do this, his sons were able to join the Ağrı Kurd rebellion in 1930 against the Turkish state (despite the notoriety of their father in Kurdish society).[80]

The alliance of the Regiments with Abdulhamid II and the CUP dwindled during the Republic because the alliance under the new regime had neither

---

[76] Olson, *The Emergence of Kurdish Nationalism*, 34.

[77] Ahmet Kahraman, *Kürt İsyanları Tedip ve Tenkil* (Istanbul: Evrensel Basım Yayın, 2013), 79.

[78] Yusuf Akçura, *Türk Yılı 1928*, 1928, 83–90, http://212.174.157.46:8080/xmlui/handle/11543/508; Mete Tunçay, *Türkiye Cumhuriyeti'nde Tek-Parti Yönetimi'nin Kurulması (1923–1931)* (Ankara: Tarih Vakfı Yurt Yayınları, 1999), 112.

[79] Eugene L. Rogan and Alişan Akpınar, *Aşiret Mektep Devlet Osmanlı Devleti'nde Aşiret Mektebi* (Istanbul: Aram Yayıncılık, 2001).

[80] Kemal Süphandağ, *Hamidiye Alayları Ağrı Kürt Direnişi ve Zilan Katliamı* (Istanbul: Pêrî Yayınları, 2012), 458; also, see Zinar Silopi, *Doza Kürdistan. Kürt Milletini 60 Sendeneberi Esaretten Kurtuluş Savaşı Hatıratı* (Beirut: Stev Basımevi, 1969), 92; Süphandağ, *Hamidiye Alayları*, 323.

existential threats (from foreign powers or Christians in the country) nor a shared ideal (the unity of Islam and the caliphate, particularly during the late Empire).[81] However, during the 1926 Koçuşağı rebellion in Dersim (Tunceli), some Alevi Kurd tribes did fight against the rebel tribes as militia forces alongside the Turkish army.[82] In addition, some pro-state tribes in Dersim supported the state's military forces as a militia during the Dersim genocide in 1937–8.[83] The state could use differences among the tribes and pull some of them into a pro-state position; when one of these tribes revolted against the state, the rival tribe or the local militia groups could help the state (the second Ağrı operation in 1927 offers another example of this).[84] Generally, however, relations between state and Kurdish tribal leaders and sheikhs sank to a minimum level because of the rigid modernist approach of the new regime.

Yet when the state elites began to perceive the continuous Kurdish revolts (the Sheikh Said and Ağrı rebellions) as expressions of nationalism, they tried to suppress them by re-establishing relations with the Kurdish feudal elites.[85] In 1927, Inspectorates-General were established in some parts of the country, particularly in Kurdish provinces.[86] These inspectorates created a dual legal system which offered impunity for paramilitary groups. The military forces, civil servants and other groups (Village Guards, militia, and perhaps pro-government tribes) that worked with them were considered to have been exempted from criminal offenses, as a result of which the crimes committed during the suppression of the Ağrı rebellion remained unpunished.[87] In this

---

[81] Mehmet Bayrak, *Kürtler'e Vurulan Kelepçe: Şark Islahat Planı* (Ankara: Öz-Ge, 2009).

[82] *Genelkurmay Belgelerinde Kürt İsyanları I*, 1. baskı (Istanbul: Kaynak Yayınları, 1992), 237–62.

[83] Tuba Akekmekçi and Muazzez Pervan, eds, *Dersim Harekâtı ve Cumhuriyet Bürokrasisi (1936-1950)* (Istanbul: Tarih Vakfı Yurt Yayınları, 2011), 257.

[84] *Genelkurmay Belgelerinde Kürt İsyanları I*, 289–310; see also Uğur Ümit Üngör, 'Rethinking the Violence of Pacification: State Formation and Bandits in Turkey, 1914–1937', *Comparative Studies in Society and History* 54, no. 4 (October 2012): 749–51.

[85] Sait Ebinç, 'Doğu Anadolu Düzeninde Aşiret-Cemaat-Devlet (1839–1950)' (PhD diss., Ankara Üniversitesi, 2008), 168.

[86] Üngör, *The Making of Modern Turkey*, 135.

[87] Engin Çağdaş Bulut, 'Devletin Taşradaki Eli: Umumi Müfettişlikler', *CTAD: Cumhuriyet Tarihi Araştırmaları Dergisi* 11, no. 21 (2015): 106.

way, the regime kept close connections to some Kurdish tribes and continued to use the Kurdish militias as paramilitary power (including, of course,
those that remained in the Regiments system during the first decade of the
Republic). Sedat Ulugana, in his work on the Ağrı rebellion, emphasises
the role of local militias collaborating with the state in the massacres,[88] while
Naif Bezwan defines the destructive violence perpetrated by state official
armed units with paramilitary groups between 1920 and 1938 as ethnocidal
and genocidal.[89]

Continuities in Paramilitary Organisation after the 1920s

Although they are different regimes, the ruling elites of the Republic were
ideologically, economically and politically connected with the paramilitary
policies of the CUP and Abdulhamid II period. The gang of Topal Osman is
the best example for this continuity. After the 1920s, the gang remained active
in violence against civilians, plunder and destruction. As a result of the partner-
ship of Topal Osman with the CUP and Mustafa Kemal, his gang eventually
became co-opted into the higher echelons of political security (and then done
away with as though to cleanse the state of its dirty work).[90] Similar examples
also emerged in western Anatolia, where members of bandit gangs, responsible
for much of the violence and massacres in the region, also fought alongside the
Teşkilat-ı Mahsusa and then became coopted by the Republican state.[91]

   Another continuity in the state paramilitary policy, although less prominent, was that of the tribal paramilitary regiments. As mentioned above, the
connection of the state to Kurdish paramilitary groups became less close,
and as a result of the suppression of Kurdish nationalism, sometimes even
antagonistic. Nevertheless, the Republican state continued to engage Kurdish paramilitaries as death squads (for assassinations of dissidents), tribal

[88] Sedat Ulugana, *Ağrı Kürt Direnişi ve Zîlan Katliamı (1926–1931)*, 2. baskı (Istanbul: Pêrî Yayınları, 2010).
[89] Naif Bezwan, 'The State and Violence in Kurdistan: A Conceptual Framework', *Kurdish Studies* 9, no. 1 (2021): 11–36.
[90] Frank Bovenkerk and Yücel Yeşilgöz, *Türkiye'nin Mafyası*, 2. baskı (Istanbul: İletişim, 2000), 130.
[91] Gingeras, 'Last Rites for a "Pure Bandit"'.

militias (for the suppression of Kurdish rebellions), Village Guards (as local informants) and youth organisations (for the indoctrination and militarisation of society, looking especially to the future). The Ankara authority worked to centralise state institutions around the country for absolute control over the territory, including its people(s). The new regime can thus be regarded as establishing these institutions to exert power through the centralisation of the state, by gaining control of inaccessible areas of the country, and via an informant network.

The *Teşkilat-ı Mahsusa* and *Karakol* paramilitary organisations also continued to exert influence, even if the *Teşkilat-ı Mahsusa* was abolished after the alleged assassination attempt (in Izmir) against Mustafa Kemal in 1926, for which former members of the *Teşkilat-ı Mahsusa* were held responsible (and subsequently eliminated). In the following year, a largely similar intelligence organisation, the National Security Service (*Milli Emniyet Hizmeti*, MEH or MAH) was established.[92] As Ryan Gingeras points out, 'it must be noted that the destruction of the *Teşkilât-ı Mahsusa*, and the elimination of its principal leaders, was not a consequence of any aversion to paramilitarism as a political or military tactic.'[93] On the contrary, the state reverted to an established method to deal with the threats of mass mobilisation and vigilantism, such as the Thrace pogrom (against the Jewish community) in 1934.[94] However, the main threats (or perceived threats) to the state continued, which now came from Kurdish nationalists, non-Muslim communities, and communists; these would also provide the rationale – and the legitimation – for the new paramilitary forces during the multi-party period.

The Multi-party Period (1950s–90s)

Even if the absolute power of Atatürk and İnönü during the Republican period was replaced after 1950 by a multi-party regime, characterised by a division of labour, if not cleavages, and conflicts between state agencies,

---

[92] Tuncay Özkan, *MİT'in Gizli Tarihi*, 9. baskı (Istanbul: Alfa, 2003), 163.

[93] Gingeras, *Heroin, Organized Crime, and the Making of Modern Turkey*, 40.

[94] Zafer Toprak, '1934 Trakya Olaylarında Hükümetin ve CHF'nin Sorumluluğu', *Toplumsal Tarih* 34 (1996): 19–25; Ayhan Aktar, 'Trakya Yahudi Olaylarını "Doğru" Yorumlamak', *Tarih ve Toplum* 155 (1996): 45–56.

much of the paramilitary policies of the previous period were continued. The main reason for this continuity was that the most effective force among the competing sections of the state was the military, together with MİT, and the political parties that supported the army's policies. Yet a new dimension was added as paramilitary forces now also became embroiled in the anti-communist agitation of the secret services of some of the NATO countries, notably the CIA.

Somewhat paradoxically, the 'multi-party' concept refers to the pluralism of a democratic state, and yet in Turkey, even as the Republic developed a multi-party system of governance, its 'security state' politics became more prominent.[95] Basically, the state developed into a dual structure, with on the one hand an elected government and a parliamentary system based on regular elections between a plurality of parties (the legal state), yet on the other hand, most of the actual power residing with the leadership of the army, which also included the leadership of the intelligence service and large parts of the state bureaucracy. This was called a 'deep state', and allegedly had control over the elected government. Until 1950, when the state administrators came from the CHP, there was no duality within the state, or at least, it had not yet appeared – with the multi-party period, however, this dual state structure started to become a problem. Basically, there were two groups claiming to govern the state: the government of the day and 'a kind of shadow or parallel system of government in which unofficial or publicly unacknowledged individuals play important roles in defining and implementing state policy'.[96] Its power became manifest during a series of military coups (in 1960, 1971 and 1980) aiming to reassert power when they thought the government was out of control (becoming too independent or 'democratic').

Almost all paramilitary forces in the post-1950s era were associated with the 'deep state' of the army and the intelligence organisation, MİT. This 'deep state' hegemony provided the ideological centre of gravity for Turkish nationalism, ethnocentric statism and right-wing militarism that constructed

[95] Ola Tunander, 'Democratic State vs. Deep State: Approaching the Dual State of the West', in *Government of the Shadows: Parapolitics and Criminal Sovereignty*, eds Eric Wilson and Tim Lindsey (London: Pluto Press, 2009), 56–72.
[96] Gingeras, 'Last Rites for a "Pure Bandit"', 152.

and delimited the democratic framework within which political parties were formed and governments elected. Thus, the governments and the military institutions used paramilitary groups extensively and in multiple ways after the 1950s against what were defined as the threats to the state. Specifically, these threats were ascried to socialist youth movements, the Kurdish leftist and nationalist organisations, and the Alevi identity and non-Muslim communities. And accordingly, the military and governments established various paramilitary organisations, such as the ÖHD and ultranationalist youth groups, which were allowed and directed to suppress these 'threats'. The paramilitary forces used various actors for this, from large-scale populist movements to highly trained death squads. Turkish nationalist masses were mobilised for the pogroms against non-Muslim and Alevi communities, youth vigilante groups were used against the dissident groups, and the extremist right-wing and Islamist paramilitary youth organisations were employed as death squads against the left-wing movements, the Kurdish leftists and the nationalist organisations and various intellectuals in different parts of Turkey (including northern Kurdistan), as well as in Europe (mostly the West, essentially in a spread and dispersion of Turkey's issues) and also in Cyprus (a special case, due to the promotion by Athens there of Greek ethno-nationalism).

The 'Deep State' Network and Paramilitarism

Scholars and journalists have discussed the secret relationships and extra-legal acts linked to the government agencies within the framework of the concept of the 'deep state'.[97] The deep state has also been long debated among members of Turkish society, state institutions and leaders of the political parties in Turkey. Essentially, the idea of depth here refers to its secret quality (hidden, underground), as formally outside the realm of public scrutiny and accountability. Thus, the 'deep state' can be defined as a secret network of relations established within the state to defend the position of (parts of) the regime and (parts of)

---

[97] Söyler, *The Turkish Deep State*; Ünver, 'Turkey's "Deep-State" and the Ergenekon Conundrum'; Can Dündar and Celal Kazdağlı, *Ergenekon: Devlet İçinde Devlet*, 10. baskı (Ankara: Can Yayınları, 2013); Cüneyt Arcayürek, *Derin Devlet: 1950–2007*, 13. baskı (Istanbul: Detay Yayınları, 2007); Belma Akçura, *Derin Devlet Oldu Devlet*, 5. baskı (Istanbul: Belge Yayınları/ Sınırötesi Yayınları, 2009).

the state bureaucracy.[98] Bezwan discusses this separation as a 'dual state' in the context of Turkey and northern Kurdistan.[99]

After the 1950s, the 'deep state', as it gradually became known in Turkish public discourses – although not, of course, in that of the 'mainstream' – was fundamentally out of reach of the law. Ayşegül Sabuktay characterises this as the 'extra-legal' activities of the state.[100] The secret network became increasingly known as a 'fact' of political life and considered responsible for political crimes, massacres and assassinations. Yet also Süleyman Demirel, seven times prime minister between 1965 and 1993, and president of the Turkish Republic for another seven years (1993–2000), asserted in an interview in 2005 that the Turkish army was the core of the deep state. He also declared that the Turkish army was responsible for the coups of 1912, 1960, 1971 and 1980; and that the army had a more prominent role in the control of the state than governments during these periods.[101]

The central paramilitary organisation within the Turkish deep state was the Special Warfare Department (*Özel Harp Dairesi*, ÖHD). According to İsmail Beşikci, it was not the Turkish parliament, the government and elected parties and individuals (MPs) that determined and enacted the politics of the Turkish

[98] Tunander, 'Democratic State vs. Deep State'; Ernst Fraenkel, *The Dual State: A Contribution to the Theory of Dictatorship* (New York: Oxford University Press, 1941); Hans J. Morgenthau, *Politics Among Nations: The Struggle for Power and Peace* (New York: Alfred A. Knopf, 1955).

[99] 'Given the frequency, recurrence and durability of emergency regimes and use of violence in dealing with the question of Kurdistan the political and administrative regimes of the states in question . . . take the form of a dual state, that is, a "normative state" approach towards the dominant ethnicity and "prerogative state" approach against the Kurds and non-core minorities at large. Whilst the former is not entirely dismissive of the principles of democratic governance, the latter operates as an apparatus of domination that denies equal rights, recognition and protection by targeting the agency, identity, territorial and communal make-up of Kurdish society through deployment of special regimes and associated policies of assimilation, displacement and social and demographic engineering.' Bezwan, 'The State and Violence in Kurdistan', 19.

[100] Sabuktay, 'Locating Susurluk Affair into the Context of Legal-Political Theory: A Case of Extra-Legal Activities of the Modern States' (PhD diss., Middle East Technical University, 2004).

[101] Akçura, *Derin Devlet Oldu Devlet*, 24–6.

state in northern Kurdistan during the 1990s – rather, it was the ÖHD that was the main authority there.[102] The beginnings of the ÖHD can be traced back to the Mobilisation Research Council (*Seferberlik Tetkik Kurulu*, STK), established in 1952. The STK was the product of the Cold War and the establishment of NATO, of which Turkey became a member in the same year. According to Daniele Ganser, a 'secret army had been set up by the US secret service Central Intelligence Agency (CIA) and the British Secret Intelligence Service (MI6 or SIS) after the end of the Second World War to fight Communism in Western Europe'.[103] According to William Blum,

> [t]he planning for this covert paramilitary network, code-named 'Operation Gladio' (Italian for 'sword'!), began in 1949, involving initially the British, the Americans and the Belgians. It eventually established units in every non-communist country in Europe—including Greece and Turkey and neutral Sweden and Switzerland—with the apparent exceptions of Ireland and Finland.[104]

The Turkish branch of this network was the STK. It was funded by the USA, in order to protect the regime against perceived communist 'threats'.[105] Yet the Turkish deep state also deployed the STK against many other groups and individuals considered enemies of the Republic. Indeed, the STK was to become one of the most controversial institutions of the Turkish military after the mid-1950s.

The STK was established in 1952 by decree of the Ministry of Defense as a department of the General Staff, but initial preparations for this can be seen in retrospect as having begun shortly after the end of World War II, in 1948, when a group of sixteen officers from the Turkish army were sent to the United States to train for irregular warfare against the communist threat.

---

[102] İsmail Beşikci, *Orta Doğu'da Devlet Terörü* (Istanbul: İsmail Beşikci Vakfı Yayınları, 2013), 72–3.

[103] Ganser, *NATO's Secret Armies*, 1.

[104] William Blum, *Killing Hope: US Military and CIA Interventions Since World War II* (London: Zed Books, 2003), 106.

[105] Ganser, *NATO's Secret Armies*, 226; Söyler, 'Informal Institutions, Forms of State and Democracy', 316.

Captain Alparslan Türkeş, later to lead the MHP, was among this group, as was Colonel Daniş Karabelen. Karabelen was engaged in the Korean War (1950–3), as commander of the Turkish troops alongside the US army, and he later became the first commander of the ÖHD.[106] It was not only his American training that prepared Karabelen for this role. In fact, he had previously had experience in irregular warfare during the late Ottoman Empire. He was trained by *Teşkilat-ı Mahsusa* during the First World War when he was in military school, and then he took part in the activities of both semi-formal paramilitary forces, the *Teşkilat-ı Mahsusa* and *Karakol*.

The first members of the ÖHD were selected from the group of sixteen US-trained officers.[107] The US also donated one million dollars to the ÖHD every year.[108] The paramilitary group's headquarters was located in Ankara, at a building shared with the Joint US Military Mission for Aid to Turkey, JUSMAT (*Türkiye'ye Yardım için Ortak ABD Askeri Kurulu*). This institution was linked to the second chief of the General Staff.[109] Kemal Yamak, commander of the force 1967–74, explained the need for the institution in his memoir, thus:

> *Özel Harp Dairesi* was an operation unit built on the basis of NATO's 'covert operation concept', especially with the support of the Americans. The geographical position and strategic location of our country made such an organisation very necessary and very useful.[110]

Turkish authorities had benefited from Germany's military and paramilitary experience in the First World War, but the authorities began to take advantage of the military – and paramilitary – experience of the USA after the Second World War. The section of the field manual of the US army regarding irregular warfare was translated by the Turkish army and used to train the ÖHD.[111] On the other hand, the ÖHD was regarded as responsible for many

---

[106] Cemal Kutay, *Beş Kıt'ada Bir Türk Paşası: Daniş Karabelen*, 2. baskı (Istanbul: Avcıol Basım Yayın, 2006); Kılıç, *Özel Harp Dairesi*, 22–47.

[107] Kılıç, *Özel Harp Dairesi*, 47–9.

[108] Yamak, *Gölgede Kalan İzler ve Gölgeleşen Bizler*, 254.

[109] Ibid., 243–8.

[110] Ibid., 248.

[111] Ibid., 245–7.

unsolved actions even by the leaders of the Turkish right-wing parties after the 1950s.[112]

Closely connected to the ÖHD was the the Turkish Resistance Organisation (*Türk Mukavemet Teşkilatı*, TMT). Founded by Rauf Denktaş and two friends against *Enosis* (union with Greece) in Cyprus in 1957, the TMT was established with the authorisation of the Turkish government and the army, with a crucial role of the ÖHD. As İsmail Lütfi Tansu, one of the founders of the ÖHD, said in an interview, 'When I was an officer in the Turkish army, I was commissioned to set up the Turkish Resistance Organisation in Cyprus.'[113] Also after it was established, the ÖHD continued to control the TMT.[114] The main aim of the TMT was the division of Cyprus. Communications between the Turkish authorities and the TMT were maintained through Denktaş, one of the leaders of the Turkish Cypriots and later President of the Turkish Republic of Northern Cyprus (*Kuzey Kıbrıs Türk Cumhuriyeti*, KKTC), as it was named in Turkey (although unrecognised internationally). Up to 1974, the TMT was responsible for many killings, which not only targeted the rival Greek paramilitary group National Organisation of Cypriot Fighters (*Ethniki Organosis Kyprion Agoniston*, EOKA), but also Turkish Cypriot leftist workers active within the Greek Cypriot trade unions on the island.[115] For much of this period, the TMT was directed by Kemal Yamak, an ÖHD commander and deputy commander between 1967 and 1974. According to Yamak, the main mission of the ÖHD in Cyprus was to support the TMT: 'the supply of TMT, particularly the supply of weapons and

---

[112] Akçura, *Derin Devlet Oldu Devlet*, 25–34. Süleyman Demirel, along with other prime ministers Bülent Ecevit, Turgut Özal and Necmettin Erbakan, the four former of Turkey, all considered the ÖHD responsible for many murders (assassinations) in the post-1950s. As leaders that could be characterised, respectively, as leftist, liberal and Islamicist, their popular democratic mandate may be considered progressive, in different ways, as outside and thus significantly in opposition to the power of the hegemonic centre, or deep state (indeed, Özal died suddenly in office, probably poisoned, and Erbakan was ousted by a 'virtual' coup).

[113] Mete Tümerkan, *Emekli Albay'dan Şok Açıklamalar!*, 21 January 2013, http://haberkibris. com/emekli-albaydan-sok-aciklamalar-2013-01-21.html; Kılıç, *Özel Harp Dairesi*, 106.

[114] Kızılyürek, 'Rauf Denktaş ve Kıbrıs Türk Milliyetçiliği'.

[115] Ibid., 338.

ammunition, were the most important and urgent issue', he stated in his memoir.[116] At the time of the Turkish invasion of Cyprus in 1974, the official Turkish army was deployed on the north of the island, which thus provided a base for the supply line. Moreover, it has also been argued, Cyprus had thus become a base for the training of Turkish paramilitaries.[117]

Because of the Turkish military and TMT actions, Greek Cypriots opened several cases at the European Court of Human Rights (ECHR). During these trials, the Court revealed several murders and disappearances for which paramilitary groups were responsible. In the 2001 judgement read on the case of Cyprus vs. Turkey, it was stated that 'the written statements of witnesses tending to corroborate the Commission's earlier findings that many persons now missing were taken into custody by Turkish soldiers or Turkish-Cypriot paramilitaries'.[118]

Political Parties and Youth Paramilitary Forces

Another of the most important paramilitary forces was the Idealist Youth (*Ülkücü Gençlik*) organisation of the MHP in the post-1950s period. Previously the Republican Villagers Nation Party (*Cumhuriyetçi Köylü Millet Partisi*, CKMP), the MHP name was taken in 1969, in the year after Alparslan Türkeş became leader.[119] Alparslan Türkeş was not only among the officers who went to US for the irregular warfare training and probably one of the founding members of the Gladio project in Turkey but also a member of the National Unity Committee (*Milli Birlik Komitesi*, MBK) established by the group of officers that organised the military coup in May 1960.[120] At the end of the 1960s, Türkeş and his friends organised an extended training camp for the party youth in different parts of the country. In fact, according to a report prepared by the security institution in 1970, the MHP organised

---

[116] Yamak, *Gölgede Kalan İzler ve Gölgeleşen Bizler*, 260.
[117] Parlar, *Osmanlı'dan Günümüze Gizli Devlet*, 244.
[118] *Case of Cyprus v. Turkey* (Council of Europe: European Court of Human Rights, 10 May 2001), 9, http://www.refworld.org/docid/43de0e7a4.html.
[119] Aydın and Taşkın, *1960'tan Günümüze Türkiye Tarihi*.
[120] Tanıl Bora and Kemal Can, *Devlet, Ocak, Dergâh: 12 Eylül'den 1990'lara Ülkücü Hareket* (Istanbul: İletişim Yayınları, 1991).

commando camps for members of the youth organisations in twenty-eight different places between 1968 and 1970. According to Türkeş, these camps were established to fight communists.[121]

There were generally three kinds of training in the camps: ideological education (predominantly rules of Islam and Turkish nationalism), combat training (karate, judo, etc.) and military training (including prevention of rallies and use of weapons). Approximately 2,000 young people were trained by retired, extreme right-wing officers in these camps, who were usually members of the MHP or close associates of Türkeş.[122] These camps were later transformed into Idealist Hearths (*Ülkü Ocakları*). As can be seen in the map of the locations of the camps organised by the MHP (Map 1.1), they were mostly sited in places where there was not much of a Kurdish population, away from the southeast of the country (i.e. northern Kurdistan). Training camps were organised in provinces such as Kars, Erzurum, Malatya and Antep, where Kurdish and Turkish populations lived together, but in these places Turkish nationalism was generally strong.

As well as retired extremist-right officers, as in the case of Türkeş and the MHP, the rise of the Idealist Youth paramilitary was a serious contributor to the legal right-wing parties, which developed symbiotically with the youth organisation. The Justice Party (*Adalet Partisi*, AP) was one of the sponsors and beneficiaries of this development. According to Canefe and Bora, this right-wing party supported the development of the youth nationalist groups:

> Particularly after the victory of the Justice Party . . . in 1965, the ultra-nationalist circles began to receive increasing support from the government as a useful force to suppress the oppositional and revolutionary left-wing movements. In some circles they were even identified as auxiliary forces of the state.

The MHP, and its youth paramilitary organisation had common ideological beliefs with both Islamists and Kemalists, such as their belief in the synthesis of

---

[121] Soner Yalçın and Doğan Yurdakul, *Reis: Gladio'nun Türk Tetikçisi*, 25. baskı (Istanbul: Doğan Kitap, 2004), 25.

[122] *Ülkücü Komando Kampları: AP Hükümetinin 1970'te Hazırlattığı MHP Raporu* (Istanbul: Kaynak Yayınları, 1997).

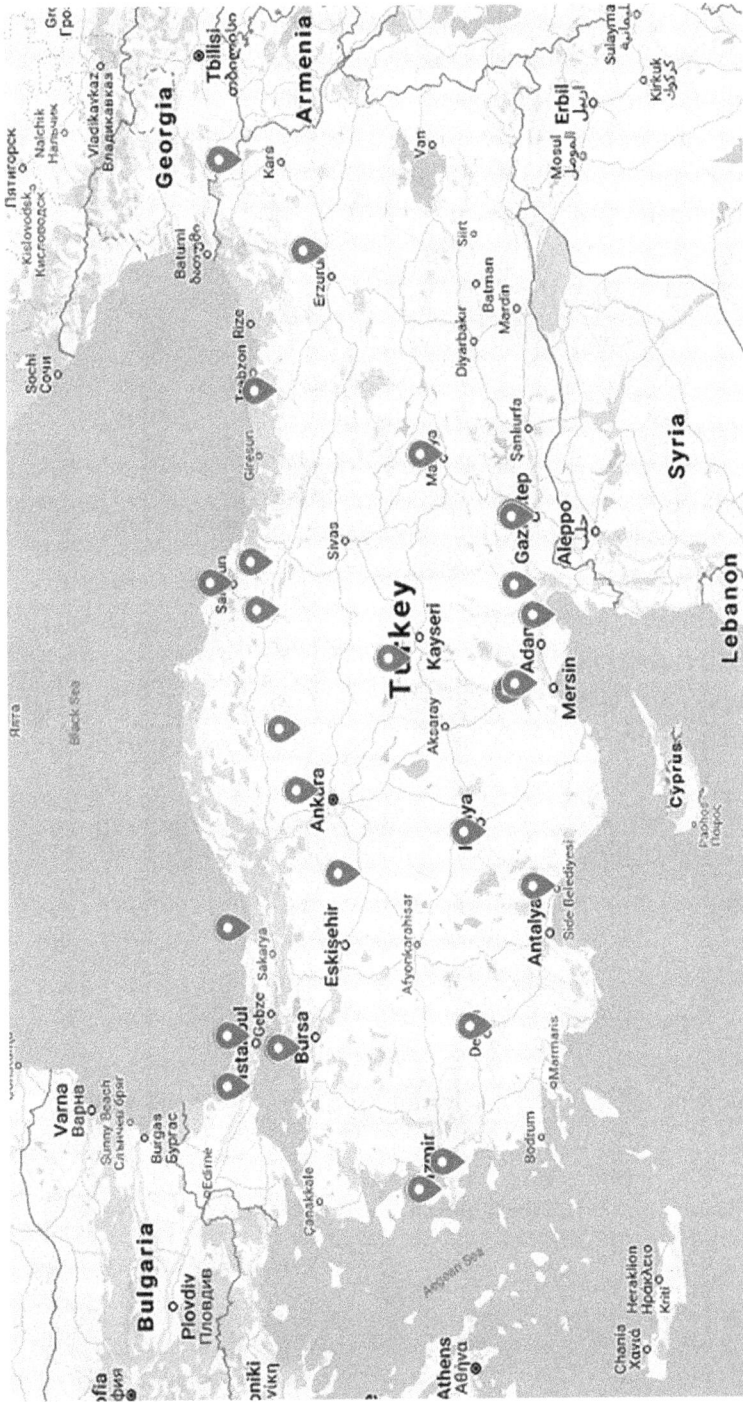

Map 1.1 Location of MHP training (commando) camps (1968–70). For a full list, camps were organised at the following places: Izmir-Gümüldür, Akrepkaya; Ankara-Eskişehir Yolu; Istanbul-Silivri; Gaziantep; Izmir-Karaburun, Balıkova; Adana-Yumurtalık, Ayaş; Kayseri-Yuvalı, Kızılırmak; Mersin-Belen, Soğukluk; Sakarya-Karasu, Kuyumculu; Konya-Çayırbağı; Çankırı-Kızılırmak Bucağı; Bursa-Mudanya, Yıldıztepe; Tokat-Yaylacık; Amasya; Adana-Osmaniye, Zorkun; Malatya-Pınarbaşı; Kars-Çıldır; Antalya-Manavgat; Samsun; Istanbul-Küçüksu, Hekimbaşı; Adana-Namrun; Erzurum-Hasankale; İzmir-Karaburun, Balıkova; Bursa-Mudanya, Yıldıztepe; Gaziantep-Erikce; Trabzon-Zigana; Ankara-Esenboğa; Denizli-Cankurtaran.

[Source: *Ülkü cü Komando Kampları: AP Hükümetinin 1970'te Hazırlattığı MHP Raporu* [Istanbul: Kaynak Yayınları, 1997, 14–19.]

Turkish nationalism and Sunni Islam.[123] Furthermore, the youth organisation was linked to Kemalists through the army (mostly, the ÖHD and the MİT), and to Islamists through the right-wing parties. Therefore, the military and intelligence institutions of the state and the right-wing parties encouraged the use of violence by youth paramilitary organisations against the threats. Tellingly, though, this also attested to the weakness of the institutional and democratic capacity of the state.

Some members of the Idealist Youth were trained in commando camps and subsequently connected to other countries' paramilitary forces. A Turkish nationalist and former member of the MHP, Turan Özbay, mentions the command camps of the MHP in his memoir. According to Özbay, these participants were usually students, and they influenced the extremist right-wing youth organisations in the universities after their training at the camps; moreover, some members of this youth organisation joined paramilitary groups in other countries as mercenaries, for solidarity and/or training. Özbay states that some high officials of the MHP went to Angola to fight with the National Union for the Total Independence of Angola (UNITA) and to Mozambique, where they opposed pro-Soviet movements at the end of the 1970s.[124] During the same decade, many members of the opposition organisations also travelled to Lebanon to the camps of the leftist Palestinian organisations.

There were many other Turkish-Islamic paramilitary forces in existence, particularly between 1960 and 1980. One of them was the Association for Fighting Communism in Turkey (*Türkiye Komünizmle Mücadele Derneği*, TKMD). This association was established in three cities of Turkey (in Zonguldak in 1950, Istanbul in 1956 and Izmir in 1963) and had many branches in different parts of the country.[125] The TKMD emerged as an anti-communist organisation during the Cold War, in accordance with the official policy and ideology of the state. Largely under the control of the Justice Party

---

[123] Nergis Canefe and Tanıl Bora, 'The Intellectual Roots of Anti-European Sentiments in Turkish Politics: The Case of Radical Turkish Nationalism', *Turkish Studies* 4, no. 1 (1 March 2003): 131.

[124] Turan Özbay, *Eve Dönmeyeceğiz* (Istanbul: Manifesto, 2006), 75, 271.

[125] Ertuğrul Meşe, 'Türk Siyasal Yaşamında Komünizmle Mücadele Dernekleri' (Masters thesis, Selçuk Üniversitesi, 2013).

during this period, organisations like the TKMD seemed to be unofficial institutions of the party.[126]

Another youth organisation, the National Turkish Students Union (*Milli Türk Talebe Birliği*, MTTB, 1916–80), operated as both a student organisation and paramilitary force; and after the 1960s, it played an important role in the ideological transformation of Kemalism from an ethno-nationalist progressive force to one of national conservatism. This transformation was partly rooted, therefore, in the right-wing student movement in the 1960s.[127] The TKMD and MTTB were both reserve forces of the state, and they participated in joint activities against leftist students. A major action of this sort was 'Bloody Sunday', in 1969, when leftist students organised a meeting to protest the arrival of the United States Sixth Fleet to Turkey. Members of the TKMD and the MTTB attacked the leftist students, killing two and injuring more than 200.[128] Also, the extreme Islamist youth group Association of Incursionists (*Akıncılar Derneği*) affiliated with the National Salvation Party (*Millî Selâmet Partisi*, MSP). Hüseyin Velioğlu, leader of Hizbullah, the extreme Islamist paramilitary group in Turkey of the 1990s, and many members of that organisation had participated in Islamist student movements and paramilitary groups in the second half of the 1970s, active then against the oppositional socialist movements in Turkey.[129]

These organisations were politically and legally (in terms of impunity) under the protection of the government. The TKMD, MTTB and Idealist Hearths were three intertwined organisations. For example, the Idealist Hearths – also known as the Idealist Youth or Grey Wolves (*Bozkurtlar*) – were established as an institution at the end of the 1960s; before that, the ultra-nationalist youth paramilitary groups had been organised in the TKMD.[130]

---

[126] Ibid., 74.

[127] M. Çağatay Okutan, *Bozkurt'tan Kuran'a Milli Türk Talebe Birliği (MTTB) 1916–1980* (Istanbul: Istanbul Bilgi Üniversitesi, 2004), 166–7.

[128] Ibid., 190; Meşe, 'Türk Siyasal Yaşamında Komünizmle Mücadele Dernekleri', 80.

[129] Faik Bulut, *İslamcı Örgütler 2*, 3. baskı (Doruk Yayımcılık, 1997), 384–5; Faik Bulut and Mehmet Faraç, *Kod Adı Hizbullah: Türkiye Hizbullahı'nın Anatomisi*, 2. baskı (Istanbul: Ozan Yayıncılık, 1999), 47–57; Ruşen Çakır, *Ayet ve Slogan:Türkiye'de İslami Oluşumlar*, 1. baskı (Istanbul: Metis Yayınları, 1990), 169–70; Cuma Çiçek, *The Kurds of Turkey: National, Religious and Economic Identities* (London: I. B. Tauris, 2017).

[130] Aydın and Taşkın, *1960'tan Günümüze Türkiye Tarihi*, 158–9.

Members of the youth paramilitary group were usually pulling the strings in the MTTB.[131] Therefore, 'threats' to the state gathered these extreme right-wing and Islamist groups together, and they could be used by other organisations, such as the ÖHD and MİT.

The state took various measures against the rise of opposition movements in the Kurdish provinces between 1975 and 1980. One such was the organisation of the paramilitary youth of the MHP in Kurdish cities. The Kurdish and Turkish populations were generally close to each other in many of these cities (Elazığ, Malatya, Erzurum, Iğdır, Maraş, Antep, Sivas, etc.), so Türkeş organised rallies in some of those where there were conflicts between the MHP paramilitary group and the Kurdish organisations.[132] Another measure was the activation of some tribes close to the state against the (perceived) threats. Pro-government tribes were determined according to the state intelligence reports, which categorised the tribes according to their 'harmful' situation (i.e. capacity to operate against the state).[133] At the end of the 1970s, there was a conflict between some of the pro-government tribes and some Kurdish leftist organisations – and most of these tribes were part of the Village Guard system in 1985. Accordingly, the state discovered many useful ways to counter 'threats', including the utilisation of some tribes in the Kurdish provinces in a similar way to that used with the ultranationalist paramilitary youth organisations.

The youth paramilitary members of the MHP and other right-wing parties created a brutal storm of violence, particularly after training in the commando camps. These parties supported their youth organisations and benefitted from their versatility: 'Conservative elements of the Justice Party (particularly those linked with small businesses and the country's religious establishment), as well as supporters within the newly established MHP, provided financial and political support to the emerging power of right wing street gangs'.[134] These youth groups did not exert violence for the political purposes of the state and its parties alone; they also organised and committed (other) crime, created illegal networks, and were involved in existing mafia networks.

---

[131] Özbay, *Eve Dönmeyeceğiz*, 75.

[132] Harun Ercan, 'Dynamics of Mobilization and Radicalization of the Kurdish Movement in the 1970s in Turkey' (Masters thesis, Koç University, 2010), 150.

[133] Ruşen Arslan, *Jandarma Genel Komutanlığının Raporu: Devletin İç Düşmanı Kürtler* (Istanbul: İsmail Beşikçi Vakfı, 2014).

[134] Gingeras, *Heroin, Organized Crime, and the Making of Modern Turkey*, 218.

The political violence of the paramilitary groups rose dramatically between 1975 and 1980. According to Hamit Bozarslan, these years were a period of violence that went out of control.[135] Polarisation (by class, ethnicity and religion) in society was at its highest level, and the paramilitary organisation of the MHP volunteered to take to the streets to protect the state against any opposition.[136] The aim of the paramilitary force was to prevent the rise of opposition movements, in support of the oppressive order that the state's regular military and police forces were seeking to impose (or rather, maintain). Thousands of people were killed. For example, 133 people, mostly leftists, were killed in the three-month period before the June 1977 election. However, the biggest massacre was committed on 1 May 1977, when around 500,000 people (trade-unions, leftist organisations, NGOs, etc.) gathered in Taksim Square, central Istanbul, to celebrate May Day, or International Workers' Day. Unidentified gunmen opened fire on the crowd (from surrounding high buildings) and from thirty-four to forty-two people were killed (mostly crushed during the dramatic police intervention made as a 'response') in what were to become and remain unsolved murders.[137] Such incidents, albeit on a smaller scale, were frequent. On 8 October 1978, for example, it was MHP's *ülkücü* militants who organised the 'Bahçelievler Massacre' in Ankara. In this violent action, seven university students and members of the Workers' Party of Turkey (*Türkiye İşçi Partisi*, TİP) were assassinated by the leaders of the Grey Wolves (Abdullah Çatlı, Haluk Kırcı and their friends).[138]

---

[135] Hamit Bozarslan, 'Bir "Bölücü" ve "Birleştirici" Olarak Şiddet', *Toplum ve Bilim*, no. 116 (2009): 15.

[136] Dündar and Kazdağlı, *Ergenekon*, 22.

[137] Aydın and Taşkın, *1960'tan Günümüze Türkiye Tarihi*, 280–1.

[138] The ultranationalist and Islamic youth organisations used different names after the assassinations and the massacres; these included the Rescue Army of Captive Turks (*Esir Türkleri Kurtarma Ordusu*, ETKO), Idealist Sharia Commando Army of Turkey (*Türkiye Ülkücü Şeriatçı Komando Ordusu*, TÜŞKO), Commander of the Turkish-Islamic Union (*Türk İslam Birliği Komandoları*, TİBKO), Turkish Revenge-Resistance and Massacre Army (*Türk İntikam-Mukavemet ve Katliam Ordusu*, TİMKO), Revenge of the Turkish-Islamic Union (*Türk İslam Birliği İntikamcıları*, TİBİ), Sharia Revenge Brigades (*Şeriatçı İntikam Tugayları*, ŞİT), and Turkish Revenge Brigades (*Türk İntikam Tugayları*, TİT). The last name was used several times in the 1990s and after. Meltem Ahıska, ed., *Sosyalizm ve Toplumsal Mücadeleler Ansiklopedisi*, vol. 7 (Istanbul: İletişim, 1988), 2340.

Abdullah Çatlı and other members of the Grey Wolves worked together with the Turkish intelligence organisation, the ÖHD or Gladio and other state institutions in many other extra-legal actions of this type between the mid-'70s and mid-'90s. Some of the state institutions also used the Grey Wolves against various political opposition movements – until the Susurluk accident brought a halt to this slide into lawlessness, as discussed in Çatlı's biography.[139]

During the early 1980s, Abdullah Çatlı and his friends were also used by the clandestine state institutions in European countries against the illegal Armenian Secret Army for the Liberation of Armenia (ASALA). ASALA militants were targeted by the state because they had carried out many assassinations against Turkish diplomats.[140] The Grey Wolves were used as an international death squad during this period.[141] The paramilitary youth was generally impelled by two motivations – anti-communism and the protection of the state as characterised by an extreme ethno-nationalism – but members of the Grey Wolves were also linked to the Turkish mafia and responsible for many organised crimes.[142] The main characteristics of this period of intense violence that was mostly perpetrated by the ultranationalist youth paramilitaries were assassinations, massacres and pogroms. Two of these are very well-known events: the attempted assassinations of Pope John Paul II, in 1981, and Prime Minister Özal, in 1988. The former was carried out by one of the members of the Grey Wolves, Mehmet Ali Ağca.[143] The latter was performed by Kartal Demirağ, who had been trained in commando camps in the 1970s.[144] Not coincidently, one might suppose, MİT was to prepare a report (the first MİT report) for Özal in 1987 that showed sophisticated relations involving organised crimes in state institutions. In other words, the state was internally fractured, with competing interests, agendas, and centres of power; or, it was

[139] Yalçın and Yurdakul, *Reis.*

[140] Ibid., 104–207; Dündar and Kazdağlı, *Ergenekon*, 30–1.

[141] Michael A. Reynolds, 'What the Assassination of the Russian Ambassador May Be Telling Us About Erdoğan's Turkey', *Foreign Policy Research Institute*, 23 December 2016, http://www.fpri.org/article/2016/12/assassination-russian-ambassador-may-telling-us-erdogans-turkey/.

[142] Gingeras, *Heroin, Organized Crime, and the Making of Modern Turkey*, 185–238.

[143] Bovenkerk and Yeşilgöz, *Türkiye'nin Mafyası*, 247–50.

[144] Dündar and Kazdağlı, *Ergenekon*, 25–6.

no longer in control of the paramilitary groups it had created – or rather inherited and recreated. Thus, according to the MİT report, many state institutions, especially police departments, were in close co-operation with the mafia, Grey Wolves and gangs in relation to money laundering, drug trafficking and various killings.[145]

The Role of Paramilitary Youth Groups during the Pogroms

The Istanbul pogrom in 1955 was probably the first business of the ÖHD. This was when the Turkish state, especially the ÖHD and intelligence services, mobilised nationalist masses for the pogroms against non-Muslim minorities during the multi-party period. Mobilisation of the masses to perpetrate a pogrom had been experienced before: the Thrace pogrom of 1934 was the first pogrom during the Republic period, organised by Turkish intelligence services and local vigilante groups against the Jews. The Istanbul pogrom of September 1955, or the 'Events of September 6–7', targeted non-Muslims, especially Greeks who lived in Istanbul, and was committed by Turkish nationalist mobs.[146] Many people were killed, injured and raped by the Turkish mobs motivated by a mix of Islam and Turkish nationalism with the collaboration of the Turkish police, militias and the press. Alfred de Zayas explains the consequence of the pogrom:

> Besides the deaths, thousands were injured; some 200 Greek women were raped, and there are reports that Greek boys were raped as well. Many Greek men, including at least one priest, were subjected to forced circumcision. The riots were accompanied by enormous material damage, estimated by Greek authorities at US$500 million, including the burning of churches and the devastation of shops and private homes. As a result of the pogrom, the Greek minority eventually emigrated from Turkey.[147]

---

[145] *T. C. Başbakanlık MİT Müsteşarlığının Banker Bako Raporudur* (Ankara, 1987); Bovenkerk and Yeşilgöz, *Türkiye'nin Mafyası*, 223–55; Arcayürek, *Derin Devlet*.

[146] Dilek Güven, *Cumhuriyet Dönemi Azınlık Politikaları Bağlamında 6–7 Eylül Olayları* (Istanbul: Tarih Vakfı Yurt Yayınları, 2005).

[147] Alfred de Zayas, 'The Istanbul Pogrom of 6–7 September 1955 in the Light of International Law', *Genocide Studies and Prevention: An International Journal* 2, no. 2 (1 August 2007): 138.

After the pogrom, many non-Muslim people were also forcibly removed from Turkey. The Turkish state argued that 'Events' – itself a euphemism – were a spontaneous mass attack by the people because of Cypriot politics, and thus that it could not have been organised by the state. However, documents that came to light later include state authority admissions of responsibility for the sequence of events. These were partly orchestrated by the secret intelligence organisation the MAH.[148] The state authorities used vigilante groups to encourage people to participate in the pogrom with economic benefits and nationalism. However, the role of the ÖHD was much more important. In an interview, the former head of the ÖHD, Sabri Yirmibeşoğlu, said 'September 6–7 was an undertaking of the Special Warfare Department [ÖHD]', which he described as 'a wonderful organisation' that 'reached its goal' (statements that he later denied).[149]

The organisation of the pogrom, mobilisation of the masses, the role of the press and so on demonstrate that this pogrom was thoroughly planned, as the former leader of the ÖHD had admitted. According to confessions of retired officers obtained later, the plan was implemented by the MAH and ÖHD together.[150] Another important issue was the relations between the ÖHD and civilians; according to Yamak, civilians could also work with ÖHD, if needed for special duties.[151] According to some sources, the civil wing of the ÖHD was known as the 'White Forces', intended to operate as an auxiliary or reserve force in times of conflict or occupation.[152] The existence of these forces was always denied by the ÖHD. Eventually, in 2012, the TBMM established a commission to investigate the military coups, and MİT sent a report to this commission.[153] According to this secret report, the ÖHD had

[148] Güven, *Cumhuriyet Dönemi Azınlık Politikaları Bağlamında*; Ünver, 'Turkey's "Deep-State" and the Ergenekon Conundrum'.
[149] NTV, '"Karakutu" Yine Ağzından Kaçırdı', *NTV*, 23 September 2010, http://www.ntv.com.tr/turkiye/karakutu-yine-agzindan-kacirdi,3Q5dK4I350OStXhyyXNcJg.
[150] Güven, *Cumhuriyet Dönemi Azınlık Politikaları Bağlamında*, 72.
[151] Yamak, *Gölgede Kalan İzler ve Gölgeleşen Bizler*, 247.
[152] Söyler, *The Turkish Deep State*, 101; Kılıç, *Özel Harp Dairesi*, 51.
[153] TBMM, *TBMM Darbe ve Muhtıraları Araştırma Komisyonu Raporu* (Ankara: Türkiye Büyük Millet Meclisi, 2012), https://www.tbmm.gov.tr/arastirma_komisyonlari/darbe_muhtira/.

prepared a secret, reserve paramilitary force with a hidden network connected to the ÖHD. There were thousands of members of the White Forces, and these civilians (usually members of the MHP and other nationalists) had a range of different professions in normal society. The main purpose of this paramilitary reserve force was – and is – to support the military institutions as and when needed.[154] Thus, the mobilisation of the masses for the Istanbul pogrom was probably fundamentally linked to this secret, state-based network.

Alevis were another target of the Turkish paramilitary forces, the extreme right-wing militias and vigilantes, especially after the 1960s. According to Kazım Ateş, this group was seen as a part of a pre-Islamic Turkish culture and considered as Turks in the categorisation of ethno-romantic citizenship for the Turk-Islam ideology of the state.[155] Although many of them were Turkish, a significant population of Alevis were Kurdish. Particularly, Kurdish Alevis were regarded as a threat. The religions and political attitudes of Alevis were important reasons for their exclusion, while ties between the Alevi and the leftist and Kurdish identities and related organisations made them a target for some paramilitaries and the nationalist, Sunni Islamic Turkish majority. The reason behind the attacks was that Alevis started to organise politically and culturally, establishing local Alevi associations in various provinces at the end of the 1950s, and increased rapidly in number in the 1960s and 1970s,[156] which was compounded by their generally 'liberal' views and thus involvement in leftist political movements.[157]

Alevi pogroms were initiated in 1978 by members of the MHP and other right-wing nationalist masses. The Malatya Alevi pogrom (17–21 April 1978)

[154] TBMM, *TBMM Meclis Araştırma Komisyonu Başkanlığı* (T. C. Başbakanlık Milli İstihbarat Teşkilatı Müsteşarlığı, 25 December 2012); Kılıç, *Özel Harp Dairesi*, 183–236.

[155] Kazım Ateş, 'Türk Milli-Kimliğinin İnşası ve Ulusal Cemaat İçinde Alevi-Yurttaşın Müphem Konumu', *İnsan Hakları Yıllığı*, no. 25/1 (2007): 73.

[156] Mehmet Ertan, 'The Circuitous Politicization of Alevism: The Affiliaton Between the Alevis and the Left Politics (1960–1980)' (Masters thesis, Boğaziçi University, 2008); Necdet Saraç, 'Türkiye'deki Alevi Örgütlenmesi', *Dersim News*, 22 July 2013, http://dersimnews.com/alevilik/alevileri-kim-temsil-ediyor.html.

[157] Emma Sinclair-Webb, 'Sectarian Violence, the Alevi Minority and the Left: Kahramanmaraş 1978', in *Turkey's Alevi Enigma: A Comprehensive Overview*, eds Paul J. White and Joost Jongerden (Leiden: Brill, 2003), 216.

started after the assassination of a local politician and continued for four days. Eight people were killed in total and almost a hundred injured. This pogrom was a sign of a new phase in the violence against Alevis. Then, in Sivas province, a similar pogrom took place in September 1978, with many Alevis being killed and injured and their buildings mostly destroyed.[158] The largest pogrom took place between 21 and 25 December 1978 in Maraş, when over a hundred people were killed (officially, 111).[159] Another Alevi massacre was perpetrated in Çorum, between May and July in 1980 – more than fifty Alevi people were killed by ultranationalist mob of people. But who organised these mobs and massacres? How did the nationalist masses come to resort to such actions?

According to some sources,[160] although the Alevi massacres were in different cities, they had many similar characteristics and followed similar organisational patterns. First, the beginning and initial development of the incidents were very similar, as if a systematic decision had been taken; generally, the pogroms began with provocations, such as bombings and assassinations. Second, members and youth paramilitary groups of the MHP and other nationalist and Islamic masses were mobilised by small, secret groups against the Alevi properties and neighbourhoods. Third, extreme right-wing masses gathered very quickly in all incidents; therefore, it is understood that a plan was in place that led to the massacres. Fourth, local authorities – including the governor, army and police – were always too late to intervene and prevent the massacres. Fifth, various inflammatory news items were published in the press before the massacres, as if for the preparation of extreme right-wing masses. And finally, weapons and bombs used in the massacres were linked to Turkish armed forces.[161] This all occurred in the context of thousands of killings

---

[158] Aydın and Taşkın, *1960'tan Günümüze Türkiye Tarihi*, 296.

[159] Sinclair-Webb, 'Sectarian Violence, the Alevi Minority and the Left'.

[160] Ertan, 'The Circuitous Politicization of Alevism'; Sinclair-Webb, 'Sectarian Violence, the Alevi Minority and the Left'; Aydın and Taşkın, *1960'tan Günümüze Türkiye Tarihi*; Bedriye Poyraz, 'Bellek, Hakikat, Yüzleşme ve Alevi Katliamları', *Kültür ve İletişim* 16, no. 1 (2013): 9–39.

[161] Özgür Açılım, *Unutturulanlar-3 Maraş Katliamı*, 2011, https://www.youtube.com/watch?v=JZ7b9J-Q5jM; Feza Erdendoğdu, 'Türkiye Basınında 1978–1980 Yıllarında Yaşanan Alevi Katliamlarına Dair Manşet Haberlerinin Karşılaştırılması Üzerıne Bir İnceleme' (Mimar Sinan Güzel Sanatlar Üniversitesi, 2014).

(of academics and journalists, leftists and right-wing students) from 1977 and until the military coup in 1980.

This period was a multi-layered and complicated process of what may be considered a civil war in Turkey. The conflicts were sometimes considered right–left, sometimes Alevi–Sunni and sometimes Kurdish–Turkish in character. Various extremist right-wing paramilitary youth organisations were associated with assaults, and masses of people were frequently employed. The true facts emerged slowly, if at all, and the effects were seen later. Many lawsuits were filed against the nationalist youth who had led the masses during the pogroms, but the paramilitary youth groups responsible for the massacres were not arrested, tried and sentenced by the police and courts. Hence, the impunity politics of the state legal system encouraged further nationalist masses for new pogroms. In 1993, another Alevi pogrom was carried out in Sivas, this one claiming the lives of thirty-seven people, mostly intellectuals and artists, burnt alive in a hotel by a mob arson attack while the police looked on.

The situation that brings together the deep state-related institutions, paramilitary groups and youth organisations of the right-wing parties was the claim of 'threats' to national security. The paramilitary groups and those not unsympathetic to their motivations sought to legitimise the actions and informal partnerships with this claim. In the 1970s, it is true, leftist groups, trade unions, Kurdish organisations and the Alevi community did themselves also make significant progress in terms of organisation, and they were interrelated, as in the case of leftist Alevi students. The leaders of the trade unions were mostly members of leftist organisations, and most of the Kurdish organisations were leftist. The development of these oppositional groups was a problem for the state, which drew various political and ideological red lines. The leftist ideology and rise of consciousness of the Kurds and Alevis meant they were targeted as communists and national threats, and left-wing political thought did indeed dominate the country in terms of progressive intellectual and social concerns. Thus, the state and right-wing parties formed and/or assisted paramilitary youth groups as a bulwark against the rise of the left and its radicalism. Much more needs to be said about the part of the left in the rise of the paramilitary right in terms of cause and effect and symbiosis. However, that would go beyond the scope of this work, which focuses just on one side of that dynamic.

Overall, the 1970s were one of the most intense periods of modern Turkish history in terms of the use of paramilitary groups. The responsibility for thousands of murders committed between 1975 and 1980 has not yet been ascertained and quite probably never will be. It is clear that the generation trained in the commando camps of the MHP became an important instrument in the increase of the violence and acts of killing from the end of the 1960s, through the '70s and '80s and into the 1990s. After the military coup of 12 September 1980, the paramilitary youth group was used in Europe against Armenian organisations and the PKK.[162] Many individuals and local groups became involved in organised crime and part of the wider mafia during the 1980s. These ultranationalist paramilitaries were included in the Special Police Teams used against the PKK after the 1980s.[163] As paramilitary groups associated with right-wing nationalist parties, some tribes in the Village Guard system also dealt with the mafia and were seen as responsible for many organised crimes. Importantly, the pro-government Kurdish tribes that had been inactive since the early Republic period were reactivated by the state against the Kurdish opposition in the late 1970s. These tribes would be a very powerful paramilitary force in the 1990s, especially under the Village Guard system.

Zones of 'threat' changed after the 1950s. During the late Empire, and early Republic periods, the most troubled region was the eastern part of the state. Between 1950 and 1975, threats against the state were particularly concentrated in the western provinces. This was because opposition groups were mostly leftist university students and the universities were usually in the wealthier, more developed western part of the country. Therefore, the state security forces and paramilitary forces affiliated with the state institutions were more active in the west of Turkey during this period. After 1975, and especially after the 1980s, however, the situation changed again. While the 'Armenian threat' supported by Russia in the north-east was expunged, that of the Kurdish provinces to the south – northern Kurdistan – grew into a major problem, dubbed 'the Kurdish issue' (from the Turkish state perspective). The Kurdish opposition organisations became quite active from the 1980s, when the PKK emerged, eventually to dominate the field and form the primary opposition force.

[162] Dündar and Kazdağlı, *Ergenekon*, 29.
[163] Ibid., 32.

Discussion

From the sultanate of the late Ottoman Empire to the twin dictatorships in the first half of the twentieth century through to the multi-party period after World War II, there are continuities. The establishment of paramilitary groups, their deployment during periods of perceived threats to the state, and their forms of political violence at different times were very similar. These similarities and continuities are perhaps best symbolised by the commander of the Turkish army, Daniş Karabelen. He was trained by the *Teşkilat-ı Mahsusa* in 1917 and worked with the subsequent paramilitary *Karakol Cemiyeti*, during 1918–20, before finally, in 1952, becoming the first commander of the ÖHD, the main paramilitary force of the Turkish army. Thus, Karabelen continued his paramilitary career through three very different governments – the sultanate, the single-party dictatorship period and the multi-party democratic period.[164] Abdullah Çatlı has a similar biography. He was one of the leaders of the Idealist Youth (or Grey Wolves, according to different sources), and then the lynchpin in many unsolved killings directed by elements of the state from the mid-1970s (against leftists) and early 1980s (against Armenian organisations in Europe) to the mid-1990s (against Kurds).[165]

There is a similar continuity in the organisation of the masses and the use of paramilitary violence in the pogroms against the non-Muslim and Alevi communities in the late Ottoman and early Republic periods and the post-1950s era (e.g. the 1894–6 Armenian pogroms, 1934 Thrace pogrom, 1955 Istanbul pogrom and 1978–80 Alevi pogroms). The Village Guard system is an important example of the institutional continuity of the paramilitary. This organisation was formally established by the state in 1924, inspired by the late Ottoman Regiments and went on to become the largest and arguably most effective paramilitary force in the 1990s. The threats of the state continued with actually rather minor changes into the last decade of the twentieth century from the end decades of the nineteenth. The longevity of these paramilitary groups was largely in accordance with the threats, some of which were short-lived but

---

[164] Kutay, *Beş Kıt'ada Bir Türk Paşası*.

[165] Massicard, 'Gangs in Uniform'; Savaş, *Susurluk Raporu*; Bozarslan, *Network-Building, Ethnicity and Violence in Turkey*.

others much longer and more in the nature of oppositions defined by the very structure of the state ideology and politics.

Although there was a continuity in terms of cadres, institutions and experiences between the periods, the names of paramilitary groups were different. Specific names were used in the late Ottoman Empire, such as the Hamidiye/Tribal Light Cavalry Regiments and the *Teşkilat-ı Mahsusa*. Such names expressed the type of armed forces or paramilitary organisations. Republican elites usually used the legacy of the CUP, but did not form very large paramilitary groups. With the multi-party period, these paramilitary forces were defined through abstract terms. The conceptualisation of Turkish paramilitary groups can be connected with four concepts during the multi-party period: the Gladio and deep state are two, which have been covered here, along with Ergenekon (the name of a Turkish founding myth and allegedly the name of a secret network or organisation in the state) and counterinsurgency (*kontergerilla*). However, these concepts are sometimes used interchangeably and all after the 1950s in Turkey, and these concepts were often used for what was, in reality, the ÖHD.

The experiences and legacies of the paramilitary organisations from the late Ottoman and Republic periods, and especially from the preceding multi-party period, were used extensively in the conflict in the 1990s. Some new paramilitary forces did emerge, while others were transformed. The Turkish army tried to reorganise the national politics with a military coup in the 1960s. The state used the ÖHD between the 1950s and 1970s in Cyprus. During the 1970s, the ÖHD was also used against Turkish and Kurdish leftist movements until the 1980 military coup. After the coup, only the PKK remained as an effective opposition. In 1984, this organisation initiated a war against the Turkish state, and the state responded by focusing on the PKK and Kurds, particularly in northern Kurdistan. To this end, the state reorganised formal and informal military institutions within the official state institutions. Some such institutions were the ÖHD and JİTEM, the best-known informal paramilitary organisation, as well as the (police) Special Operations Department – of which many members belonged to the paramilitary youth organisation of the MHP – and the Village Guards. Different groups may be added to this list, such as the repentants and Turkish Hizbullah. The relations and structures of hierarchy among these organisations at the end of the century were very complex (with further dynamic factors over time, local tribal, historical, etc. issues, specifics related to families and individuals, etc.). They were mostly used against the PKK and Kurdish civilians who were pro-PKK.

A similarity of continuity for the (mainly Kurdish) Village Guard and Hizbullah might be mentioned. For example, in the second half of the 1970s, the leader of Hizbullah, Hüseyin Velioğlu, was involved in pro-state radical Islamist groups such as the MTTB and the *Akıncılar* as mentioned (above), and Velioğlu also played an active role against oppositional political movements. Similarly, the Bucak tribe, which was based in Urfa province, adopted a pro-state position against the Kurdish-identity political parties from the late 1970s, and later, in the '90s, continued and reaffirmed this position by entering into the Village Guard system.

The reasons for the establishment and continuity of the Turkish paramilitary policy can be stated simply as the 'security state' mentality. Formal and informal state institutions could also have carried out informal acts in the democratic periods because of the threat to the state. The reason for the continuity of paramilitary groups can be explained by two concepts: one of them is lack of confrontation and another is impunity. Regarding the lack of confrontation (referred to above), Turkish society had long fostered paramilitary forces, especially those drawing their motivational source from ideological grounds.[166] Regarding impunity, the actions of the paramilitary forces rarely went punished by the courts for their wrong-doing, especially not in a timely and appropriate way. For instance, Abdullah Çatlı and many members of the Grey Wolves, large numbers of Village Guards who committed crimes, and leaders of the tribes and countless people who were responsible for pogroms were either unpunished or else released from detention with negligible punishment. As a result of this lack of societal confrontation and the associated culture of impunity, paramilitary organisations were used very effectively again in the 1990s.

Conclusion

Throughout both the late Ottoman and Republican periods, state elites created and utilised paramilitary formations with different characteristics in different periods. It can be argued that the origins for the emergence of

[166] Barış Ünlü, 'Türklüğün Kısa Tarihi', *Birikim Dergisi*, no. 274 (2012): 23–34.

paramilitary groups in the late Ottoman and the Republic period lay not just in internal conflicts but also in a lack of military and administrative institutional local capacity of the state. In terms of the origin of the paramilitary forces in Turkey, the governments, military institutions and the deep state network constituted and used irregular forces that had a paramilitary character during internal conflicts and to deal with perceived threats. In other words, the deep state, which was organised as a secret network in the bureaucracy, the army and the governments, can be said to have constituted the general politics of the state and to have established or used paramilitary forces due to the lack of democratic capacity of the state institutions. The paramilitary forces in Turkey connected mostly with the Turkish army rather than governments, and military institutions were widely involved in the establishment and maintenance of paramilitary forces. Moreover, the policies of the right-wing parties were consistent with the aims of the state. Hence, young members of the right-wing parties could easily be included in paramilitary groups coordinated through a secret network of relationships, quite reasonably referred to as the 'deep state', especially after 1950.

The Turkish state and society have never properly confronted the hegemonic political violence of their dark history and pre-history, which has been an important reason for the continuity of paramilitary groups. The paramilitary groups used very different types of political violence/mass violence: from genocide, pogroms and massacres to individual political assassinations and lynchings. At the same time, these processes were crucial in the re-establishment of the nationalist-Islamic identity in Turkish society; the state's institutions used violence to intimidate dissidents, while paramilitary groups used these kinds of violence to 'protect' the state and for economic and other gains. For example, the Istanbul pogrom was of economic interest for the masses but also an intimidation of certain non-Muslim communities for the state. There were two motivations for the violence that extremist right-wing paramilitary groups used in the 1970s and 1980s: defending the state's official ideology and material profit. According to Bozarslan, the violence was both separatist and unifying.[167] For the dissidents, it was exclusionist, which held also for the state and pro-state nationalist and Islamic groups. Consequently,

---

[167] Bozarslan, '*Bir 'Bölücü' ve 'Birleştirici' Olarak Şiddet*'.

this mutual benefit and support (the ideological and political objectives of the state and the ideological and economic motivation of society) is the main factor that ensures the continuity of paramilitary politics.

Table 1.1 illustrates the continuity via ideology, institutions and cadres as discussed in this chapter.

Table 1.1 Continuity of the paramilitary legacy.

Ideology	Sunni Islam and Turkish nationalism				
Institutions (Turkish)	*Teşkilât-ı Mahsusa*	Special Warfare Department	Idealist Hearths (*Ülkü Ocakları*)	JİTEM	Special Police Team
Militias (Kurdish)	Hamidiye/Tribal Light Cavalry Regiments		Tribal Militias	Hizbullah	Village Guards
Cadres	Daniş Karabelen during WWI and the 1950s	Abdullah Çatlı 1970s–1990s	Sedat Bucak 1970s–1990s	Hüseyin Velioğlu 1970s–1990s	Members of Idealist Youth since 1968

2

PARAMILITARIES AND STATE RELATION: ESTABLISHMENT OF THE PARAMILITARY FORCES IN THE 1980s

Introduction

Four important organisations emerged in the 1980s. In 1982, the Special Police Teams were established (and reorganised in 1993); in 1985 the system of Village Guards (established in 1924) was reorganised (and again in 1991); and in the late 1980s, JİTEM was established, which included repentants. These paramilitary groups were all formed by state institutions, primarily to deal with the situation in the Kurdish provinces (northern Kurdistan). Also, during 1991–5, the extreme Islamist Hizbullah organisation that had emerged in early 1980 in a Kurdish province, Batman, was utilised by state agencies, particularly against pro-PKK Kurdish civilians and politicians. The questions addressed here concern how and why these paramilitary organisations were established and what explains their characteristics.

On the basis of secondary literature, interviews, memoirs and newspaper reports focusing on the 1990s, it appears that these paramilitary organisations were established for three main reasons: (1) the threat to the national security of the Turkish state (as perceived), (2) the weakness of the military in irregular warfare and the institutional capacity of the state, and (3) the plausible deniability they afforded regarding violence carried out against civilians. The political conditions in which these paramilitary groups emerged were those of (1) ethnic conflict (more clearly, political demands of the Kurds), (2) the army and party politics, (3) tribal politics and (4) organised crime.

I use the concept of state rather than particular regimes or governments since, as mentioned above, the role of governments in the state administration was not determinant of the ideology and politics of the Turkish state, simply because of the network of hidden relations called the 'deep state', and the temporary placeholders on the democratic scene did not have real power. I make a distinction between immediate causes and deeper conditions because, first, I consider the reasons why the paramilitaries were actually set up, and then I analyse the conditions of the political, military and economic environment that reveal these. Developing an assumption implicit in the first chapter, the conditions are taken to be the more important. These conditions resulted in both small-scale, informal organisations and large-scale, hierarchically ordered organisations. Some of the organisations were an extension of the secret services, others of the army and of organised crime. They were active in different regions, and the nature of their main activities also varied, from those of vigilantes to covert death-squad operations.

This chapter first examines the causes for the emergence of paramilitary organisations and the conditions of ethnic conflict (i.e. the nationalist politics of the state, tribal politics and organised crime). Then follows a consideration of similarities and differences among the JİTEM, Special Action Police Units, Village Guards and Hizbullah as paramilitary organisations.

Establishment of Paramilitaries

Why and how did paramilitary organisations emerge? There is significant literature on the formation of paramilitary groups from different conflicts and war zones in the world. These offer a variety of reasons for the formation of paramilitary forces. Among them, three explanations recur: paramilitary groups are said to be established in support of the official armed forces in their struggle against internal enemies, when the capacity of core institutions is too limited to sustain the continued existence of the state, and for plausible deniability.[1] These three reasons can be used to explain the formation of paramilitary groups in Turkey, particularly in the 1980s.

---

[1] Campbell, 'Death Squads'; Kowalewski, 'Counterinsurgent Vigilantism and Public Response'; Mazzei, *Death Squads or Self-Defense Forces?*; Jentzsch *et al.*, 'Militias in Civil Wars', 755–69; Mason and Krane, 'The Political Economy of Death Squads'; Carey and

Paramilitary forces have often emerged in response to internal threats to the state.[2] The rise of both armed and unarmed opposition groups in the country may be considered as threats to the security of the nation. Colating the information on militias and irregular armed groups that are connected to government authorities between 1981 and 2007, Carey, Mitchell and Lowe have shown that these were present in 81 per cent of all countries affected by civil war.[3] Therefore, it can be said that in situations where internal conflicts arise, the state tends to deploy paramilitaries as an important deterrent instrument.

This was obviously exemplified in Turkey by the rise of guerrilla warfare as instigated by the PKK and the response of the state to it. The MGK periodically redefines the organisations, ethnic and religious groups that threaten national security.[4] It defines internal and external threats in the National Security Policy Document known as 'The Red Book' (*Milli Güvenlik Siyaset Belgesi*) and sets policies accordingly.[5] According to the MGK, an internal threat is constituted by the class, ethnic or religious armed and unarmed groups that do not accept state authority in state-controlled lands. This definition was used to legitimise the state violence that was persistently employed against opposition groups. Accordingly, internal opposition as threats to the

Mitchell, 'Progovernment Militias'; James Ron, 'Territoriality and Plausible Deniability: Serbian Paramilitaries in the Bosnian War,' in *Death Squads in Global Perspective – Murder with Deniability*, eds Bruce B. Campbell and Arthur D. Brenner (Basingstoke: Palgrave Macmillan, 2002), 287–312, //www.palgrave.com/us/book/9780312213657.

[2] Campbell, 'Death Squads'; Mazzei, *Death Squads or Self-Defense Forces?*; Kowalewski, 'Counterinsurgent Vigilantism and Public Response'.

[3] Sabine C. Carey, Neil J. Mitchell and Will Lowe, 'States, the Security Sector, and the Monopoly of Violence: A New Database on Pro-Government Militias', *Journal of Peace Research* 50, no. 2 (2013): 249–58.

[4] Egemen B. Bezci and Güven Gürkan Öztan, 'Anatomy of the Turkish Emergency State: A Continuous Reflection of Turkish *Raison d'état* between 1980 and 2002', *Middle East Critique* 25, no. 2 (2 April 2016): 165; Hamit Bozarslan, '"Neden Silahlı Mücadele?" Türkiye Kürdistan'ında Şiddeti Anlamak', in *Türkiye'de Siyasal Şiddetin Boyutları*, eds İbrahim Şirin and Güney Çeğin, 1. baskı (Istanbul: İletişim Yayınları, 2014), 152–5.

[5] İlhan Uzgel, 'Ordu Dış Politikanın Neresinde?', in *Bir Zümre, Bir Parti: Türkiye'de Ordu*, eds Ahmet Insel, Ali Bayramoğlu and Ömer Laciner, 2. baskı (Istanbul: Birikim Yayınları, 2004), 89–92.

state can be identified as ranging from small, informal opposition groups to large-scale national resistance movements. These internal 'enemies' were generally defined by the state in the context of ethnic, religion and class conflicts. And the origin of this threat perception has been related to the Turkish state's acceptance of northern Kurdistan as a colony since the foundation of the Republic. These statements are contained in secret reports on the Kurds prepared by state bureaucrats in the early Republican period.[6]

Another reason for the emergence of paramilitary organisations is the weakness of the state's institutional capacity. According to Ann Hironaka, the lack of an autonomous, rationalised bureaucratic structure, of military capability and of territorial control, and also a (relative) cohesion and organisation of the opposition, are the characteristic features of a weak state.[7] It can be said that Turkey's 1980s partially fits this definition. In this condition, paramilitary groups might emerge to compensate for the 'lack of means to respond to rebellious movements' and/or also including a need by the state to 'compensate for a lack of economic means'; compared to regular armed forces, militias are a 'cheap instrument for the projection of state power'.[8]

In Turkey, the weakness of the state's democratic capacity was expressed in such problems and deficits as the repeated interruption and prevention of parliamentary work by military coups, the inability to represent social differences in parliament and the obstruction of the work of NGOs. Moreover, following Michael Mann,[9] the Turkish state can be adjudged to have mainly used *despotic power* against the Kurds and other opponents, which was due to the weakness of its infrastructural power, or to the lack of democratic capacity in the country. Despotic power is when state elites act without considering civil society, and in general other non-state institutions, in any of their actions and policies. This should not be taken to mean that the state does not use its infrastructural

[6] Mehmet Bayrak, ed., *Kürtler ve Ulusal-Demokratik Mücadeleleri Üstüne: Gizli Belgeler – Araştırmalar – Notlar*, 2. baskı (Ankara: Öz-Ge Yayınları, 2013).

[7] Ann Hironaka, *Neverending Wars: The International Community, Weak States, and the Perpetuation of Civil War* (Cambridge, MA: Harvard University Press, 2009), 69–80.

[8] Jentzsch *et al.*, 'Militias in Civil Wars', 764.

[9] Michael Mann, 'The Autonomous Power of the State: Its Origins, Mechanisms and Results', *European Journal of Sociology/Archives Européennes de Sociologie/Europäisches Archiv Für Soziologie* 25, no. 2 (1984): 185–213.

power or did not have any ideological tinge to it. On the contrary, the Turkish state employed despotic power and the influence of ideology at the same time, but mostly because its infrastructural power was insufficient. Despotic power was used against those groups considered to be threatening, and this was due to the shortfall in the democratic capacity of the state.

Therefore, this political atmosphere of lack of the requisite democratic, bureaucratic and military capability of the state institutions was an important reason for the extra-legal state violence including the emergence of paramilitary groups in Turkey. In addition, in the following pages I will discuss, through the memoirs of high-ranking soldiers, that the military institutions, historically the instruments of the state's despotic power, were also weak before and during the 1990s, particularly regarding their capacity for irregular warfare. This was also one of the reasons for the establishment of paramilitary groups.

Plausible deniability is another of the main terms employed in discussions about the formation of the paramilitary groups. As Campbell argues, although some states maintain the monopoly of violence, they establish death squads to which the use of violence is delegated in order to suppress armed opposition movements without the liability of being accused of war crimes or human right violations.[10] In other words, the state can use paramilitaries against oppositions to operate outside the law – to commit crimes – without serious risk of punishment. Carey and Mitchell argue that pro-government militias (PGMs) can generally be placed into one of two categories: 'semi-official' and 'informal'.[11] It is the semi-formal or informal relations with the state that allows for the state's deniability in respect of the paramilitary groups, their actions and the consequences of these. 'One way to establish deniability is to have the killing organised and done by people who are not formally or officially associated with the state', writes Campbell.[12] Moreover, according to Wolpin, states establish death squads against leftist and ethnic opposition movements, and one of the most important features of these forces is deniability.[13] Accordingly, the denial

---

[10] Campbell, 'Death Squads', 17.

[11] Carey and Mitchell, 'Progovernment Militias', 130.

[12] Campbell, 'Death Squads', 6.

[13] Miles D. Wolpin, *State Terrorism and Death Squads in the New World Order* (Dundas: Peace Research Institute-Dundas, 1992), https://search.library.wisc.edu/catalog/999715854402121.

of the actions and violence of paramilitary groups is used as an important tool to eliminate dissidents without modifying the legal boundaries of the state.

The state in Turkey enjoyed such deniability in northern Kurdistan during the 1990s through all the paramilitaries listed that it created and employed and whose actions it denied, disowned and otherwise distanced itself from. This was the case in particular with JİTEM.[14] JİTEM would fall under Carey and Mitchell's informal category, since this was a state-established institution without legal status and whose very existence was denied. Indeed, the type of shadowy, 'deep state' structure that can conduct murderous acts with impunity because of its state origins and sponsorship but which does not have any publically recognised status (indeed does not even officially exist), may be said to afford the state its greatest level of deniability. This can hold regardless of how 'plausible' the deniability or rather how *im*plausible it actually becomes, to the point where it is an open secret and yet still officially denied.

Existing Explanations of the Emergence of the Paramilitary Groups in Turkey in 1980–90

The origins of the paramilitary groups active in Turkey in the 1990s are generally traced to the 1970s. There were different reasons for the establishment of these groups. As indicated, the causes of the emergence of the paramilitary groups can also be regarded as explanatory points for the example of Turkey. One of the main reasons was the emergence of opposition groups, in other words, of perceived threats to the state, both external (the Soviet Union) and internal (communist, Kurdish leftist and nationalist movements).[15] These threats were ideologically and politically determined after 1980 by the MGK; in other words, the MGK *produced* enemies and target groups. The perception of communism as a threat derived from NATO membership and ideological reasons rooted in Kemalism as it had developed, while the threat of Kurdish movements had ideological, political and colonial (right-wing statist and ethno-nationalist) reasons. Another important reason was the weakness

---

[14] Biner, 'From Terrorist to Repentant: Who Is the Victim?'; Söyler, *The Turkish Deep State*.

[15] Özar *et al.*, *From Past to Present*; Evren Balta Paker and İsmet Akça, 'Askerler, Köylüler, Paramiliter Güçler: Türkiye'de Köy Koruculuğu Sistemi', *Toplum ve Bilim*, no. 126 (2013): 7–34; Söyler, *The Turkish Deep State*.

of the irregular warfare capacity of government agencies in terms of internal conflicts. And to these reasons should, of course, be added that of deniability, one of the main reasons for the establishment of paramilitaries around the world. Although there are many factors that led to the establishment of paramilitary groups in Turkey, particularly towards the 1990s, these elements can be expressed as the most important.

As mentioned in Chapter 1, the paramilitary groups of the late Ottoman and early Republic periods were largely established by the state during the emergence of internal opposition movements. Similar conditions existed for groups established during the post-World War II Republic and particularly after the 1970s. According to Aydın and Taşkın, the extreme nationalist and right-wing paramilitary youth groups founded in the 1970s were actively mobilised to protect the state and its official security forces from dissident movements.[16] These nationalist youth groups were related to intelligence and paramilitary groups affiliated to the government and military. In the 1970s, the leftist movements were the priority in terms of threats to the state, and they thus became the primary target of paramilitaries. Political violence reached unprecedented levels in the late 1970s, as the MHP developed into a political party that formed and supported a paramilitary organisation with its 'modern bandits' recruited from the Grey Wolves and the massacres and unknown assailant murders of the ÖHD and MİT rose dramatically, according to Söyler.[17]

Over time, however, the state's internal threat perception shifted because of the guerrilla warfare launched by the PKK, which the MGK then began seeing as the biggest internal ethnic threat since 1984. High-ranking officers were thus pushed into discussing the lack of military capacity of their security forces to combat the guerrilla warfare, both in interviews at the time and later in their memoirs.[18] Doğan Güreş, who was the chief of the general staff between 1990 and 1994, openly expressed this in an interview: 'Initially, the main tasks of the gendarmerie units were not sufficient for the organisation, equipment and

[16] Aydın and Taşkın, *1960'tan Günümüze Türkiye Tarihi*, 284.
[17] Söyler, *The Turkish Deep State*, 200.
[18] Kışlalı, *Güneydoğu*; Fikret Bilâ, *Komutanlar Cephesi*, 2. baskı (Istanbul: Detay Yayıncılık, 2007); Hasan Kundakçı, *Güneydoğu'da Unutulmayanlar*, 4. baskı (Istanbul: Alfa Yayıncılık, 2004).

training needed for this kind of struggle.'[19] Accordingly, the military institutional capacity of the state was updated for non-conventional warfare, as the Turkish army had been equipped and organised as a conventional force aimed at repelling a Soviet invasion before. This restructuring process continued until 1993. The new concept was expressed as a 'low-intensity war' doctrine – an 'insurgency', 'guerrilla war' and (nowadays) 'asymmetric warfare', as well as the state 'terrorism' perception. Many semi-formal and informal paramilitary groups emerged and/or reorganised in northern Kurdistan particularly and Turkey more widely during this period.[20]

The emergence of internal threats to the state was also very important with regard to the military, bureaucratic and democratic capacity of the state. Although the single-party system had transitioned to a multi-party system,[21] the army continued to dominate politics until the 2000s, when it was finally eased out, apparently, by a combination of a popularly mandated, somewhat anti-Kemalist Islamicist government party, Justice and Development Party (Adalet ve Kalkınma Partisi, AKP), that was able to grow in political strength, aided by economically as well as politically liberalising internal and external forces and institutions.[22]

The emergence of paramilitary organisations (especially Village Guards) in Turkey was related to the local perception of threat to the state; although paramilitary groups were established due to threats to the state, the role of micro-level power relations was also very important. According to the authors, the 'central capacity and decisions of the state may not always be parallel with its local capacity and practices'.[23] Indeed, like any other states, the Turkish state was not a monolith, especially in northern Kurdistan – where it was very far from that – and paramilitary emergence should also be analysed through the various dynamics among central and local political actors (including

---

[19] Kışlalı, *Güneydoğu*, 216.

[20] Balta Paker and Akça, 'Askerler, Köylüler, Paramiliter Güçler', 16–17.

[21] Kemal H. Karpat, *Turkey's Politics: The Transition to a Multi-Party System* (Princeton, NJ: Princeton University Press, 2015); John M. Vanderlippe, *The Politics of Turkish Democracy: Ismet Inonu and the Formation of the Multi-Party System, 1938–1950* (Albany: State University of New York Press, 2006).

[22] Cizre Sakallıoğlu, 'The Anatomy of the Turkish Military's Political Autonomy'.

[23] Balta Paker and Akça, 'Askerler, Köylüler, Paramiliter Güçler', 9.

Kurdish tribes, extended families and their social relations, etc.). Hence, the lack of its military (irregular warfare) capacity in the Kurdish provinces led to the formation of paramilitary groups jointly with pro-state local micro-power networks.

Programmes of assassination requiring deniability require paramilitary groups if they are to be scaled up beyond the single take-outs of standard state espionage secret services. The actions of the most well-known death squad used by the state in Kurdish provinces in the 1990s, the JİTEM,[24] were discussed in many parliamentary research commissions and cases.[25] However, the state authorities still denied its existence, a continuing refusal to acknowledge the truth about JİTEM that allowed a continued impunity for its actions.[26] In the report prepared by Kutlu Savaş, the Prime Minister's Inspector-General, about the Susurluk accident and the dark relationship networks within the state, there was also a debate about the deniability of the paramilitary forces, as described by Öznur Sevdiren:[27]

> The report by Kutlu Savaş offers the following observations on JİTEM: 'Although the Gendarmerie General Command denies its existence, the fact of JİTEM cannot be forgotten. JİTEM might indeed have been disbanded, liquidated, its staff might be employed in other units, and its records might have been sent off to archives. Yet, several individuals who worked for JİTEM are alive. In fact, the existence of JİTEM is actually not a problem. JİTEM came into being due to a need . . .'[28]

[24] Göral et al., *The Unspoken Truth: Enforced Disappearances*; Özar et al., *From Past to Present*; van Bruinessen, 'Turkey's Death Squads'.

[25] Serap Işık, *JİTEM Ana Dava Geniş Özeti* (Hakikat Adalet Hafıza Merkezi, 2014), http://failibelli.org/wp-content/uploads/2013/01/JİTEM_Ana_Dava_Genis_Ozet.pdf; TBMM, *Ülkemizin Çeşitli Yörelerinde İşlenmiş Faili Meçhul Siyasal Cinayetler Konusunda Meclis Araştırma Komisyonu.*

[26] Özlem Has, 'Structured Agencies of Paramilitaries in the Kurdish-Turkish Conflict: The JİTEM Case' (PhD diss., University of Copenhagen, 2021), 128.

[27] Savaş, *Susurluk Raporu.*

[28] Öznur Sevdiren, 'The Recognition of Enforced Disappearance as a Crime Under Domestic Law and the Statute of Limitations: A Problematic of International Criminal Law', in *Enforced Disappearances and the Conduct of the Judiciary*, edited by Gökçen Alpkaya (Istanbul: Truth Justice Memory Center, 2014), 94.

This section in the report is highly relevant because a state-sanctioned report itself confirmed that JİTEM was set up for deniability purposes. Despite these types of reports from the administrative bureaucracy, the military bureaucracy has always denied the existence of JİTEM. In 2009, in a case related to unsolved murders in Diyarbakır, the court asked the chief of general staff about JİTEM. The response received from the general staff was as follows: 'There is no unit named JİTEM established in our organisation.'[29]

Further to the three main causes mentioned above – the threat to the state, the weakness of the military and the employment of deniability – the following sub-reasons also led to the establishment of these groups. First, the state did not know the conflict areas in which it was engaged when fighting with the PKK; hence, it needed local forces to control the conflict zones, which was quite separate from the strengthening of the police and the army. The local forces were supplied by militias and pro-state Kurdish tribes who had detailed knowledge of their traditional lands, the territorial setting for armed engagements. In this respect, the relationship established by the state with the local micro-power networks was crucial and played a major role in the formation of the paramilitaries.

Another sub-reason for this was the historical or traditional reflex of the state against oppositional movements. The Turkish state had been liquidating dissident movements through vigilantes and death squads since the late Ottoman period. Without veering toward essentialism, there was an unmistakable tradition of these groups that were used together with the official armed forces of the state, which continued as a known technique. As mentioned, the use of extreme right-wing youth groups for threats to the state in the 1970s, '80s and '90s in different historical contexts was an example of this continuity. A third sub-reason was the motivation to establish paramilitary groups to gather intelligence on issues such as the social structure in northern Kurdistan, the political preferences of Kurds, the number of people supporting the PKK, provisioning and supply routes and other human resources available to the enemy, and types of opposition to the state likely to be encountered in each area. The state created paramilitary forces consisting mostly of Kurds due to a lack of local military and intelligence capacity.

[29] 'Genelkurmay'dan Açıklama: "JİTEM Diye Bir Birim Yok"', *Cumhuriyet Gazetesi*, 30 December 2009.

The formation of paramilitary groups relates in part to the arming of pro-state civilians, of social groups and of tribes against the armed opposition groups – and these groups could become one of the biggest obstacles in terms of ending conflicts, consolidation of the peace processes and democratic institutions. Thus, the paramilitaries effectively perpetuated the situation that had brought them into being or brought about their contemporary (re)organisation. Additionally, the state established paramilitary groups to fight against dissidents, but these organisations themselves became the greatest threat for ordinary Kurdish civilians during the 1990s. In other words, they took on a life of their own, independent of their origins.

Conditions of the Establishment of Paramilitary Organisations in Turkey

Looking to the deeper causes or underlying conditions for the establishment of paramilitary organisations in Turkey during the 1990s, four factors that may be identified are the demands of the Kurds, the army and party politics, tribal politics and crime.

Ethnic/Political Demands of Kurds

Ethnic conflicts provide an important political context for the establishment and use of paramilitary groups. Ethnic violence increased in general in the post-Cold War period. The ethnicisation of political violence was also related to the changing perception of threats (from communism to ethnic conflicts, from class movements to nationalist movements).[30] The conflict between the Turkish state and the Kurdish movements in Turkey was expressed as ethnic and national demands by the Kurds, but successive Turkish governments did not accept the claim of a different nation and ethnic group within the Turkish nation-state. Yeğen and Ünver analyse how the Kurdish issue is discussed both in state discourse and in the national and international institutions.[31]

---

[30] Rogers Brubaker and David D. Laitin, 'Ethnic and Nationalist Violence', *Annual Review of Sociology* 24 (1 January 1998): 424.

[31] Mesut Yeğen, 'The Kurdish Question in Turkish State Discourse,' *Journal of Contemporary History* 34, no. 4 (1999): 555–68, https://www.jstor.org/stable/261251; Hamid Akin Ünver, *Turkey's Kurdish Question: Discourse & Politics Since 1990* (Abingdon: Routledge, 2015).

Beşikci, Yarkın and Bayrak discuss this issue in the context of colonialism.[32] As Yarkın analyses, the Turkish state authorities have ruled northern Kurdistan using colonial methods since the state's foundation.[33] These colonial methods have been applied in various fields such as law, politics, culture and ecology.[34] Especially after 1980, Kurdish people became more ethnically discriminated against and denied any political space through which to manage this. Therefore, some were led to initiate an armed struggle, which caused them to be seen as the greatest threat to the state and thus its main target.[35]

Although the ideological framework of the national struggle of the Kurdish political movements first emerged during the early Republic, it began to become apparent in the late 1960s.[36] The primary Kurdish demands were cultural rights, and in 1969 an association was established for this, the Revolutionary Cultural Hearts of the East (*Devrimci Doğu Kültür Ocakları*).[37] The government's response was uncompromising; commando operations were organised by the Turkish military throughout the Kurdish villages and towns in 1970 and '71. According to the state authorities, the justification for these commando raids was the gathering of illegal weapons in Kurdish villages and the 'hunting of bandits'.[38] However, these military operations

---

[32] İsmail Beşikci, *Devletlerarası Sömürge Kürdistan* (Istanbul: İsmail Beşikci Vakfı Yayınları, 2013); Güllistan Yarkın, 'İnkâr Edilen Hakikat: Sömürge Kuzey Kürdistan,' *Kürt Araştırmaları*, no. 1 (2019): 45–69; Bayrak, ed., *Kürtler ve Ulusal-Demokratik Mücadeleleri Üstüne*.

[33] Yarkın, 'İnkâr Edilen Hakikat', 45–69.

[34] Rênas Cûdî, 'Kürdistan–Türkiye İlişkilerine Yönelik Eleştirel Bir Okuma,' *YeniOzgurPolitika.com*, accessed 20 July 2022, https://www.ozgurpolitika.com/haberi-kurdistan-turkiye-iliskilerine-yonelik-elestirel-bir-okuma-156972.

[35] Namık Kemal Dinç, ed., *Stories of Migration 'One Who's Seen Pain doesn't Inflict Pain upon Others'*, trans. Kolektif Atölye (Istanbul: Göç Der Yayınları, 2008), http://www.gocder.com/sites/default/files/proje-photo/goc-hikayeleri-en.pdf.

[36] Ahmet Hamdi Akkaya, 'Ulusal Kurtuluş, Ayaklanma ve Sınırların Ötesi: 1970'lerden 1990'lara Kürt Hareketi'nin Değişim Dinamikleri', *Toplum ve Kuram*, no. 9 (2014): 75–98; Ahmet Alış, 'The Kurdish Ethnoregional Movement in Turkey: From Class to Nation (1959–1974) and from Nation to "Revolution" (1974–1984)' (PhD diss., Boğaziçi University, 2017).

[37] Alış, 'The Kurdish Ethnoregional Movement in Turkey', 89.

[38] Ahmet Özcan, 'The Missing Link in the Chain of Oppression and Resistance: Last Era of Kurdish Banditry in Modern Turkey, 1950–1980' (PhD diss., Boğaziçi University, 2014), 147.

were an important factor in the politicisation of the Kurds.[39] According to Ismail Beşikci, villagers, especially men, were tortured intensively during these operations, whose main purpose was to frighten the Kurds and to prevent their national awakening.[40]

The national liberation discourse became an ideological framework in the Kurdish movements in these years, with slogans like 'Kurdistan is a colony'.[41] This discourse became the basic ideological argument of almost all Kurdish parties through the 1970s. The national Kurdish awakening largely began to develop ideologically in the western universities of Turkey and in Kurdish intellectual circles. This meant a significant threat to the state's official policy. Therefore, Kurdish political movements were targeted in the west of the country not by commando raids, as in northern Kurdistan against civilians, but by right-wing paramilitary youth groups.[42]

Turkish governments had used paramilitary forces against different leftist Kurdish parties since the mid-1970s. Kurdish political activism was born again after the 1960s and took on a socialist character in the '70s, an activism that turned into a Kurdish national liberation movement with many different political parties aligned against the Turkish state.[43] Bozarslan argues that Kemalism and post-1960 neo-Kemalism redefined enemies of the state (especially Kurds and Alevis) for the sake of maintaining a homogeneous Turkish nation. Also, he describes how the state had attacked internal enemies – in the case of the Kurdish rebellions – with violent methods, including death squads, to pursue this official doctrine and maintain maximum homogeneity.[44]

[39] Ercan, 'Dynamics of Mobilization and Radicalization of the Kurdish Movement', 101–5.

[40] İsmail Beşikci, *Rejimin Niteliği ve Kürtler* (Istanbul: İsmail Beşikci Vakfı Yayınları, 2013), 36–7.

[41] Cengiz Güneş, *The Kurdish National Movement in Turkey: From Protest to Resistance* (New York: Routledge, 2012), 81–100; Akkaya, 'Ulusal Kurtuluş, Ayaklanma ve Sınırların Ötesi'.

[42] Celal Temel, *1984'ten Önceki 25 Yılda Kürtlerin Silahsız Mücadelesi*, 1. baskı (Istanbul: İsmail Beşikci Vakfı Yayınları, 2015), 251.

[43] Emir Ali Türkmen and Abdurrahman Özmen, eds, *Kürdistan Sosyalist Solu Kitabı* (Ankara: Dipnot Yayınları, 2013); Güneş, *The Kurdish National Movement in Turkey*, 49–80.

[44] Hamit Bozarslan, 'Why the Armed Struggle: Understanding the Violence in Kurdistan of Turkey', in *The Kurdish Conflict in Turkey: Obstacles and Chances for Peace and Democracy*, eds Ferhad Ibrahim and Gülistan Gürbey (Münster: LIT Verlag, 2000), 17–30.

The intensive use of violence did not result in the realisation of the official doctrine, however. After the 1980 military coup, Kurdish political movements, particularly the PKK, started its armed struggle and became the single opposing force against the state.[45] This was the condition or state of affairs that determined the re-emergence of old and establishment of the new paramilitary groups composed of Turkish nationalists and pro-state Kurdish tribes.[46]

Although the PKK was founded in 1978 and began various armed conflicts against the Turkish state and pro-state tribes from 1979, the official declaration of war was not made until 1984 and the conflicts not intensively escalated until the 1990s.[47] The conflict had different characteristics for the two sides. While the Turkish state executed the war with its military and paramilitary institutions, the PKK has co-executed the war with mass popular support of the Kurdish society. This made Kurdish civilians the main target of the forces of the state and many Kurdish civilians were killed through extra-judicial executions, enforced disappearances and unsolved murders. Turkish society outside of northern Kurdistan was quite removed and not directly involved in the war in real terms, other than through the young men drafted by military conscription, many into the war zone.[48] Also, Kurdish civilians were sometimes threatened, pressured, and even killed by gangs in the PKK in the late 1980s and early 1990s.[49]

Regarding the response of the Turkish state, it was to create different irregular forces to support the military forces, but a divide-and-rule policy was able to be deployed against Kurdish society, through the Village Guard system.[50] The illegal, armed Islamic-Kurdish group Hizbullah also used intense violence against Kurdish civilians who were pro-PKK in the first half of 1990s and allegedly cooperated with other militia groups. In addition to JİTEM, members of

---

[45] Ercan, 'Dynamics of Mobilization and Radicalization of the Kurdish Movement'.
[46] Massicard, 'Gangs in Uniform', 52–3.
[47] Ahmet Hamdi Akkaya, 'The Kurdistan Workers' Party (PKK): National Liberation, Insurgency and Radical Democracy Beyond Borders' (PhD diss., Ghent University, 2016).
[48] Dinç, *Stories of Migration*.
[49] Murat Karayılan, *Bir Savaşın Anatomisi Kürdistan'da Askeri Çizgi* (Diyarbakır: Aram Yayıncılık, 2014), 157–79.
[50] Özar *et al.*, *From Past to Present*.

the special police teams trained by the ÖHD were sent to the conflict zones.[51] Thus, the ethnic conflict dynamic was one of the most important conditions for the establishment of the paramilitaries. In the global context generally, ethnic tensions and violence increased significantly after the Cold War as changing conditions impacted on the structure of conflicts in many countries. Both the PKK and Turkish governments were ideologically and militarily influenced by this transformation. For its part, the Turkish military responded by consolidating its irregular warfare capacity with paramilitary forces.

The Army and Party Politics

What was the role of nationalist policies of the state institutions (army, governments and parties) regarding the establishment of the paramilitary forces? One of the fundamental conditions in the emergence of paramilitary groups in Turkey was the nationalist policy of the state institutions. Two different institutions that promoted this state nationalist policy must be mentioned: first and foremost, the Turkish military, and second, the Turkish nationalist parties and their different characters (Kemalist, right-wing, Islamist and ultranationalist) that formed most of the governments after 1950.

Undoubtedly, the army had undisputed domination over governments and state institutions during the period in question. It led the armed forces, was active and autonomous in the state administration and, in the MGK, had created a pressure mechanism for the realisation of state politics in the direction of military coups and nationalist ideology. As discussed, the army was at the same time a main actor of the deep state network, which partly emerged due to the lack of the capability of the democratic institutions of the state, precisely because of the army's power.[52] The emergence of paramilitary groups was related to this fragmented structure of state institutions and different power elites along with the general ethno-nationalist or Kemalist militarising of state institutions underpinned by the army. Given the formation of paramilitary groups by nationalist political parties from their youth groups (as mentioned

---

[51] Soner Yalçın, *Binbaşı Ersever'in İtirafları*, 8. baskı (Istanbul: Kaynak Yayınları, 1994); Kılıç, *Özel Harp Dairesi*, 272–3.

[52] Söyler, *The Turkish Deep State*; Ünver, 'Turkey's "Deep-State" and the Ergenekon Conundrum'.

in Chapter 1), nationalist ideologies were one of the main conditions of the emergence of paramilitary organisations from the 1970s to '90s.

The influence of Turkish military institutions on politics has been analysed by several authors. According to these works, the army had an autonomous role in state administration.[53] Cizre Sakallıoğlu argues that this autonomy took place on two levels, institutional and political. The institutional autonomy refers to military education and doctrine, which was concerned 'primarily with internal insurgencies caused by rising ethnic and nationalist aspirations', while the political autonomy was defined as the direct or indirect influence of military institutions on democratically elected governments.[54] The state elites even created a constitutional institution for military influence in the MGK,[55] which significantly created the threat perceptions of the political parties and Turkish society and thus restricted the political space.

Following the 1980 coup, which severely limited the political space and freedom of civil society, the new constitution of 1982 had a clearly extreme nationalist tone.[56] Moreover, the military institutions did not allow political parties to open discussion on some important issues – notably, the problems of groups belonging to different religious and ethnic identities – under the blanket phrasing of 'these are security issues'.[57] This political process caused a rigidification and stagnation of state institutions, political parties and civil society. Growth was curtailed, development prevented. Yet, although the military had strong control over the state institutions, this did not mean that the state was strong. On the contrary, this revealed the low capacity of the state's democratic institutions. Summarising, it can be said that the main political

---

[53] Cizre Sakallıoğlu, 'The Anatomy of the Turkish Military's Political Autonomy'; Uzgel, 'Ordu Dış Politikanın Neresinde?'; Söyler, *The Turkish Deep State*.

[54] Sakallıoğlu, 'The Anatomy of the Turkish Military's Political Autonomy', 152–3.

[55] Gülistan Gürbey, 'The Kurdish Nationalist Movement in Turkey Since the 1980s', in *The Kurdish Nationalist Movement in the 1990s: Its Impact on Turkey and the Middle East*, ed. Robert W. Olson (Lexington: University Press of Kentucky, 1996), 12–13; Uzgel, 'Ordu Dış Politikanın Neresinde?', 77–9.

[56] Mithat Sancar, *'Devlet Aklı' Kıskacında Hukuk Devleti*, 4. baskı (Istanbul: İletişim, 2008); Aydın and Taşkın, *1960'tan Günümüze Türkiye Tarihi*.

[57] İsmet Akça, '1960'lardan 2012'ye Türkiye'de Devlet: Hegemonya Krizleri, Sol Hareket Ve Kürt Meselesi', *Toplum ve Kuram* 6–7 (2012): 93.

actor in Turkey, which determined the nationalist policy of the state after the multi-party period, was the military, and the emergence of paramilitary groups was directly related to the state-power of the army.

After the single-party dictatorship period, many political parties formed elected governments, but these parties all exhibited versions of Turkish nationalism (Kemalist nationalism, Islamist nationalism, ultranationalism).[58] Accordingly, these governments conducted quite similar nationalist politics while managing government institutions, directed against the various dissident groups (the internal enemies/threats). There was one exception, the legal left and democratic parties, but these were quite marginal in parliament. The Workers Party of Turkey (*Türkiye İşçi Partisi*) was founded in 1961 and then gained entry into parliament in the 1965 election.[59] However, it was closed down in 1971 because of decisions it took on the rights of Kurds in its fourth congress.[60]

The underlying reason for this uniformity of ideological politics was the military inheritance of the single-party dictatorship period and the consequent influence of the military institutions over the governments in the multi-party period. Thus, even though the parties were different, their ideological arguments were similar in terms of threats to the state, because the army limited all political space. The ideological and political similarities of these parties were effectively expressions of the inherited and ongoing delimitation of the democratic space by the military. Nevertheless, the parties in parliament did play an important role in the re-production of nationalist politics, and they had a prominent role in the emergence of paramilitary groups in accordance with nationalist and Islamist ideology during the 1970s and after.[61] The nationalist ideologies of these parties fostered and stoked the polarisation of society and the clash of different groups.

It was during this period that a paramilitary group was formed through the relations of the army and an ultranationalist party, the MHP. It also showed

---

[58] Temel Demirer and Sibel Özbudun, *Derin Milliyetçiliğin Siyasal İktisadi* (Ankara: Ütopya Yayınevi, 2006), 109.

[59] Aydın and Taşkın, *1960'tan Günümüze Türkiye Tarihi*, 136.

[60] Mesut Yeğen, 'Türkiye Solu ve Kürt Sorunu', in *Modern Türkiye'de Siyasi Düşünce*, 2. baskı, Sol (Istanbul: İletişim Yayınları, 2008), 1218.

[61] Aydın and Taşkın, *1960'tan Günümüze Türkiye Tarihi*, 269–86.

their employment of pro-state individuals and groups in actions for which they did not want to take responsibility. The MHP as a movement had a 'long history of involvement with paramilitary counterinsurgencies, organised political violence and state-centric totalitarian political scenarios'.[62] The trainers of its young recruits in the commando camps in different regions of Turkey between 1968 and 1980 were retired officers, former colleagues of the founder-leader, Alparslan Türkeş. Thus, a political party that was ideologically intolerant of oppositions was given constitutional direction of the military institutions which themselves already had an ideological motivation against oppositions. Türkeş and his officer-trainers had militarised the party and moved it towards to the ultranationalist ideology. In this process, the MHP and the army, nationalism and militarism were intertwined.

The youth organisations of the nationalist right-wing parties carried out many actions against dissident groups throughout the 1970s. Some of the members of these youth organisations were employed in Kurdish provinces as a new irregular unit under the police special action unit after 1980 and especially in the 1990s.[63] The boundaries of the politics determined by the army had a strongly nationalist framework; therefore, the MHP and its radical youth groups could find a place under the protective umbrella of the state where they could act freely. There was a fuzziness and interaction at the intersection between party politics, the military and the paramilitary – and among all security forces, for that matter, including the militarised rural police (*jandarma*) and regular urban police (*polis*).

Tribal Politics

After the 1980s, the relations established by state institutions with Kurdish tribes played an important role in the emergence of paramilitary organisations in Turkey. As described (Chapter 1), the Ottoman state had armed the Kurdish tribes that were loyal to the state against Armenians during the late Empire period and the Turkish state similarly had used pro-state Kurdish

---

[62] Canefe and Bora, 'The Intellectual Roots of Anti-European Sentiments in Turkish Politics', 126.

[63] Tim Jacoby, 'Fascism, Civility and the Crisis of the Turkish State', *Third World Quarterly* 32, no. 5 (1 June 2011): 912.

tribes in the suppression of Kurdish rebellions in the early years of the Republic. This was a win-win policy, because the tribes were also accepted by the state as political actors. The Turkish state played an important role in the re-establishment of traditional relations among the Kurds for pragmatic reasons, even though it has a modernist ideal.

There are contradictions between the tribal politics of the state and the ideal of a 'modern' country, modelled after the developed West.[64] Although the Turkish state had the intent to be a modern country, it was unable to realise this, especially in northern Kurdistan. There were at least three reasons for this. First, the capacity of state institutions in northern Kurdistan had been weak for a long time;[65] second, the state had strengthened traditional relations with pro-state tribes, constituting some tribes, armed by the state, as a political power in the local area;[66] and third, the Kurds had frequently rebelled in different ways against the state, so the stability of state institutions had been delayed or prevented. Further, state institutions had always maintained connections to the loyal tribes and families, partly in order to prevent the politicisation of Kurds as a whole, yet not all of the 'loyal' tribal members/families had been pro-state or loyal. Thus, the Village Guards that were loyal to the state could similarly count on a number of tribal families clustered around the tribal leader, not all of them. One of the interviewees gives the following example from the 1990s:

> There was Kamil Atağ in Cizre, and there weren't even twenty families around him. Less than twenty families were acting together with the state. They were with the state to maintain their power, not because they are loyal to the state or because they loved the state. They depended on the state for what it gave them.[67]

[64] Levent Köker, 'Kemalizm/Atatürkçülük: Modernleşme Devlet ve Demokrasi', in *Modern Türkiye'de Siyasi Düşünce Cilt 2 – Kemalizm*, ed. Ahmet İnsel (Istanbul: Iletisim Yayincilik, 2009), 97–112.

[65] Balta Paker and Akça, 'Askerler, Köylüler, Paramiliter Güçler', 11; Ahmet Özcan, 'Son Kürt Eşkıyaları: Kürt Meselesinde "Adi" Şiddetin Olağanüstülüğü, Siyasallığı ve Yasa Yapıcı Mirası', in *Türkiye'de Siyasal Şiddetin Boyutları*, eds Güney Çeğin and İbrahim Şirin (Istanbul: İletişim Yayınları, 2014), 183.

[66] Martin van Bruinessen, *Kürdistan Üzerine Yazılar*, 6. baskı (Istanbul: İletişim Yayınları, 2008), 181. And see also, for early Republic period, Üngör, *Rethinking the Violence of Pacification*.

[67] Interview #28, conducted in Spaubeek, 28 June 2017.

Several scholars explain how, when the Kurdish socialist movements rose in the 1970s, they declared the feudal tribes and landlord class who had political and economic patronage relations with the state to be 'collaborators' and 'traitors'.[68] Thus, the families, tribes and individuals in society were divided with a logic of 'either–or', (re)interpreted as pro-state or anti-state.[69] This was not just a political but also a social fragmentation, which suited the state authorities. The state elites in contact with Kurdish tribes and landowners loyal to the government were military institutions and governments, parties and local bureaucrats, such as governors. Joost Jongerden describes the government's management mechanism in Kurdish provinces as a 'Dual Administrative System', in which the military institutions were dominant; in other words, local civil bureaucrats and governors were under the control of military institutions.[70] Thus, it was the army institutions that were mostly in contact with the pro-state local Kurdish elites and the relations between the pro-state Kurdish tribes and state institutions mainly concerned security issues. The reorganisation of the Village Guard as the state's largest paramilitary force in northern Kurdistan was the result of this relationship. Also, new opportunities were offered to the leaders of these tribes and local elites, involving, for example, inclusion in the bureaucracy, positions such as deputy in the parliament, and local economic opportunities.

Stathis Kalyvas argues that during the conflict between the Turkish state and the PKK, being loyal to the state for the Kurdish population comprised a defection in terms of ethnic identity. In other words, according to Kalyvas, the ethnic belonging did not remain stable, and the perception of identity changed among the Kurdish population during the war. Therefore, 'ethnic defection takes place when a one-dimensional political space (ethnic identity: Turk or Kurd) is replaced by a two-dimensional space (loyal or disloyal to the

[68] Jongerden, *The Settlement Issue in Turkey and the Kurds*, 55; Ercan, 'Dynamics of Mobilization and Radicalization of the Kurdish Movement', 132–33; Güneş, *The Kurdish National Movement in Turkey*, 86.

[69] Adnan Çelik, '1990'lı Yılların Olağanüstü Hal Rejimi ve Savaş: Kürdistan Yerellerinde Şiddet ve Direniş', *Toplum ve Kuram*, no. 9 (2014): 107.

[70] Jongerden, *The Settlement Issue in Turkey and the Kurds*, 145–7.

Turkish state)'.[71] This understanding can be nuanced, however, with the further consideration that the defection was not an ideological Turkification on the part of the Village Guards, but rather a temporary, political and pragmatic adoption of this identity. This transformation was actualised in several ways.

First, there was the long-standing relationship established by some tribes and pro-state local elites with state institutions. Adnan Çelik argues that the majority of Kurdish tribes that cooperated with the state during the Sheikh Said rebellion in Diyarbekir province in 1925 joined the Village Guards system after 1985.[72] Thus, there was a continuity in the positions of pro-state tribes and families across time. Second, the state authorities also established the Village Guard system by force (approximately one-third of the guards),[73] by making the peasants and tribes decide between the two options: 'either you will become Village Guards or leave your village'.[74] Third, the relation of some tribes to the state was determined through the political position of a rival tribe. If there was an opponent pro-state or pro-PKK tribe, its rival/enemy tribe could acquire weapons as the part of the Village Guard system. Fourth, there were important economic reasons to be a Village Guard. This position provided regular salaries to the individual Village Guards as well as opportunities for organised crime relations, such as smuggling in the local area.[75] Therefore, state loyalty was not only based on volunteerism, but also gained by the state authorities through military, social and economic pressure.

The Village Guard system as a paramilitary force consisting of pro-state tribes emerged as a result of the lack of state military capacity in northern Kurdistan. As Balta Paker and İsmet Akça explain, the state renewed its institutional capacity in the fight against the PKK during the early 1990s, and the number of guards was greatly increased in this process – from 18,000 in 1990 to 64,000 in 1994. The Village Guards system assumed a LIC doctrine

---

[71] Stathis N. Kalyvas, 'Ethnic Defection in Civil War', *Comparative Political Studies* 41, no. 8 (1 August 2008), 1050.

[72] Çelik, '1990'lı Yılların Olağanüstü Hal Rejimi ve Savaş', 107.

[73] Mehmet Seyman Önder, 'Geçici Köy Korucuları Üzerine Sosyolojik Bir Araştırma' (PhD diss., Fırat Üniversitesi, 2013), 164.

[74] Özar *et al.*, *From Past to Present*, 149.

[75] Nur Tüysüz, 'Geçici Köy Koruculuğu Sisteminin Toplumda Yarattığı Dönüşüm ve Korucu Olmanın Kişisel Gerekçelendirmeleri', *Toplum ve Kuram*, no. 9 (2014): 177–201.

and played an important role in the rise of the local capacity of the state.[76] Researchers explain that in the Turkish state tradition, irregular militias from the Kurdish tribes were established especially during internal threats and that the tribal Regiments in the late Ottoman period and the Village Guard system a century later showed considerable similarities.[77] State authorities frequently renewed their relations with pro-state Kurdish tribes through various methods, both to strengthen the influence of the state in the local area and to utilise local populations as armed militia.

Paramilitarism, Organised Crime and the State

There was a complex relationship between paramilitary groups, criminal organisations and secret networks within the Turkish state, and these were in co-operation to further the state's political agenda.[78] Organised crime is an important phenomenon in Turkey and northern Kurdistan: the main types of organised crime between 1970 and 2000 were smuggling (especially weapons trafficking), drug trafficking, illegal gambling, racketeering, prostitution and large-scale theft. This sub-section focuses on the relationship of criminal organisations with state institutions, and particularly the effect of this on paramilitary organisations in the conflict with the PKK.

After the 1970s, the connection of organised crime to state authorities in Turkey rose dramatically, for various reasons. One of them was that employers who supported the right-wing parties and some units of the police and intelligence agencies began to economically and militarily support the extreme right gangs against opposition movements.[79] This had the effect of legitimising the presence of the right-wing gangs in government institutions (because they were fighting against common threats). Another reason for the increase

---

[76] Balta Paker and Akça, 'Askerler, Köylüler, Paramiliter Güçler', 16–17.

[77] Klein, 'Power in the Periphery', 349; David McDowall, *A Modern History of the Kurds* (I. B. Tauris, 2004), 424; Özar *et al.*, *From Past to Present*, 9; Aytar, *Hamidiye Alaylarından Köy Koruculuğuna*.

[78] Gingeras, *Heroin, Organized Crime, and the Making of Modern Turkey*; Bozarslan, *Network-Building, Ethnicity and Violence in Turkey*; Bovenkerk and Yeşilgöz, 'The Turkish Mafia and the State'; Massicard, 'Gangs in Uniform'.

[79] Gingeras, *Heroin, Organized Crime, and the Making of Modern Turkey*, 218; Bovenkerk and Yeşilgöz, *Türkiye'nin Mafyası*, 242–3.

in state-crime relations was the increase in the importance in Turkey of drug trafficking, which created enormous economic profits.[80] Combined with the fragmentation of state institutions and the weaknesses of institutional capacities, the threats of opposition movements and huge economic benefits to be gained led some units of the army, members of the political parties and the bureaucracy to become part of the organised crime network.

Bovenkerk and Yeşilgöz argue broadly that the attitudes of the police and other state institutions determine the structure, character and sphere of influence of criminal organisations.[81] A former member of the Turkish intelligence agency, Mehmet Eymür, explains in his memoir that the policymakers of MİT were multi-headed (the army, the government and the MGK), and therefore its capacity was fragmented and insufficient.[82] This can be said to be similar in many state institutions during 1970–90. Thus, when oppositional movements against the regime arose, the reactions of state institutions were different.

The Grey Wolves was not only a youth organisation of the MHP but also a criminal organisation with an important role in drug trafficking,[83] and one that was used by the security and intelligence agencies of the state for many years (although governments denied it).[84] One of the most important reasons for the members of this group to stay in a relationship with state institutions for a long time despite its criminal acts was the widespread impunity provided by the security services. A major reason for this was that illegal actions against dissidents have been perpetrated by the group. It appears that this ultranationalist, paramilitary youth group was responsible for many murders from the 1970s through to the 1990s – and many murder suspects were released shortly after they had been arrested, essentially patronised by the official authorities and secret forces of the state because they were acting against oppositions.[85] This impunity guarantee led to the emergence of new paramilitary groups and strengthened existing ones that were also major actors in organised crime.

[80] Gingeras, *Heroin*, 205–38.

[81] Bovenkerk and Yeşilgöz, *Türkiye'nin Mafyası*, 30–1.

[82] Mehmet Eymür, *Analiz: Bir Mit Mensubu'nun Anıları*, 9. baskı (Istanbul: Milenyum Yayınları, 2006), 47.

[83] Gingeras, *Heroin, Organized Crime, and the Making of Modern Turkey*, 2.

[84] Massicard, 'Gangs in Uniform', 53; Savaş, *Susurluk Raporu*.

[85] Aydın and Taşkın, *1960'tan Günümüze Türkiye Tarihi*, 158–9.

By way of example of the relationship between government officials and gang members, there was the notable event of one-time security chief, Interior Minister and Deputy Mehmet Agar signing a fake identity for gang leader Abdullah Çatlı.[86] As Söyler put it,

> The state consolidated by upgrading the 'modern bandits' in the service of the state. [There was a] correlation between the rise of corruption, drug trafficking, and political terror . . . The state subcontracted prominent ultranationalist mafia bosses and gunmen from the 1970s that were recruited from Gray Wolves, such as Abdullah Çatlı, Turgay Maraşlı, Oral Çelik, and Hadi Özcan. Protected by the shield of impunity, these gunmen were later deeply involved in the lucrative drug business.[87]

The relations between the chiefs of the Turkish police department and members of these extremist right-wing gangs provide quite descriptive information for an understanding of the relationships between organised crime, the state and the war. Hüseyin Kocadağ, who died with Çatlı in the Susurluk accident, was ane important founder of one of the special units in the police department, founded in the mid-1980s and used in the Kurdish provinces alongside other military and paramilitary forces during the 1980s and '90s.[88] The members of this unit were selected from those who had an ultranationalist background. Under the order of the General Director of Security, Mehmet Ağar,[89] some members of this unit became the guardians of Sedat Bucak, head of the Village-Guard Bucak tribe and one of the key actors in organised crime in Kurdish provinces.[90] 'These special forces were quickly re-named "death units" (*ölüm timi*) because of the often very brutal nature of the operations they were involved in.'[91]

---

[86] Massicard, 'Gangs in Uniform', 47.

[87] Söyler, *The Turkish Deep State*, 136.

[88] Bovenkerk and Yeşilgöz, 'The Turkish Mafia and the State', 585.

[89] For the rise of Mehmet Ağar within the general directorate of security affairs and his relationship with the extra-legal activities, see also: 'Mehmet Ağar: Devlete Doğmak ve Devletten Olmak', *Toplum ve Kuram*, no. 6–7 (2012): 66–9.

[90] Dinçer Gökçe and Enis Tayman, 'Susurluk'un İtirafları İfade Verecek!', *Radikal*, 26 March 2011, http://www.radikal.com.tr/turkiye/susurlukun_itiraflari_ifade_verecek-1044155/.

[91] Massicard, 'Gangs in Uniform', 52–3.

More specifically, Abdullah Çatlı and those with a similar role did not just act as assassins in Turkey. An interview I made in the Netherlands, shows that in the early 1990s, Çatlı worked on Kurdish Alevi associations to make them pro-state and carried out activities to assimilate them into Turkishness:

> [The first] Alevi association in the Netherlands was opened in 1990. We later found out that Abdullah Çatlı, who was killed in Turkey [found dead in the Susurluk accident], came here and had a meeting with the people who founded the Alevi association. With the particular aim of alienating the Kurd-Alevis from their own identity, such a team came from Turkey and followed a conscious policy. I know this from those who take part in the administration of Alevi-Bektaşi associations.[92]

The extensive relations of the police chiefs with gangs and criminal organisations meant that they could not remain hidden. Political and economic competition between state institutions caused a report prepared by MİT to be leaked to the press on 7 February 1988.[93] Known as MİT's first report to focus specifically on Istanbul, this revealed the corruption in play among several state institutions, including members of the army, the police department, the governorate and the mafia.[94] Arguably the most important feature of this report was that it showed that gangs associated with state institutions were being used both as death squads and to control drug trafficking. Government officials initially denied the report, in which the economic relations between the state/provincial bureaucracy and organised crime networks were particularly emphasised. Subsequent MİT reports (in 1996 and 1997) showed that these particularly economic relations in the 1980s had gained a political character in the 1990s.

According to the 1996 and 1997 reports, a secret unit had been established in the police force composed of former ultranationalist Grey Wolves and under the command of Mehmet Ağar. This unit, which was allegedly found

---

[92] Interview #42, conducted in Amsterdam, 21 October 2020.

[93] Sinan Doğan, ed., *Mit Raporu Olayı*, 1. baskı (Ist[anbul]: Sistem Yayıncılık, 1988), 7; TBMM, *TBMM Susurluk Komisyonu Raporu* (Ankara, 3 April 1997), 138, https://www. tbmm.gov.tr/sirasayi/donem20/yil01/ss301.pdf.

[94] Doğan, *Mit Raporu Olayı*.

to be acting against illegal dissident organisations, was mainly engaged in drug trafficking in European countries.[95] After the Susurluk accident in 1996, a commission was established in the TBMM to research this secret network. According to the commission report, such units were established not only in the police force, but also in MİT and JİTEM.[96] In addition, journalist İsmet Berkan claimed that in a MGK document he had seen, it was indicated that these secret units had been formed by a decision taken by the MGK in the autumn of 1993. This new informal force was established to counter PKK members, and their civilian supporters in particular.[97]

The reports prepared by the various agencies of the state and the parliament can be evaluated from two perspectives in terms of the relations of the criminal organisations and the state. Firstly, criminal organisations were politicised with the conflict between the PKK and the state. Secondly, Turkish mafia/organised crime took over Kurdish mafia/organised crime; or rather, the Kurdish mafia was liquidated by Turkish mafia with government support.[98] In this process, the role of the extreme right-wing gangs that the state used for secret operations was prominent. For example, these units had important roles in the killing of Kurdish businessmen, some of whom were involved in organised crime.[99] There were several key reasons for these units affiliated to the security forces of the state to kill Kurdish businessmen.

In 1993, Prime Minister Tansu Çiller made the following statement: '[W]e will cut down the logistical support of the PKK, we have a list of the businessmen that provide this support, we know about it.'[100] This statement was a very clear legitimation of the killing of Kurdish businessmen and seems to have functioned as a first step towards the murders, because it was immediately afterwards that many Kurdish businessmen were killed in unsolved murders. In short, the political decision from Ankara was the first reason for the liquidation of Kurdish businessmen. Also, according to Bovenkerk and Yeşilgöz, Kurdish

---

[95] Bovenkerk and Yeşilgöz, 'The Turkish Mafia and the State', 586.

[96] *TBMM Susurluk Komisyonu Raporu*, 170.

[97] İsmet Berkan, 'Gladio'ya MGK Onayı', *Radikal*, 6 December 1996.

[98] Bovenkerk and Yeşilgöz, *Türkiye'nin Mafyası*, 223–303; Soner Yalçın, *Behçet Cantürk'ün Anıları*, 7. baskı (Istanbul: Su Yayınları, 2000).

[99] *TBMM Susurluk Komisyonu Raporu*, 170.

[100] Ibid., 217.

102 | TURKISH PARAMILITARISM IN NORTHERN KURDISTAN

cities such as Van, Yüksekova and Hakkari, which had an important strategic location in the drug trade and were thus centres of great economic interest, became particular targets for the state. After the beginning of the conflict with the PKK, state units took control of these territories and thus the major drug-trafficking routes.[101] A second reason for the killing of Kurdish businessmen after 1993 was economic, therefore, related to this transition and involving elimination of the Kurdish mafia.

The emergence of paramilitary organisations when internal conflicts begin is importantly related to the lack of capacity on the part of the state's armed institutions. Within this causal framing, conditions that led to the emergence of paramilitary organisations in Turkey between 1970 and 1990 were related to the state's nationalist politics and the ethno-political demands of the Kurds (for self-determination) and then tribal politics and organised crime. Since the mid-1980s when it initiated an armed struggle, the PKK had been regarded as the most important threat to the state, but the state's security forces did not have the capacity to resist guerrilla movements. Basically, the guerrillas used small-movement units operating in the countryside, while the Turkish army, established with the threat from Moscow in mind, was still using a conventional method of warfare. It was not until some nine years into the conflict that the Turkish army was reorganised in the context of a LIC doctrine. Thus, during this period years (1984–93), government agencies tried to resolve the lack of capacity of the state institutions, which they did by creating various paramilitary forces.

Active Paramilitary Organisations during the 1990s

The Turkish state established several paramilitary groups immediately after the beginning of the conflict in 1984. In developing the paramilitaries, government agencies took advantage of conditions that were considered a basis of legitimacy for the creation of those groups (the emergence of political movements for the demands of Kurdish political rights, the common actions of the military and right-wing political parties against opposition movements, the establishment of local allies in northern Kurdistan that cooperate with the state, and the use of criminal organisations and paramilitary

---

[101] Bovenkerk and Yeşilgöz, *Türkiye'nin Mafyası*, 258.

groups for the purposes of state politics). Some of the units were organised as special forces within the army and police, and others were created by the government to support the army as an auxiliary force. As a result, JİTEM (including repentants), the Special Police Teams, the Village Guards and Hizbullah emerged as semi-formal and informal paramilitary organisations active particularly in northern Kurdistan. However, these forces had quite different characteristics. Some operated as death squads, others as auxiliary to the regular security forces; three of the four groups were established by state institutions and thus directly accountable (in theory), while Hizbullah was not and was consequently surreptitiously used by, but technically independent of the state.

Although JİTEM was one of the most well-known paramilitary organisations in Turkey, its existence was long denied by the state and the date of its establishment is still unclear.[102] Arif Doğan, a colonel in the Turkish army, has claimed to have founded it. According to Doğan, the JİTEM hierarchically was under the Gendarmerie Public Security Corps Command (*Jandarma Asayiş Kolordu Komutanlığı*), established in Diyarbakır in 1987 (see Figure 2.1).[103] Another Turkish officer, however, Major Ahmet Cem Ersever, gave an interview in June 1993 in which he claimed to be the boss of JİTEM and to have founded the institution.[104] Ersever was killed in November of the same year, his murder unsolved.[105] One view was that his killing was a revenge action undertaken by different paramilitary units (ÖHD) within the state.[106] The contradicting claims of the two officers about the establishment of the JİTEM may have been related to the names of formal and informal gendarmerie intelligence institutions. There had been an intelligence unit in the gendarmerie previously, which was used to fight against smuggling in general, but when the PKK emerged as a threat, a more active new organisation, with a new political and military mission, began to be established. Thus, the unit was transformed or renewed, making either

---

[102] Çetin Ağaşe, *Cem Ersever ve JİTEM Gerçeği* (Istanbul: Pencere Yayınları, 1998), 11.

[103] Arif Doğan, *JİTEM'i Ben Kurdum*, 1. baskı (Istanbul: Timaş Yayınları, 2011), 22–5.

[104] Yalçın, *Binbaşı Ersever'in İtirafları*, 45.

[105] Ibid., 17–18.

[106] *TBMM Susurluk Komisyonu Raporu*, 216.

one or two units that were set up, depending on one's perspective. Regardless of the details of the claims of the two officers, this paramilitary group was certainly operative in the second half of the 1980s, and although the officers presented different narratives about the establishment of the JİTEM, it is clear from their testimonies that they were responsible for atrocities committed and human rights violations.[107]

The army governed the country under martial law from the 1980 military coup until 1987. When martial law was abolished, a state of emergency was declared in the Kurdish provinces.[108] In the same year, the Gendarmerie Public Security Corps Command was established in Diyarbakır, where the JİTEM office was located, according to a repentant.[109] The interview with Ersever covered discussions about why this unit was founded. Apparently, government institutions, especially the intelligence agency, had failed to prevent the growth of the PKK, so Ersever wanted to introduce counter-guerrilla tactics.[110] Accordingly, the emergence of the JİTEM is related to the ineffectiveness of the existing armed forces of the state in the war against the PKK.

JİTEM members consisted of ultranationalist officers within the gendarmerie as well as repentants. There were also some people who worked in JİTEM but were neither officers nor repentants. Mahmut Yıldırım, a Sunni Kurd, was one. Operative under the code name 'Yeşil' (Green), he had worked with MİT and been affiliated with the MHP since the 1970s before becoming a very effective member of the paramilitary.[111]

A year after the PKK began its armed struggle, the TBMM introduced the 'Law of Repentance' (Pişmanlık Yasası).[112] This provided for courts to reduce the sentences of former members of the PKK who surrendered to the state.

---

[107] Yaprak Yıldız, '(Dis)Avowal of State Violence', 135–47.

[108] Bezci and Öztan, 'Anatomy of the Turkish Emergency State', 174.

[109] Uğur Balık, Kerberos: PKK'dan JİTEM'e Bir Tetikçinin Anatomisi, 1. baskı (Istanbul: Timaş Yayınları, 2011), 40, 173.

[110] Yalçın, Binbaşı Ersever'in İtirafları, 67, 107, 123.

[111] TBMM Susurluk Komisyonu Raporu, 229; Savaş, Susurluk Raporu; Ecevit Kılıç, JİTEM: Türkiye'nin Faili Meçhul Tarihi, 2. baskı (Istanbul: Timaş, 2009), 122–5.

[112] Biner, 'From Terrorist to Repentant: Who Is the Victim?', 340; 'Kaçakçılık Yasası Çıktı', Milliyet Gazetesi, 8 May 1985, http://gazetearsivi.milliyet.com.tr/Ara.aspx?araKelime=Pi%C5%9Fmanl%C4%B1k%20Yasas%C4%B1%20%C3%A7%C4%B1kt%C4%B1&isAdv=false.

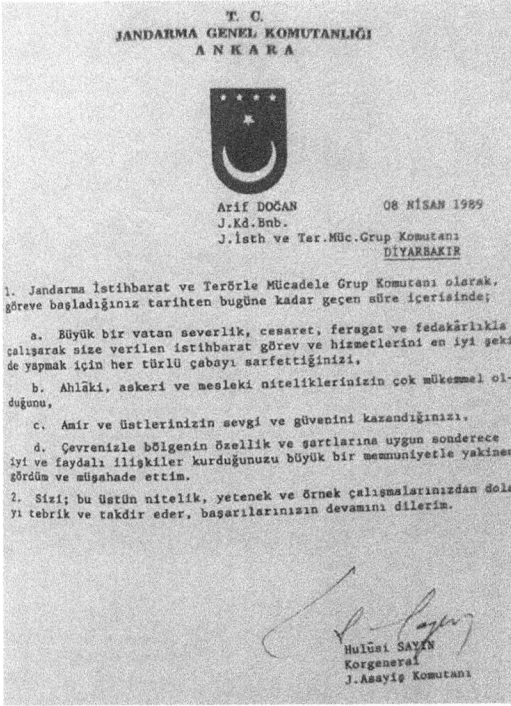

Figure 2.1 Arif Doğan's Certificate of Appreciation (given by Hulusi Sayın, then commander of the Gendarmerie Public Security Corps Command, 1989).

[Source: Arif Doğan, *JİTEM'i Ben Kurdum* (Istanbul: Timaş Yayınları, 2011), 205.]

Some repentants were hired as Village Guards and civil servants,[113] but they were also often used as assassins in JİTEM operations, mainly against Kurdish civilians and politicians. According to Yaprak Yıldız, 'the PKK repentants who worked as the hitmen and torturers of JİTEM's death squads [were] used by the state to deny and individualise the killings, disappearances, abductions and extortions, as people to put the blame on'.[114] The repentants were hierarchically positioned within JİTEM, because they were not an autonomous paramilitary organisation. Although the law was passed in 1985, its employment in combination with JİTEM began a little after that, in the late 1980s.[115]

---

[113] Özar *et al.*, *From Past to Present*, 186; Balık, *Kerberos*, 40.

[114] Yaprak Yıldız, '(Dis)Avowal of State Violence', 172.

[115] Balık, *Kerberos*.

Soldan sağa: Abdulkadir Aygan, Hüseyin Tilki (en üstte), İbrahim Babat, Recep Tirili, Ali Ozansoy, Adil Timurtaş (alta oturan)

Figure 2.2 Former PKK repentants recruited to JİTEM.
[Source: Timur Şahan and Uğur Balık, *İtirafçı: Bir JİTEM'ci Anlattı . . .* (Diyarbakır: Aram Yayınları, 2004), 148]

The Village Guards organisation was the largest and most widespread paramilitary group, but its emergence was nevertheless influenced by local dynamics. Pro-state militias in the regions of northern Kurdistan where the conflict was most intense were mainly established for intelligence gathering and military operations.[116] Specific local and regional circumstances – such as social divisions during the conflict, the state's traditional tribal politics and the organised crime network in northern Kurdistan – played a significant role in the emergence of the Village Guards. Established in March 1985 as a semi-legal paramilitary organisation under the 'Temporary Village Guard System', this paramilitary organisation emerged in conditions of an increase of violence in villages and their peripheries.[117] Therefore, it was established as one of the first reactions to the appearance of the PKK as a threat against the state, through revision of an old law:

[116] Mehmet Seyman Önder, *Devlet ve PKK İkileminde Korucular*, 1. baskı (Istanbul: İletişim Yayınları, 2015), 48–54.
[117] GÖÇ DER, *Türkiye'de Koruculuk Sistemi: Zorunlu Göç ve Geri Dönüşler* (Istanbul: GÖÇ DER, 2013), 3.

The legal basis of the Temporary Village Guard System was the Village Law numbered 442 that was legislated in 1924. On March 26, 1985 with the amendment made to the Article 74,3 a paramilitary structure comprising temporary and voluntary Village Guards was established ... The Village Guards were under the command of the village headman administratively and the Commander of the Gendarmerie Squad in professional matters.[118]

Balta Paker and Akça analyse the emergence of the Village Guard system as having three main aims: (1) to establish a force capable of struggling against a small number of guerrillas in the local area without changing the conventional structure of the army; (2) to gather quick information about conflicts and the enemy through local actors; and (3) to identify loyal and 'enemy' groups through this local cooperation system.[119] As a result of the formation of the Village Guard system, there was a dramatic rise in pro-state/anti-state polarisation in the Kurdish social structure, alongside the conflict between state and the PKK. In this context, one can speak of a bilateral relationship between Village Guards and the state. The state's security forces did not trust local guards as an ally. In the same way, a significant part of the Village Guards were not ideological allies of the state, but motivated by economic and political interests.[120] Thus, the establishment of the Village Guards may be regarded as intended to divide the Kurdish population socially and politically, as well as to gather intelligence from the rural areas and control conflict zones, which were well known to the Village Guards.

The image in Figure 2.3 is a photo taken by Ercan İpekçi and published in pro-state *Cumhuriyet* newspaper as its 'Photo of the Day' on 23 September 1989. We see the Village Guards here mostly lined up in civilian clothes with military-type, official-issue flak jackets, and armed. Behind them, the children are watching, lined up in the same way; hence the title used by Ipekçi referring to 'Future Village Guards'.

Due to insufficient local and irregular warfare capacity of the Turkish security forces, special action police units were established as an irregular force

---

[118] Özar *et al.*, *From Past to Present*, 9.

[119] Balta Paker and Akça, 'Askerler, Köylüler, Paramiliter Güçler', 11.

[120] Interview #22, conducted in Istanbul, 18 May 2017; Interview #28, conducted in Spaubeek, 28 June 2017.

GÜNÜN FOTOĞRAFI

Korucular ve İstikbaldeki korucular (Fotoğraf: Ercan İpekçi/AA)

Figure 2.3 'Village Guards and future Village Guards'.
[Source: Ercan İpekçi, 'Korucular ve İstikbaldeki Korucular', *Cumhuriyet* newspaper 'Photo of the Day', 23 September 1989, 11.]

to join the operations in cities alongside the police and in rural areas alongside the army, gendarmerie and Village Guards.[121] This group was a paramilitary organisation formed by the state during the conflict and consisted of the youth of nationalist political parties. The police Special Operations Department had been established in 1982 against the Armenian nationalist organisation ASALA.[122] With the development of the conflict between the PKK and the state, the members of this unit were allegedly trained by another paramilitary

[121] Former police academy member Ertan Beşe expresses the purpose and functions of the special police teams as follows: 'Special Operation Police Teams (Polis Özel Harekât Timleri, PÖHT) were organised in 1983 within the Presidency of the Department of Public Order (Asayiş Dairesi Başkanı) under a central Special Operations Branch Directorate (Özel Harekât Şube Müdürlüğü) and Special Operations Group Authority (Özel Harekât Grup Amirliği) in the cities of Ankara, Istanbul and Izmir as specially-trained units for sensitive operations requiring special skills such as forestalling the armed actions of terrorist organisations in inhabited or rural areas, overpowering or capturing the perpetrators of terrorist actions that were carried out and rescuing hostages in closed areas such as planes, vehicles and buildings'. He does not, however, emphasise the role of the special teams in human rights violations in the Kurdish provinces, or he expresses it as a claim of the Susurluk Report. Ertan Beşe, 'Special Operations Unit', in *Almanac Turkey 2005: Security Sector and Democratic Oversight*, ed. Ümit Cizre, 1st edn (Istanbul: TESEV Publications, 2006), 118–19.
[122] Kılıç, *Özel Harp Dairesi*, 272.

organisation, the Special Warfare Department (*Özel Harp Dairesi*).[123] Thus, this unit, together with the army, was able to begin small-unit operations against the PKK. Hasan Kundakçı, one of the former commanders of the Department, explained in his memoir that these units were first sent to the conflict zone to perform special operations in late 1985 to early '86.[124] The members consisted of persons following an ultranationalist ideology. Former member of this special unit Ayhan Çarkın stated the following in an interview:

> I was in the special operations group of 320 people who were first sent to the Southeast [Kurdish provinces] in 1986. I stayed in the region until 1990. We were all covered with blood. Terrible things have been done to those people.[125]

Figure 2.4 Newspaper report on 1993 Ministry brochure looking for 'Turks' to join up to the Special Police Teams.

[Source: *Cumhuriyet* newspaper, 3 November 1993.]

---

[123] Ibid., 273.

[124] Kundakçı, *Güneydoğu'da Unutulmayanlar*, 157–60.

[125] Gökçe and Tayman, 'Susurluk'un İtirafları İfade Verecek!'

In 1993, the Special Police Teams were reorganised. The government sent a brochure to the police departments of all provinces in November of that year stating that the main criterion for recruits was that they were Turks. In other words, only people who identified with (and/or had adopted) Turkish nationalism were recruited (the role of the ultranationalist MHP during this period, as well as other right-wing parties, is further discussed in the chapters below).[126] Mehmet Ağar, the General Director of Security and Gendarmerie Command in the Kurdish provinces, under which the teams were assigned, reorganised the structure with Tansu Çiller, Prime Minister between 1993 and 1996, when the violence was at its peak.[127] Reorganisation of the Special Police Teams was one of the issues that concerned Çiller most during those years. She would visit their training centres, as shown in the photo below (Figure 2.5).

Nadire Mater had interviewed soldiers who took part in the conflicts between the Turkish state and the PKK and published them in a book. In the

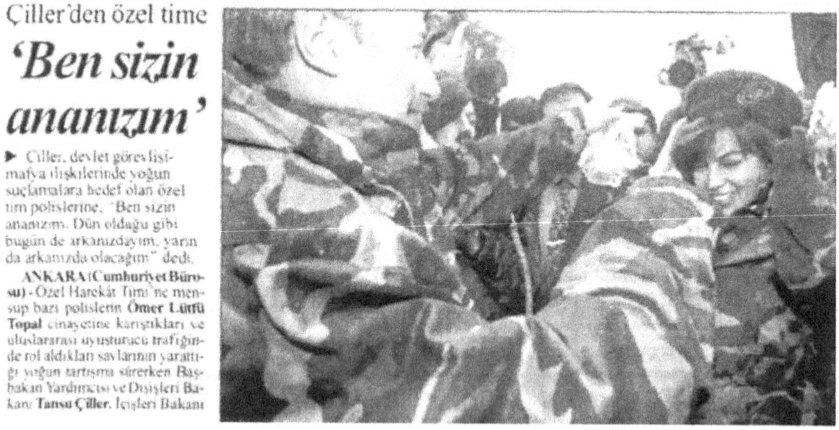

Çiller'den özel time

'Ben sizin ananızım'

▶ Çiller, devlet görevlisi-mafya ilişkilerinde yoğun suçlamalara hedef olan özel tim polislerine, "Ben sizin ananızım. Dün olduğu gibi bugün de arkanızdayım, yarın da arkanızda olacağım" dedi.

ANKARA (Cumhuriyet Bürosu) - Özel Harekât Timi'ne mensup bazı polislerin **Ömer Lütfü Topal** cinayetine karıştıkları ve uluslararası uyuşturucu trafiğinde rol aldıkları savlarının yarattığı yoğun tartışma sürerken Başbakan Yardımcısı ve Dışişleri Bakanı **Tansu Çiller**, İçişleri Bakanı

Figure 2.5 Newspaper report on a Special Police Team visit made by Çiller (under the headline 'I am your mother', quoting her as saying also 'I am standing behind you today as I did yesterday, and I will also stand behind you tomorrow').

[Source: 'Tansu Çiller'den Özel Time: Ben Sizin Ananızım', *Cumhuriyet Gazetesi*, 28 December 1996, 1, 19.]

126 Göksel Polat, 'Özel Time "Türk" Aranıyor', *Cumhuriyet Gazetesi*, 3 November 1993.

127 'Bölücülere Karşı "Özel Polis"', *Milliyet Gazetesi*, 7 October 1986; 'EGM – Özel Harekat Daire Başkanlığı', EGM, https://www.egm.gov.tr/Sayfalar/%C3%96zel-Harekat-Daire-Ba%C5%9Fkanl%C4%B1%C4%9F%C4%B1.aspx.

soldiers' narratives, the differences and ideological attitudes of the paramilitary Special Forces are frequently emphasised. The following testimony of a soldier who served in the Special Forces during the 1990s is quite striking:

> We occasionally came into contact with the Special Forces. I am a friendly type, but I did not seek to make friends with them much. From what I saw, the Special Forces are God, the Prophet, everything in that region. Anyway, they had special training, these were the people who sliced off the ears and noses of the corpses and nailed them on the walls. In this respect, they are very different from us. I don't believe they are soldiers, they were men sent by MHP on a special mission. You would be frightened when you saw them; they were big and heavy and without feeling because they believed in a cause. They believed that they would be heroes if they died, so they would attack to become heroes.[128]

The special teams were the most known paramilitary group that the state's top officials (Prime Minister Çiller and Director-General of Public Security Mehmet Ağar) supported openly. It was also stated, however, that army officers and the ÖHD trained these special units[129] and that army officers and the ÖHD also provided training for Hizbullah members.[130]

Hizbullah has been shown to be responsible for the many killing of pro-PKK Kurdish civilians in northern Kurdistan in the 1990s.[131] Thus, it can be included in paramilitary groups as employed by the state military and paramilitary forces in the first part of the 1990s.[132] According to Ruşen Çakır, Hizbullah emerged as an Islamic illegal organisation in the Kurdish provinces in the early 1980s,[133] although Mehmet Kurt claims that it was established in 1979.[134] Both authors refer to the 1980s as the early period of Hizbullah and the 1990s as the period of violence with the building of an Islamic state

[128] Nadire Mater, *Voices from the Front: Turkish Soldiers on the War with the Kurdish Guerrillas* (Basingstoke: Palgrave Macmillan, 2005), 79–80.

[129] Bilâ, *Komutanlar Cephesi*, 50.

[130] Orhan Gökdemir, *Pike: Bir Polis Şefinin Kısa Tarihi* (Istanbul: Chiviyazilari, 2001), 87–8.

[131] Funda Danışman and Rojin Canan Akın, *Bildiğin Gibi Değil:90'larda Güneydoğu'da Çocuk Olmak* (Istanbul: Metis Yayınları, 2011), 32–9; Dinç, *Stories of Migration*, 108.

[132] *TBMM Darbe ve Muhtıraları Araştırma Komisyonu Raporu*, 98.

[133] Çakır, *Derin Hizbullah*, 58.

[134] Kurt, *Din, Şiddet ve Aidiyet*, 45.

as the purpose of the organisation, motivated by the Islamic revolution in Iran.[135] Almost all the members of this group were or can be characterised as extremist Islamist Kurds.

A former minister of the state, İsmet Sezgin has said that Hizbullah was used in some way by the state,[136] while Arif Doğan has gone further and stated that it was *founded* by the state (to fight against the PKK).[137] Indeed (as mentioned), the first Hizbullah leader was an active member in the 1970s and early '80s of two radical Islamic organisations, the paramilitary student's union MTTB and the MSP youth group *Akıncılar*.[138] The relationship between Hizbullah and state institutions appears quite complex, but Hizbullah claims that they are neither part of the state institutions (including JİTEM), nor dependent on state institutions officially.[139] Nevertheless, this group and the state collaborated against the 'common enemy, the PKK' – so while there may have been no agreement between the state and Hizbullah officially, there was certainly cooperation. After all, Hizbullah mostly fought against the PKK and pro-PKK civilians, politicians and other rival Kurdish Islamic communities. For this reason, this group can be handled separately from the other paramilitary groups. Overall, one could argue that it operated as a volunteer and a subcontractor paramilitary force that was used by the Turkish state in northern Kurdistan. It seems to have played an important role in trying to eliminate members of the PKK and killing many civilians.

Thus, two paramilitary organisations were founded in the 1980s, the JİTEM and the Special Police Teams, under the umbrella of two state institutions, the Gendarmerie Public Security Corps Command, based in Diyarbakır, and the Special Warfare Department, a more experienced and former paramilitary group. Thus, while many NATO members lifted or deactivated their secret armies established in the 1950s due to the end of the Cold War, this great

[135] Ibid., 47; Çakır, *Derin Hizbullah*, 55.

[136] '90'larda Ne Olmuştu? Ismet Sezgin: Birtakım Öldürmeler, Hapsetmeler, Bir Mücadele', BBC, 4 September 2015, http://www.bbc.com/turkce/haberler/2015/09/150903_90lar_3_ismet_sezgin_roportaj.

[137] Doğan, *JİTEM'i Ben Kurdum*, 156.

[138] Kurt, *Din, Şiddet ve Aidiyet*, 41, 121.

[139] İ. Bagasi, 'Kendi Dilinden Hizbullah ve Mücadele Tarihinden Önemli Kesitler', Husayni Sevda, n.d., 217–29, http://huseynisevda.biz/viewpage.php?page_id-33.

political transformation did not end the ÖHD in Turkey. Only its name was changed, and its focus of engagement. On the contrary, the conflict with PKK meant that the former paramilitary group established and/or led several new militia groups.[140]

Conclusion

At the beginning of the conflict between the PKK and the Turkish state in 1984, paramilitary organisations with different characteristics were formed. Primarily, this was in response to what was regarded as the main threat to the state, namely, the insurgency and political demands of the Kurdish political movements, which already had a decades-long history. Secondly, the ruling elite determining the perception of threat consisted mainly of the army and right-wing parties, which espoused a strongly and even extremist Turkish nationalist ideology. Thirdly, when threats to the state arose, 'loyal' Kurdish tribes and families were used, when necessary, as local militias, which was due to the low level of the state's capacity in northern Kurdistan.

In general, relations among state institutions, bureaucrats, politicians and criminal organisations were quite complex. Armed gangs were used both for extra-legal activities of the state and supported to intimidate opposition political movements. The Susurluk scandal and some similar cases have revealed these relations as entirely standard practice of state institutions. Thus, there was a direct and indirect state sponsorship of the various paramilitary organisations that were formed in the late 1980s and early '90s, ranging from death squads to auxiliary forces (JİTEM, including the repentants, the Special Police Teams, the Village Guards and Hizbullah). Broadly, the conditions discussed created a political and military atmosphere conducive to the establishment of paramilitary groups.

The actual formation of some of these paramilitary organisations can be explained as a top-down process in which the state created or reorganised paramilitary groups when faced with threats because of their previous experience. The history of the state (its 'memory'), existing institutions and traditions were employed. The JİTEM, Special Police Teams and Village Guards can be evaluated in this framework precisely because the state had created

---

[140] Kılıç, *Özel Harp Dairesi*, 267–80; Serdar Çelik, *Türk Kontr-Gerillası*, 2nd edn (Köln: Ülkem Presse, 1995), 415–16.

similar organisations in previous periods. However, a bottom-up process may be better descriptive of the relationship between Hizbullah and the state. Hizbullah was similar to the paramilitary groups that the state had established or benefited from in the previous period (before the PKK). It resembled earlier state-sponsored paramilitary groups used against the Kurdish and leftist oppositions, such as the *Akıncılar* and Grey Wolves, established and used in the mid-1970s. These groups may not have been established directly by the state, but there were clear relationships between the leaders of these groups and the various institutions of the state.

In general, though, we can conclude that the formation or activation of paramilitary groups occurred as a top-down process. Therefore, the formation of paramilitary forces was especially established as the first intervention force against the PKK due to the inadequacy of the institutional capacity of the Turkish army and the lack of irregular warfare capabilities – because these groups were both ideologically reliable and institutionally deniable for the state elite. Although the Turkish army changed its conventional structure in 1993 to an LIC doctrine, the paramilitary groups were not deactivated. On the contrary, although established in the 1980s, they were specially developed and strengthened in the first half of the 1990s.

Table 2.1 illustrates the history and formation of the paramilitary groups discussed in this chapter.

Table 2.1 Establishment and transformation of the paramilitary groups.

← 1950	1960	1970	1980	1990	2000 →
Village Guard (1924)				Village Guard System (1985)	→
	Mobilisation Research Council (1952)	Special Warfare Department (1965)		Special Forces Command (1991) →	
		Grey Wolves or Idealist Youth (1968)			→
			Special Action Office (1982)	Special Police Team (1993) →	
				Hizbullah (particularly 1991-95)	?
				JİTEM (inc. repentants) (1987)	?

3

THE CHANGING MILITARY STRATEGY
AND REORGANISATION OF
PARAMILITARY FORCES

Introduction

There was a major reorganisation and development of the paramilitary formations in Turkey in the early 1990s. Between 1991 and 1996, the Turkish security forces sought to improve their irregular warfare capacity by implementing the low-intensity conflict doctrine. While the PKK declared a unilateral ceasefire in March 1993, and some steps were taken by state representatives toward a democratic solution of the Kurdish question, the leadership of the Turkish army remained adamant that it could only be settled by military means.[1] This, it was convinced, required a transformed organisation and development of paramilitary forces.

Three aspects distinguished the political and military atmosphere in Turkey in the early 1990s from the previous period. The conditions before 1990 were: (1) Kurdish civilians were not made direct targets of the war, (2) the public space in Turkey had not yet been made supporter of the war by the nationalist political parties and the state, and (3) the violence used by the paramilitary forces was lower than in the 1990s and the paramilitary formations were smaller and predominantly intelligence groups. These military, political

---

[1] Akkaya, 'Ulusal Kurtuluş, Ayaklanma ve Sınırların Ötesi', 92–3; Ümit Özdağ, *Türkiye'de Düşük Yoğunluklu Çatışma ve PKK* (Ankara: Üç Ok Yayınları, 2005), 72–3; Jongerden, *The Settlement Issue in Turkey and the Kurds*, 44–51.

and ideological features began to change from the beginning of the 1990s. First, the war was not only between the security forces and the PKK, as in the previous period, primarily since the state authorities adopted a more complex war doctrine that also targeted Kurdish civilians, politicians and human rights advocates. Almost all the security and paramilitary forces were reorganised structurally and numerically within the framework of this doctrine. Second, the ideological propaganda of Turkish nationalism was heavily used; political parties became the cornerstone of the war with this nationalist campaign and the protectors of certain paramilitary formations. Finally, particularly intensive types of violence (unsolved murders, enforced disappearances, burning of villages, etc.) were put into effect, intimidating and threatening Kurdish civilians, whether they were pro-PKK or not. The violence of paramilitary groups was unrestricted and went out of control. This chapter addresses the question of how these paramilitary forces developed and reorganised and which were the causal factors in this transformation.

When the PKK began its armed struggle, the government and the army had established paramilitary forces as the first armed groups to be sent to war with the gendarmerie. These forces were transformed together with the reorganisation of the army and police forces in the early 1990s. The paramilitary groups were developed, and the types of violence used was diversified and increased. This chapter discusses the role of the LIC doctrine as a reason for the increase and reorganisation of paramilitary groups and the violence they perpetrate, as well as the role of political parties in the transformation of paramilitary organisations.

First of all, I examine the role of LIC doctrine in the reorganisation of the paramilitary forces and the changing nature of the war. The LIC doctrine provided important conditions in terms of the reorganisation and development of paramilitary groups during the period of its implementation. Second, the LIC doctrine was essentially a political concept rather than a military one. Hence, I evaluate the role of political parties in the adoption of the new doctrine of war and the reorganisation of paramilitary forces. The state institutions were administered by a more nationalist and more radical political and military elite during 1991–6, and this political atmosphere played an important role in the reorganisation of paramilitaries. Third, I discuss the changes in the nature of paramilitary formations, both quantitative and qualitative. I argue that the changing nature of paramilitary forces was a result of the new war doctrine, and I discuss the results in terms of the dramatic increases in the numbers of members of these formations, their development into predominantly death squads and their becoming more autonomous.

Fourth, I analyse the changes in the nature of the violence that the paramilitary groups perpetrated. I discuss the different characteristics of the paramilitary groups in terms of the types of violence they used. Specifically, I argue that there was a division of labour between different paramilitary forces, which were separated both according to their geographical coverage (city vs. countryside) and their functions (death squads vs. auxiliary forces). Finally, I argue that the new strategy executed by state authorities since 1991 was not only a military strategy but also a political strategy, which included the political parties in addition to the whole state security apparatus. Therefore, I dub this period, particularly between 1991 and '96, the *paramilitarisation of the state*.

The LIC Doctrine and Paramilitarism

This section argues that the LIC doctrine created an important transformation in the reorganisation of paramilitary forces and a major change in their functions. Restructuring the Turkish army through the LIC doctrine had a determinant role in the reorganisation and development of paramilitary formations. Regarding the idea of LIC, there are different concepts that are employed to describe civil wars or non-international conflicts in which paramilitary groups are active. Kaldor gives a few examples – 'hybrid wars', 'degenerate wars', 'small wars', 'LICs' and 'new war' – and then famously settles on the 'new wars' concept.[2] Smith, however, critically approaches these different types of war, stating simply that 'War is war, regardless of what tactics are used'.[3] That may be the case, and there was indeed a war between the Turkish state and the PKK, but it is equally true that this war had shifted into a different dimension by the beginning of the 1990s and it is therefore necessary to characterise this difference. Accordingly, I argue that the term 'low-intensity conflict' better describes the changing characteristics of the war from 1991 and

---

[2] Kaldor, *New and Old Wars*, 2–3.

[3] M. L. R. Smith, 'Guerrillas in the Mist: Reassessing Strategy and Low Intensity Warfare', *Review of International Studies* 29, no. 1 (January 2003): 37.

evaluate the reorganisation of paramilitary forces through this concept. Although there are different debates about the transformation of the conflict, I discuss it in terms of the LIC doctrine. This provides an important framework for an understanding of the war strategy that the state began to implement against the PKK and particularly pro-PKK Kurdish civilians in the early 1990s.

What is the LIC doctrine and how did it emerge? John Collins, senior specialist in national defence of the US, distinguishes conflict intensity in three groups:

> High (nuclear wars: global, regional, conventional war (major)); Mid (limited wars: nuclear, conventional and insurgency (phase III)); and Low (a. violent conflicts: insurgency (phases I, II), counterinsurgency, coups d'etat, transnational terrorism, anti/counterterrorism, narco conflict, conventional war (minor); b. nonviolent conflicts: political warfare, economic warfare, technological warfare, psychological warfare, peacekeeping).[4]

According to this listing, LICs have a much more complex and wider framework than other conflict types. LICs also, we should note, involve strategies that target not only an armed enemy but also the civilians in its periphery. Historically, the phrase 'low intensity conflict' was an American national security term that came into usage during the late 1970s.[5] It was primarily employed for *internal* conflicts (rather than war between states) and involved a preventive strategy against the rise of leftist revolutionary and national liberation movements in 'Third World' countries, prepared during Reagan's presidency, in the 1980s.[6] However, this idea of conflict itself did not emerge in the 1980s; there was a long historical background, including the cases of the Philippines in the 1940s and Angola in the 1980s, through which the doctrine was developed.[7] This new strategy was implemented not through direct intervention

---

[4] John M. Collins, Frederick Hamerman and James P. Seevers, *U.S. Low-Intensity Conflicts 1899–1990* (Washington, DC: Committee On Armed Services House of Representatives, 1990), 5.

[5] Richard H. Shultz, 'The Low-Intensity Conflict Environment of the 1990s', *Annals of the American Academy of Political and Social Science* 517 (1991): 121.

[6] Ibid., 122–3; Jochen Hippler, ed., *Düşük Yoğunluklu Çatışma: İlân Edilmemiş Savaş* (Istanbul: Belge Uluslararası Yayıncılık, 1996), 12–14.

[7] Collins *et al.*, *U.S. Low-Intensity Conflicts*, 29; Hippler, *Düşük Yoğunluklu Çatışma*, 14–20.

and occupation, as in Vietnam, but through more complicated, unconventional and domestic preventive measures. As a strategy of war, it was used in US operations in various parts of the world, such as in Bolivia, Beirut, Grenada and Libya. It 'included a comprehensive range of political and psychological operations, sometimes referred to as "special operations," sometimes "special activities" and "unconventional warfare"'.[8]

During and especially after the Cold War, conventional armies in general were transformed into more mobile, irregular forms and smaller units, particularly in the context of internal conflicts and civil wars. Thus, the LIC doctrine came to refer usually to internal conflicts rather than wars between states. Rather than a conventional war against other armies/enemies, LIC describes a method of warfare, one that typically targeted pro-insurgent civilians (making it a form of 'asymmetric' war). In other words, the doctrine became a prominent counterinsurgency strategy. Kaldor argues that the new types of organised violence had many different names that came to define the new characteristics of armed forces and that LIC doctrine was one of them.[9]

The UK and France – such as in Malaysia and Algeria, respectively – had developed irregular and asymmetric warfare strategies, but it was US leadership that had become the most significant factor and example in the suppression of opposition movements for other NATO countries, including Turkey. The anti-communist secret paramilitary organisations established by NATO member-states also illustrated the prevalence of this strategy of war.[10] Ramsey Clark thus describes the main purpose of this doctrine as follows: 'The LIC strategy has two sides: first, to support the sovereignty of a pro-Western state, and second, to destabilise a state affiliated with the Eastern Bloc or a neutral state.'[11] The pro-Western, NATO member Turkey was also supported in different ways during the war with the PKK.[12] With the collapse of the Soviet Union, the main threat for NATO had disappeared, and these military experiences began to be used to liquidate mostly leftist and national opposition

[8] Hippler, *Düşük Yoğunluklu Çatışma*, 11.
[9] Kaldor, *New and Old Wars*, 2–3.
[10] Ganser, *NATO's Secret Armies*; Yamak, *Gölgede Kalan İzler ve Gölgeleşen Bizler*.
[11] Ramsey Clark, 'İnsan Hakları ve "Low Intensity Conflict"', in *Düşük Yoğunluklu Çatışma: İlân Edilmemiş Savaş*, ed. Jochen Hippler (Istanbul: Belge Yayınları, 1996), 43.
[12] Bilâ, *Komutanlar Cephesi*, 43–6.

movements in pro-Western countries or together with pro-Western regimes, which were both supported and installed. The adoption of the LIC doctrine by the Turkish state was also a result of this process.

The LIC doctrine began to be debated in Turkey by high-ranking soldiers, members of parliament and journalists in the late 1980s through the concept of a 'territorial army'. A territorial militia force was proposed by the MGK, and the government began to work on legislation.[13] Journalist Ali Sirmen argued that a territorial army could not be established because of the dark relations between the existing paramilitary force, the Special Warfare Department, the nationalist youth of the MHP, and the US.[14] However, at the beginning of the 1990s, the discussions about a special army came to the fore again with the LIC doctrine. The establishment of a special army was also debated in various political and military institutions of the state. High-ranking commanders (including Cem Ersever, co-founder of JİTEM) suggested a special army of tens of thousands of people.[15] President Özal, shortly before he died in April 1993, wrote a secret letter to Demirel, then prime minister, suggesting that a new path should be followed in the conflict with the PKK. Among the suggestions in the letter was an idea for the establishment of a special force of 40–50,000 people.[16]

The discussion about a new army – a 'territorial', 'special' or 'people's army' – that had alternative, local and mobile features itself indicated the lack of irregular warfare capacity in the conventional army. The military force described in these discussions included the creation of a very large paramilitary group, but instead, state authorities reorganised and consolidated existing groups. The army was to be structurally transformed and made more mobile. In the same period, the state authorities were also preparing a different liquidation plan against the pro-PKK civilians associated with the LIC doctrine (see below). Moreover, a report of the parliamentary research commission on the military coups mentions a different secret plan, named the 'Castle Plan'

---

[13] Haldun Armağan, 'Ordu Kontrolünde Yerel Savunma', *Milliyet Gazetesi*, 31 October 1988, 7; Nilüfer Yalçın, 'Sivil Orduya Asker Komutan', *Milliyet Gazetesi*, 11 May 1988, 8.
[14] Ali Sirmen, 'Teritoryal Tartışması', *Cumhuriyet Gazetesi*, 13 November 1988.
[15] Yalçın, *Binbaşı Ersever'in İtirafları*, 137–9.
[16] Jongerden, *The Settlement Issue in Turkey and the Kurds*, 46.

(*Kale Planı*). According to the report, the Castle Plan was prepared by the General Commander of the Gendarmerie, Eşref Bitlis, and submitted to the government and involved the establishment of new paramilitary groups and/or use of existing groups (including Hizbullah and the repentants) for the liquidation of businessmen and deputies who were allegedly supporting the PKK.[17]

Several authors argue that the LIC doctrine was adopted by the Turkish state in 1991 but not fully implemented until 1993.[18] The Chief of the General Staff, Doğan Güreş, one of the founding actors of the LIC doctrine in Turkey, stated that he investigated the types of irregular warfare by various countries (the US, UK and Spain) to use against the PKK in 1991, and that after this research, the Turkish army and government began to implement the doctrine.[19]

The first change was made after the end of the Cold War, when the Special Warfare Department was transformed into a Special Forces Command.[20] Güreş explains this transformation as follows:

> One of my significant decisions was to disband the Special Warfare Department. Why did I disband it? The reason I did this was that it remained left over from the Second World War. It had been established to organise civil society behind the possible areas to be occupied after that War . . . However, the Second World War was long over. The threats had changed. When the condition in the 1990s was taken into consideration, the Special Warfare Department had no function. I disestablished it and said the 'Special Forces Command' would be established because when I looked at the world, I saw that the struggle against organisations like the PKK was carried out by means of special forces. We also had to apply this.[21]

---

[17] *TBMM Darbe ve Muhtıraları Araştırma Komisyonu Raporu*, 98.

[18] Massicard, 'Gangs in Uniform', 53; Jongerden, *The Settlement Issue in Turkey and the Kurds*, 67.

[19] Kışlalı, *Güneydoğu*, 222–3.

[20] Söyler, *The Turkish Deep State*, 101; Balta Paker, 'Dış Tehditten İç Tehdide', 414.

[21] Bilâ, *Komutanlar Cephesi*, 44. 'Bir önemli kararım da Özel Harp Dairesini lağvetmekti. Neden Lağvettim? Çünkü, Özel Harp Dairesi, İkinci Cihan Harbi'nden kalmıştı. İkinci Cihan Harbi'nden sonra işgal edilmesi muhtemel yerlerin arkasında sivil halkı örgütlemek için kurulmuştur . . . Ama ikinci Cihan Harbi çok geride kaldı. Tehditler değişti. 1990'lardaki duruma bakıldığında Özel Harp Dairesi'nin bir işlevi yok aslında. Ben bunu lağvettim ve dedim ki yerine "Özel Kuvvetler Komutanlığı" kurulacak. Çünkü PKK gibi örgütlerle mücadele özel kuvvetler aracılığıyla yürütülüyor. Bizim de buna geçmemiz lazım.'

In other words, the Special Warfare Department, which was a secret paramilitary formation, was transformed into an irregular but official unit of the army. This force was among the first special groups sent to the war in small units against the PKK.[22] It was reorganised as a division in 1992, technically improving its power and increasing its strength in numbers.

Meanwhile, it was also argued that this military and political transformation caused conflicts between the state institutions and the elites. Former Turkish intelligence officer Hüseyin Oğuz alleged that there were contradictions among different cliques in the state about the implementation of the new strategy.[23] Between 1991 and 1993, many high-ranking soldiers and politicians were either killed or died in a suspicious way, and several journalists claimed that this was related to the strategic transformation within the state.[24] For instance, in 1993, when the transformation took place, gendarmerie general commander Eşref Bitlis died in a highly suspicious way in a case that remains unsolved. Some journalists and former intelligence officer Oğuz discuss similar deaths in terms of the liquidation of the clique that had not accepted the strategic transformation within the state institutions.[25] Based on these observations, it seems quite likely that there were objections among state elites about the implementation of the new war strategy, and that some politicians, officers and bureaucrats were liquidated as a result.

Nine years after the PKK had declared its armed struggle and the state authorities had set up paramilitary groups and given their first response to the new conflict, the Turkish government and armed forces finally began to implement a new strategy. The lack of irregular warfare capacity of the state's security forces was one of the major reasons for the loss of control in conflict zones.[26] The situation eventually led the state to form a new

---

[22] *TBMM Meclis Araştırma Komisyonu Başkanlığı.*

[23] Emin Demirel and Ali Burak Ersemiz, *Ömrüm: Bir İstihbaratçı Askerin Anıları* (Istanbul: Lagin Yayınları, 2010), 170–2.

[24] Ercüment İşleyen, 'Eşref Bitlis Zinciri', *Milliyet Gazetesi*, 17 February 1994; Adnan Akfırat, *Eşref Bitlis Suikastı: Belgelerle* (Istanbul: Kaynak Yayınları, 1997); 'Özal'ın Ölümü İçin Araştırma Önergesi', *Cumhuriyet Gazetesi*, 22 May 2002.

[25] Akfırat, *Eşref Bitlis Suikastı*; Demirel and Ersemiz, *Ömrüm*, 170–2.

[26] Kalyvas distinguishes three main areas of conflict zones in civil wars: full control, no control and contestation zones (with three separate stages). Kalyvas, *The Logic of Violence in Civil*

strategy.[27] According to several sources, in 1993, the army, police and para-military organisations fighting against the PKK totalled more than 300,000 members.[28] Jongerden argues that in spite of this enormous armed force, the Turkish armed forces were still faced with serious problems in the fight against 15,000 to 20,000 guerrillas. The main reason for this was the structure of the conventional and unwieldy Turkish army positioned against the Soviet threat, despite the mobile guerrilla warfare.[29] According to Balta Paker, state authorities thus reorganised and strengthened the Second Army, which was deployed in Kurdish cities for 'internal threats', instead of the First Army, which remained aimed at external threats.[30] Jongerden analyses the main features of the strategy as follows:

> The Turkish armed forces thus formulated an integrated doctrine of area control, named the 'field domination doctrine', and aimed at the production of a new (contracted rural and urban) war space. The doctrine had been laid down in 1991, but not put into practice until after the reorganisation of the army, initiated in 1992, was completed in 1993. The PKK was recognized as the first priority threat, and a change was announced from 'search and destroy' sweeps to a 'clear and hold' penetration strategy.[31]

The name of this new strategy of the Turkish state and army varied, but academics and journalists conducting research on the subject generally prefer

War, 218–32. For the northern Kurdistan situation, we may think of it as divided into two basic conflict areas: the cities/towns and their peripheries, where the state enjoyed a great deal of control, and the rural area, which was mainly in the control of the PKK in until 1993. There were also timing differences between the state and PKK control areas: the military troops were generally in control during the daytime and the PKK at night. Therefore, the LIC doctrine was a strategy that the state initiated to break this balance. Kışlalı, *Güneydoğu*, 8; Murat Karayılan, *Bir Savaşın Anatomisi Kürdistan'da Askeri Çizgi* (Neuss: Mezopotamya Yayınları, 2011), 267.

[27] Bezci and Öztan, 'Anatomy of the Turkish Emergency State', 173.

[28] 'Weapons Transfers and Violations of the Laws of War in Turkey', Human Rights Watch, November 1995, https://www.hrw.org/legacy/reports/1995/Turkey.htm; Jongerden, *The Settlement Issue in Turkey and the Kurds*, 64.

[29] Jongerden, *The Settlement Issue in Turkey and the Kurds*, 66–7.

[30] Balta Paker, 'Dış Tehditten İç Tehdide', 410–13.

[31] Jongerden, *The Settlement Issue in Turkey and the Kurds*, 67.

to use the LIC designation.[32] The strategic transformation was probably named differently among the commanders of the Turkish army. Former Turkish Commander Kundakçı, who served in different regions of northern Kurdistan for many years, expressed the transformation in his memoir thus: 'The Turkish Armed Forces took a series of measures to improve the situation in the region with the government. This package of measures was called "the 1993 Strategy".'[33] Turkish Lieutenant General Altay Tokat characterised the strategy implemented against the PKK through two separate concepts, one being LIC and the other 'field domination'.[34] Metin Gürcan, a former soldier in the Turkish army, used the name 'Doctrine of Areal Control',[35] while Murat Karayılan, a PKK leader, called the strategy that the state used against them 'Total War'.[36] Authors, army and guerrilla commanders have conceptualised the strategic transformation that occurred at the beginning of the early 1990s in various ways.

The LIC doctrine may be argued for as the most appropriate conceptualisation since, unlike other concepts, it does not indicate a predominantly military strategy. It allows for a political dimension and use of the paramilitary forces. However, due to the use of intense violence, especially against civilians, this war strategy has been popularly described as a 'dirty war' of the state in public space, especially since the early 1990s. The reason for use of the term 'dirty war' was the many acts of secret, mostly state-sponsored brutality that constituted war crimes but went largely uninvestigated and generally unpunished, so outside the bounds of law and legal redress.

The LIC doctrine created a legal void in terms of the actions of the (para) military forces. Many states (including the Turkish) fighting with armed opposition movements prefer the concept of the 'fight against terrorism' to conflict and war concepts. This delegitimises the opposition and enables

---

[32] Bezci and Öztan, 'Anatomy of the Turkish Emergency State', 173; Balta Paker, 'Dış Tehditten İç Tehdide: Türkiye'de Doksanlarda Ulusal Güvenliğin Yeniden İnşaası', 414; Kışlalı, *Güneydoğu*, 8.

[33] Kundakçı, *Güneydoğu'da Unutulmayanlar*, 219.

[34] Bilâ, *Komutanlar Cephesi*, 177, 192.

[35] Metin Gürcan, 'Arming Civilians as a Counterterror Strategy: The Case of the Village Guard System in Turkey', *Dynamics of Asymmetric Conflict* 8, no. 1 (2 January 2015): 10.

[36] Karayılan, *Bir Savaşın Anatomisi Kürdistan'da Askeri Çizgi*, 2011, 218, 249.

the violence used by paramilitary organisations against the opposition movements and civilians to go unconsidered under the Geneva Convention.[37]
Protocols I and II, adopted in 1977, supplement the Geneva Conventions of
1949; Protocol II concerns non-international conflicts, thus including civil or
internal wars.[38] Turkey has made reservations for these two additional protocols.[39] The result is an undeclared war that is not constrained by international
war conventions.

What was the effect of the LIC doctrine on the reorganisation of the
paramilitary forces? The LIC doctrine is predominantly a form of irregular
warfare. As the paramilitary groups are also characteristically composed of
irregular forces, these groups were significantly developed and legitimised
with the LIC doctrine. The transformation in the armed forces also seriously
affected the structure of the paramilitaries, with their actions and members
increasing greatly. Further, the new doctrine of the war meant that the paramilitary groups became more powerful and gained characteristics of autonomy. Thus, the violent actions (unsolved killings, enforced disappearances,
burning of villages, etc.) of the armed forces and paramilitary formations
increased markedly between 1991 and 1996.[40]

---

[37] Hüsnü Öndül, 'İnsancıl Hukuka Giriş', in *Her Zaman Yaşamak*, ed. Cennet Ayhan (Ankara: SES Yayınları, 1998), 16–40, http://www.ihd.org.tr/insancil-hukuka-g/.

[38] 'Protocols I and II Additional to the Geneva Conventions', ICRC, 1 January 2009, icrc.org/en/resources/documents/misc/additional-protocols-1977.htm.

[39] Melike Batur Yamaner *et al.*, *12 Ağustos 1949 Tarihli Cenevre Sözleşmeleri Ve Ek Protokol-leri* (Istanbul: Galatasaray Üniversitesi Hukuk Fakültesi Yayınları, n.d.), III, 265–76; Selahat-tin Esmer, 'Uluslararası İnsancıl Hukukta Çatışma Kategorileri Ve Minimum Silahlı Şiddet Eşiği', İnsan Hakları Derneği, 2 July 2016, http://www.ihd.org.tr/uluslararasi-insancil-hukukta-catisma-kategorileri-ve-minimum-silahli-siddet-esigi/.

[40] İHD, 'Ocak 1990–Mart 2009 Döneminde Köy Korucuları Tarafından Gerçekleştirilen İnsan Hakları İhlallerine İlişkin Özel Rapor', 2009, 4–18, http://www.ihd.org.tr/images/pdf/ocak_1990_mart_2009_koy_koruculari_ozel_raporu.pdf; HRW, 'Weapons Transfers and Vio-lations of the Laws of War in Turkey'; Dilek Kurban *et al.*, *Coming to Terms with Forced Migra-tion: Post-Displacement Restitution of Citizenship Rights in Turkey* (Istanbul: Tesev-Turkish Economic and Social Studies Foundation, 2007), 169–311, http://tesev.org.tr/wp-content/uploads/2015/11/Coming_To_Terms_With_Forced_Migration_Post-Displacement_Restitution_Of_Citizenship_Rights_In_Turkey.pdf; Göral *et al.*, *The Unspoken Truth: Enforced Disappearances*, 24; *Göç-Der Zorunlu Göç Raporu* (Istanbul: Göç Der, 2001).

During the beginning of the implementation of the LIC doctrine, the boundaries between military units and paramilitary forces became porous. One of the most important points of the strategy was the transformation of two brigades of the army into groups with paramilitary characteristics. Thus, some troops of the army were paramilitarised. From 1984 to 1993, the gendarmerie was responsible for internal security and the main actor in the war, but with the new strategy, the army was transitioned from large unwieldy divisions to flexible brigades and replaced the gendarmerie[41] The most important units of the army for this new strategy were the Bolu and Kayseri special commando brigades.[42] The dedicated mobile troops, especially the commandos, were brought to the region to fully control the rural area and evacuated thousands of Kurdish villages and hamlets. As Jongerden has described, this strategy was aimed at the control of space, and the inhabitants of the territory were forced to leave (migrating to city centres and the western cities).[43] During these military operations, not only were villages evacuated, but also burned, along with crops and orchards, and many civilians were killed and injured.[44] Such a rural evacuation was not only implemented in the 1990s in Turkey; this strategy of forced population transfer ('ethnic cleansing') was also deployed in many other countries.[45] And in Turkey, paramilitary

---

[41] Jongerden, *The Settlement Issue in Turkey and the Kurds*, 68–9.

[42] Kundakçı, *Güneydoğu'da Unutulmayanlar*, 220–304; Kışlalı, *Güneydoğu*, 191.

[43] Jongerden, *The Settlement Issue in Turkey and the Kurds*, 67–91.

[44] Namık Kemal Dinç, ed., *Stories of Migration 'One Who's Seen Pain doesn't Inflict Pain upon Others'* (Istanbul: Göç Der Yayınları, 2008); Kurban *et al.*, *Coming to Terms with Forced Migration*, 77–105.

[45] Benjamin Valentino, Paul Huth and Dylan Balch-Lindsay, '"Draining the Sea": Mass Killing and Guerrilla Warfare', *International Organization* 58, no. 2 (2004): 385, 389. Valentino *et al.* suggest that the majority of mass killings in 147 wars between 1944 and 2000 occurred as a part of such strategies. They argue that the evacuation of the rural areas where supporters of guerrilla movements live is part of the counterinsurgency strategy through various country examples: 'Thus, as many political leaders and military commanders engaged in counterinsurgency warfare have openly acknowledged, if the civilian population is the 'sea' in which the guerrilla 'fish' swim, the surest way to catch the fish is by draining the sea.' This argument contextualises the mass violence against civilians by the military and paramilitary formations of Turkey.

organisations were also involved, along with the mobile army units (commando troops), in the strategy.[46]

Although there was a clear difference in the fortunes of war after the implementation of this strategy and the transformation of the army into mobile and smaller groups similar to paramilitary groups, this did not diminish the role of the paramilitary groups. In fact, some units of the army began to resemble the paramilitary formations in terms of their function. In other words, the differences between the actions of the paramilitary groups and the actions of some units of the regular army diminished.[47] Thus, the strategic transformation introduced in the early 1990s, did not eliminate the paramilitaries at all; on the contrary, some units of regular armies gained paramilitary characteristics, especially in the Kurdish provinces. Clearly, there could be an intertwined relationship between the troops of the army and paramilitary formations as a direct result of the favourable conditions for this substantially created by the new strategy. Human Rights Watch (HRW) prepared a report in 1995 about the weapons transfer and conflict in northern Kurdistan which focused on the human rights violation perpetrated by the Bolu and Kayseri Commando Brigades:

> Witnesses interviewed by Human Rights Watch said they were able to identify Bolu and Kayseri soldiers, and reported that they were involved in numerous violations of the laws of war, including village destructions, indiscriminate fire, and kidnapping civilians who were then forced into serving as porters during Army patrols.[48]

The LIC doctrine was a very important restructuring strategy in terms of both army and paramilitary formations. The existing paramilitary forces were enlarged and were more actively used by state authorities, and the strategy was not only adopted for military purposes but also aimed at psychological

---

[46] 'Kulp'u Asker İnceleyecek', *Milliyet Gazetesi*, 24 December 2004; *Yavuz Ertürk (Kulp) Davası*, accessed 4 April 2017, https://www.failibelli.org/pec-events/yavuz-erturk-kulp-davasi-7/. One such example took place in 1993 in Diyarbakır: the former commander of the Bolu commando brigade, Yavuz Ertürk, is still being tried for the forced disappearances of eleven civilians in the Kulp district of Diyarbakir in October 1993.

[47] Joost Jongerden, 'Village Evacuation and Reconstruction in Kurdistan (1993–2002)', *Études rurales*, no. 186 (29 March 2010): 9–15; Kundakçı, *Güneydoğu'da Unutulmayanlar*, 220.

[48] HRW, 'Weapons Transfers and Violations of the Laws of War in Turkey'.

and economic oppression. Therefore, one of the most important pillars of its implementation was politics. Governments also created the legal framework of the strategy with new 'anti-terror laws'.[49] The period of war 'hawks' began in the army and in politics in 1993.[50] Consequently, it becomes necessary to look at the developments and changes in politics in order to more fully appreciate this structural transformation in paramilitary formations.

The Role of Political Parties in the Reorganisation of Paramilitary Forces

This section argues that right-wing and nationalist political parties played important roles in the development and consolidation of the paramilitary formations and the implementation of the LIC doctrine in the first part of the 1990s. The military transformations and preparations for the new strategy between 1991 and 1993 also included political parties. In particular, two political parties, the True Path Party (*Doğru Yol Partisi*, DYP) and MHP, played key roles in the reorganisation of the paramilitary groups with the LIC doctrine, while the legal pillar of the strategic transformation, begun in 1991, was made by the Motherland Party (*Anavatan Partisi*, ANAP), which formed the government of that period.

The TBMM adopted the 'Law on the Fight against Terrorism' in April 1991.[51] The legal foundation of the new strategy was created with this law, which was based on a very broad definition of terrorism.[52] Legal freedoms, including that of the press and expression, were severely restricted by the new law and members of the security forces made very difficult to prosecute.[53] In the election of that year, in the autumn of 1991, ANAP lost power to the DYP,

---

[49] Bezci and Öztan, 'Anatomy of the Turkish Emergency State'.

[50] Beşe, 'Special Operations Unit', 120.

[51] 'Terörle Mücadele Kanunu', *T.C. Cumhurbaşkanlığı Resmi Gazete*, 12 April 1991, http://www.resmigazete.gov.tr/; 'Teröre Yeni Tanım', Cumhuriyet Gazetesi, April 13, 1991.

[52] Kurdish Human Rights Project: KHRP, *Turkey's Anti-Terror Laws: Threatening the Protection of Human Rights*, KHRP Briefing Paper 11 August (London: KHRP, 2008).

[53] *Türkiye İnsan Hakları Raporu 1991* (Ankara: TİHV-Türkiye İnsan Hakları Vakfı, 1992); Ali Yılmaz, *Karanlık Vardiya 90'lı Yılların Politik Arşivi* (Istanbul: Doğan Kitap, 2015), 122; Mark Muller, 'Nationalism and the Rule of Law in Turkey: The Elimination of Kurdish Representation during the 1990s', in *The Kurdish Nationalist Movement in the 1990s: Its Impact on Turkey and the Middle East*, ed. Robert W. Olson (Lexington: University Press of Kentucky, 1996), 179.

whose name now became mentioned as responsible for the intense violence carried out against civilians in northern Kurdistan and the building of the gangs within state institutions. Therefore, after ANAP, both the MHP – as detailed, a highly influential nationalist party in the state institutions, even if it was not part of the government – and the DYP were instrumental in legitimising the use of paramilitary forces and recruiting members of paramilitary groups.

The year 1993 was a milestone in Turkish politics. President Turgut Özal died on 17 April, and a major bureaucratic and political transformation began within state institutions. Tansu Çiller became the DYP party leader and then Prime Minister. Mehmet Ağar also became the General Director of Security, and these two actors took over the political responsibility for the realisation of the new political and military strategy.[54] Kutlu Savaş, author of the Susurluk Report, describes this fundamental change as the beginning of the period of the 'hawks', referring to a radical elite group of politicians, officers and bureaucrats, among others, who wanted a more intense use of violence to gain the upper hand in the conflict.[55] This strategy, co-chaired by the Chief of General Staff and Prime Minister,[56] transformed both the manner of the conflict and the lives of the civilians in northern Kurdistan. This period saw the numbers and training, effect and influence of the paramilitary organisations increase dramatically.

The first effect of the political parties in the reorganisation of paramilitary forces during the LIC doctrine was related to the role of the MHP in recruiting members of the Special Police Teams. One of the most important advocates of a fascist ideology in Turkey, the MHP was not a partner of the government in the early 1990s, but it had leveraged a militia force (the *Ülkücü* movement) since the late 1960s (as detailed above), which was organised against left-wing and Kurdish opposition movements.[57] In other words, the 1970s was a period of mass violence used by these extremist-right militias, and the MHP was the

[54] Massicard, 'Gangs in Uniform', 53–4.
[55] Savaş, *Susurluk Raporu*, 6; Beşe, 'Special Operations Unit', 120.
[56] Kışlalı, *Güneydoğu*, 220.
[57] Bora and Can, *Devlet, Ocak, Dergâh*, 64–74, 90; 'Faşist Hareket ve MC İktidarları', in *Sosyalizm Ansiklopedisi* (1988), 8:2216–31; Vasfi Can Yazıcı, 'Anti-Communism and the Making of Ülkücü Paramilitary Identity, 1974–1980' (Masters thesis, Boğaziçi University, 2012), 57–63; Haluk Kırcı, *Zaman Süzerken (Hatıralar)* (Istanbul: Burak Yayınevi, 1998).

mainstream organiser of post-1970s fascism in Turkey.[58] While this movement had probably been organised bottom-up in the 1970s,[59] the paramilitaries were organised top-down by the MHP and governments in the 1990s, an important distinction that former police chief Hanefi Avcı confirmed in his statement to the TBMM's Susurluk commission.[60] As a part of this development, the *Ülkücü* movement was transformed from the vigilante groups of the 1970s to a paramilitary formation of the 1990s.

It was as an informal employer of a paramilitary force that the MHP proposed a law in parliament to establish a special army to fight against the PKK in the autumn of 1993.[61] However, the government and General Director of Security reorganised its existing Special Police Teams instead of creating a new special army – a reorganisation that was carried out in cooperation with the MHP. A newspaper reported that those who wanted to be a police officer (thus, a member of the Special Police Teams) applied to the MHP.[62] It was also reported that the MHP listed the names of the applicants; although the MHP was not part of the government, it was probably sending its list to the government for recruitment.[63] It was also stated in news reports that the relations of the MHP, army and police were not new and that there had been similar relations before the 1980 coup. Thus, it was reported that *Ülkücü* members connected to the MHP were now employed through the MHP in the paramilitary force formed to deal with the situation in northern Kurdistan.[64] The special police units launched in 1982, institutionalised in 1985 and numbering up to 5000, were restructured as the Special Police Teams as part of the

---

[58] Bora and Can, *Devlet, Ocak, Dergâh*, 542.

[59] As Mann discusses, the development of fascism is a bottom-up process: 'What essentially distinguishes fascists from the many military and monarchical dictatorships of the world is this "bottom-up" and violent quality of its paramilitarism'. Michael Mann, *Fascists* (Cambridge: Cambridge University Press, 2004), 16.

[60] *TBMM Susurluk Komisyonu Raporu*, 170.

[61] Necdet Pekmezci and Nurşen Büyükyıldız, *Ülkücüler Öteki Devletin Şehitleri* (Istanbul: Kaynak Yayınları, 1999), 193; 'PKK'yı 1 Yılda Kazırız', Milliyet Gazetesi, August 8, 1993, 23.

[62] Kemal Yurteri, 'Polis Olmak İsteyen MHP'ye Başvuruyor', *Cumhuriyet Gazetesi*, 21 September 1994, 4.

[63] 'Özel Time "Bozkurt" Referansı', *Özgür Ülke*, September 1994.

[64] Pekmezci and Büyükyıldız, *Ülkücüler Öteki Devletin Şehitleri*, 194–7.

strategic transformation of 1993, with the political party (MHP) connection maintained throughout this process.[65]

The second effect of the political parties in the reorganisation of para-military forces during the LIC doctrine was that the MHP and DYP both legitimised paramilitary groups in terms of both public opinion, politics and military roles. This legitimisation was effected for two main purposes: to present the paramilitary formations as legitimate forces through the media and to include the leaders of paramilitary groups in the political sphere (especially Village Guard leaders) during the elections. DYP leader and Prime Minister Çiller was an important political figure in strengthening and legitimising two separate paramilitary groups (the units of the Special Operations Department [Special Police Teams] and the Village Guards) in the context of the implementation of the new strategy. Çiller visited the Special Operations training camp in the autumn of 1993 and publically stated that it had an important role in working against 'terrorism' and that its numbers would be increased.[66] As the severity of war increased, state authorities were further developing this special unit in the Kurdish provinces, eventually increasing its numbers to some 20,000 members.[67] The logic of this strategy was to create special, well-trained units and to reorganise the existing paramilitary organisations rather than use less-trained soldiers on compulsory military service. As stated in the previous chapter, the MGK had taken the decision to set up a secret organisation affiliated to the Special Warfare Department in the same year.[68]

The DYP and the MHP wanted to control and to legitimise the Village Guards like the other paramilitary force, the special operation units. The MHP was unable to establish a special army, but it actively took part in the reorganisation of the special operations units and wanted to increase its influence on the Village Guards. Some pro-state Kurdish tribes that were part of the Village Guards joined the ultranationalist party in 1994.[69] Almost all the

---

[65] Çelik, *Türk Kontr-Gerillası*, 87–93; Gökdemir, *Pike*, 94.

[66] 'Çiller'den Özel Time Övgü', *Milliyet Gazetesi*, 7 November 1993.

[67] Massicard, 'Gangs in Uniform', 53; Jongerden, *The Settlement Issue in Turkey and the Kurds*, 70.

[68] Gökdemir, *Pike*, 95; Berkan, 'Gladio'ya MGK Onayı'.

[69] Namık Durukan, 'MHP'li Aşiretler DYP'ye Transfer', *Milliyet Gazetesi*, 10 November 1994; Pekmezci and Büyükyıldız, *Ülkücüler Öteki Devletin Şehitleri*, 202.

chiefs of the Village Guards who stood as mayoral candidates had indicated their preference for the right-wing parties in 1994.[70] Journalist Celal Başlangıç provided important information about the development of the Village Guards while conveying observations from Siverek about local elections in 1994:

> There is a 'state within the state' here. The official number of the Village Guards is around 1100. We heard that the state gave weapons to only 600 people. The rest is the tribes' own weapons (through weapons smuggling)! But people are talking about five to ten thousand. When you ask 'What are these?', the official response is ready; 'They are the volunteer Village Guards'.[71]

The state authorities strengthened the Village Guards in northern Kurdistan through the new strategy, and the security forces and politicians ignored the uncontrolled arming of these tribes due to the fact that they were fighting against the PKK. During the conflicts, sub-paramilitary gangs associated with prominent political figures (e.g. Sedat Bucak and Salih Şarman) emerged as smaller scale gangs derived from the largest paramilitary formation, the Village Guards. The DYP deputy Sedat Bucak was one of the chiefs of the huge armed forces around Siverek.[72] In Batman, another Kurdish province, Governor Salih Şarman had created a similar force. The name of this unit, formed by 700–800 guards, was the Batman Combined Special Operations Unit (*Batman Karma Özel Harekat Birliği*). Unlike the Village Guards, it consisted of specially selected young men and was connected hierarchically to

---

[70] Celal Başlangıç, 'Korucular Aday Oldu', *Cumhuriyet Gazetesi*, 3 July 1994.

[71] Ibid., 5.

[72] Sedat Bucak was the chief of the Bucak tribe, in the district of Siverek, Urfa province. In 1996, Bucak was injured in the Susurluk accident that revealed the secret relationships among the police, mafia and politicians. When the accident happened, he was a deputy of the True Path Party and a member of the TBMM. According to several sources, there were thousands of Village Guards in Bucak's command, and these guards, who were very active in the 1990s, were involved in serious violations of human rights. Savaş, *Susurluk Raporu*, 33–6; Bozarslan, *Network-Building, Ethnicity and Violence in Turkey*, 12–15; Massicard, 'Gangs in Uniform', 44–5; Michael M. Gunter, 'Susurluk: The Connection between Turkey's Intelligence Community and Organized Crime', *International Journal of Intelligence and CounterIntelligence* 11, no. 2 (1 June 1998): 121, https://doi.org/10.1080/08850609808435368.

the provincial gendarmerie command.[73] According to Şarman, the formation of this local sub-paramilitary force was allowed by Çiller. Similar units were established in many other provinces and districts of northern Kurdistan after the end of 1993; or, the existing Village Guard units were restructured within the framework of the new strategy.

The relationship between the MHP and the Special Operations Units was criticised by another right-wing Islamist party, the Welfare Party (*Refah Partisi*, RP), which made the following statement on the Kurdish issue in a report prepared in 1994: 'Many commandos in the Special Teams affiliated to the Ministry of Interior are making political shows with a very racist attitude to the region.'[74] According to the report, these commandos were related to the MHP. The greatest impact of this new strategy, in which the paramilitary formations were reorganised with the MHP and DYP substantially legitimising the paramilitary formations as useful armed forces, was that the intensity of paramilitary violence against civilians in northern Kurdistan increased greatly.

All in all, in the process of reorganisation of the paramilitary formations that started with the LIC doctrine, it can be said that the government and major political parties supported this transformation of the security forces. The effects of the MHP and DYP in the strengthening of paramilitary formations were important in respect of their direct and indirect roles in the recruitment of paramilitary group members and of their legitimisation of the paramilitary forces through distribution of political largesse, by making the leaders of paramilitary forces deputies, mayors and party executives in the Kurdish provinces. It can also be added that the political parties (including the ANAP) prepared the legal framework of the new strategy. All these political, legal and military changes transformed the autonomy, features, member-numbers and structure of the paramilitary groups as a whole.

Changes in the Nature of Paramilitary Forces

There were several changes in the nature of war in the early 1990s, and these affected the transformation of paramilitary forces. Most obviously, as indicated,

---

[73] Salih Şarman, *Rutin Dışı: Jitem-Kayıp Silahlar ve Harcanan Hayatlar* (Istanbul: Pozitif yayınları, 2007), 41–70.

[74] Faik Bulut, *Kürt Sorununa Çözüm Arayışları: Devlet ve Parti Raporları, Yerli Ve Yabancı Öneriler (1920–1997)* (Istanbul: Ozan Yayıncılık, 1998), 149.

the Turkish state authorities established various paramilitary groups against the PKK. Until 1990, the Turkish government had thought it would defeat the PKK with the support of paramilitary groups alongside the gendarmerie. The role of paramilitary groups in the conflicts before 1991 was mostly as auxiliaries to the gendarmerie forces. However, from 1991 onwards, as Turkish elites changed their war strategy, they became one of the main instruments of the war, especially against civilians allegedly to be supporting the PKK. However, the PKK grew rapidly in terms of both its number of guerrillas and mass support from the Kurdish civilians; as the 'Turkish army forces were rapidly losing control of an undeclared war', the state responded with a new concept of war.[75] Thus, we can view the Turkish Republic and the PKK as locked in a vicious circle of escalation, violence, and counter-violence.

According to Ersever, the army had faced a serious lack of capacity against the guerrilla war carried out by the PKK at the beginning of the 1990s, a strategic and tactical insufficiency of the Republic that had to be changed.[76] Hence, the army and paramilitary formations were transformed through the new war strategy during 1991–3.[77] This transformation radically changed the nature of war, violence and the paramilitary forces. The new war concept in the military field led to the reorganisation of the paramilitary forces, which affected the nature of previously established paramilitary groups in various ways. These can be analysed as follows: (1) the existing paramilitary force numbers increased substantially, (2) these forces became even more autonomous, and (3) they became predominantly death squads in terms of their function.

In the first half of the 1990s, the number of paramilitary groups increased dramatically with the new war concept. Of the four major paramilitary forces in the 1990s, two of them (the Village Guards and the Special Action Police Units) were semi-formal paramilitary forces whose existence the government had legislated for and whose numbers were more or less known. The numbers of the other two informal forces, JİTEM and Hizbullah, on the other

---

[75] Güneş, *The Kurdish National Movement in Turkey*, 102–11; Karayılan, *Bir Savaşın Anatomisi Kürdistan'da Askeri Çizgi*, 2011, 190–5; Jongerden, *The Settlement Issue in Turkey and the Kurds*, 43.

[76] Yalçın, *Binbaşı Ersever'in İtirafları*, 47.

[77] Jongerden, *The Settlement Issue in Turkey and the Kurds*, 67.

hand, were not known. The most significant increase in the number of para-military groups was to the Village Guards. The Village Guard system can be divided by membership into two categories, the temporary and the voluntary Village Guards:

> Temporary village guards acquire licensed guns, a monthly salary in which they are obliged to join the guard duties and operations in return. On the other hand, voluntary village guards do not receive any payment.[78]

The number of temporary Village Guards who received salaries was consider-ably increased in the first half of the 1990s. In twenty-one provinces with signif-icant numbers of Kurds (so, including but beyond northern Kurdistan), there were 14,818 guards in 1988, a number that by 1995 had increased four-fold, to 62,186.[79] The Special Police Teams, like other units, was transformed numeri-cally and institutionally in the early 1990s. However, this institutional trans-formation was carried out secretly and numbers never publicly announced.[80] According to the Susurluk Report, the total number of personnel trained in this unit was 8,443.[81] According to scholars, the real number was over 20,000.[82] The increase in the number of semi-formal paramilitary forces gives some indi-cation regarding the other two (informal) paramilitary formations.

There is not much information about the number of members of JİTEM and Hizbullah. However, co-founder of JİTEM Arif Doğan argues that together with the informants, it had some 10,000 people in total.[83] If this claim is true, a very large part of this number consisted of informants because the number of JİTEM members active in death squads probably did not exceed a few hundred, even in the early 1990s. There is no clear information on the number of members of Hizbullah, which started an intense period of acts of violence in 1991. Although the number of Hizbullah members is not known,

---

[78] Özar *et al.*, *From Past to Present*, 10.

[79] Ibid., 56.

[80] Beşe, 'Special Operations Unit', 118–19.

[81] Savaş, *Susurluk Raporu*, 6; Beşe, 'Special Operations Unit', 121.

[82] Bozarslan, 'Why the Armed Struggle: Understanding the Violence in Kurdistan of Turkey', 21; Jongerden, *The Settlement Issue in Turkey and the Kurds*, 70.

[83] Doğan, *JİTEM'i Ben Kurdum*, 25.

between 1992 and 1999 more than 4,000 of its members were detained because of actions against Kurdish civilians and members of other Kurdish Islamist groups.[84] Acknowledging the cover they would have enjoyed from state forces and authorities, we can only speculate as to how much to raise the 4,000 figure for a true idea of total Hizbullah members. As mentioned above, the Special Warfare Department was also transformed as part of the new war doctrine. This power was transformed from brigade to division and also from a paramilitary group to a formal unit of the army in 1992. The number of members of this unit was greatly increased, and the name was changed into Special Forces Command (*Özel Kuvvetler Komutanlığı*).[85] Based on the above (quantitative) assessment, it can be inferred that the growth of the membership of the paramilitary formations was fundamental to a transformation of their functioning.

Another important point in the change of nature of paramilitary groups with the introduction of the new war concept was that they became more autonomous. This autonomy was likely two-sided: (1) the paramilitary forces achieved more autonomy when they became stronger (as testified by the numbers along with formal recognition in the political space), and (2) they became relatively independent of the local military units of the state. This autonomy did not mean they were outside of the military hierarchy, however; on the contrary, because they were stronger, their relations with high-ranking soldiers, bureaucrats and powerful politicians intensified.[86] One of my interviewees clearly explained this autonomy of paramilitary groups with an impressive example:

> For example, a typical Siverek family event, the two families from our tribe are fighting because of a blood feud, and conflict will arise because people were armed. My dad is calling the gendarmerie and he says, 'You have to intervene; people will kill each other'. 'You hang up the phone and I will call Mr. Sedat' says the commander, 'I need to call Mr. Sedat'.[87]

---

[84] Çakır, *Derin Hizbullah*, 88; Kurt, *Din, Şiddet ve Aidiyet*, 61–71.

[85] Hale Akay, 'Türk Silahlı Kuvvetleri: Kurumsal ve Askeri Boyut', in *Güvenlik Sektörü ve Demokratik Gözetim: Almanak Türkiye 2006–2008*, ed. Ahmet İnsel and Ali Bayramoğlu (Istanbul: TESEV Yayınları, 2009), 121–2; Kılıç, *Özel Harp Dairesi*, 289–92; Söyler, *The Turkish Deep State*, 101.

[86] Balık, *Kerberos*, 168–71.

[87] Interview #22, conducted in Istanbul, 18 May 2017.

The person mentioned in the interview is Sadat Bucak, leader of paramilitary Village Guards in the Kurdish-dominated province of Siverek, and at the same time a deputy in parliament.[88] He and his tribe became an autonomous paramilitary power in the local area. This example is important because the state authorities would ignore certain actions by pro-state tribes in the local area. As they were fighting against the PKK, the state allowed them a type of fiefdom in which to conduct illegal actions and gain economic profit.

The TBMM's Susurluk Report also refers to the autonomy of the paramilitary forces. According to the report, the repentant and local elements that were employed in JİTEM became a source of many problems over time. Not only local elements, but also those working in the intelligence services have been omitted from the military hierarchy, for instance. JİTEM Commander Erseyer was able to act independently in high-ranking environments.[89] Hizbullah's situation was different, of course, since it was never a state structure and thus a formal part of the military hierarchy; there was probably a subcontractor relationship in this case, mostly with the state and due to the common enemy.[90]

As the role of paramilitary forces in the war grew in importance, it can be said, the paramilitary groups were increasingly able to ignore the local military and political hierarchy, to control gun and drug smuggling and become economically strong.[91] Their increases in numbers and connections to official doctrine, institutions and individuals further insulated them from any real accountability and enabled them to become fairly autonomous units. Hamit Bozarslan analyses the autonomous armed forces, which emerged as the main actors of the war with the LIC doctrine, their 'military solution' and the relationship with economic benefit as follows:

> In fact, one has to admit that the gangs were a price that Turkey had to pay for its inability to deal with the Kurdish question as a political issue. If the war, and particularly the 'Low Intensity Conflict' doctrine, have weakened the PKK,

[88] Massicard, 'Gangs in Uniform', 43–4.
[89] Savaş, *Susurluk Raporu*, 14–16.
[90] Adnan Çelik, 'Kürdistan Yerellerinde 90'ların Savaş Konfigürasyonu: Baskı, Şiddet ve Direniş', in *İsyan, Şiddet, Yas 90'lar Türkiye'sine Bakmak*, ed. Ayşen Uysal (Ankara: Dipnot Yayınları, 2016), 100–8.
[91] Özar *et al.*, *From Past to Present*, 60; Kılıç, *JİTEM*, 188.

they have also created the conditions for the emergence or reinforcement of the paramilitary gangs. The political options in the Kurdish issue have been eliminated, because, among other reasons, for many involved actors, the so-called 'military solution' meant financial benefits and a total independence from the central power.[92]

Radical military, bureaucratic and political elites who defended the military solution in the Kurdish question had probably calculated the results when they planned to use paramilitary groups. In other words, in Bozaslan's analysis, the political and military consequences (weakening of the PKK and strengthening of paramilitary groups), which seemed to be a dilemma for the state elite, were actually the main idea of the strategy carried out since 1991. This was quite likely neither an unpredicted nor undesired consequence.

With the new concept of war, the functions of paramilitary forces changed and unrestricted violence that they used, especially against civilians, reached enormous dimensions.[93] Also, many units of the paramilitary forces began to transform into death squads. The paramilitary groups that the state created against the PKK in the 1980s had been mainly used by security forces to better understand the conflict areas and to gather intelligence. After 1991, however, the number of unsolved political murders increased steadily until, in 1995, the TMBB formed a commission to investigate them.[94] The report shows the unsolved political murders as mostly of pro-PKK Kurdish civilians and their numbers as rising in a very obvious way: 1990: 6, 1991: 24, 1992: 316, 1993: 314.[95] The annual balance sheets prepared by the İHD similarly showed the numbers of unsolved murders and enforced disappearances as escalating in the early 1990s.[96]

An interview I made with a Kurdish journalist working during the 1990s showed both how one of their journalist friends was forcibly disappeared and how paramilitary groups and official state institutions worked in cooperation, with a division of labour:

---

[92] Bozarslan, *Network-Building, Ethnicity and Violence in Turkey*, 17–18.

[93] *Zorla Kaybedilenler, Faili Meçhul Cinayet-Yargısız İnfazlar, Toplu Mezarlar Raporu* (Diyarbakır: İnsan Hakları Derneği, 2014), 79–124, 130–227.

[94] TBMM, *Ülkemizin Çeşitli Yörelerinde*.

[95] Ibid., 161–5.

[96] 'Bilançolar', İHD, http://www.ihd.org.tr/sample-page-2/.

This friend (Nazım Babaoğlu) was told by the distributor in charge there to come urgently by concocting an excuse, and he reluctantly went to the Siverek on 12 March 1994. We found the witnesses. The paramilitary forces had taken him into custody and at the police station. The people who had taken him were undercover Village Guards, and all of them died later.

The Nazım Baba case put a lot of pressure on the state. Some people say that Babaoğlu was brought to the Sedat Bucak for a second time, and there are others who say that Bucak said to him, 'Didn't I say you not to come back?' and then killed him. Some say he was killed on March 21st, Newroz Day. On the other hand, some say that he was killed by a group from the police officers. We couldn't figure out how it happened, but some people saw who kidnapped him. The prosecution didn't even call them as witnesses. So, someone, paramilitary forces, disappeared him.

The prosecutor didn't hear from the witnesses. The governor says, 'I can't do anything to the police,' and, the police department says should I use violence to make the witness talk? . . . The thing is, everybody knows everything. You can come to that conclusion because paramilitary forces conduct their operations under the auspices and control of the police department. Look, this is important. No paramilitary force can take a step, go into the public, and go out without doing this.

Let me make it very simple – to catch someone, the cop at the police station blocks the street, checks identities and a panzer [armoured vehicle] is deployed, so the whole place is completely surrounded. The paramilitary knocks on the door, shows himself, takes him away and this person will never be heard from again. That's it. No counterinsurgency operations are possible without official state forces creating such a security zone. I mean, they [paramilitary forces] become involved in the operations after cutting roads, laying siege to the villages and blockading the neighborhood. The police knows that a group comes and disappears someone but doesn't know who they are.[97]

According to a HRW report, the Turkish government began implementing a new counterinsurgency strategy against the PKK in 1992 in which the paramilitaries (particularly the Village Guards) played a major role.[98] Reports prepared at different times by the TBMM also referred to JİTEM and

---

[97] Interview #8, conducted in Diyarbakır, 25 July 2016.
[98] HRW, 'Weapons Transfers and Violations of the Laws of War in Turkey'.

'counter-guerrilla' (the Special Warfare Department) as responsible for the unsolved murders in the 1990s.[99] The Human Rights Investigation Commission of the Assembly prepared a report in 2013 which found that in the thirty-year conflict, 5557 civilians had been killed (additionally, that is, to the deaths of security force members and PKK militants).[100] Most of the civilians were Kurds, many of them killed in unsolved murders or just 'disappearances'. NGO works on this issue show that the paramilitary groups were largely responsible for the increasing number of civilian murders from the early 1990s.[101] This characteristic increase in the norm of political violence (murders, disappearances, etc.) was not new in terms of the paramilitary politics of the Turkish state, but it was a new phase of the conflict that started in 1984.

The fundamental changes in the nature of the paramilitaries appeared in relation to the introduction of the new war concept in the early 1990s through three striking conversions, namely, the increase of members of the paramilitaries, the autonomy of these formations and their transformation into death squads. This transformation was a preference of the state authority that launched the new war concept. In other words, the state *shared* the monopoly of violence with the paramilitary forces in the new war strategy. Therefore, the paramilitary formations established as an auxiliary force for intelligence purposes were to become one of the main components of the conflict.

Reorganisation of Paramilitary Forces and the Changing Nature of Violence

From the early 1990s, state authorities substantially transformed the existing paramilitary formations from intelligence gathering units to death squads.

---

[99] TBMM, *Ülkemizin Çeşitli Yörelerinde*; *TBMM Susurluk Komisyonu Raporu*; *TBMM Darbe ve Muhtıraları Araştırma Komisyonu Raporu*.

[100] TBMM İnsan Haklarını İnceleme Komisyonu, *Terör ve Şiddet Olayları Kapsamında Yaşam Hakkı İhlallerini İnceleme Raporu*, 78.

[101] Gülçin Avşar, *The Other Side of the Ergenekon: Extrajudicial Killings and Forced Disappearances* (Istanbul: TESEV Yayınları, 2013), http://tesev.org.tr/wp-content/uploads/2015/11/The_Other_Side_Of_The_Ergenekon_Extrajudicial_Killings_And_Forced_Disappearances.pdf; Göral *et al.*, *The Unspoken Truth: Enforced Disappearances*; İHD, 'Ocak 1990–Mart 2009 Döneminde Köy Korucuları Tarafından Gerçekleştirilen İnsan Hakları İhlallerine İlişkin Özel Rapor'.

Thus, the limits of violence expanded significantly compared to the previous period; an environment of intense violence emerged in the conflict zones. In this section, I look at the paramilitary formations as an important part of the intense violence of various types, including the unsolved political murders, enforced disappearances and evacuation of villages, in which it was civilians who were made the main target of the new strategy.

The conflict with the PKK had caused the perception of 'internal threat' (separation of the Kurdish region) to reach the highest levels of the state authorities. The state violently suppressed and tried to eliminate opposition movements. Thus, violence had become almost the single policy mediating between the state and its dissidents, especially against the Kurdish opposition.[102] The use of violence as a first resort by the authorities was a traditional path; for almost a century, violence had always been the most obvious instrument of the Turkish state in relation to the Kurds. According to the nationalist/Kemalist ideology as published in the (supposed) National Security Policy Document (*Milli Güvenlik Siyaset Belgesi*) known as 'The Red Book', the Turkish nation state was in danger and this internal danger had to be removed. In this document, prepared in November 1992, 'separatism' was identified as the main threat.[103] Therefore, the military transformation of the new strategy, which began in 1991, would be completed militarily and politically in early 1993. One of the most prominent features of this new concept was the increase in violence that had been used by previously established paramilitary formations. In fact, the main characteristic of the 1990s was the flourishing of different varieties of paramilitary violence.

We may think that one of the most important goals of this new strategy was the liquidation of the pro-PKK civilians by the use of intense violence. These forms of violence were mostly carried out by paramilitary groups and aimed to scare Kurdish civilians into keeping away from the PKK. Due particularly

---

[102] Bozarslan, 'Why the Armed Struggle: Understanding the Violence in Kurdistan of Turkey'; Bahar Şahin Fırat, 'Türkiye'de "Doksanlar": Devlet Şiddetinin Özgünlüğü ve Sürekliliği Üzerine Bir Deneme', in *Türkiye'de Siyasal Şiddetin Boyutları*, by Güney Çeğin and İbrahim Şirin (Istanbul: İletişim Yayınları, 2014).

[103] Zeynep Şarlak, 'Atatürkçülükten Millî Güvenlik Rejimine: 1990'lar Türkiye'sine Bir Bakış', in *Bir Zümre, Bir Parti: Türkiye'de Ordu*, eds Ahmet İnsel and Ali Bayramoğlu (Istanbul: Birikim Yayınları, 2004), 290.

to the absence of bodies, the disappearances were probably the most common type of crime in terms of both physical and symbolic violence, and they occupied an important place in the memory of the relatives of the disappeared and Kurdish people in the 1990s (and after). According to the tentative list of a study made by the Truth Justice Memory Centre (*Hakikat Adalet Hafıza Merkezi*), the number of enforced disappearances was 1353, and they overwhelmingly (95%) occurred between 1991 and 1999.[104] Because the conflict is still ongoing and there is no government-created research commission to investigate, these figures are not certain. Most of the disappearances as reported did occur in northern Kurdistan, with others in the western provinces, like Istanbul, where Kurds were also populous.[105]

Table 3.1 The numbers of disappeared (by year). [Data from: Özgür Sevgi Göral et al., *The Unspoken Truth: Enforced Disappearances* (Istanbul: Truth Justice Memory Center, 2013), 24.]

1980–90	1991	1992	1993	1994	1995	1996	1997	1998	1999	after 2000	date unknown
33	18	22	103	518	232	170	94	50	76	33	4

There are probably many reasons for the enforced disappearances and this issue is discussed in more detail below (Chapter 5).[106] Two intentions are quite clear, however; to scare the families and to show the consequences of being pro-PKK, in the most severe form. Shortly before being disappeared, the victims were usually taken into custody, both from their homes or from public spaces.[107] Sometimes they were taken into custody by the formal security forces, sometimes directly by paramilitary groups.[108] The main suspect in these events were paramilitary formations (the JİTEM, the Special Operation Teams, the Village Guards):

[104] Göral et al., *The Unspoken Truth: Enforced Disappearances*, 24.

[105] Ibid., 25.

[106] Gökçen Alpkaya, '"Kayıp"lar Sorunu Ve Türkiye', *Ankara Üniversitesi SBF Dergisi* 50, no. 3 (1995): 36.

[107] Ibid., 47.

[108] *Zorla Kaybedilenler, Faili Meçhul Cinayet-Yargısız İnfazlar*, 79–124; Ayhan Işık, '1990'larda Devletin "Sivil Siyaseti" Olarak Zorla Kaybetmeler', *Toplum ve Kuram*, no. 9 (2014): 49.

When they talk about the time of the disappearance, the relatives of the disappeared always emphasise the extraordinary powers of the team they call 'JİTEM', or 'The Team', and the powerlessness of the other institutions of the state, or of other social sections that wanted to intervene.[109]

Enforced disappearances were the most violent phenomenon and harshest punishment that the state implemented with the new strategy, by both official security forces and paramilitary forces.

A commission was set up in the TBMM to investigate unsolved political murders in 1995, due to the extraordinary increase in the numbers of political killings in the first half of the 1990s. This commission found that Village Guards, repentants and JİTEM members were involved in many illegal actions and thus that the Ministry of Justice should carry out investigations into them.[110] According to this report, 908 unsolved political murders had been committed.[111] According to Human Rights Foundation of Turkey (*Türkiye İnsan Hakları Vakfı*, TİHV) reports, the number of unsolved political murders in 1991 was 152 but increased to 467 in 1993.[112] According to İHD reports, a total of 1964 political killings were recorded as committed between 1989 and 1999, with 80 per cent of them having occurred in the Kurdish provinces.[113]

In another report made by the same institution, 3,566 unsolved political killings were found to have been committed between 1980 and 2011. According to this report, the state had had great difficulties in fighting the PKK, for which it formed and used various special units (including the Bolu and Kayseri Commando Brigades, along with JİTEM, the Special Operations Teams and Special Forces Command) and launched these against civilians under the name

[109] Göral *et al.*, *The Unspoken Truth: Enforced Disappearances*, 44.
[110] TBMM, *Ülkemizin Çeşitli Yörelerinde*, 159.
[111] Ibid., 16.
[112] *Örneklerle Türkiye İnsan Hakları Raporu 1991* (Ankara: TİHV-Türkiye İnsan Hakları Vakfı, 1992), 52; *Türkiye İnsan Hakları Raporu 1993* (Ankara: THİV-Türkiye İnsan Hakları Vakfı, 1994), 149–58.
[113] Hüsnü Öndül, 'Faili Meçhul Siyasal Cinayetler', İnsan Hakları Derneği, 24 January 2000, http://www.ihd.org.tr/faili-mel-siyasal-cinayetler/,

of the 'struggle against terrorism'.[114] Most of the murdered civilians were politicians, journalists, NGO members and students.[115]

Table 3.2 Unsolved political murders and extrajudicial executions (by decade). [Data from: *Zorla Kaybedilenler, Faili Meçhul Cinayet-Yargısız İnfazlar, Toplu Mezarlar Raporu* (Diyarbakır: İnsan Hakları Derneği, 2014).]

1980–90	1991–2000	2001–11	Total
103	3285	228	3566

The murder of Vedat Aydın is usually considered as a starting date for the unsolved political killings in the 1990s.[116] Aydın was the head of the Diyarbakır branch of the pro-Kurdish People's Labour Party (*Halkın Emek Partisi*, HEP). According to Abdulkadir Aygan, a repentant member of the JİTEM, he was taken and killed by JİTEM, on 5 July 1991.[117] A few days after his detention, Aydın's dead body was found, tortured, in a rural area of Elazığ province.[118] Finding the dead body of a person after being taken into custody is one of the most frequently used methods of the security forces, particularly of the paramilitary forces.[119] State violence against dead bodies has a long history. In his doctoral study, Hişyar Özsoy analyses the state's policy towards the dead bodies of Kurdish leaders, civilians and militants since the foundation of the Republic.[120]

In January 2000, the security forces carried out an operation against Hizbullah and killed its leader, Hüseyin Velioğlu. Later, the main case against Hizbullah was opened in Diyarbakır; several Hizbullah members

---

[114] *Zorla Kaybedilenler, Faili Meçhul Cinayet-Yargısız İnfazlar*, 130–227.

[115] Yılmaz, *Karanlık Vardiya 90'lı Yılların Politik Arşivi*, 306–26.

[116] 'The First Bullet: Murder of Vedat Aydın', *ANF English*, July 2017, https://anfenglish.com/news/the-first-bullet-murder-of-vedat-aydin-20886.

[117] Balık, *Kerberos*, 52–3.

[118] 'HEP İl Başkanı'nın Kuşkulu Ölümü', *Cumhuriyet Gazetesi*, 9 July 1991, 5.

[119] Yılmaz, *Karanlık Vardiya 90'lı Yılların Politik Arşivi*, 306–7.

[120] Hişyar Özsoy, 'Between Gift and Taboo: Death and the Negotiation of National Identity and Sovereignty in the Kurdish Conflict in Turkey' (PhD diss., The University of Texas at Austin, 2010).

were punished for a total of 181 murders. These actions had mainly started in 1991 and continued until 2000.[121] Therefore, these deaths continued for about ten years, importantly due to state institutions providing Hizbullah freedom of action. Figures in the İHD and Hizbullah case documents show that violence directed against civilians in the 1990s was much higher than that of the pre-1990 and post-2000 years. Ümit Özdağ, an academic and former member of the MHP, also prepared a report on unsolved murders, covering the twenty years from 1984 to 2004. According to this report, a total of 840 unsolved murders were committed, which is much lower than the number given by NGOs. In his report, Özdağ tries to make invisible the role of the state and paramilitary groups in the unsolved murders. However, even if the information in the report is taken as a basis, the unsolved murders are still seen to increase dramatically after 1991.[122] These differences were related to the LIC doctrine, which created an unrestricted field of action for paramilitary groups.

Another issue that illustrates the intense violence perpetrated by state security forces and paramilitary groups in the 1990s is that of the mass graves. According to a report prepared by the Diyarbakir branch of the İHD in 2014, there are many mass graves, mostly in the Kurdish provinces.[123] Some of these graves have been opened, but the vast majority are still waiting to be opened. The İHD report argues that people from three different groups were buried in these mass graves. The first ones had the bodies of guerrillas who died during the conflicts with the state's security forces; the second group contained those killed by Hizbullah, both in northern Kurdistan and in Turkey's western provinces; and the third group of mass graves were filled with the bodies of civilians, disappeared by security forces and paramilitary groups.

[121] 'Esas Hakkında Mütalaa-Hizbullah Terör Örgütü', Diyarbakır 6. Ağır Ceza Mahkemesi Esas No: /171 C. Sav. Es. No: 2000/559 2000; 'Gerekçeli Karar-Hizbullah Davası', Diyarbakır 6. Ağır Ceza Mahkemesi Esas No: /171, Karar No: 2009/727 2000.
[122] Ümit Özdağ, 'Faili Meçhuller', Yüzyıl Türkiye Enstitüsü, 2013, https://stratejisite.files.wordpress.com/2015/10/faili-mehuller-tarihe-gre-sral-liste.pdf.
[123] Türkiye'de Toplu Mezarlar Raporu (Diyarbakır: İnsan Hakları Derneği Diyarbakır Şubesi, 2014).

Table 3.3 Mass graves (numbers of sites, graves and people buried). [Data from: *Türkiye'de Toplu Mezarlar Raporu* (Diyarbakır: İnsan Hakları Derneği Diyarbakır Şubesi, 2014).]

	Graves	People
Mass graves: claimed	303	3920
Mass graves: opened	45	281
Total	348	4201

The investigations into the opened mass graves show that most of the killings were committed in the 1990s. However, the report also has certain points that need to be emphasised. One is related to outside the Kurdistan conflict areas, namely, the mass graves in Turkey's western cities, such as in Konya, Ankara and Istanbul, containing the bodies of people killed by Hizbullah. Another belongs to the pre-conflict period: some mass graves in Dersim/Tunceli and Erzincan remain from the time of the genocide committed in 1938 against the Kurdish-Alevis there. If all of the mass graves could be opened, identification of the bodies and identities of many of the disappeared (by the formal and informal armed forces) might be possible, as well as a more accurate totalling of the numbers involved. In terms of evidence, these mass graves clearly reveal that the perpetrators used certain locations as killing sites. Map 3.1 shows the geographic distribution of mass graves. These places are also the places where conflicts, enforced disappearances and village evacuations were most intense.

The forced evacuation and burning of villages in the Kurdish provinces was another, different step in the implementation of intense violence against civilians following the LIC strategy. The evacuation of villages was directly related to the state's paramilitary policy, particularly the Village Guards. State authorities gave civilians in the countryside of northern Kurdistan 'two options' – either to stay and become Village Guards or to leave.[124] These options comprised the choice between loyalty and hostility to the state. According to the TİHV report in 1997, 3,500 villages and hamlets had been evacuated and

---

[124] Özar *et al.*, *From Past to Present*, 43.

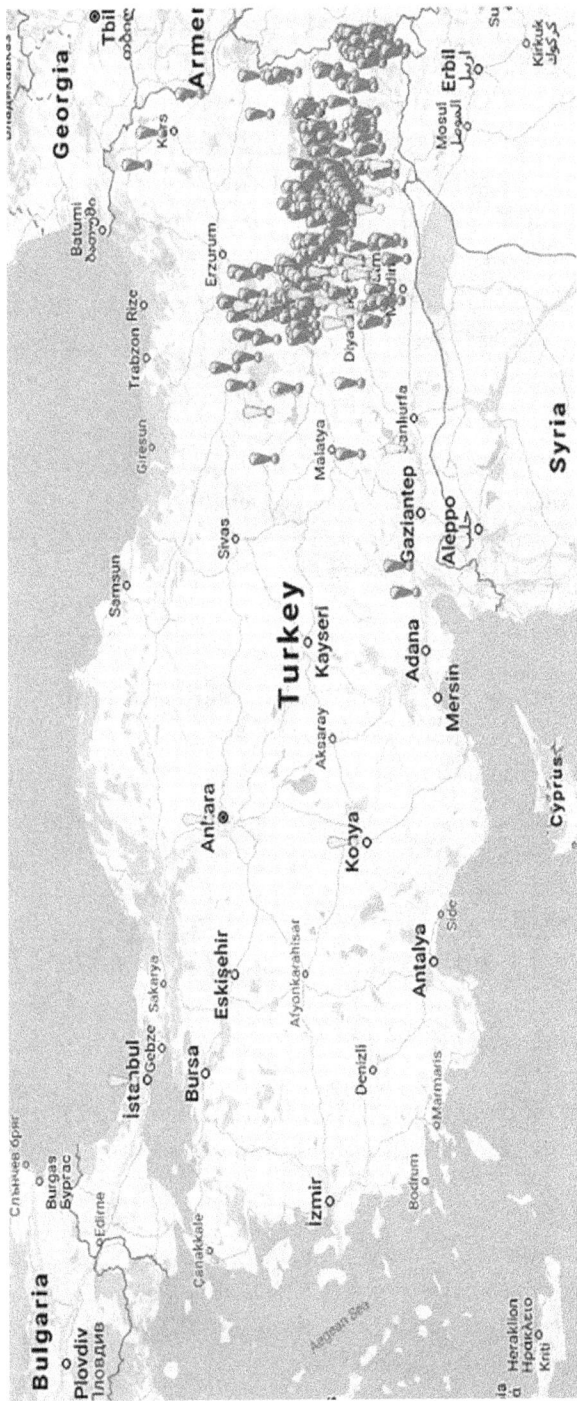

Map 3.1 İHD mass grave map, Diyarbakır branch (dark: mass grave claimed; light: mass grave opened).

[Source: *İnsan Hakları Derneği Diyarbakır Şubesi Toplu Mezar Haritası* (Diyarbakır: İHD Diyarbakır Şubesi, n.d.), http://map.ihddiyarbakir.org/Map.aspx.]

approximately 3 million people had been forced to emigrate.[125] Other research on the subject gives different figures for the number of evacuated villagers and displaced people (from 300,000 to 3 million).[126] According to research of the Migrants' Association for Social Solidarity and Culture (*Göç Edenler Sosyal Yardımlaşma ve Kültür Derneği*), the movement of people in Kurdish provinces during 1970–2000 was as follows: 18.3 per cent of the migrations had been made from the province and district centres, and 81.7 per cent of them were from the village-hamlet settlements.[127] Moreover, from the beginning of the 1990s, when the LIC doctrine began to be implemented, these figures changed dramatically.

Table 3.4 Migrations from Kurdish cities and villages (by decade). [Data from: *Göç-Der Zorunlu Göç Raporu* (Istanbul: Göç Der, 2001), 9–12.]

1970–80	1981–90	1991–2000
2.5%	21.8%	75.7%

Table 3.5 Evacuated and destroyed villages in Northern Kurdistan (1991–2001). [Data from: Joost Jongerden, 'Village Evacuation and Reconstruction in Kurdistan (1993–2002)', *Études rurales*, no. 186 (29 March 2010): 3–4; Kerim Yıldız, *Ülke İçinde Göç Ettirilen İnsanlar: Türkiye'de Kürtler*, trans. Emin Soğancı (London: KHRP, Haziran 2002), 22–39.]

1991	1992	1993	1994	1995	1996	1997	1998	1999	2000	2001
109	295	874	1531	243	68	23	30	30	–	3

Jongerden explains the evacuation of the villages:

> The objective of the new doctrine was the destruction of the PKK environment, both by contraction (resettlement of the population) and penetration

---

[125] *Türkiye İnsan Hakları Raporu 1997* (Ankara: TİHV-Türkiye İnsan Hakları Vakfı, 1999), 181.

[126] Kurban *et al.*, *Zorunlu Göç Ile Yüzleşmek*; *Göç-Der Zorunlu Göç Raporu*; *Türkiye Göç ve Yerinden Olmuş Nüfus Araştırması* (Ankara: Hacettepe Üniversitesi Nüfus Etütleri Enstitüsü, 2006), http://www.hips.hacettepe.edu.tr/TGYONA-AnaRapor.pdf; *TBMM Göç Araştırma Raporu* (Ankara: TBMM, 1998).

[127] *Göç-Der Zorunlu Göç Raporu*, 9–12.

(deployment of special forces, applying the principles of a war of movement, and penetrating the spaces of the PKK, as well as drafting the civilian population in PKK areas into the Village Guard system).[128]

The authorities were using paramilitarised army units (especially the Bolu and Kayseri special commando brigades)[129] to target civilians and thus gain control of the rural territory where the war was being waged. Therefore, one of the biggest changes of the period was that civilians were directly exposed to the violence of the new strategy, with the evacuation and burning of their villages and hamlets.

The new strategy also produced significant changes in politics as well as the army. The army and paramilitary groups were restructured in the direction of an irregular war strategy, and, as a result, intense violence against civilians began to be implemented. But if politics (government, parties and parliament) had not been a part of this new strategy, such intense violence against civilians could not have been implemented. For example, when the figures for the consequences of violence before and after the 1990s are compared, a huge change can be seen. Therefore, the increasing violence imposed by paramilitary groups was clearly realised through agreements between figures and institutions from the world of politics and of the military.

Conclusion

In the late 1980s and early 1990s, during the war between the PKK and the state, paramilitary forces were created or existing groups with paramilitary characteristics were activated by state agencies. This process can be defined as the first period in which paramilitary groups took an active role in the conflict. The paramilitary groups' duties during this period had mainly been to support the gendarmerie forces fighting in the conflicts. However, Turkish state authorities made important decisions to change the character of the war after 1991. These military and political transformations of government agencies were mostly completed in 1993, a strategic transformation referred to by different names. I have argued that the doctrine of LIC is the most appropriate

---

[128] Jongerden, *The Settlement Issue in Turkey and the Kurds*, 91.
[129] HRW, 'Weapons Transfers and Violations of the Laws of War in Turkey'.

concept for this period since it facilitates understanding not only of the military transformation but also of the war strategy performed against civilians.

The state's strategic change and the target of this new strategy were predominantly focused on Kurdish civilians. They concerned the political attitude of a major part of the Kurdish population between 1989 and 1991, years when civilians in many cities and towns of northern Kurdistan rebelled against the state.[130] Thus, while the state authorities determined the new strategy, they began to explore ways to separate civilians and the PKK guerrillas. Accordingly, the realisation of the new strategy hindered the PKK's relationship with the Kurdish population living in cities. Thus, while the villages in rural areas were burned and emptied, public leaders prominent among the civilians in the cities were killed or else 'disappeared' in various ways.

Among the most distinctive features of the paramilitary violence of the 1990s were the actions of death squads targeting human-rights activists and local leaders. A lawyer in the 1990s who later became the mayor of a district in a big city in northern Kurdistan describes the working mechanism of the death squads and how he survived the death list they prepared:

> Repentants had once had high-level positions in the PKK . . . and began to turn against the PKK as they were intimidated by torture and threats. While this process continued, they would be taken out the jail with the permission of the court [supposedly] for interrogation.
>
> JİTEM took the decision to kill me in 1992. They declared that. How? Hizbullah published 24–26 names. Besides my name, Mehmet Sincar's, Hatip Dicle's and Musa Anter's name were on the list. This list was in the magazine of *Towards 2000* (*2000'e Doğru*) published at that time. I was on the deathlist for having been an advocate for and having taken on a PKK case . . . Hizbullah also took their place on the stage. In addition to the repentants and Village Guards, there was now also Hizbullah. Repentants were making various plans to assassinate us.
>
> According to the court file, they had a group that gathered the information on your address and the times you came and went. In other words, they were making the reconnaissance. After that, this group disappears, and a group of hitmen comes and makes its plan, and later on it comes and shoots you . . .

---

[130] Güneş, *The Kurdish National Movement in Turkey*, 109–11.

My life was not very organized as I read from the files [of unsolved murders]. I didn't go in and out of the house at the same time every day. Sometimes I went out at eight, sometimes at ten and sometimes at nine. I didn't go straight to the office directly; sometimes I went to the courthouse. So irregular living became something that saved us.

After I became the mayor, I met with someone on a plane who had been police chief during the period of unidentified murders and was about to retire at that time. He swore that I'd had a narrow escape. JİTEM was going to shoot me, but they missed by two or three minutes thanks to my irregular life. At that time, we didn't stay at the same house for three days in a row. Sometimes I stayed at my sister's home and sometimes at a friend's home. Sometimes I was lodging in different neighborhoods, and if you look at the profile of those who were assassinated, they were the ones who were living regularly. As we knew about this, we were cautious.[131]

The features of this transformation of the war can be summed up as follows: the main military unit in the conflict was the army rather than the gendarmerie, and the conventional and unwieldy army was divided into smaller and more mobile units; besides the PKK's guerrillas, civilians, especially those living in rural areas and supporting the PKK, were massively targeted; the paramilitary formations, which had previously had intelligence gathering as their main task, were strengthened and were turned into death squads. Hence, we can define the years between 1991 and 1996 as the second period in terms of the active role of the paramilitary formations. During this period, these forces were reorganised in terms of their positions in the LIC doctrine, their relationship to politics, their changing characteristics and the types of violence they used. In order to better understand the role of the paramilitary groups in this second phase of the conflict, the following two chapters address two different local examples as case studies, Batman province and the city-district of Cizre.

---

[131] Interview #11, conducted in Diyarbakır, 28 July 2016.

4

BUREAUCRACY AND POLITICAL VIOLENCE (1992–7): PARAMILITARISM IN BATMAN PROVINCE

Introduction

The relationships of paramilitary formations to one another and to state institutions is best understood at the local level. Focusing on paramilitarism in a small area, makes the relations between the influential political, military and bureaucratic actors more visible and concrete, on the one hand, while illuminating the micro-dynamics of tribes, families and individuals loyal to the state, on the other. As the workspace or perspective narrows, relationships and actions become crystallised. At the same time, gaining an understanding of the nature of paramilitarism through local examples also provides an entry point to an appreciation of the similarities and differences between paramilitary policies in different regions. Therefore, in the last two chapters of the book, I offer a comparative discussion of two different areas.

Batman (province) and Cizre (city-district) provide good examples to understand the paramilitaries as operative at the local level in northern Kurdistan during the 1990s. Batman and Şırnak were both previously districts in Siirt province and were made provinces on 16 May 1990, mainly for military reasons in combating the PKK.[1] Administratively restructuring ('upgrading') a place from district to province meant that more troops could be deployed there. In that same month, May 1990, a state of emergency was declared in both

[1] *Türkiye Büyük Millet Meclisi 18. Dönem Tutanak Dergisi*, TBMM, 23 May 1990, 245–55.

provinces.[2] These territories were administratively restructured upon the proposal of the MGK. The reasons for the change were not the socio-economic conditions of the locals there, but military and political factors.[3] Batman also had a unique paramilitary force, which was created by the administrative bureaucracy, while Cizre was one of the clearest local examples of paramilitarisation of the state.

Additionally, the following two chapters focus on Batman and Cizre based on (1) the embeddedness in the local administrative bureaucracy, (2) the structure of the paramilitary formations, and (3) the level of violence. Considering these in turn, first, in terms of the conduct of government institutions in the region with regard to paramilitary forces, the role of the governor of Batman and the mayor of Cizre in relation to the paramilitary forces was quite strong and unambiguous. Both the bureaucrat and the politician (the governor was appointed from Ankara, the mayor was elected locally) had important roles in directing the paramilitary forces. One had set up a new paramilitary group from existing forces in Batman, and the other was a chief of the Village Guards in Cizre. Second, the case of Batman was a specific example in terms of bureaucracy and paramilitary relations because, under the Governor's control, a new special paramilitary group was created. The case of Cizre resembled most others, but it was one of the rare areas where the four paramilitary formations (JİTEM, the Special Police Teams, Village Guards and Hizbullah) intensively and 'constructively' cooperated. Third, both regions were particularly brutal areas, where different forms of violence against civilians (murders and disappearances) were intensively experienced. Of course, Diyarbakır, Mardin, Dersim and Hakkari provinces were also regions where violence was intensively experienced in the 1990s, but Batman and Cizre were different insofar as they had characteristics that facilitate a better understanding of the intense violence, by looking at the relations of paramilitary groups and state institutions, as well as the relations among the paramilitary groups.

---

[2] Bezci and Öztan, 'Anatomy of the Turkish Emergency State', 174.

[3] From the establishment of the MGK to the amendment of the constitution in 2001, soldiers who were high ranking members of the National Security Council were both more in number and more powerful than government officials in this institution. Uzgel, 'Ordu Dış Politikanın Neresinde?', 106–7.

There were similarities and differences in the nature of the violence in each province, but the violence of the paramilitary formations against the Kurdish civilians can, I suggest, be sufficiently well understood through the examples of Batman and Cizre. Historically, the political and symbolic violence that the Turkish state had used in the Kurdish provinces dated back many decades (see Chapter 1) but there were two major categories that distinguished the violence used in the 1990s from other violent periods: the mass occurrence of unsolved murders and the enforced disappearances. These two cases were the regions where these two forms of violence were most intense. This chapter examines the relationship between the state's local government bureaucracy and paramilitary formations through the case of Batman province in the context of intense violence.

Batman was a small village called 'Îluh' until 1955. Situated on the northern Mesopotamian plains near the confluence of the Tigris and Batman rivers, it is a dry and hot settlement. With the discovery of oil in the 1940s, the population started to increase and in 1955 under the name of 'Batman' became a small town. In 1957, it became a centre of a district, and in 1990, the capital of a province.[4] Batman experienced an extremely rapid growth and urbanisation, and its socio-political structure was quite complex compared to other Kurdish cities. In 1950 the population of Îluh village was only 915 people; when it became a province in 1990, this population had increased to 168,779.[5]

In the 1979 local elections, the majority of Batman's voters elected Edip Solmaz, an independent candidate supported by the PKK, to the mayorship.[6] These elections were important in terms of showing the PKK's power in Batman, and Solmaz's victory was one of its first political achievements. Then, on 12 November, just twenty-eight days after he had become mayor,

---

[4] Faruk Alaeddinoğlu, 'Batman Şehri, Fonksiyonel Özellikleri ve Başlıca Sorunları', *Doğu Coğrafya Dergisi* 15, no. 24 (14 September 2011): 19–42; Murat Sunkar and Sadettin Tonbul, 'Batman Şehrinin Kuruluş ve Gelişmesi', *Coğrafya Dergisi*, no. 21 (2010): 18–38.

[5] Sunkar and Tonbul, 'Batman Şehrinin Kuruluş ve Gelişmesi', 23.

[6] Ercan, 'Dynamics of Mobilization and Radicalization of the Kurdish Movement', 163; Nejat Uğraş, 'Unutulan Bir Özyönetim Deneyimi: Batman ve Edip Solmaz (1979)', *Gazete Karınca*, 15 November 2017, http://gazetekarinca.com/2017/11/unutulan-bir-ozyonetim-deneyimi-batman-ve-edip-solmaz-1979/.

Map 4.1 Location of Batman province.

[Source: https://www.mapsland.com/asia/turkey/large-detailed-administrative-divisions-map-of-turkey-2006]

Edip Solmaz was murdered in an armed attack.[7] This political assassination went unsolved, and was effectively to become a prototype for Batman in the 1990s. That same year, Hüseyin Velioğlu, a Kurdish Islamist who took part in radical Islamist youth organisations in the second part of the 1970s, came to Batman from Ankara and started to develop his political and religious organisation in the city. This group would later be called Hizbullah, and was responsible for countless murders in Batman.[8]

After the local political successes of the PKK, Turkish state elites allowed the Islamist movements to organise and expand their power bases in Kurdish provinces. After the 1980 military coup, some groups distributed Islamist-related leaflets in various parts of northern Kurdistan and encouraged political Islam against the PKK. In *2000'e Doğru*[9] (*Towards 2000*) magazine, which reported many of these developments, it was claimed that these were part of a state attempt to mobilise Islamic sentiments against the PKK as a counterweight.[10] On the other side of the political spectrum, an article in the pro-Hizbullah *Hira* magazine included information about the leaflets that were distributed and their contents.[11] Thus, since the end of the 1970s, the main political and social cleavage among the Kurds in Batman was secular versus religious.

Batman in the 1990s is remembered for violent, unsolved murders which were widely assumed to be perpetrated by Hizbullah and the paramilitary group the governor set up. These three aspects were directly and/or indirectly related to each other. The governor of Batman, Salih Şarman, was appointed in 1993 during the government period of Çiller's DYP.[12] He created a new

---

[7] Uğraş, 'Unutulan Bir Özyönetim Deneyimi'.

[8] Kurt, *Din, Şiddet ve Aidiyet*, 42–60.

[9] It was a weekly political magazine published between 1987 and 1993 by the political group led by Doğu Perinçek. It mainly published articles on topics such as the Turkish army, the Kurdish issue, the PKK and Hizbullah. They published highly critical news, articles and interviews during the period when the conflicts were very intense.

[10] 'Laik Devlet Cihada Çağırıyor: Doğuda Dağıtılan Bildiri ve Afişler', *İkibin'e Doğru* 1, no. 1 (10. Ocak 1987): 8–9.

[11] Selman Dilsoz, 'İslami Değerler Çiğnetilmedi', *Hira*, 1993, 3–4.

[12] 'Salih Şarman was born the son of an officer in Çorum in 1948. In 1970, he graduated from the Mülkiye and entered the Ministry of Interior in 1971. After serving as district governor in many districts, he was assigned as governor in 1993 during the Çiller's government period and he was appointed as a volunteer to Batman. He worked as Governor of Batman until 1997. The former governor entered into one-to-one conflicts with the PKK and participated

combined militia force at the end of 1993 and early 1994.[13] Because the term of office of the governor was very problematic, he wrote a memoir to explain it in 2007. According to this remarkably candid text, a special unit was formed consisting of young Village Guards and members of the Special Police Team and hierarchically linked to the gendarmerie.[14] The memoir was entitled 'Out of Routine' (Rutin Dışı), referencing a sentence uttered in 2000 by then President Süleyman Demirel, who said that 'the state can go out of its routine when necessary', when talking about missing weapons in Batman.[15]

The role of the governor in violence against civilians and his relationship with paramilitary groups was a distinguishing feature of this episode in the war, but the formation of the local militia group coincided with (occurred as a part of) the period of reconstruction of the existing paramilitary groups within the framework of the LIC doctrine. Thus, we can relate the creation of a smaller, more adept force within the current paramilitary groups to the reorganisation process.

At the same time, it appears that the Turkish political and military elites tried to use some of the Village Guards as part of the death squads, like JİTEM.[16] Accordingly, the discussion in this chapter focuses on understanding the relationship between the administrative bureaucracy, the paramilitary forces and the use of violence in Batman between 1992 and 1997.

Local Bureaucrats and the Paramilitary Forces

The governor of Batman was one of the governors imposed during the State of Emergency (Olağanüstü Hal, OHAL) in thirteen provinces in south-east Turkey (northern Kurdistan). The town was ruled under martial law as a

---

in the military operations. He was recognized by public opinion in Turkey with his private army and secret weapons he brought. Some of the weapons received from Bulgaria are missing, while Şarman, who was allegedly taking Mercedes as a bribe from a company, went to jail. According to the Hurriyet newspaper, he was the first governor to be jailed in Turkey.''Derin Vali'den Derin Açıklamalar', Hürriyet, 11 December 2007, http://www.hurriyet.com.tr/gundem/derin-validen-derin-aciklamalar-7673014.

[13] Nihat Ekinci, Faili Meçhul Cinayetler: (Batman'ın 1990–2000 Tarihi) Akan Katran Değil Kandı (Istanbul: Do, 2012), 51–2.

[14] Şarman, Rutin Dışı, 41.

[15] '"Rutin" Tartışma', Milliyet Gazetesi, 15 February 2000, 17; Şarman, Rutin Dışı, 17.

[16] Özar et al., From Past to Present, 9–10; Batman Barosu Faili Meçhul Cinayet ve Kayıpları Araştırma Komisyonu 2011 Yılı Çalışma Raporu (Batman: Batman Barosu, 2011).

district of Siirt between 1978 and 1987, and it fell under the State of Emergency legislation after 1987. The State of Emergency continued when Batman became a new province in 1990. Hierarchically, the thirteen governors were under the Governor of the State of Emergency.[17] There was a general governorship of 'the Region in State of Emergency', which was based in Diyarbakır, to which the governors were subject. Therefore, this dual political and legal system in northern Kurdistan also had a legal distinction. In effect, it comprised another, parallel political and legal system within the country that functioned as an administration dedicated to northern Kurdistan exclusively.

The Kurdish provinces were generally governed by extraordinary regimes during the post-republic period. There were the periods of the General Inspectorates (1927–52), the Martial Laws (during the 1960, 1971 and 1980 military coups) and the State of Emergency (1987–2002).[18] Further to these, moreover, a large number of martial laws were declared on other dates.[19] The purpose of the parallel legal structure for northern Kurdistan was to provide the administrative and military bureaucrats there with more power during the conflict. The newspapers referred to the Governor of the State of Emergency Region as 'super-governor' because of the power he wielded.[20] The governors in northern Kurdistan, including the governor of Batman, were very strong because of this special authoritarian regime and were able to take extensive initiatives in the local areas. In order to examine the role of the Batman governor – Salih Şarman – we need first to establish the significance of the local bureaucrats in relation to violent crimes and the paramilitary forces more generally.

The idea of creating an elite class to govern the state is a very old one, a tradition found, for example, in the late Ottoman Empire under Sultan Abdulhamid II, who gave particular importance to certain bureaucrats in order to carry

---

[17] Bezci and Öztan, 'Anatomy of the Turkish Emergency State'.

[18] Naif Bezwan, 'Kuzey Kürdistan'da Devletin Değişen Savaş Stratejileri', in *1990'larda Kürtler ve Kürdistan*, eds Ayhan Işık *et al.*, 1st edn (Istanbul: İstanbul Bilgi Üniversitesi Yayınları, 2015), 43–8; Cemil Koçak, *Umumi Müfettişlikler (1927–1952)* (Istanbul: İletişim, 2003); Doğan Özgüden, *File on Turkey, Democratic Resistance of Turkey* (France, 1972), http://www. info-turk.be/File%20on%20Turkey.pdf; Serdar Şen, *Türkiye'de Sıkıyönetimler: 1925–1980* (Propaganda Yayınları, 2016); Bezci and Öztan, 'Anatomy of the Turkish Emergency State'.

[19] Zafer Üskül, *Siyaset ve Asker* (Ankara: Imge Kitabevi, 1998).

[20] Zafer Üskül, 'Olağanüstü Hal Türkiye'nin Yazgısı Mı?', *Cumhuriyet Gazetesi*, 19 July 1992, 4.

out the political strategy of the state. Certain names in the bureaucracy were assigned to strategic locations, especially at politically historical turning points. For example, the Ottoman Civil Service Academy (the *Mülkiye*) in the late nineteenth century trained the bureaucrats of the CUP by instilling in them a nationalist ideology.[21] Kieser argues that the Military School of Medicine was one of the centres where Turkish nationalist bureaucrats were trained during the late Ottoman Empire[22] – later to be assigned as military and administrative bureaucrats in the period of intense violence (1912–18 and the early Republic period). Most of the bureaucrats studying in these schools remained active in the Republican period.

Mehmet Bayrak argues that in the first years of the Republic, in the reports they prepared, the Turkish state elites and bureaucrats said that northern Kurdistan should explicitly be regarded as a colony (*müstemleke*) and governed in this way.[23] The military and administrative bureaucrats assigned in Kurdish provinces carried out their duties with this mentality. In the form of General Inspectorates, martial law, military coups and the State of Emergency, northern Kurdistan was ruled by these extraordinary politics and legal apparatuses more or less consistently through the twentieth century. Moreover, many of the military bureaucrats, especially those serving in strategic positions in Kurdish provinces in the 1980s and '90s, had served in Cyprus, which had been under a similar rule.[24] In other words, the same bureaucrats served at different times in (the) two extraordinary regions of the country.

Several bureaucrats who served during the 1990s received their training in a small number of important institutions, such as the *Mülkiye* (now the Faculty of Political Sciences of Ankara University).[25] State bureaucrats had been trained at this higher education institution since 1859.[26] However, the *Mülkiye*

[21] Şerif Mardin, *The Genesis of Young Ottoman Thought: A Study in the Modernization of Turkish Political Ideas* (Princeton, NJ: Princeton University Press, 1962); M. Şükrü Hanioğlu, *The Young Turks in Opposition* (Oxford: Oxford University Press, 1995); Mann, *The Dark Side of Democracy*, 122.
[22] Kieser, 'Dr Mehmed Reshid', 247.
[23] Bayrak, ed., *Kürtler ve Ulusal-Demokratik Mücadeleleri Üstüne*, 452–80.
[24] Yamak, *Gölgede Kalan İzler ve Gölgeleşen Bizler*; Kılıç, *JİTEM*, 80.
[25] Şarman, *Rutin Dışı*; Gökdemir, *Pike*.
[26] Cumhur Ferman, 'Kuruluş Günümüzde', *Mülkiyeliler Birliği Dergisi* 1, no. 1 (1965): 4, 36.

was also a place in which leftist students and professors had dominated, particularly after the 1950s, and from the late 1960s it became one of the places where socialist student movements were organised.[27] Nevertheless, it tended to be the right-wing students and politicians that had graduated from the *Mulkiye* who were selected and positioned as bureaucrats in the state's strategic institutions.

Kılıç argues that the Special Warfare Department of the army and the people who worked in that unit were usually assigned to strategic conflict zones in the Kurdish provinces.[28] While the security forces and paramilitary groups of the state practised intense violence in Kurdish provinces in the 1990s, there were certain administrative and military bureaucrats who graduated and served from these agencies and ruled the strategic institutions of the state in the region. Governor of the State of Emergency Hayri Kozakçıoğlu, Governor of Batman Salih Şarman, Director General of Public Security Mehmet Ağar[29] and Commander of Gendarmerie Public Security Hasan Kundakçı[30] were prominent among the many bureaucrats, officers and politicians who followed this route. And it was this generation that descended upon the Kurdish regions of Turkey in the 1990s to implement its vision.[31] The role of civilians (bureaucrats, civil servants, politicians) in Turkish politics has been generally assumed as under the shadow of the military.[32] However, the civilians mentioned above all adopted the radical political and military strategy defined as the LIC doctrine and thus ought to be regarded as an integral part of its implementation.

During the intense conflicts in the 1990s, the roles and initiatives of the OHAL governors and bureaucrats were very important in the implementation of the political strategy against civilians and the use of paramilitary groups. While the formation and strengthening of paramilitary groups was a

---

[27] 'Kitlesel Mücadeleler ve Dev-Genç', in *Sosyalizm ve Toplumsal Mücadeleler Ansiklopedisi*, vol. 7, ed. Ertuğrul Kürkçü (Istanbul: İletişim Yayınları, 1988), 2134–65.

[28] Kılıç, *Özel Harp Dairesi*.

[29] Gökdemir, *Pike*; Şarman, *Rutin Dışı*; 'Evinde Ölü Bulunan Hayri Kozakçıoğlu'nun Eşi İfade Verdi', *t24.com.tr*, 23 May 2013, http://t24.com.tr/haber/turkiyenin-ilk-ohal-valisi-hayri-kozakcioglu-intihar-etti-iddiasi/230493.

[30] Kundakçı, *Güneydoğu'da Unutulmayanlar*.

[31] '"Devlet Hatırası" Albümü: Ulus-Devletin Portresini Çizmek', *Toplum ve Kuram*, no. 6–7 (2012): 29–81.

[32] Cizre Sakallıoğlu, 'The Anatomy of the Turkish Military's Political Autonomy'.

state policy, the names of certain bureaucrats came to the fore in regions where the violence was particularly intense. Following the 1991 murder of HEP provincial head Vedat Aydın, who was also head of the Diyarbakir branch of the İHD, the number of unsolved murders in many Kurdish provinces escalated rapidly.[33] The bureaucrats in Diyarbakır at that time were OHAL Governor Hayri Kozakçıoğlu, Chief of Police Ramazan Er, Deputy Chief of Police Responsible for Counterterrorism Hüseyin Kocadağ and Deputy Chief of Police Responsible for Intelligence Hanefi Avcı. In 1994, these bureaucrats were mostly serving in and around Istanbul – the Istanbul bureaucrats were Governor Hayri Kozakçıoğlu, Chief of Police Necdet Menzir, Deputy Chief of Police Responsible for Counterterrorism Hüseyin Kocadağ and Deputy Chief of Police Responsible for Intelligence Hanefi Avcı (i.e. three of the four were in identical positions)[34] – and similar acts of violence against Kurdish civilians began to occur there too. The unsolved murders of Kurdish businessmen, such as of Savaş Buldan, Behçet Cantürk and Hacı Karay, started in Istanbul around that time. It is hard to credit this as a coincidence. The perpetrators of the 1991 and 1994 murders in Diyarbakır and Istanbul were never found. It was alleged that the crimes were committed by paramilitary groups, especially JİTEM.[35] A further link between paramilitary forces and the bureaucracy is strongly implied.

Not only in the administrative bureaucracy, but also in the military bureaucracy some officers have been identified as most likely having played a vital role in the use of violence against the Kurdish civilians. Veli Küçük, a high-ranking military officer, was one. He was always thought to use intense violence against Kurdish businessmen and civilians in the places where he served.[36] JİTEM co-founder Arif Doğan stated that Veli Küçük began active duty in the Gendarmerie Intelligence Group Command, in other words JİTEM,

[33] Van Bruinessen, 'Turkey's Death Squads'; Yılmaz, *Karanlık Vardiya 90'lı Yılların Politik Arşivi*, 304–26.

[34] Hikmet Çetinkaya, 'Yüzü Kapanmış Yara', *Cumhuriyet Gazetesi*, 12 February 2000, 5.

[35] Hatip Dicle *et al.*, 'Hüseyin Baybaşin İle Röportaj', in *Çete Devlet – Susurluk Dosyası*. (Mezopotomya Yayınları, 1997), 192–5; Balık, *Kerberos*, 52–61; Soner Yalçın, *Behçet Cantürk'ün Anıları – Beco*, 7. baskı (Istanbul: Su Yayınları, 2000).

[36] *TBMM Susurluk Komisyonu Raporu*, 229; Savaş, *Susurluk Raporu*, 36; Ergenekon İddianamesi [Ergenekon indictment], No. 2009/188 (n.d.).

in 1990,[37] which coincided with the beginning of the unsolved political murders linked to that paramilitary unit.[38] Küçük was appointed as the Kocaeli Gendarmerie Commander on August 1993. Kocaeli was one of the regions where the bodies of murdered Kurdish businessmen were found, particularly in 1994.[39] Therefore, in addition to the administrative bureaucracy, certain police and military officials were identified as having played an important role in determining the level of violence in the Kurdish provinces.

Another intelligence officer allegedly responsible for the unsolved political murders was Abdulkerim Kırca. He was held responsible for unsolved killings in Batman as head of the branch of JİTEM there in 1990–2.[40] Kırca was then appointed to the head of the group command of the JİTEM in Diyarbakir.[41] According to the report of the unsolved murders prepared by the Batman Bar Association in 2011, dozens of unsolved murders were committed in Batman between 1990 and '92 (especially in 1992).[42]

For the state authorities, these radical bureaucrats and officers were very useful in the atmosphere of a war conducted against civilians. As discussed in the previous chapter, the Turkish military and political elite determined civilians who supported the PKK guerrillas in line with the LIC doctrine as their primary target. Therefore, the state elites gave important roles to the experienced military and administrative bureaucrats in order to carry out this political and military strategy. The above-mentioned administrative and military bureaucrats were those who were active in this strategy, and the governor of Batman was another.

Salih Şarman was one of the bureaucrats who implemented a politics in the local area (province) that involved, as an important strategic element, the use of paramilitaries to target Kurdish civilians in line with and as a part of the LIC doctrine. Moreover, he was a part of a nationalist elite created (educated) for just such a specific purpose. Governor Şarman was the most senior bureaucrat

---

[37] Ibid., 126.

[38] *Türkiye İnsan Hakları Raporu 1997*, 6.

[39] Kılıç, *JİTEM*, 163–76.

[40] Ibid., 140.

[41] Savaş, *Susurluk Raporu*, 18; Kılıç, *JİTEM*, 139–41.

[42] *Batman Barosu Faili Meçhul Cinayet ve Kayıpları Araştırma Komisyonu 2011 Yılı Çalışma Raporu*.

in Batman, appointed and operating in the context of the State of Emergency during the fight against the PKK and pro-PKK civilians. The reports of both the Batman Bar Association and the İHD show that most of the unsolved murders and enforced disappearances there coincided with his period of office (1993–7).[43] The information gathered from different government agencies and the İHD by the Batman Bar Association puts the number of unsolved murders at 513 people. According to state sources in the report, the PKK was responsible for 151 of these killings. The other 362 unsolved murders – so 70 per cent – were the work of unknown groups (which seems to indicate JİTEM), and Hizbullah.[44]

A New Paramilitary Group in Batman

During his period in office in northern Kurdistan, Batman governor Salih Şarman established a new paramilitary group alongside the army, police and the other already existing paramilitary forces. For the history behind this, we need to recall that state authorities had sought to create a special army against the PKK in the late 1980s, and in 1987 both the Gendarmerie Public Security Corps Command and JİTEM were established, the former as a military institution to provide the main coordination against the PKK during the war and the latter as an intelligence organisation under this Corps Command.[45] However, when JİTEM was founded, the main issue of the discussions was not the establishment of a narrow intelligence organisation but of a counter-guerrilla army (as mentioned, above).[46] This counter-guerrilla army was to be well-trained and consist of 100,000 people to be deployed against the PKK.[47] Such a huge counter-guerrilla army could not be established for political or military reasons, and using smaller and semi-formal/informal groups was more useful for reasons like political deniability and impunity of actions. Yet, discussions about the establishment of a large army against the PKK always remained

---

[43] Ibid.; *Zorla Kaybedilenler, Faili Meçhul Cinayet-Yargısız İnfazlar.*

[44] *Batman Barosu Faili Meçhul Cinayet ve Kayıpları Araştırma Komisyonu 2011 Yılı Çalışma Raporu.*

[45] Kılıç, *JİTEM*, 49–53.

[46] Kundakçı, *Güneydoğu'da Unutulmayanlar*, 157–60; Çelik, *Türk Kontr-Gerillası*, 73–93; Kılıç, *JİTEM*, 55–6.

[47] Yalçın, *Binbaşı Ersever'in İtirafları*, 138; Kılıç, *JİTEM*, 56.

on the agenda. This is observed in the case of Batman. The state elites kept an irregular army alternative on the agenda through the paramilitary groups established during the war. The Batman case was one of them. Therefore, even if this unit was established on the initiative of the governor, the governor said that he received the authority from the prime minister.[48]

The establishment of this special, local unit by the governor developed out of ideological motivation, state security perceptions, and the opportunities created by the war economy. In addition, two other conditions for establishing the paramilitary group were local dynamics (the Village Guards and the Hizbullah were effective in the province), and the governor's initiative directly through the prime minister (outside the bureaucratic and military hierarchy at the local security institutions). In his memoirs, Şarman explained Batman's political situation in 1993 and the ambition to change it as follows:

> As an appointed governor, I'm going voluntarily to a province that is one of the most troubled regions of our country, which is experiencing additional problems besides the general issues of the region, under the heavy conditions of the day. In this province, which started to be known as the city of unsolved murders, a deputy was killed in the middle of the city only a few weeks ago. This city is at the focal point of the state of emergency region as it is at the intersection of all the transit routes of terrorist organisations, and it is where the people who are joining these groups are organised. My wishes had come true, and I was now part of this war my country had been fighting.[49]

The governor further stated that a new paramilitary force needed to be set up due to the lack of the capacity of the security forces and the existing paramilitary forces, and he elaborated the reasons as follows: the existing military and police force was inadequate; the Special Police Team could only be used for

---

[48] Şarman, *Rutin Dışı*, 49–50.

[49] 'O günün ağır şartlarında ülkemizin en sorunlu bölgesine ve bölgenin sorunlarına ilave olarak ekstra sorunlar yaşayan, adı faili meçhuller şehrine çıkmış, daha birkaç hafta önce orta yerinde bir milletvekili öldürülmüş, olağanüstü hal bölgesinin tam odak noktasında, terör örgütlerinin bütün geçiş yollarının üzerinde ve bu örgütlere yapılan tüm katılımların organize yeri olan bir ile, Vali olarak ve de gönüllü gidiyorum. Dileklerim kabul olmuştu, artık ülkemin verdiği bu mücadelede ben de vardım'. Ibid., 29.

spot operations, not for field domination; large military units (division and brigade) were still not available, despite Batman being made a province; and the Village Guards were disorganised and lacked training and equipment.[50] Hence, according to the governor, the security forces and existing paramilitary groups in Batman had a serious lack of capacity for the conflict with the PKK. Moreover, the governor said that Prime Minister Tansu Çiller had told administrative and military bureaucrats: 'You must finish off terrorism, regardless of how'.[51]

This instruction implied the realisation of many illegal acts and the establishment of a brutal programme to accomplish this objective at any cost. When the governor of Batman founded this special paramilitary unit, he did not consider the hierarchy in the bureaucracy, including the ministry of interior. Furthermore, Governor of the State of Emergency Region (OHAL) Ünal Erkan, who was the direct superior of the governor, said he rejected the proposal for the establishment of these special units, but the governor of Batman established these units through the government. In other words, the governor of OHAL, Ünal Erkan, said that he rejected the project that the Batman governor wanted – to establish a new paramilitary group – but the Batman governor bypassed him and negotiated directly with Prime Minister Çiller.[52] In addition, Commander of Gendarmerie Public Security Hasan Kundakçı said that he was not consulted about the special armed units.[53] Thus, upon the instructions and support of the prime minister and due to the adoption of the LIC doctrine, the governor created a paramilitary formation as a prototype of the special army that had been conceived in the late 1980s. In an interview, the governor said that this model was planned for other provinces too.[54]

The paramilitary group in Batman was a unique example, different from the other paramilitary groups in the State of Emergency region. Formed with

---

[50] Şarman, *Rutin Dışı*, 34–5.

[51] Yılmaz Ekinci, '"Rutin Dışı" Vali'den Özel Tim Gerçeği', *haber7.com*, 13 November 2007, http://www.haber7.com/guncel/haber/280001-rutin-disi-validen-ozel-tim-gercegi.

[52] 'Kimseyi Dinlemedi', *Cumhuriyet Gazetesi*, 11 February 2000, 1, 19.

[53] Ercüment İşleyen, '"Valiye Özel" Tabur', *Milliyet Gazetesi*, 11 February 2000, http://www.milliyet.com.tr/2000/02/11/haber/hab02.html.

[54] Ahmet Dirican, 'Eski Vali: Jitem'le Çalıştık', *Sabah Gazetesi*, 17 April 2006, http://arsiv.sabah.com.tr/2006/04/17/gnd106.html.

a combination of members from different paramilitary groups (Village Guards and special teams) and from the official armed forces, the Batman Combined Special Operations Units was the only paramilitary formation established by a governor during the 1990s conflicts.[55] The use of the two paramilitary groups may be taken as indicating that the governor preferred to include radical members in terms of ideological and political background. However, there were already various allegations about the recruitment of members for this unit. Among these claims was an accusation that members were selected from pro-Hizbullah tribes and that a part of the missing weapons that belonged to the army was given over to Hizbullah by the governor.[56]

Journalist Aydın Engin interviewed Rıfat Demir, one of the leaders of the Habizbin tribe, while researching Hizbullah in Batman in 1993. Demir said in this interview that he had close ties with bureaucrats and politicians in Ankara and made other statements that were instructive in relation to the state–Hizbullah relationship:

> The regular policeman does not know about these issues. But there is the Special Team, then Counterterror [JİTEM] they know. They allow [Hizbullah] . . . If Hizbullah's path were opened better, Batman would be cleansed in one day . . . Most Hizbullah [members] are boys of our tribe, namely of the Habizbin tribe.[57]

The Village Guards in Batman consisted mainly of the members of two tribes, one of them being the Habizbin.[58] It is highly probable that members of this pro-Hizbullah and pro-state tribe, which was one of the biggest suppliers of Village Guards in Batman, were part of the new paramilitary group. One

---

[55] Şarman, *Rutin Dışı*, 41.

[56] Aydın Engin, 'Hizbullah'ı Devlet Kurdurdu', *Cumhuriyet Gazetesi*, 20 February 1993; 'Devlet Menfaati Icabı', *Hürriyet*, 13 February 2000, http://www.hurriyet.com.tr/devlet-menfaati-icabi-39133096.

[57] Aydın Engin, 'Devlet Hizbullah'a Göz Yumuyor', *Cumhuriyet Gazetesi*, 19 February 1993, 14: 'Karakol polisi ne bilsin bu işleri? Ama Özel Tim var, sonra Terörle Mücadele var. Onlar göz yumuyor . . . Hizbullah'ın yolu iyice açılsa, Batman bir günde temizlenir . . . Hizbullah [üyeleri] bizim aşiret çocuğu çoğu, Habizbin yani.'

[58] Önder, *Devlet ve PKK İkileminde Korucular*, 65.

interviewee, a journalist in Batman and nearby places in the 1990s, explains the claim about the state–Hizbullah relationship thus:

> The attacks are so public that the men [members of Hizbullah] did not feel the need to hide them. For example, they get military training in the Mervaniye village of the Gercüş district of Batman . . . From a distance we look, hundreds of people are receiving military training, and the Gercüş garrison command is two kilometres away. So they almost see each other. I do not see who gives them training, but I see they have been trained. So it was very public.[59]

This brings up another point, that Batman was somewhat separated geographically in terms of paramilitary group activities.[60] The rural area, as indicated in the above citation, was mainly used for training and intelligence, while the urban centres were used mainly for assassinations.

Regarding the missing weapons that had been issued, the governor was accused of illegally importing weapons from Bulgaria and China. Some of these weapons disappeared and were allegedly used in assassinations by Hizbullah hitmen.[61] Later, the governor was tried by the Council of State (*Danıştay*) because of missing weapons and equipment and taking bribes, and received a prison sentence for illegally smuggling weapons into the country.[62] Another discussion that strengthens the allegations of relations between certain state institutions and Hizbullah can be found in Arif Doğan's memoirs. Doğan claimed that some Village Guards were deployed in

---

[59] Interview with C.M., 29 June 2017, Netherlands: 'Saldırılar o kadar ayyuka çıktı ki, adamlar kendilerini saklama gereği de görmüyorlardı. Mesela Batman'ın Gercüş ilçesine bağlı Mervaniye köyünde … orada diyelim askeri eğitim alıyorlar. Uzaktan biz bakıyoruz, yüzlerce insan askeri eğitim alıyor ve Gercüş garnizon komutanlığı da iki kilometre ileride. Yani neredeyse birbirlerini görüyorlar. Onlara kimin eğitim verdiğini göremiyorum ama verdiklerini görüyorum. Öyle yani çok aleniydi.'

[60] *Batman Barosu Faili Meçhul Cinayet ve Kayıpları Araştırma Komisyonu 2011 Yılı Çalışma Raporu.*

[61] 'Hizbullah'ı Koman ve Küçük Kurdu', *Birgün Gazetesi*, 29 July 2008, https://www.birgun.net/haber-detay/hizbullah-i-koman-ve-kucuk-kurdu-41968.html; 'Batman'da Kayıp Silah Bilmecesi', *Cumhuriyet Gazetesi*, 10 February 2000, 19.

[62] 'Valiye Rüşvetten Mahkumiyet', *Cumhuriyet Gazetesi*, 14 February 2004.

Hizbullah during its first propaganda period.[63] The Combined Special Operations Units were actively used between 1993 and 1997, during Governor Şarman's term of office. The governor claims that military operations were undertaken with this mixed paramilitary group, which were very successful and continued until 1997.[64]

The governor's personal ambition, motivation and initiative played an important part in the establishment of the Batman force. Although Şarman was an administrative bureaucrat, he states that he participated in an armed engagement during a military operation and carried a firearm himself.[65] And it is clear that as head of the provincial state bureaucracy, Şarman was responsible for Batman's most bloody period. The combined paramilitary formation was used alongside other paramilitary groups during his term of office as governor, particularly between 1994 and 1997. The governor indicates these relations in an interview: 'We worked very well with the JİTEM. I never understood why they said it didn't exist. It did exist, and it was useful. For us, the model was correct, it can be applied again.'[66]

The former repentant Murat Demir made the interesting claim that the name 'Hizbullah' was first used for the actions of JİTEM, and only later was it used by Islamic groups.[67] In fact, according to researchers Faik Bulut and Mehmet Faraç, there were many different Hizbullahs, although they probably take 'Hizbullah' to name all radical Islamist groups. They argue that one of these was Hizb-ül-Kontra, an active group in Diyarbakir and Batman that was responsible for many political killings there in the 1990s.[68] Even though the governor claimed that the new paramilitary group was operating only against the PKK, the years that this group was active coincided with a period of intense violence used against civilians. Therefore, the paramilitary group the Combined Special Operations Units established by the governor can also be cited as one of the actors that used intense violence in the province besides and in addition to JİTEM and Hizbullah.

---

[63] Doğan, *JİTEM'i Ben Kurdum*, 158.

[64] Şarman, *Rutin Dışı*, 60.

[65] Ibid., 104.

[66] Dirican, 'Eski Vali: Jitem'le Çalıştık'.

[67] Bulut and Faraç, *Kod Adı Hizbullah*, 75.

[68] Ibid., 117–18.

The Level of Political Violence in Batman

Batman is remembered as a city that experienced very high levels of political violence in the 1990s, including arrest, torture and extrajudicial killings (unsolved murders and enforced disappearances). Almost every day, there was a profoundly fearful climate in the streets, where people would be publicly killed. Before the 1990s, Batman was a region where there was violence for political, social and economic reasons, which included conflicts between tribes.[69] The leaders of one of the most well-known tribes in Batman, the Raman, had formed gangs from some of the tribe members and cooperated with the governor of Diyarbakir during the Armenian genocide,[70] and the tribe maintained its pro-state position against the Kurdish political movements in the 1970s.[71] According to several sources, the Raman later became part of the Village Guard system, and there were conflicts between this tribe and the PKK from 1979.[72] The Turkish-nationalist and Islamist youth organisation the MTTB, which was associated with right-wing parties, also operated in Batman and carried out acts of violence against members of various Kurdish and leftist opposition movements in the second half of the 1970s.[73]

A major point separating Batman from other Kurdish cities during the conflict between the state forces and paramilitaries and the PKK was the social, economic and religious polarisation there. One reason was the oil industry. Batman was a place where the working-class and trade union struggle was more active than in other Kurdish provinces due to the presence of oil refineries.[74]

[69] Van Bruinessen, *Agha, Shaikh, and State: The Social and Political Structures of Kurdistan* (London: Zed Books, 1992), 53–4; İsmail Beşikçi, *Doğu'da Değişim ve Yapısal Sorunlar Göçebe Alikan Aşireti* (Istanbul: İsmail Beşikçi Vakfı Yayınları, 2014); Hasan Biçim, 'Aşiretlerin Kente Eklenlenme Tarzı: Batman Örneği' (PhD diss., Ege Üniversitesi, 2018), 329–30.
[70] Demirer, *Ha Wer Delal Emine Perixane'nin Hayatı*, 75–89.
[71] Mazlum Doğan, *Toplu Yazılar* (Weşanen Serxwebun, 1982), 115.
[72] Adnan Çelik, 'Temps et Espaces De La Violence Interne: Revisiter Les Conflits Kurdes En Turquie à L'échelle Locale (Du Xixe Siècle à La Guerre Des Années 1990)' (PhD diss., de l'École des hautes études en sciences sociales (EHESS), 2018), 326–7; Önder, *Devlet ve PKK İkileminde Korucular*, 65, 91; Karayılan, *Bir Savaşın Anatomisi Kürdistan'da Askeri Çizgi*, 2011, 103; Uğraş, 'Unutulan Bir Özyönetim Deneyimi'.
[73] Enver Sezgin, *Batman Bolşoy* (Istanbul: Vapur Yayınları, 2018), 66–9, 76–7.
[74] 'Batman' Da Durum Nedir ?', *Xebat*, Kürdistan-1977/1979 Bildirileri (1980): 19–22.

This social separation between pro-PKK Kurds and Islamist Kurds began in the late 1980s.[75] The PKK was quite strong in the province at the beginning of the 1990s, which led the state elites to find alternative means in the conflict. These included the strengthening of pro-state tribes, and the creation of a space to organise for religious communities. The informal Islamist groups that saw the PKK and pro-PKK civilians as threats and enemies started to organise by opening bookstores in the town. Thus, these Islamic groups (later called 'Hizbullah') found an informal route to fighting against the PKK and pro-PKK civilians as a common enemy, alongside the state's armed forces.

One of my interviewees from Batman describes an event that his friend witnessed during the intense violence to explain the politics of the state:

> I was waiting in front of the telephone box in Batman . . . There was either a police officer or a member of a special team in front me. He was the state's security guard. He was talking on the phone, probably to someone from his family. He said, they [members of the PKK and the Hizbullah] shoot each other like dogs, we just collect the bodies.[76]

This comment vividly illustrates the operation of the general politics of the Turkish state employed against Kurdish civilians during the war. Batman province is almost exclusively populated by ethnic Kurds, but during the conflict of the 1990s, there was a very serious social polarisation, and this created an atmosphere of violence. It was not a distinction between different ethnic groups, but the division of society as religious or pro-PKK under the direction of state institutions. Arif Doğan claimed that this polarisation in Batman was implemented as a state policy. State authorities had realised that in Batman there was a situation of potential division among the Kurds that they could use in the developing war. The basis of this social differentiation began with the Village Guard system in the mid-1980s.

[75] Bagasi, 'Kendi Dilinden Hizbullah ve Mücadele Tarihinden Önemli Kesitler', 23–49.
[76] Interview #34, conducted in Den Haag, 28 February 2018. 'Batman'daki telefon kutusunun önünde bekliyordum . . . Önümde ya bir polis ya da bir özel tim vardı. Devletin güvenlik görevlisiydi. Telefonda muhtemelen ailesinden biriyle konuşuyordu. Şöyle dedi 'itler birbirlerini vuruyor, biz sadece ceset topluyoruz.'

One of the most effective Village Guard tribes in Batman was the Habizbin tribe.[77] Both the leader of Hizbullah and many cadres of the organisation were members of this tribe. The violence spectrum in Batman was quite complicated and there were several interconnected reasons for the intense violence, but one was certainly the social polarisation and conflict that started after 1991 and continued until 1997 involving the PKK and Hizbullah, in which the direct and indirect state–Hizbullah relationships were implicated in deadly violence.

Hizbullah was ideologically opposed to the PKK; hence, it implemented violence against pro-PKK civilians, particularly between 1991 and 1995. Hizbullah also began to use serious violence against rival Islamic movements from 1993, and Batman was one of the places where these attacks occurred. PKK leader Abdullah Öcalan argued that Hizbullah was formed as a version of the MHP in northern Kurdistan against the PKK.[78] The pro-Kurdish *Yeni Ülke* newspaper also argued that the counter-insurgency was organised under the name of Hizbullah.[79] As the governor stated (above), JİTEM was very active in the province, there were thousands of Village Guards, and a further paramilitary power had been newly established by the governor.[80] As a result of this, Batman become a place where violence against Kurdish politicians and civilians was intensively practised by the security forces of the state and especially by paramilitary groups.

Many people were killed in Batman as a result of the violence perpetrated by the state's official security forces, but the unsolved murders were mainly thought to have been perpetrated by paramilitary groups.[81] The unsolved murders were aimed at specific targets: assassinations were committed against executives of Kurdish political parties, such as Mehmet Sincar;[82] journalists investigating the murders and human rights violations in Batman;[83] human rights activists and

[77] Bulut and Faraç, *Kod Adı Hizbullah*, 89; 'Hizbullah'ın Militan Deposu: Habizbin Aşireti', *Sabah Gazetesi*, 23 January 2000.

[78] 'Öcalan: "Hizbullah", MHP'nin Kürdistanlılaştırılmış Biçimidir', *Yeni Ülke*, Şubat 1993.

[79] 'Kontrgerilla Hizbullah Kılığında', *Yeni Ülke*, 11 Ocak 1992.

[80] Özar *et al.*, *From Past to Present*, 62.

[81] *Türkiye İnsan Hakları Raporu 1994* (Ankara: TİHV-Türkiye İnsan Hakları Vakfı, 1995), 62.

[82] Aydın Bolkan, *Faili Meçhul Bir Milletvekili Cinayetinin Öyküsü Mehmet Sincar* (Istanbul: Aram Yayınları, 2005).

[83] *Türkiye İnsan Hakları Raporu 1991*, 144.

NGO members;[84] tradesmen who closed their shops in response to PKK calls; and Assyrians living in the State of Emergency region. Generally, attacks were carried out against those who were thought to have had relations with the PKK but could not be arrested because of lack of evidence, such as people whose relatives had joined the PKK. And according to TİHV reports, the paramilitary groups had important roles in all these attacks in Batman.[85]

Enforced disappearances featured prominently in the Batman catalogue of crimes and violence. The way paramilitary groups collaborated with the state's official security forces in this respect involved the targets – from among above-mentioned groups – being detained by the official security forces, which later denied the arrest: 'there is no such person under interrogation' became a familiar refrain.[86] Indeed, the 'first and perhaps most significant technique that various representatives and institutions of the state agree upon and which renders the strategy of enforced disappearance possible is denial'.[87]

There was a pattern to the time period of such attacks in Batman. In general, people were targeted when they went to work in the morning and towards evening. So, in general, the murders were committed during the day. An obvious reason for this is that when it was dark there was no-one on the street – it was simply too unsafe to go out in Batman at night. Therefore, the paramilitary state forces or forces acting for the state would pick out and pick up individuals during the day and bundle them into vehicles in broad daylight. White Renault Toros models became murderously iconic with this type of action. Essentially, one can say, the unsolved murders took place in public. Such attacks on pro-PKK civilians thus effected both a punishment and intimidation. Also, murders were committed in the city centre, where the streets were more suitable for the hitmen to escape afterwards. The daytime urban environment was transformed into a zone of killing with fear and suspicion that fostered and heightened the social divisions.

---

[84] HRW, 'The Kurds of Turkey: Killings, Disappearances and Torture', Human Rights Watch-Helsinki Watch, March 1993, 16, https://www.hrw.org/report/1993/03/01/kurds-turkey/killings-disappearances-and-torture.

[85] *Türkiye İnsan Hakları Raporu 1993*, 143, 305–6.

[86] *Türkiye İnsan Hakları Raporu 1994*, 202–5.

[87] Göral *et al.*, *The Unspoken Truth: Enforced Disappearances*, 38.

One of the striking examples of violence in which paramilitary groups were central was the September 1993 murders of a Kurdish MP and party executives. This narrative starts with the killing of Habib Kılıç, one of the Batman executives of the Kurdish party (then known as the Democracy Party [*Demokrasi Partisi*, DEP], following closure of the HEP). Kılıç was murdered on the street by unknown persons on 2 September. The next day, eight DEP deputies and executives went to Batman to investigate the murder. The delegation was under police protection throughout, from the moment it arrived, but the following day (4 September), there were no police in sight. After the delegation divided into two groups to investigate the murder, unknown persons attacked the group with Mehmet Sincar MP and Metin Özdemir, chairman of the Batman DEP, shooting them both dead.[88]

DEP deputies frantically discussed the situation, and MP Nizamettin Toğuç observed that 'the state has handed us over to the counter guerrilla [JİTEM]'.[89] Leyla Zana, a member of the delegation, went to the hospital to visit the injured immediately after the attack and reported an undercover policeman as having said to her, that 'Yesterday we followed your delegation all the day' but that their superiors 'gave us the order this morning not to follow you'.[90] Despite the unsolved murders in Batman, security measures were not taken to protect the MPs that day.[91] After Sincar was killed, his family told government officials that they wanted to bury his body according to their tradition, but state officials refused and had the funeral performed without family members.[92] Then, during the condolence period, on 9 September, a bomb was thrown at night at the home of Mehmet Sincar's father, in Kızıltepe, Mardin, injuring six more.[93]

The killings of Kılıç, Sincar and Özdemir were similar to other political killings in Batman in that they were murdered in the middle of the street

---

[88] Ekinci, *Faili Meçhul Cinayetler*, 106–12; Tuncay Şur, 'Mehmet Sincar Cinayeti ve DEP'in Legal Siyasete Dâhil Olma Çabası: Anaakım Basın Üzerinden Bir İnceleme', *Kültür ve İletişim* 19, no. 38 (2016): 42–63.

[89] Bolkan, *Faili Meçhul Bir Milletvekili Cinayetinin Öyküsü*, 103.

[90] Ibid., 108–9.

[91] Ekinci, *Faili Meçhul Cinayetler*, 109; TBMM, *Ülkemizin Çeşitli Yörelerinde*, 28.

[92] Bolkan, *Faili Meçhul Bir Milletvekili Cinayetinin Öyküsü*, 151–62.

[93] Ibid., 169.

in broad daylight. Who were the perpetrators; who was responsible? The discussions that followed pointed the finger at JİTEM and at Hizbullah.[94] That it was these two organisations which were considered as perpetrators of the murders gives an important clue about the responsibility of the unsolved murders in Batman generally in the 1990s. It is alleged that the two assassins in the second killing – the attack on the investigating group of the delegation – were JİTEM members Alaattin Kanat and Adem Yarkın. JİTEM co-founder Cem Ersever gave these two names in an interview.[95] When the delegation had arrived at Diyarbakır from Ankara, these two JİTEM members followed (i.e. from Diyarbakır airport). MP Sincar even pointed out Alaattin Kanat to the other deputies and gave his name, saying 'We're from the same village, we were children together.'[96] In an interview given in 1997, the repentants Murat İpek and Murat Demir also explained that a team from JİTEM had been sent to Batman and that the murder order came from Ankara. According to this account, the target was all the deputies in the delegation, but only one was killed.[97]

Such unsolved political murders as these increased dramatically with the new war strategy of the state implemented from 1991. High-level state officials admitted at various times that this violence against civilians was a state policy. Retired Vice-Admiral Atilla Kıyat participated in a TV programme in 2010 in which he said this of the unsolved murders between 1990 and 2000.[98] Various reports prepared by state institutions further support this argument.[99]

---

[94] Yalçın, *Binbaşı Ersever'in İtirafları*, 171–5; Ekinci, *Faili Meçhul Cinayetler*, 114.

[95] Yalçın, *Binbaşı Ersever'in İtirafları*, 173.

[96] Bolkan, *Faili Meçhul Bir Milletvekili Cinayetinin Öyküsü*, 98–100. In this respect, the murder of Sincar in particular recalls the book 'Chronicle of a Death Foretold' by Gabriel Garcia Marquez, in which a murder was predicted by everyone but not prevented.

[97] *Murat İpek ve Murat Demir'in İtirafları*, Interview by Şanar Yurdatapan (Istanbul, 1997).

[98] 'Atilla Kıyat'tan Şok Edici Açıklamalar', *Haberturk*, 3 August 2010, http://www.haberturk.com/polemik/haber/538375-atilla-kiyattan-sok-edici-aciklamalar.

[99] Savaş, *Susurluk Raporu*; *Yasadışı Örgütlerin Devletle Olan Bağlantıları İle Susurluk'ta Meydana Gelen Kaza Olayının ve Arkasındaki İlişkilerin Aydınlığa Kavuşturulması Amacı İle Kurulan Meclis Araştırması Komisyonu (10/89, 110, 124, 125, 126) Tutanakları* (Ankara: TBMM Basımevi, 1998); *TBMM Darbe ve Muhtıraları Araştırma Komisyonu Raporu*.

Table 4.1 Unsolved murders and forced disappearances in Batman (1992–7). [Data from: *Türkiye İnsan Hakları Raporu 1991*, 65–70; *Türkiye İnsan Hakları Raporu 1993*, 149–58; *Türkiye İnsan Hakları Raporu 1994*, 130–8; *Türkiye İnsan Hakları Raporu 1995*, 169–72; *Türkiye İnsan Hakları Raporu 1996*, 228–30; *Türkiye İnsan Hakları Raporu 1997*, 138–46, all (Ankara: TİHV-Türkiye İnsan Hakları Vakfı); Özgür Sevgi Göral *et al.*, *The Unspoken Truth: Enforced Disappearances* (Istanbul: Truth Justice Memory Center, 2013), 24–5.]

	1992	1993	1994	1995	1996	1997	Total
Unsolved political murders	57	103	80	20	8	9	277
Forced disappearances	0	7	30	11	7	5	60

The figures in Table 4.1 show pro-PKK civilians reported as killed by paramilitary groups (including Hizbullah) and state security forces according to data mainly collected from the annual reports of the İHD. Nihat Ekinci puts the number higher, stating that the number of unsolved murders in Batman between 1991 and 1998 came to 449 people (and that 126 villages and hamlets were partially or completely evacuated in Batman in that period).[100] Another important point is that forced disappearances, which had not occurred there before, started to increase in 1993.[101] The disappearances occurred particularly between 1993 and 1997. Therefore, all forms of intense violence that symbolised the 1990s were experienced in Batman, and the shadow cast by this violence meant that people could not easily leave their homes for many years after.

Conclusion

Batman experienced intense violence in the period 1993–7, for which paramilitary forces were primarily responsible. The violence decreased in the second

---

[100] Nihat Ekinci, *Faili Meçhul Cinayetler: (Batman'ın 1990–2000 Tarihi) Akan Katran Değil Kandı* [Murders by Unknown Persons (Batman 1990–2020) Not Oil Flowing but Blood], 25, 74–5. Nihat Ekinci's book examined the unsolved murders and village guard system through the Batman case. Ekinci worked as a civil servant in both the municipality and different state institutions in Batman, and also as a journalist and has written articles for various local newspapers since the 1990s. In other words, he was a witness to the political violence in Batman.

[101] Ibid., 129–31.

half of the 1990s.[102] In the 1990s, the city was known as the 'city of unsolved murders', but the violence did not end there, because Batman also came to be known as the 'city of suicides'.[103] Journalist Müjgan Halis has argued that the suicides should be understood as a post-war syndrome.[104] Following this analysis, we can divide the periods and level of violence in Batman into three: the social polarisation before 1990, the intense political violence of the 1990s, and the post-conflict syndrome starting from the second half of the 1990s.

The editor-in-chief of the Batman newspaper *Batman Çağdaş Gazetesi* summarised the period of Salih Şarman well: '[It] was full of nightmares for me, for the Batman press and most importantly for the people of Batman.'[105] The intense violence in Batman did not start with Şarman's arrival, and it did not end with his departure, but the years in which he was in Batman coincided with the years when violence was its most intense. The points discussed above indicate that the role of the governor in this violence was quite prominent. He enthusiastically took on the task the state gave to the local military and administrative bureaucracy to 'solve' or suppress the longstanding Kurdish issue and established a unique paramilitary unit at the local level (with functions, weapons and relations with other paramilitary groups as discussed).

Batman became a province in 1990 and was included in the region of northern Kurdistan, where the extraordinary law of the State of Emergency was implemented and which saw intense violence directed at civilians under the name of the 'fight against terrorism'. There were various reasons motivating the bureaucrats and officers that enacted this: ideological motivations (extreme Turkish nationalism), solution methods (believing that the Kurdish issue had to be resolved and that could only be achieved violently), and economic interests.

---

[102] Abdurrahman Altindag, Ozkan Mustafa and Oto Remzi, 'Suicide in Batman, Southeastern Turkey', *Suicide and Life-Threatening Behavior* 35, no. 4 (7 January 2011): 478–82, https://doi.org/10.1521/suli.2005.35.4.478.

[103] Ayşe Durukan, 'Batmanda Kadınlar Hala İntihar Ediyor', *Bianet – Bagimsiz Iletisim Agi*, 21 June 2005, http://www.bianet.org/bianet/kadin/62684-batmanda-kadinlar-hala-intihar-ediyor.

[104] Müjgan Halis, *Batman'da Kadınlar Ölüyor* (Istanbul: Metis Yayınları, 2001).

[105] 'Salih Şarman dönemi, benim, Batman basınının ve en önemlisi Batman halkının en kabus dolu yıllarıydı.' Ekinci, *Faili Meçhul Cinayetler*, 158.

The bureaucrats were appointed to the Kurdish provinces by state institutions, but the rigidity of the politics in northern Kurdistan was also related to the personal ambitions, economic interests and ideologies of these bureaucrats. In other words, these individuals had it in their power to shift the state's general Kurdish politics by applying further pressure and thus cause the situation to turn even more violent. The fact that the governor of Batman saw 'the armed struggle against terrorism' as a personal duty can be cited as an example of this bureaucratic type. The governor was clearly expressing this approach in a TV programme that is still publically available.[106] Many of these bureaucrats were rewarded in their retirement by deputyships or by being made consultants in important institutions, but the end of some was less comfortable or happy. Two of the military and civilian bureaucrats later committed suicide or died a suspicious way. Abdulkerim Kırca, the JİTEM commander of Batman and Diyarbakir, committed suicide in 2009.[107] Hayri Kozakçıoğlu, the first Governor of the State of Emergency Region was said to have committed suicide in 2013, but his parents alleged it was murder.[108] These suspicious deaths have been much discussed but little clarified in Turkey's recent public debates.

When considering what distinguished the governor of Batman and other bureaucrats in northern Kurdistan from those in Turkey's western provinces, it is to be noted that those in the Kurdish provinces had more latitude and authority than did those in other provinces because of the needs of 'national security' and 'sensitivity of the region'. One of the initiatives they were thus able to take was the control and use of paramilitary groups and establishment of new groups when necessary, as seen in the Batman example. It was with the permission of the prime minister that the governor there formed this paramilitary unit, further to the existing paramilitary formations and set apart from the regular bureaucratic hierarchy. Accordingly, this was at the same time a factor that reduced accountability mechanisms in the local area in terms of the criminal acts of this force.

---

[106] 'Kayıp Silahlar Salih Şarman', *Satranç Tahtası* – MPL TV, 25 November 2007, https://www.youtube.com/watch?v=IxaFqhb_Mj0.

[107] Kılıç, *JİTEM*, 233–7.

[108] 'Hayri Kozakçıoğlu İntihar Etmedi, Öldürüldü', *Radikal*, 19 November 2013, http://www.radikal.com.tr/turkiye/eski_ohal_valisi_hayri_kozakcioglunun_olumunde_kritik_gelisme-1161646/.

Salih Şarman was eventually brought to court, but the subject of the trial was not the unsolved murders, evacuation of villages, and such like, but smuggling. After the Susurluk accident, it was revealed that he had bought weapons in illegal ways and that some of these weapons were missing.[109] There is still debate about whether some of the weapons purchased for his paramilitary unit were given to Hizbullah. Therefore, it can be said that the establishment of the paramilitary group and its relationship with other paramilitary groups were 'out of routine' even in a region where extraordinary law was implemented.

---

[109] 'Valiye Rüşvetten Mahkumiyet'.

5

LOCALISED PARAMILITARISATION OF THE STATE (1992–9): THE CASE OF CİZRE

Introduction

İhsan Aslan[1] and Ali Karagöz[2] were detained in their homes in Cizre in the early morning on 27 December 1993. Both were originally from the village of Şax (Çağlayanköy) at the foot of the Cudi mountain in Cizre, in the neighbouring district of Şırnak. The state security forces had burned and evacuated their villages and homes because they refused to be Village Guards, so they had to move to Cizre centre, a small city (or large town) with a population of more than 100,000 people.[3]

İhsan was working in his brother's shop, and Ali was an animal dealer. They were detained by a group from the Special Police Teams, the Village Guards and the gendarmerie commander, who was known as the commander of JİTEM in Cizre. Their wives said that they saw İhsan and Ali being taken to the Village Guard's shelter, not to the gendarmerie or police station. After being detained, their families never heard from them again. Their bodies have still not been found. When family members insisted on asking about the fate of those disappeared, they were threatened by Village Guards, and the

---

[1] Interview conducted with A.Ş. in Cizre, Archive of Truth Justice Memory Centre, 3 September 2012, Hafıza Merkezi Arşivi.

[2] Interview conducted with K.A. in Cizre, Archive of Truth Justice Memory Centre, 2 September 2012, Hafıza Merkezi Arşivi.

[3] Cizre is officially designated as a city, the administrative centre of a district of the same name, one of six and the second largest by population (to Şırnak) in the province (of Şırnak).

prosecutors repeatedly rejected their petitions. For years they were unable even to search for their disappeared relatives due to fear.

Beşir Bayar (1993), İzzet Padır (1994), Abdullah Özdemir (1994), Ramazan Elçi (1994) and Abdullah Efelti (1995) are just a few examples of the many people disappeared in the same way as İhsan Aslan and Ali Karagöz in Cizre at that time. Their fate was part of a general pattern of enforced disappearances and unsolved murders that became routine in Cizre.[4] In order to understand the paramilitary violence in Cizre in the 1990s, the working methods of paramilitary groups, their relations with each other and their policies against civilians, the stories of those who disappeared are important.

In the incident described above, members of three different paramilitary groups were involved: JİTEM, the Special Police Teams and the Village Guards. This also determined the characteristics of paramilitary groups active in Cizre in the 1990s. There are a few factors that present as important in examining Cizre as a case study. First, Cizre was located in a critical geographical area. It had a militarily strategic position because it was on the Syrian and Iraqi borders, as well as in the region where the PKK started the armed struggle. Its location was vital for the PKK to maintain contact with the Kurds living in the other parts of Kurdistan and as a key transit point on the border of the region.

Second, and against that, a mixed team – or death squad – was active in Cizre, recruited from members of local paramilitary groups – the special police unit, Village Guards and JİTEM, by which it was led. The mixed team did not include members of Hizbullah, which, although active in Cizre since 1991, was not as active there as in other regions, like Diyarbakır, Batman and Mardin. According to an interviewee, this was because the PKK and its supporters did not allow Hizbullah to strengthen in Cizre.[5] After the PKK began its armed struggle, it was in Cizre and the surrounding area that the state's military units first used irregular warfare tactics and the prototypes of paramilitary groups.[6] Therefore, Cizre was a prominent centre in the development and deployment

---

[4] Court documents: 'Temizöz ve Diğerleri Davası – İddianame' (indictment), No. 2009/906-1040-972, https://www.failibelli.org/dava/temizoz-davasi/.

[5] Interview #38, conducted in Amsterdam, 25 May 2018.

[6] *TBMM Darbe ve Muhtıraları Araştırma Komisyonu Raporu*, 125.

of counterinsurgency tactics and paramilitary violence, which served as an example to other regions.[7]

Third, the death squad was acting administratively and militarily quite autonomously from 1993 and had considerable control of the region's state security through its links to local leaders and groups. Gendarmerie Commander Cemal Temizöz was head of the local JİTEM group and allegedly responsible for many unsolved murders and enforced disappearances. The mayor of the district, Kamil Atağ, was leader of both the Village Guards and the Kurdish Tayan tribe in the region. Cizre was one of the rare places – along with Kızıltepe, Kulp, Dargeçit, and so on[8] – where the mayor, the leader of the Village Guards, JİTEM (and repentants) and the special police team worked smoothly together. Not only the paramilitary leaders but also regular members of the group were well known by everyone. Finally, Cizre was one of the most prominent areas in which state-sponsored paramilitary groups used extreme violence in different forms. The most distinguishing feature of this intense violence was the enforced disappearances of Kurdish civilians.[9] Cizre district had one of the highest numbers of enforced disappearances in Turkey (although the actual figures are still uncertain, of course).

Thus, Cizre can be examined as a very highly contested territory. Kalyvas analyses the control of conflict areas in several stages according to the conflict capacities of both sides and their areas of full control, contestation and no control (his analysis of control of conflict zones can also be applied more widely, to the various areas and centres of conflict across northern Kurdistan).[10] The military circumstances in Cizre (the urban centre and surrounding rurality) during the 1990s provide an important example in this respect. From the late 1980s to 1993, neither the PKK nor the military units of the state were able

---

[7] Özgür Sevgi Göral Birinci, 'Enforced Disappearance and Forced Migration in the Context of Kurdish Conflict: Loss, Mourning and Politics at the Margin' (PhD diss., École des Hautes Études en Sciences Sociales Histoire et Civilizations, 2017), 125; Kılıç, *JİTEM*, 62–5; Yalçın, *Binbaşı Ersever'in İtirafları*.

[8] 'Davalar', *FAİLİ BELLİ*, http://failibelli.org/tum-davalar/. Gendarmerie commanders of districts like Cizre are also examples of individuals who have been sued regarding their activities with JİTEM.

[9] Göral *et al.*, *The Unspoken Truth: Enforced Disappearances*, 33.

[10] Kalyvas, *The Logic of Violence in Civil War*, 218–43.

to control Cizre entirely. Cizre and its surroundings themselves may be considered as a contested zone. Conflicts around Cizre might be interpreted as being situated in a contestation zone – until 1993, when the LIC doctrine began to be violently implemented.[11] The state's armed forces did not fully dominate the region during this period, and the PKK were especially effective there at night. The state elites considered this as a weakness in terms of national security. Accordingly, the role of the paramilitary groups in the new war strategy was relevant also to the development of hostilities more generally, and one of their main objectives there was to break apart the relationship between the PKK and the people. In particular, their role was to terrorise the area and to punish those civilians (with torture, murder and disappearance) who supported the PKK in various ways (offering shelter, provisions, etc.).

The military and political control of the conflict areas in northern Kurdistan differed between the urban centres, which were generally under the control of the state military and paramilitary forces, and the rural areas, controlled by the PKK. This rural–urban (spatial) split was a significant characteristic of Cizre. Control of the conflict area in Cizre also differed over time: from the late 1980s until 1992, the state security forces and paramilitary formations generally controlled Cizre during the daytime, while at nights it was the PKK that dominated.[12] This bifurcated control of the space according to time of day and as a narrative through time (over years) demonstrated the lack of military and institutional capacity of the state in Cizre. Thus, with the new war strategy implemented in 1993, civilians suspected as supporters of the PKK were directly targeted. One of my interviewees who lived in Cizre in the 1990s stated in our conversation that Cizre was bombed with tanks and howitzers in early December 1993, even though there were civilians inside.[13]

The pro-PKK population in the Cizre rurality had begun moving to the urban centre in the late 1980s after their villages were burned.[14] The military troops frequently and randomly bombed the houses of civilians.[15]

[11] Jongerden, *The Settlement Issue in Turkey and the Kurds*, 67.
[12] Kışlalı, *Güneydoğu*, 8.
[13] Interview #38, conducted in Amsterdam, 25 May 2018.
[14] Interview #28, conducted in Spaubeek, 28 June 2017.
[15] *Türkiye İnsan Hakları Raporu 1993*, 126; *Türkiye İnsan Hakları Raporu 1994*, 86.

In 1992, seven people from the same family had died in one such bombing.[16] From 1993, the attacks against civilians had resulted in further displacement of the pro-PKK population – but at the same time, the Village Guards from outside the town were moved to the centre. This movement comprised a straight-forward scheme of localised, security-determined social engineering; it constituted what was a change of forced migration policy, attempting to shift the urban population demographics in the state's favour, at least sufficiently so. Displacement, forced migration and emptying of the rurality was the policy that the state began to enforce in the early 1990s.[17] Thus, from 1993, paramilitary groups began to exert control over Cizre.

What was the nature of paramilitary violence, their working methods, their relations with state institutions and their policies against civilians in Cizre in the 1990s? I argue that the aim of paramilitary violence was to target civilians including active PKK supporters. This was carried out by a death squad developed in Cizre from different paramilitary formations and directed by two government officers. This group played a major role in carrying out the enforced disappearances and unsolved murders.

Accordingly, the chapter is divided into three main sections. The first section considers the importance of space. Here, Cizre's differences from other regions, geographical importance and socio-cultural structure (in terms of the emergence of the paramilitary groups) are discussed. The second section contains an analysis of the roles of Gendarme Commander Temizöz and District Mayor Atağ in the functioning of the paramilitary groups and their relations with state institutions. The third section focuses on the levels and forms of violence implemented by the paramilitary groups. Cizre was a place where torture and enforced disappearances became commonplace. The discussion of this type of violence is also important in terms of understanding the purpose, intensity and level of violence meted out by the state authorities.

---

[16] *Türkiye İnsan Hakları Raporu 1991*, 37.

[17] Göral Birinci, 'Enforced Disappearance and Forced Migration in the Context of Kurdish Conflict', 143–8; Jongerden, 'Village Evacuation and Reconstruction in Kurdistan', 1–22 (77–100).

Cizre as Focal Point: Towards the Paramilitarisation of the State in the Local Area

As mentioned in the previous chapters, after the reorganisation of the military and political strategy of the state, I have argued that the official military units took on paramilitary features. Cizre was one of the extreme places where this transformation occurred. Why was Cizre important and how did it transform into an area controlled by paramilitary groups?

Cizre is an ancient settlement on the edge of the river Tigris in northern Kurdistan.[18] It is one of the six districts of Şırnak and is larger than the other five districts in terms of population, including Şırnak where the capital of the province is located. Cizre seems to be a peninsula because of the curves of the Tigris River around it. Therefore, the name Cizre comes from 'jazira' which means 'island' in Arabic. And this, in the time of Caliph Omar, coincides with the period when Islamic armies invaded the region.[19] When the borders of the nation state were drawn in the Middle East in the early twentieth century, Cizre remained on the Turkish side, on the Syrian border. The city was the centre of the Cizre-Bohtan Emirate, one of the 'most known Kurdish Emirates during the Ottoman Empire, between the 16th and 19th centuries'.[20] It was one of the important stops of trade caravans between East and West. In addition, Cizre was one of the centres of the trade route on the Tigris River from north to south until the beginning of the twentieth century.[21] The importance of Cizre in terms of the PKK and the state began to be heard mostly in the 1990s in Turkish public opinion. Cizre was a district of Mardin until 1990. In the same year, as mentioned in the previous chapter, when Şırnak became a

---

[18] Birgül Açıkyıldız Şengül, 'Cizre Kırmızı Medrese: Mimari, İktidar ve Tarih', *Kebikeç*, no. 38 (2014): 164–98; Süheyl Sâbân, 'Tarih ve Medeniyet Bağlamında Cizre', trans. Hüseyin Güneş, *Şırnak Üniversitesi İlahiyat Fakültesi Dergisi* 4, no. 7 (2013): 154–62; Muhammed Yusuf Gandur, *Ortaçağ Cizre Tarihi (M.S. 815–1515)*, trans. Fadıl Bedirhanoğlu (Ankara: Beşir Ant Yayınları, 2008).

[19] Metin Tuncel and Abdülkerim Özaydın, 'Cizre', *TDV İslam Ansiklopedisi* (Ankara: Türkiye Diyanet Vakfı Yayınları, 1993), 37.

[20] Ahmet Kardam, *Cizre-Bohtan Beyi Bedirhan* (Ankara: Dipnot Yayınları, 2011).

[21] Tuncel and Özaydın, 'Cizre'; Cabir Doğan, 'Cizre ve Bohtan Emiri Bedirhan Bey (1802–1869)' (PhD diss., Afyon Kocatepe Üniversitesi, 2010), 23–4.

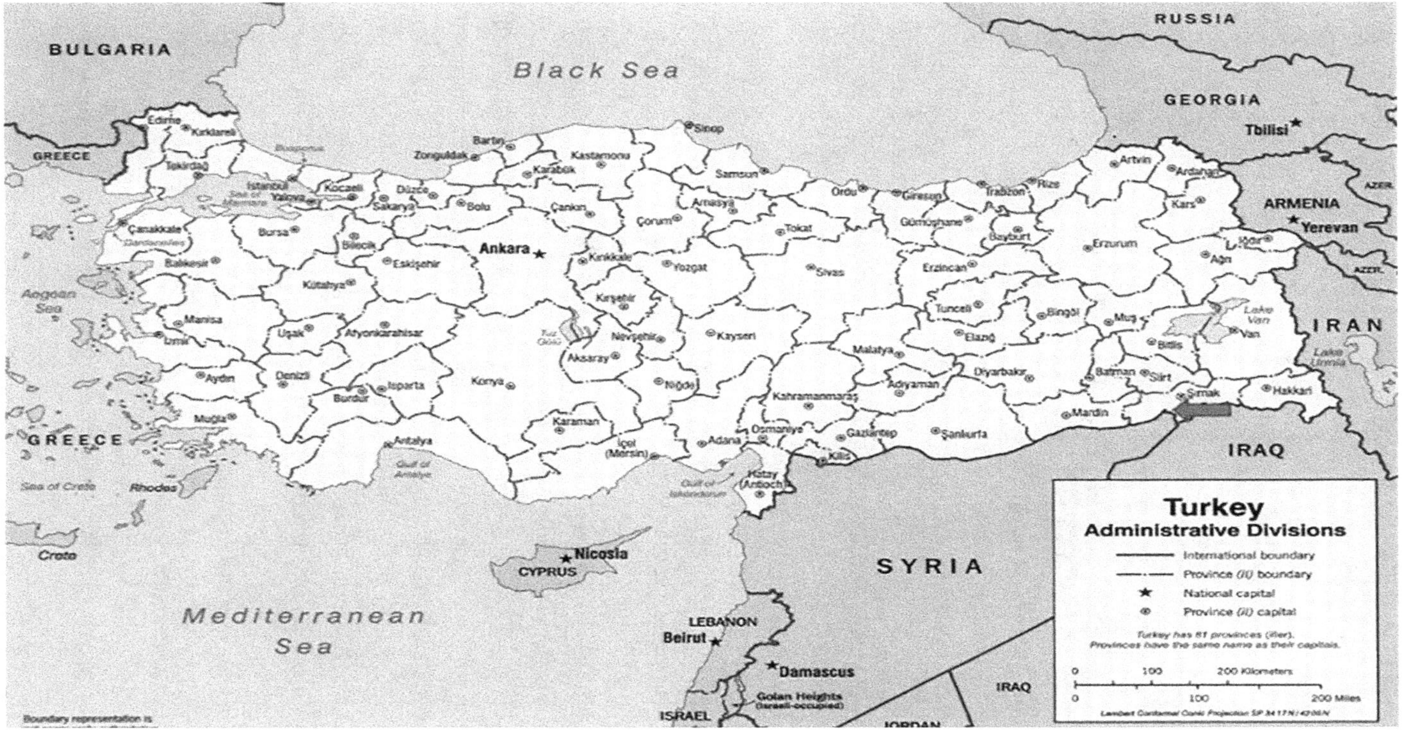

Map 5.1 Location of Cizre city and district.

province for military reasons, Cizre was made a district of Şırnak and it is still the largest district by population.

Because of its historical background and geostrategic position, Cizre was a place of special interest for both the PKK and the state. The PKK had begun to be quite active in Cizre by the late 1980s. At the same time, popular uprisings, called 'serhildan' in Kurdish, occurred in many parts of northern Kurdistan.[22] In 1992, *Newroz*, one of the most important festivals for Kurds, was celebrated in Cizre as a *serhildan*,[23] this being the first major attack on military and paramilitary groups in Cizre.[24] There were various reasons that this mass act of mobilisation emerged in Cizre. One was that other than the military and civil servants of the state, the population there was almost entirely Kurd. Regarding the population and social structure of Cizre, residents in the local area can be separated into three categories: settled residents of the urban centre or city (Kurdish: *bajarî*); villagers (*gundî*), resettled in the city after evacuation of their villages; and nomads (*koçer*), seasonal residents living in Cizre in the winter and the highlands (mountains) in the summer.[25]

Regarding the demography of Cizre, the seasonal settlement of semi-nomadic tribes in Cizre had transformed the social structure of the city, and the relations of these tribes with the state and with the PKK were complex. The majority of the city's population consisted of three tribes (the Batuyan, Kiçan and Tayan), which were also the politically influential semi-nomadic tribes there. The semi-nomadic peoples began to settle seasonally in the centre of Cizre in the early 1990s, due to the village evacuations – which is actually shorthand, in the Cizre case at least, but also elsewhere, for the state imposition of its spatial dominance programme through the bombing of houses, the burning of villages and also orchards and crops and the ban on the use of pastures in order to force the evacuation of villages and village lands and imposition of the Village Guard system. The tribes that accepted the Village Guard

---

[22] Güneş, *The Kurdish National Movement in Turkey*, 104.

[23] Aydın Orak, *Bir Başkaldırı Destanı: Cizreli Berivan* [documentary], 2010, http://archive.org/details/CIZRELRBERVAN.

[24] *Türkiye İnsan Hakları Raporu 1992* (Ankara: TİHV-Türkiye İnsan Hakları Vakfı, 1993), 22; 'Kürtler Katledildi', *Yeni Ülke*, 27 Haziran 1992; 'Ji Tirkiye Teror û İşkence Ji Gel Berxwedan', *Welat*, 29 Gulan 1992.

[25] Interview #38, conducted in Amsterdam, 25 May 2018.

system had relations with different paramilitary groups; while the Tayan tribe had relations with JİTEM, the Batuyan tribe had relations with Hizbullah.[26] But the fact that the PKK was so strong in the region indicates that these tribes were not Village Guards or pro-state in their entirety. Tribal leaders and some families became Village Guards and held a pro-state position, but the general populations of the tribes were pro-PKK.[27] For example, while the leader of the Kiçan tribe was a Village Guard, his niece[28] joined the PKK and became a female commander.[29]

Bozarslan argues that if a tribe or an extended family wanted to win a violent economic, political and military competition, it had to establish a nationwide economic and political network and develop something other beyond the blood solidarity of kinship relations to keep social ties and maintain itself as a cohesive structure.[30] That was indeed what some tribes did, such as in Cizre, through linkages to wider systems of power. Since the nationwide economic and political actors during the 1990s were predominantly nationalist Turkish right-wing politicians and their gangs, making up an extended network of extreme-right relations that had come to largely control the state, it followed that the tribes in cooperation with the state were also affiliated with this network through the Village Guard system. In connection with this, the relationships of the Tayan tribe with JİTEM, the Special Police Teams and the nationalist political parties can be considered as a whole.

Another issue was the political and historical memory of the people in Cizre, which had been the centre of one of the most important Kurdish emirates in the Ottoman period. Many Kurdish intellectuals were descended from the dynasty-family of this emirate, while others were among the most important founding actors of Kurdish nationalism in the late Ottoman period.[31]

---

[26] Haydar Darıcı, 'Savaş Zamanında Aşiret Hukuku', unpublished article, 2018.

[27] Interview #28, conducted in Spaubeek, 28 June 2017.

[28] Vedat Yıldız and Jihat Akşa, 'Ailesi, Çiçek Botan'ı anlattı', *Yeni Özgür Politika*, 28 October 2011, http://www.yeniozgurpolitika.com/index.php?rupel=nuce&id=3212.

[29] Interview #38, conducted in Amsterdam, 25 May 2018.

[30] *TBMM Darbe ve Muhtıraları Araştırma Komisyonu Raporu*, 125.

[31] Yener Koç, 'Bedirxan Pashazades Power Relations and Nationalism (1876–1914)' (Unpublished thesis, Boğaziçi University, 2012).

Other factors that account for the *serhildan* attack in Cizre – further to its near total Kurdish demographic – were its geographical position and state actions. Located on the Syrian border (and close to Iraq), Cizre was directly influenced by Kurdish political movements in both western and southern (Syrian and Iraqi) Kurdistan. Then, especially after the PKK began its armed struggle, the people of Cizre regularly experienced the violence and political pressure of the government's formal and informal security forces.[32] For all these reasons, Cizre was a strategically important region for both the PKK and the state.

The Turkish state paid special attention to Cizre in the 1990s. In Batman, state institutions and Hizbullah had been able to create an Islamic community against the pro-PKK population.[33] This social stratification was not economic but ideological. However, since Hizbullah was not as strong in Cizre as in Batman, and, moreover, local state institutions had not been very successful in creating social polarisation, state agencies determined to seek to create stratification in Cizre through tribal affiliations and oppositions using leadership loyalties to the state.[34] Ultimately, of course, it was as a result of the imposition of the LIC doctrine that there was a gradual increase of violence with the actions of paramilitary groups in Cizre after 1993, the main purpose of which was to intimidate and/or eliminate those civilians who supported the PKK and thus reduce its human and material resource base.[35]

Unlike in Batman, some of the members and the leaders of the military and administrative bureaucracy in Cizre (particularly Temizöz and Atağ) were directly involved in paramilitary groups, which were a part of the system of paramilitarism. In Batman, although the governor formed a new paramilitary group, he was not one of the leaders of the irregular forces; rather, he was the

---

[32] Celal Başlangıç, '90'ların İşaret Fişeği: Yeşilyurt Köylülerine Yedirilen Dışkı', *Bianet – Bağımsız İletisim Ağı*, Aralık 2014, https://www.bianet.org/bianet/medya/160934-90-larin-isaret-fisegi-yesilyurt-koylulerine-yedirilen-diski.

[33] Bulut and Faraç, *Kod Adı Hizbullah*, 107–26.

[34] Interview #28, conducted in Spaubeek, 28 June 2017; Interview #38, conducted in Amsterdam, 25 May 2018.

[35] Serap Işık, *Temizöz ve Diğerleri Davası Geniş Özeti* (Hakikat Adalet Hafıza Merkezi, 2013), 1, http://failibelli.org/wp-content/uploads/2013/02/Temizoz_Genis_Ozet.pdf; Göral Birinci, 'Enforced Disappearance and Forced Migration in the Context of Kurdish Conflict', 108–14.

state's top bureaucrat in the local area. The formal and informal lines between the paramilitary leaders and the state's military–administrative bureaucracy in Cizre were rather unclear and transitional. For example, the same person could hold a position in the state's official bureaucracy and in the death squads, which were part of the paramilitary system. Batman, on the other hand, had relatively discrete boundaries between paramilitary groups and the bureaucracy.

When the paramilitary groups in Cizre are examined, two names stand out. One of them was Cemal Temizöz, who served as the commander of the gendarmerie troops between 1993 and '95. The other was the Head Village Guard, Kamil Atağ, who was the mayor of Cizre between 1994 and 1999. These two actors, both official bureaucrats of government and army institutions as well as leaders of semi-formal and informal paramilitary groups, determined the political climate in Cizre from 1993 to 1999. In other words, the military and political actors at the head of state's official institutions were personally and professionally responsible in particular for effecting the paramilitarisation of these institutions of the state.

Just before this intense period of violence, the state armed forces and paramilitary groups, and in particular the special police unit, carried out a massacre during Cizre's Newroz celebration in 1992. Kurds traditionally celebrate Newroz as their New Year's Day on 21 March, the first day of spring. On this day in 1992, the security forces and paramilitary groups of the Turkish state attacked the celebrations (in Cizre and many other places).[36] Various numbers of dead and wounded after the attacks are given. According to the TİHV 1992 report, which carried out the most comprehensive investigation of the attacks at that time, twenty-four people were killed and sixty injured in Cizre.[37] The report states:

> Observations made in Nusaybin, Cizre and Şırnak, and as a result of interviews with local authorities and the people; It was judged that during the Newroz that the people were fired on randomly and when the people sat on the ground they were crushed by a *panzer* [armed, tank-like military vehicle, i.e. with caterpillar tracks].[38]

[36] Orak, *Bir Başkaldırı Destanı* [documentary], 2010; 'Kanlı Nevruz: 38 Ölü', *Cumhuriyet Gazetesi*, 22 March 1992, 19.

[37] *Türkiye İnsan Hakları Raporu 1992*, 22.

[38] Ibid., 26.

The Newroz day attacks were carried out against civilians, resulting in the deaths of some ninety-four people in total (included three police).[39] The state and paramilitary violence carried out during the 1992 Newroz became a sign of what was ahead in the coming years for Cizre.

The local paramilitary leaders working in government institutions during the period of the intense use of violence in Cizre were highly visible. These leaders were strong in the local area precisely because the state institutions afforded them freedom of action and flexibility in the hierarchy. Thus, they enjoyed the power of the state to act as they saw fit in response to the opposition threat, both real and perceived. Temizöz was one of the officers who served in Cyprus, trained in special and irregular warfare and had been placed in strategic positions in northern Kurdistan in the 1990s;[40] Atağ, meanwhile, was one of the leaders of a family and tribe historically loyal to the state.[41] The political and ideological background of those actors and the opportunities provided by the state's local military and administrative institutions help us to understand the extreme violence in Cizre.

Relationships between Paramilitary Groups and the State: Temizöz and Atağ

The paramilitary violence of the 1990s in Cizre is largely remembered with two names: Cemal Temizöz and Kamil Atağ. The most important characteristic of these men was that they were the highest positioned political and military

---

[39] Ibid., 21.

[40] Göral *et al.*, *The Unspoken Truth: Enforced Disappearances*, 20, 21. 'Putting the debate over the exact name of this organization aside, it is a known fact that certain mixed groups both within the gendarmerie and the police forces formed of village guards, informants and security forces, carried out systematic human rights violations including murder without facing any legal barrier, that they were protected by a perfect shield of impunity, and that they operated lawlessly in the OHAL region especially when it came to "those who were suspected of supporting the PKK" . . . Some members of this team are being tried within the scope of the Balyoz and Ergenekon cases, some have deceased, and some have never been tried. The team reportedly includes Cem Ersever, Veli Küçük, Mahmut Yıldırım (known by the code name Yeşil), Arif Doğan, Cemal Temizöz, Cahit Aydın, Eşref Bitlis, Mete Sayar, Necati Özgen, Hulusi Sayın and Hasan Kundakçı. The most striking common trait of the military personnel is that all have at one point during their careers served in the current Turkish Republic of Northern Cyprus.'

[41] Interview #38, conducted in Amsterdam, 25 May 2018.

officials of the state in Cizre. One was the gendarmerie commander, the other was the mayor and a local political actor, and they were founders of JİTEM in Cizre. They constructed a group of radical members of different paramilitary groups and official units that were known to be the perpetrators of innumerable acts of intense violence, enforced disappearances, and unsolved murders.

Cemal Temizöz was born in 1958 in Çorum (a province in central Anatolia). He graduated from the Turkish Military Academy in 1979[42] and served as gendarmerie intelligence officer. He served in Cizre when political murders and enforced disappearances were at their highest, as a gendarme station commander between 1993 and 1995.[43] Later, he became the Gendarmerie Intelligence Commander (JİTEM Group Commander) in Diyarbakir.[44] He, then, served in Tekirdağ, Denizli and Kayseri provinces in the position of gendarmerie regiment command.

Many years later, in 2009, while serving in Kayseri, Temizöz was arrested, accused and brought to stand trial for his role in (criminal responsibility for) the killings in Cizre. He was also tried in the later 'Balyoz' case, known as the case of the 'Turkish deep state'.[45] Temizöz retired from the army while in prison in 2010, and he was released in 2014. In the court documents, memoirs of repentants, and narratives of the victims' relatives, the commander of the gendarmerie, Major Cemal Temizöz, was regarded as the leader of the paramilitary gangs, or death squads, that were active in Cizre between 1993 and 1995.[46]

In Cizre, it is claimed that Major Temizöz was one of the persons who prepared the list of those to be killed or disappeared – Kamil Atağ was the other. In the 2009 trial, some witnesses reported that the identification papers of those killed were given to Major Temizöz by the repentants after the executions.[47] The death squads, allegedly created by Temizöz, consisted mostly

[42] 'Temizöz ve Diğerleri Davası – İddianame'.

[43] Işık, *Temizöz ve Diğerleri Davası Geniş Özeti*.

[44] Kılıç, *JİTEM*, 191.

[45] Gülçin Avşar, Levent Pişkin and Hande Özhabeş, *Ergenekon'un Öteki Yüzü: Faili Meçhuller ve Kayıplar: Ergenekon Dosyaları İncelemesi* (Istanbul: TESEV Yayınları, 2013), 14.

[46] 'Temizöz ve Diğerleri Davası – İddianame'; Balık, *Kerberos*, 162–3; Interview conducted with Ö.H. in Cizre, Archive of Truth Justice Memory Center, 1 September 2012, Hafıza Merkezi Arşivi.

[47] 'Temizöz ve Diğerleri Davası – İddianame', 10.

of low-ranking officers along with repentants and Village Guards. In addition, since he was a local gendarmerie commander, the Gendarmerie and the Special Police Teams acted together. Also, Temizöz played an important role during the 1994 election of Kamil Atağ as mayor. Temizöz threatened other candidates, thus creating favourable conditions for Atağ to become mayor.[48] During the same period, repentants who were members of JİTEM in Cizre also stated that members of paramilitary groups intervened in the parliamentary elections and threatened the people to elect pro-state candidates.[49] Also, in an interview I conducted with the wife of one of the enforced disappeared people in Cizre, she argued that 'he started the murders in Cizre', referring to Cemal Temizöz.[50] As this short biography of him demonstrates, he was one of many military bureaucrats who led informal paramilitary groups while he was part of the formal army hierarchy.

The other person who prepared the list of those to be killed or disappeared in Cizre – along with Temizöz – is thought to be Kamil Atağ. Kamil Atağ was born in 1952 in the village of Heym, in Cizre, as a member of the Tayan tribe. Elected mayor of Cizre in 1994 as the candidate of the (Islamic, right-wing) RP, Atağ continued in this position until 1999. He was arrested in 2009 for political murders committed in Cizre in the 1990s and released in 2012. Kamil Atağ's younger brother Mehmet Nuri Binzet (the surname is different because his birth was registered to his uncle) gave very detailed information about Atağ in the 'Case of Temizöz and Others', begun in 2009, regarding the political killings in Cizre between 1993 and 1995. Binzet stated that Kamil Atağ was wanted for two murders in Van province and for the bombing of an oil pipeline between Cizre and Silopi in the mid-1980s.[51]

Atağ was a member of the Tayan tribe. This tribe had several conflicts with the PKK that led to its joining the Village Guard system, although one interviewee said that the tribe was already loyal to the state before the PKK emerged.[52] In Silopi, 1987, Atağ met with Cem Ersever, who offered him

[48] Avşar *et al.*, *Ergenekon'un Öteki Yüzü*, 172–3.
[49] *Murat İpek ve Murat Demir'in İtirafları.*
[50] Interview conducted with K.A. in Cizre, 2012.
[51] 'Temizöz ve Diğerleri Davası – İddianame'.
[52] Interview #38, conducted in Amsterdam, 25 May 2018.

the position of Village Guard with his tribe.[53] In 1989, the tribe settled in Cizre; there were no clashes between the Village Guard (tribe) and the PKK because they made a deal that lasted until 1993. At the end of 1993, the tribe broke the deal and the PKK attacked its leaders. Atağ's brother claims that Hasan Kundakçı, commander of the Gendarmerie Security Corps based in Diyarbakir, came to Cizre and authorised Atağ to establish checkpoints and identity control in the district.[54] In 1994, with the support of Major Temizöz, Atağ was elected mayor as a candidate of RP. Atağ, along with his brothers, the repentants and JİTEM, controlled Cizre in every aspect until 1999.

Atağ is generally regarded as one of those responsible for the large numbers of murders and disappearances in Cizre. During his court defence, he said that what was done in the 1990s was done for the state and by order of the state. Although he won the mayorship again in 1999, it was aborted because of his murder case in Van province and also because of the absence of his high-school graduation diploma (a requirement for this office).[55] Atağ's biography is also an important example of tribal leaders, who were loyal to the state, demonstrating their relations with the informal and semi-formal paramilitary groups of the state and their role during the 1990s violence.

The paramilitary groups established in other parts of northern Kurdistan in the early 1990s were also established in Cizre, but when Cemal Temizöz started to serve there in 1993, he formed a new team from the members of the existing paramilitary groups.[56] It is not clear whether this was an officially formed unit or not. However, there are many court documents, testimonies and narratives from the victim's relatives testifying to their work together as members of different armed units during actions such as unsolved murders and enforced disappearances in the region. Cemal Temizöz was quite obviously the leader of the group and also, at the same time, commander of the gendarmerie station. Together with his brothers, Kamil Atağ was a part of this

---

[53] 'Devletin Derebeyi: Korucu Kamil Atak', *Birgün Gazetesi*, 19 March 2009, https://www.birgun.net/haber-detay/devletin-derebeyi-korucu-kamil-atak-45222.html.

[54] Işık, *Temizöz ve Diğerleri Davası Geniş Özeti*.

[55] 'Devletin Derebeyi'.

[56] Balık, *Kerberos*, 252; Kılıç, *JİTEM*, 188–9.

team, as leader of the Tayan tribe and of the Village Guards.[57] The guards were Adem Yakın, Abdulhakim Güven (Fırat Altın) and Hıdır Altuğ, the repentants who usually served as hitmen in JİTEM.[58] In addition to these, there were the special sergeants, Yavuz Güneş, Selim Hoca, Cabbar and Tuna were their code names, together with a member of a special police unit known as Ramazan Hoca.[59] This combined paramilitary group also controlled the district administratively. The district governor did not have a function, and the mayor's office passed into the hands of this team a year later.

Many victims' fates and the narratives of their relatives demonstrate how Atağ and Temizöz worked together. For example, İhsan Aslan was one of the people who disappeared after he was taken into custody by a group including Temizöz and Atağ. The two representatives – one appointed (Temizöz) and the other elected (Atağ) – and their teams were responsible for many similar actions, including disappearances and political murders. Moreover, these paramilitary leaders threatened the relatives of the disappeared people so they would not investigate their fate. When A.Ş. asked Kamil Atağ about her husband's fate after he was detained and disappeared, Atağ threatened her:

> I went there [Kamil Atağ's house] and he said that, by God, he could not release him [İhsan Arslan]. His wife also told me that they would not let him go and that my coming was pointless . . . Again, I went and he came and sat there. I said: 'My uncle Kamil, I am at the mercy of you and please, on behalf of God, set İhsan free.' He said: 'Go away,' and by God, I will kill you if you stay here one more hour.[60]

Kamil Atağ continued to threaten the relatives of disappeared people during his trial in 2009: 'My son's name is "Tarih" (lit.: history). Tarih will write history; no-one should testify comfortably [about me].'[61] The fact that the Village Guards' leader would threaten people in such a casual and comfortable

---

[57] Interview conducted with A.Ş. in Cizre, 2012.
[58] 'Temizöz ve Diğerleri Davası – İddianame'.
[59] Işık, *Temizöz ve Diğerleri Davası Geniş Özeti*; 'Temizöz ve Diğerleri Davası – İddianame'.
[60] Interview conducted with A.Ş. in Cizre, 2012.
[61] Özar *et al.*, *From Past to Present*, 135.

manner in court was probably due to his belief in the politics of impunity (as it related to his personal history).

In the case that was opened in 2009, the soldiers who served in the gendarmerie station in Cizre in the 1990s also testified. Mehmet Aksoy, for example, served as a commander at the Cizre district central gendarmerie station in 1994–6, and he testified to the Chief Public Prosecutor of Diyarbakır on 30 April 2009. The information he gave to the prosecutor's office clearly illustrates the function of the paramilitary group and its relation to other military units in Cizre:

> On July 17, 1994, I started working as the commander of the central gendarmerie station in the district of Cizre . . . When I started the task, Major Cemal Temizöz was the commander of the district gendarmerie station. When I was on my duty, there were Selim Hoca, Tuna, Yavuz, Cabbar and two or three other people, whose names I didn't know, in civilian clothes, and they were known as the interrogation team. They took care of all the interrogations. The team, which consisted of 6–7 civilians, as I mentioned, were involved in all judicial procedures related to terrorism [so, political cases], namely, detaining, releasing, interrogation, statement-taking and taking them to the courthouse. We had to take care of normal judicial cases [non-political cases], and we'd take care of security . . . This interrogation team had a white Renault, but this car wasn't in our gendarmerie inventory. I don't know how that car was supplied, but they usually used it. I met the team probably once or twice a week. Because we had no familiarity with the group, I didn't know the real names of these people. We didn't have a unit designated for interrogation in our squad at the time, though there was such a unit that was actually involved in it. I don't know why. When I went there, Kamil Atağ was both the leader of the Village Guard and mayor. Kamil Atağ and our commander Cemal Temizöz met regularly and I knew they were sincere, but I did not know what they were talking about.[62]

This quotation clearly exposes the relations between the paramilitary formations and the official institutions of the state, and the division of labour between the informal and formal institutions. It has been previously argued that government agencies were paramilitarised, especially with the new (LIC)

---

[62] 'Temizöz ve Diğerleri Davası – İddianame'.

war strategy. As the testimony above shows, the state institutions in Cizre, particularly the gendarmerie forces, were under the control of the local paramilitary group. Members of the local paramilitary group, who did not use their real names, appear to have taken over many official duties (from detaining to taking the suspect to the court) that the gendarmerie unit normally has to do. This means that some kind of authority or monopoly of violence was transferred from official state institutions to the local informal forces. At the same time, this mechanism mentioned by the witness also enabled the easy deniability of the relationship between the state and the informal units, because members of the paramilitary group had the code names and also used a vehicle that was unregistered. Accordingly, although the military and political control of Cizre was in the hands of this paramilitary force, its members could easily be made invisible on official documents. Moreover, there are many claims that Temizöz, managed the relations between those different formal and informal institutions.[63]

Consequently, we can state without reservation that the members of formal and informal military institutions of the state worked together in Cizre. The above-mentioned testimony, the interviews I conducted and the reports prepared by many national and international organisations all indicate the extreme violence used by paramilitary groups and demonstrate the relations between these groups and the official state institutions in Cizre.[64] Therefore, both the actions (the extra-legal activities of the paramilitaries) and the military and political positions (gendarmerie commander and mayorship) of these two actors demonstrate the most obvious example of the state–paramilitary relationship. I would argue that the division of labour between those formal and informal units in Cizre was also important in terms of being an example of plausible deniability. In other words, there were paramilitary cadres that benefitted from the state's official institutions and who served in units that were not legally part of the official institutions.

[63] '9 Kez Müebbet İstemi', *Cumhuriyet Gazetesi*, 16 July 2009, 4; Işık, *Temizöz ve Diğerleri Davası Geniş Özeti*, 3.

[64] HRW, 'Weapons Transfers and Violations of the Laws of War in Turkey'; HRW, 'The Kurds of Turkey: Killings, Disappearances and Torture'; *Türkiye İnsan Hakları Raporu 1994*; *Zorla Kaybedilenler, Faili Meçhul Cinayet-Yargısız İnfazlar*.

Therefore, the official institutions of the state were enabled to deny their relations with the paramilitary groups during the investigations of acts of paramilitary violence.

Torture and Disappearances as Method of State Terror

Cizre was one of the places where the main characteristics of the conflict between the PKK and the Turkish state on a local scale became manifest. The most obvious aspect of this was the methods of violence used against civilians, such as torture and extrajudicial killings (as well as enforced disappearances and unsolved political murders). Taken as a whole, these comprised the methods of state terror as applied via semi-formal and informal forces, which, as a matter of public policy enacted by people in important administrative and military/security offices, amounted to a paramilitarisation of the state.

Unsolved political murder is used to identify the victims of murder assumed to be committed due to their political affiliation or thought, where the unknown perpetrator is thought to have committed the act of murder either for political reason or in the employ of someone or something that did have such a motive.[65] This definition is actually quite close to the definition of enforced disappearances, as will be discussed below. Victims often disappeared without leaving a trace, but in other instances their bodies were found in the countryside, near the places where they were apparently taken to be murdered. In the words of a repentant, when the perpetrators wanted the bodies to be found, they threw them randomly around in the countryside.[66] Some of the areas where the bodies were randomly thrown were around the killing sites in the countryside. This means that the perpetrators made the bodies disappear if they did not want the bodies to be found and did not bother with this otherwise (if there was no pressing reason to make extra effort to hide the deed or – more darkly, perhaps, a benefit of fear – terrorising the public – to be gained by the gruesome finds of the human remains). Thus, in fact, the enforced disappearances were mainly both

---

[65] TBMM, *Ülkemizin Çeşitli Yörelerinde İşlenmiş Faili Meçhul Siyasal Cinayetler Konusunda Meclis Araştırma Komisyonu* (Ankara: TBMM, 1995), 12.

[66] *Murat İpek ve Murat Demir'in İtirafları.*

unsolved murders and extrajudicial killings, certainly in terms of the result of the violence applied.

In Cizre, two methods of terror were used. Many people were tortured, others were murdered. The first method of terror during the conflict was torture.[67] According to the UN definition, the term 'torture' specifies actions done to punish, intimidate, or force a person to confess something.[68] Scholars discuss the purpose of torture through different models but similar meanings. Darius Rejali, for example, categorises torture according to three models: national security (to gain any kind of information that threatens national security), juridical (to force the confession of criminals and political opponents) and civic discipline (to discipline specific groups in society).[69] Ruth Blakeley analyses torture in terms of security (againstthreats), stability (as a tool of state terror to discipline and suppress potential or actual political opposition) and legitimacy (to claim the right to use torture is legitimised in certain circumstances, such as the 'War on Terror').[70]

The analyses of torture made by both these scholars refer to the gathering of information that could be a threat to national security, the intimidation and the punishment of certain groups of the population. Therefore, it should be emphasised that torture may be employed as an instrument of the state, so be a form of state terror that it implements for certain purposes. Scholars analyse

---

[67] See Başak Can's PhD dissertation for more detail on torture and its denial after the 1980 military coup in Turkey: 'State-Making, Evidence-Making, and Claim-Making: The Cases of Torture and Enforced Disappearances in Post-1980 Turkey' (PhD diss., University of Pennsylvania, 2014).

[68] *Convention Against Torture and Other Cruel, Inhuman or Degrading Treatment or Punishment*, No. A/RES/39/46 (Meeting no. 93, 10 December 1984). 'Torture means any act by which severe pain or suffering, whether physical or mental, is intentionally inflicted on a person for such purposes as obtaining from him or a third person information or a confession, punishing him for an act he or a third person has committed or is suspected of having committed, or intimidating or coercing him or a third person, or for any reason based on discrimination of any kind, when such pain or suffering is inflicted by or at the instigation of or with the consent or acquiescence of a public official or other person acting in an official capacity. It does not include pain or suffering arising only from, inherent in or incidental to lawful sanctions.'

[69] Darius Rejali, *Torture and Democracy* (Princeton, NJ: Princeton University Press, 2009).

[70] Ruth Blakeley, 'Why Torture?', *Review of International Studies* 33, no. 3 (2007): 373–94.

torture in Turkey similarly.[71] Discussions on the methods and purposes of torture in Turkey can also be considered using this three-pronged analysis (i.e. to acquire information, to punish and to intimidate).

Many of the people who were arrested in Turkey as a part of its new war strategy were subjected to intense torture. According to a HRW report published in 2000, 'more than 450 people have died in police custody, apparently as a result of torture in the two decades since the 1980 military coup'.[72] Table 5.1 shows the number of people who died as a result of violence during detention or interrogation.

Table 5.1 Suspicious deaths and deaths by torture in detention and prisons in Turkey (1992–2000). [Data from: *Türkiye İnsan Hakları Raporu 1991*, 77; *Türkiye İnsan Hakları Raporu 1992*, 107; *Türkiye İnsan Hakları Raporu 1993*, 178; *Türkiye İnsan Hakları Raporu 1994*, 187; *Türkiye İnsan Hakları Raporu 1995*, 259; *Türkiye İnsan Hakları Raporu 1996*, 322; *Türkiye İnsan Hakları Raporu 1997*, 233; *Türkiye İnsan Hakları Raporu 1998*, 221; *Türkiye İnsan Hakları Raporu 1999*, 115–21; *Türkiye İnsan Hakları Raporu 2000*, 85, all (Ankara: TİHV-Türkiye İnsan Hakları Vakfı).]

1991	1992	1993	1994	1995	1996	1997	1998	1999	2000
23	17	29	34	19	32	14	15	10	3

Cizre was one of the places where many detainees were tortured. People arrested in Cizre were frequently tortured by members of paramilitary groups, in some instances working together with official military and police units.

For example, the group responsible for the torture and disappearance of Selami Çiçek on 10 June 1994 was a JİTEM unit. When his family found his

---

[71] Gilles Dorronsoro, 'La Torture Discrète: Capital Social, Radicalisation Et Désengagement Militant Dans Un Régime Sécuritaire', *European Journal of Turkish Studies – Social Sciences on Contemporary Turkey*, no. 8 (31 December 2008), http://journals.openedition.org/ejts/2223; Murat Paker and Burcu Buğu, 'Türkiye'de İşkence Mağdurlarının Psikolojisi Üzerine Yapılmış Araştırmaların Gözden Geçirilmesi', *Türk Psikoloji Yazıları*, no. 19 [Özel Sayı] (Kasım 2016): 76–92.

[72] 'Preventing Torture', Human Rights Watch, 2000, https://www.hrw.org/reports/2000/turkey2/Turk009-01.htm.

body, two days later after he had been picked up, it was clear that he had been exposed to intense torture. According to a relative of Selami Çiçek, he had been taken from a crowded bus station by a group of people in civilian clothes who had arrived in a white Renault car and stated, 'We'll take Selami to the police station.'[73] Later, when the brothers of Selami went to the police station in Cizre, officials at the station said that there was no such person there. The brothers went on to the Cizre gendarmerie station and then to two other police and gendarmerie stations, in İdil and Silopi (both in the Şırnak province), to no avail.

Selami Çiçek's body was found in an unmarked grave in Silopi after indications by officials of the municipality:

> [A man] had been killed in Çatak Yolu, a rural area between Cizre and Silopi. His body had been thrown in there somewhere. Nitric acid had been spilt on his body. They put a bullet in his head and burnt his face, eyes and body. They told Çiçek's family that the nameless man they had buried had a scar on his belly.[74]

For a relative of Çiçek, this was proof it was him. They took the body of Selami to Cizre and buried him there. The torture of Selami and the appearance of his body after two days show that the paramilitary group specifically aimed at two of the purposes of the torture mentioned above. The first purpose was to punish Selami. The second was to threaten his family and friends (i.e. send a message of warning to his social environment). His brother said that they were, indeed, later threatened.[75] Forcing Selami to confess or getting information from him was probably the last option of the perpetrators. In Turkey in the 1990s, interrogations would sometimes take weeks, even months, so the appearance of the body in just two days indicates that the perpetrators' intent was not to gain information, to punish the person and warn those connected to him more than to interrogate him.

The emphasis here is placed on the observations of those who were tortured for allegedly being pro-PKK. People who had been arrested and sent

---

[73] Interview conducted with Ç.T. in Cizre, Archive of Truth Justice Memory Centre, 4 December 2012, Hafıza Merkezi Arşivi.
[74] Ibid.
[75] Ibid.

to prison said in my interviews that the torture methods of the military and paramilitary groups were various and very heavy. One interviewee was shot and wounded by JİTEM members outside of Cizre. He said that those who shot him had repeatedly threatened him and that he had to flee to Europe.[76] Two other interviewees said that they had been tortured by JİTEM.[77] Some of the torture methods can be listed as follows: being kept in custody for a long time (beyond the official detention period), removal of teeth, electric shocks, being kept in a very small cell for days, verbal abuse, listening to the torture of others, beatings, being forced to become a confessor, removal to a rural area, being threatened with death with a gun at their head, being left hungry or thirsty, being prevented from going to the toilet, sexual assault, threats of rape, being kept in the cold, being given leftover food, *strappado* (Palestinian hanging),[78] the burning of parts of the body with electricity. The list goes on.[79] The implementation of these torture methods probably varied according to the purposes of the torture. When the interviewees questioned for this study mentioned similar methods, however, these were generally used during the interrogations in the 1990s, suggesting a level of commonality, or standard practices. The repentants and Village Guards who knew the local dynamics and PKK cadres played a very important role in the interrogation teams.[80]

The main purposes of these torture sessions were the gathering of intelligence, the punishment of opponents and intimidation of those who were thought to sympathise with the PKK. However, the long periods of interrogation demonstrate that – beyond pure 'sadism', that is, assuming rationality, a logical purpose – people were tortured mainly for gathering intelligence.

---

[76] Interview #13, conducted in Cologne, 14 February 2017.

[77] Interview #38, conducted in Amsterdam, 25 May 2018; Interview #28, conducted in Spaubeek, 28 June 2017.

[78] The victim is secured to a rope and made to fall from a height almost to the ground before being stopped with an abrupt jerk.

[79] Interview #28, conducted in Spaubeek, 28 June 2017; Interview #38, conducted in Amsterdam, 25 May 2018.

[80] 'Village guards and informants play a special role in the "interrogation team": The "localization" of the mechanism of killing and the transmission of local relationships, social texture and its information is essentially carried out by village guards and informants.' Göral *et al.*, *The Unspoken Truth: Enforced Disappearances*, 32.

At the end of this torture process, people were sometimes released; mostly though they were arrested, and many were forcibly disappeared. The interrogations of the security forces thus resulted in three distinct consequences: the target (victim) was either released after the interrogation, arrested and sent to prison, or killed. Some of the people killed during the interrogation disappeared and their bodies remained unfound.

The second method of state terror during the civil war was the widespread implementation of enforced disappearances. In order to better understand the specific example of the enforced disappearances in Cizre, an overview may be first gained by looking at the definition in the literature and some examples from elsewhere in the world.

Enforced disappearance by security forces of the state or by groups associated with the state is one of the most extreme methods of violence against an individual who is thought to be threatening the regime.[81] In 1978, the situation of disappeared persons was discussed by the General Assembly of the United Nations.[82] 'The disappeared are stripped of all their rights and placed, defenseless, at the mercy of their victimisers, with no legal protection,' was the characterisation given by the Geneva Commission.[83] The lack of a grave is also included in the lack of human rights:

> Leaving a dead person unburied is a political act as much as it is tragic. Although burial rites show diversity in different cultures and religions, in most societies, the burial of the dead is a tradition, law or obligation.[84]

Therefore, to leave a person without a grave creates a serious break in the cultural continuity of the individual and society.[85] In this respect, the absence

[81] Jeremy Sarkin and Grażyna Baranowska, 'Why Enforced Disappearances Are Perpetrated against Groups as State Policy: Overlaps and Interconnections between Disappearances and Genocide', *Catholica Law Review*, 2018.

[82] 'Disappeared Persons', Pub. L. No. UN-General Assembly, 33/173 158 (1978), http://www.un.org/documents/ga/res/33/ares33r173.pdf.

[83] *Enforced Disappearance and Extrajudicial Execution: Investigation and Sanction: A Practitioners Guide* (Geneva: International Commission of Jurists, 2015), 5.

[84] Göral *et al.*, *The Unspoken Truth: Enforced Disappearances*, 70–1.

[85] Ibid., 69–76.

of a grave separates enforced disappearances from extrajudicial killings and unsolved murders. Many military juntas, dictatorships and one-party regimes across the world have implemented enforced disappearances as a systematic method of violence to maintain their control of state power.[86] The most well-known example of enforced disappearance as a policy and programme was that of the military junta regime in Argentina in 1976–83.[87] Enforced disappearances are mainly defined in law, but are also a historical and sociological phenomenon.[88]

The disappearance of the opponents forcibly removed by the regime not only extinguishes the lives of the individuals themselves but also operates as a warning to and punishment of the entire social and political community they belonged to. In other words, it involves the intimidation of the relatives, friends and associates of the disappeared, and thus a part of the

---

[86] Alpkaya, '"Kayıp"lar Sorunu Ve Türkiye', *Ankara Üniversitesi SBF Dergisi* 50, no. 3 (1995): 34–5; Göral *et al.*, *The Unspoken Truth: Enforced Disappearances*, 15; Marthe Lot Vermeulen, *Enforced Disappearance: Determining State Responsibility under the International Convention for the Protection of All Persons from Enforced Disappearance* (Cambridge: Intersentia, 2012), 2–5.

[87] Francesca Lessa, 'Beyond Transitional Justice: Exploring Continuities in Human Rights Abuses in Argentina between 1976 and 2010', *Journal of Human Rights Practice* 3, no. 1 (1 March 2011): 25–48; Emilio Crenzel, 'Argentina's National Commission on the Disappearance of Persons: Contributions to Transitional Justice', *International Journal of Transitional Justice* 2, no. 2 (1 July 2008): 173–91, https://doi.org/10.1093/ijtj/ijn007; Nazan Üstündağ, *Dealing With the Past: Argentinean Experience* (Istanbul: Anadolu Kültür-Truth, Justice and Memory Studies, 2011), https://hakikatadalethafiza.org/wp-content/uploads/2015/02/ARG_Report_EN.pdf.

[88] United Nations, *International Convention for the Protection of All Persons from Enforced Disappearance* (Geneva: United Nations Human Rights Office of the High Commissioner, 1992), https://www.ohchr.org/EN/HRBodies/CED/Pages/ConventionCED.aspx. 'Enforced disappearance' is defined according to the 'Declaration on the Protection of All Persons from Enforced Disappearance adopted by the General Assembly of the United Nations in its resolution 47/133 of 18 December 1992' as follows: 'Enforced disappearance is considered to be the arrest, detention, abduction or any other form of deprivation of liberty by agents of the State or by persons or groups of persons acting with the authorization, support or acquiescence of the State, followed by a refusal to acknowledge the deprivation of liberty or by concealment of the fate or whereabouts of the disappeared person, which place such a person outside the protection of the law.'

enactment of state terror as a weapon. Gökçen Alpkaya, who was one of the first scholars to analyse the cases of enforced disappearance in Turkey in the mid-1990s, argues that the purpose of this type of violence is as follows. The first purpose is to neutralise the 'enemy'. Secondly, it is the choice of a shorter way rather than elimination/punishment of opponents within the bounds of the legal system, which will take a (relatively) long time. Third, it functions to pacify the relatives of disappeared persons, whose subsequent actions are constrained by the possibility that the disappeared is still alive. Finally, it exempts the perpetrators from accountability and punishment and thus provides them with a freedom of action.[89] The chilling of the social and political environment of the disappeared person can be added to these purposes. Thus, this method of eliminating the opposition was frequently implemented by the Turkish state and paramilitary groups in the 1990s.[90] We might very reasonably argue that the enforced disappearances were one of the most important forms of violence carried out as a result of the (LIC) war approach from 1991 onwards.

Cizre had a distinctive characteristic in terms of the type and level of paramilitary violence (as compared to other areas in northern Kurdistan). In terms of quantity, it was among the places where the most enforced disappearances took place.[91] The method of elimination of the civilians was mainly carried out by paramilitary groups.[92] Turkish military and paramilitary forces were reorganised with the new war concept both numerically and 'qualitatively'.[93] In addition, paramilitary groups were predominantly transformed from intelligence units into death squads, which was mostly denied.[94] Therefore, enforced disappearances were carried out outside the law by groups that did not have any responsibility under the law, enabling plausible deniability for the state authorities.

[89] Alpkaya, '"Kayıp"lar Sorunu Ve Türkiye', 36.

[90] Göral et al., The Unspoken Truth: Enforced Disappearances.

[91] Ibid., 24.

[92] Göral Birinci, 'Enforced Disappearance and Forced Migration in the Context of Kurdish Conflict', 64.

[93] Balta Paker, 'Dış Tehditten İç Tehdide', 407–32.

[94] Kılıç, JITEM, 203–10.

Table 5.2 Enforced disappearances in Cizre (1991–9). 'As for figures regarding the disappeared in Şırnak, according to our tentative data, a total of 211 people were forcibly disappeared in Şırnak province and its districts since 12 September 1980; Cizre is the district where the highest number of enforced disappearances took place with 79 people . . .' [Data from: Özgür Sevgi Göral *et al.*, *The Unspoken Truth: Enforced Disappearances* (Istanbul: Truth Justice Memory Center, 2013), 92–104, quote 31.]

1991	1992	1993	1994	1995	1996	1997	1998	1999
1	–	11	28	2	–	–	–	–

Table 5.3 Unsolved murders and extrajudicial executions in Cizre (1991–9). [Data from: *Zorla Kaybedilenler, Faili Meçhul Cinayet-Yargısız İnfazlar, Toplu Mezarlar Raporu* (Diyarbakır: İnsan Hakları Derneği, 2014), 126–227.]

1991	1992	1993	1994	1995	1996	1997	1998	1999
8	21	39	58	7	4	12	–	3

The figures in Tables 5.2 and 5.3 were taken from two different NGOs. They may not provide exact information and numbers. Possible reasons for any inaccuracies include a lack of a research commission to investigate officially, inaccessible state archives, lack of adequate investigation by tribunals and prosecutors, and the attempt by state institutions to prevent NGO work. Some of the names of people who were disappeared or killed in this way are not listed, and some names are given both in the list of enforced disappearances and in that of unsolved murders. The point to be emphasised with these numbers is the years when violence escalated. Between 1992 and 1997 (peaking in '94) was the most intense period of paramilitary violence. These years coincide with the time when the two paramilitary actors, Temizöz and Atağ controlled Cizre, politically and militarily.

Beyond the geostrategic importance of Cizre, a primary purpose of the implementation of very intense violence in Cizre was to break the political ties between the PKK and civilian population. Haydar Darıcı argues that military and paramilitary forces killed the PKK's militia or its supporters in the city to purposefully break the opposition relationship with the Kurdish community in Cizre.[95] The main intention of the paramilitaries was to frighten the pro-PKK populace, and also to eliminate people who had the characteristics of being public leaders and thus the potential to lead a future 'threat'. For this reason, well-known people in Cizre society were targeted. The disappearance and murder of politically active public leaders in Cizre was a form of violence that the paramilitary group frequently implemented.[96]

Interviews with people who lived in Cizre in the 1990s demonstrate that there were two main methods of enforced disappearances. First, the military, police and paramilitary groups would take one person into custody, who would then disappear.[97] This was the most common method. The missing person was first followed by official and/or unofficial units of the state and captured and then disappeared outside the city, or else they were detained and disappeared when crossing military or police checkpoints.[98] The arrest and disappearance of Ali Karagöz was a very clear example of the first, frequently practised method.

Ali Karagöz was detained in December 1993 and then disappeared, but his family did not find the body, even though the team that came to detain Ali Karagöz was quite large, including as it did elements of the gendarmerie, JİTEM, Special Police Teams and the Village Guards. The wife of Ali Karagöz narrates the moment of detention:

> Our house was in Cudi neighbourhood . . . It was Kamil Atağ's period and he was leader of Village Guard at that period which was the period of Cemal Temizöz. As you know, he was a Village Guard at that time and they came and invaded my house while my husband was sleeping. They came and took away him at six o'clock. They took him out of the house, and I asked 'What will you do him?' and they answered that they would take him there and after speaking to him they'd let him go. They said he would come now. I thought they were being honest . . . Cemal Temiz[öz] was the sergeant of that time . . . At those

---

[95] Haydar Darıcı, 'Savaş Zamanında Aşiret Hukuku', unpublished article, 2018.

[96] Interview #12, conducted in Cologne, 13 February 2017.

[97] Interview conducted with Ö.T. in Cizre, Archive of Truth Justice Memory Centre, 2 September 2012, Hafıza Merkezi Arşivi.

[98] Interview conducted with B.G. in Cizre, Archive of Truth Justice Memory Center, 4 September 2012, Hafıza Merkezi Arşivi.

times, all of these places were under his control. They came and invaded my house by taking my husband. They did it. Kamil Atağ, Kukel Atağ, Temel Atağ and Cemal Temiz[öz] took my husband away.[99]

The case and quotes obviously show that those people who disappeared were detained by the paramilitary forces. As mentioned earlier, Selami Çiçek had been detained by a small JİTEM group and his severely tortured body was later found. However, Karagöz had been detained by Temizöz, Atağ and their teams, and his body has never been found.

The other method of disappearance was that people left their homes and were simply never heard from again. Usually, witnesses informed the family of the disappeared person. Sometimes, the family heard about their fate from people who were detained at the same time and released afterwards. In other cases, witnesses reported how the disappeared person was detained at a checkpoint. Sometimes, the security forces acknowledged they had detained the missing person and then released him. But if there were no witnesses, they would say, 'We don't know, we don't have any information.' Some information about disappearances came to light through the release of the repentants' memoirs.[100] Failing any evidence, this second method of disappearance could be more easily denied by the state institutions.

Although the main form of violence in Batman was the unsolved murders, the forced disappearances were the most obvious method of paramilitary violence used against civilians in Cizre. Comparing Batman and Cizre directly may be problematic because Batman is a province and Cizre is a district. However, a consideration of the numbers available for the 1990s does enable a basic comparison of the violence. In Batman, between 1992 and 1997, 277 unsolved murders and sixty enforced disappearances were committed.[101] In Cizre, there were 152 unsolved murders and forty-two enforced disappearances in that

[99] Interview conducted with A.K. in Cizre, Archive of Truth Justice Memory Center, 2 September 2012, Hafıza Merkezi Arşivi.
[100] Nevzat Çiçek, İtirafçı, 1. baskı (Istanbul: Timaş Yayınları, 2009); Balık, Kerberos.
[101] Türkiye İnsan Hakları Raporu 1992, 65–70; Türkiye İnsan Hakları Raporu 1993, 149–58; Türkiye İnsan Hakları Raporu 1994, 130–8; Türkiye İnsan Hakları Raporu 1995, 169–72; Türkiye İnsan Hakları Raporu 1996, 228–30; Türkiye İnsan Hakları Raporu 1997, 138–46; Göral et al., The Unspoken Truth: Enforced Disappearances, 24–5.

period. Also, there were certain places around Cizre where unsolved political murders were probably committed since bodies were found. In other words, the bodies of the murdered and disappeared were sometimes found. This may be taken as evidence to suggest the impunity enjoyed, since there was little to no fear of any 'justice' being done, but it may equally point to the aim to terrorise, since the message that was sent became crystal clear when mutilated, tortured bodies were located.

In Batman, the assassins or death squads were hidden, and they usually came from other regions. But everyone in Cizre knew the members of JİTEM and the Village Guards who cooperated with them, and it is possible to follow the traces of this relationship in court documents.[102] In this respect also, there were differences between the two places. Every aspect of the violence (the form of violence, the perpetrators, the killing zones and so on) was quite public in Cizre. This is what most distinguishes Cizre from other regions, that the semi-official and informal paramilitary groups were an entirely open secret.[103] The interviewers knew the perpetrators' names, their faces and their methods of violence. The four paramilitaries all took an active role in human rights violations in Cizre (including the unsolved murders and disappearances). That the Village Guards leader was the mayor enabled a political control that allowed the guards to operate with considerable ease. The special police units collaborated with other paramilitary groups in the detention of civilians. Also, the power of the repentants in the Cizre JİTEM was greater and, despite their being members of JİTEM, the entire population of the town knew them. Consequently, although many of the disappeared peoples' bodies were not found, the mechanism of the paramilitary groups that carried out the acts was quite visible.

One of the features of the violence in Cizre was the existence of certain killing sites (Botaş, Kuştepe village and the surroundings of military garrisons in the area). According to the testimonies of the repentants, people who were detained were sometimes killed during interrogation and disposed of in particular places in the countryside, but sometimes people who were detained

[102] 'Temizöz ve Diğerleri Davası – İddianame'.

[103] Interview conducted with Ü.F. and Ü.A. in Cizre, Archive of Truth Justice Memory Center, 5 September 2012, Hafıza Merkezi Arşivi; Interview conducted with A.Ş. in Cizre, 2012.

were taken to the countryside, interrogated and killed there.[104] These killing sites used by paramilitary groups in and around Cizre were well known by the local population. The bodies of those killed by the paramilitary groups in Cizre were usually found in the rural area, outside the city centre. According to the security rules in Turkey, police are responsible for the security of the urban areas and the gendarmerie for the rural.[105] The official division of labour of the security forces could not occur in Cizre, because the semi-formal and informal forces were controlling the district (i.e. as a whole). However, the rural area was the responsibility of the gendarmerie, and the bodies of the murdered people were generally found in the rural area. The reason for this was that JİTEM, the most active paramilitary force, was affiliated to the gendarmerie.

There were two places in particular where the bodies of those that had been killed were found.[106] One of these killing sites was between Cizre and Silopi, where bodies and bones were found in and around the well of the state-owned Petroleum Pipeline Company (*Boru Hatları ile Petrol Taşıma*, BOTAŞ), where there was also a military area.[107] The other known killing site was at Kuştepe, a small village opposite the military garrison just north of Cizre where Hizbullah supporters lived.

JİTEM had its repentants. One describes their actions as 'doing the job' and summarises the process from detention to murder: '*Doing the job* means taking a man illegally, taking him to JİTEM, interrogating him, then executing him, throwing his dead body out, burning or burying him.'[108] Another repentant recruited around Cizre said, 'We randomly threw out the bodies we wanted people to find.'[109] Whether or not the body was to be found could be

---

[104] Balık, *Kerberos*; Çiçek, *İtirafçı*, 125–41; Neşe Düzel, 'JİTEM İtirafçısı Abdülkadir Aygan Anlatıyor', *Taraf Gazetesi*, 29 January 2009; *Murat İpek ve Murat Demir'in İtirafları*.

[105] 'Jandarma Teşkilatı Görev ve Yetkileri Yönetmeliği', accessed 12 September 2018, http://www.kanuntr.com/kanunlar/20109.html.

[106] 'Cizre'deki Kayıp Kazısında da 20'ye Yakın Kemik Bulundu', *Bianet – Bağımsız İletişim Ağı*, 17 March 2009, http://www.bianet.org/bianet/insan-haklari/113182-cizre-deki-kayip-kazisinda-da-20-ye-yakin-kemik-bulundu.

[107] Göral et al., *The Unspoken Truth: Enforced Disappearances*, 43.

[108] Düzel, 'JİTEM İtirafçısı Abdülkadir Aygan Anlatıyor'.

[109] *Murat İpek ve Murat Demir'in İtirafları*.

determined by the position and importance of the murdered person in society as well as the message to be sent to the family and others.

The violence carried out by the perpetrators in Cizre did not end with the killing or disappearance of the targeted person. In almost all interviews at the Truth Justice Memory Centre (*Hakikat Adalet Hafıza Merkezi*), the relatives of disappeared people were warned not to follow the fate of their lost ones. The experiences of the family of Selami Çiçek were quite dramatic in this regard. According to his brother, Selami's family was warned to stop following the case:

> We got a secret call. They said, 'Don't investigate, don't show any interest, or we'll kill you, too.' . . . We didn't know what to do now. We waited. Then we went to the public prosecutor's office and said we had a problem. The prosecutor said, 'Go back home, the whole world [i.e. northern Kurdistan] is like that, we can't do anything.'[110]

Similarly, a relative of Ali Karagöz submitted many petitions to find out the whereabouts of her husband after he was disappeared, but she did not receive a response:

> I went and gave my petitions in to the government office. They lost my petitions. I gave almost twenty petitions, and they lost them.[111]

Statements by relatives like these and the narratives of other missing families demonstrate that various institutions of the state cooperated to hide what was happening in the 1990s. In the search for justice after the incident, the attitude relatives faced at the prosecution office, district governorship office and the police station could all be characterised as follows: the petitions were not accepted; the relatives were threatened. Beyond this even, members of the paramilitary group in Cizre would demand a ransom from relatives in exchange for the release of the detained person, but after the money was taken, the detained person was not released.[112] In fact, acquiring ransom

---

[110] Interview conducted with Ç.T. in Cizre, 2012.
[111] Interview conducted with K.A. in Cizre, 2012.
[112] Interview conducted with M.Ö. in Cizre, Archive of Truth Justice Memory Centre, 12 October 2012, Hafıza Merkezi Arşivi; Interview conducted with İ.B. and İ.İ. in Cizre, Archive of Truth Justice Memory Centre, 12 October 2012, Hafıza Merkezi Arşivi.

monies was an important economic gain and thus part of the process of the disappearances.

Although these paramilitary groups acted autonomously in the local area, they still took instructions from the Ankara-based institutions of the state. The actions they committed were the local consequences of a general state strategy. Here, a shopkeeper from Cizre describes the disappearance of his neighbour and the relationship between paramilitary groups and state institutions in a conversation with a high-ranking soldier:

I was a shopkeeper in Cizre, and I witnessed an incident at that time. I was living in the Yafes neighborhood. We had a very young and wonderful neighbor
and friend named L. One day L got sick, bought medicine from the shop and
came home . . . There were witnesses who saw him. He was taken away in a
military vehicle. There are people who saw this. We did some research and his
father went to the chief of police. At that time there was Mr. Hayri [as chief of
police], I think that was his name. [The father] said 'You are the police chief . . .
They've kidnapped my son, please help me, hand him over to me . . .'

'If he's here, if I learn anything, I'll let you know', replied the police chief.
However, there are some dangerous [lit.: transgressor] people, no one can play
with them. If it's them who kidnapped him, there's nothing I can do.'

He meant the JİTEM. That is what he told the father. In the morning, we
found L murdered on the road between Cizre and İdil. He used to took care of
his whole family. That's how they killed him. There were officers and polices in
JİTEM. And, it was headed by Cemal Temizöz.

They were operating in the knowledge of the state. It was a state politics;
they were not gangs. One day, I had a conversation with a major in İdil battalion.
We talked about what was happening. He said that they didn't really have anything in their control, the orders came from above. If they were told to go and
bury Cizre and Silopi alive, they had to do it. Anyone who spoke would have his
head chopped off. They didn't do what they wanted; they did what they were
ordered to do. He said it was not their fault. It was a major who said this.[113]

Conclusion

Cizre differed from other Kurdish provinces in terms of the type of parami-li-
tary violence that occurred there. Paramilitary violence in Cizre continued

---

[113] Interview #17, conducted in Istanbul, 10 May 2017.

intensively throughout the 1990s. The period from 1993 to 1996 was when the perpetrators used the most intense violence, particularly unsolved murders and enforced disappearances. This was related to the implementation of the new war strategy, but its distinguishing characteristics in Cizre were the dominance of the paramilitary group, its control over the state institutions in the district and the autonomy the group's leaders enjoyed. Therefore, Cizre was one of the regions where paramilitarisation of state institutions was observed most prominently. The intensity of this strategy decreased after 1996.

Importantly, the members and leaders of the paramilitary groups were quite autonomous, sanctioned from Ankara and acting independently of the authority of the state's military and administrative institutions (but able to rely on their support for their 'work'). They established a separate, informal organisation, arranging for members of the different groups to work together as a large, loose-knit team. One of the leaders of this organisation of paramilitary groups in Cizre was the gendarmerie regional commander of the state, and the other was a leader of the local tribe and the Village Guards. Intertwined relations between state-sponsored informal and semi-formal armed forces under the leadership of those two actors resulted in the freedom of action of what was to be realised as a death squad. This unit was the most responsible for the extreme violence in Cizre.

Indeed, one of the most important aspects for Cizre's consideration as a case was the form and level of violence that took place there. Although Cizre became a place of violence as a whole, certain areas are still known in the memory of those living there as the killing sites. Demonstrably expressing impunity as a weapon of terror, the paramilitary groups in Cizre were known by everyone. The violence they meted out was extremely public. The extrajudicial killings, unsolved murders and enforced disappearances created a wave of state violence enacted through paramilitary groups. The paramilitary groups and their violence were so obvious in Cizre that it appears they were purposely sending a public message to the area where the PKK started its armed struggle. The message stated that, first, there was a price for civilians in supporting the PKK, and second, state power was active in the local area.

The torture, unsolved murders and enforced disappearances as forms of violence are still very clear in the minds of the relatives of the victims and witnesses. They remember because their pain is still very much alive; not

just because of the brutalising trauma but also because of how this was compounded when the state institutions denied the mass violence implemented
by the state-backed paramilitary forces, refused to investigate properly and
avoided any responsibility. The plausible deniability of state-backed paramilitary violence has been adopted by many states.[114] It naturally has a role that
prevents the investigation of murders and disappearances.

Therefore, transitional justice remained as the sole demand of the relatives
of the victims (of disappearances, unsolved murders and the other human
rights violations).[115] Impunity forces people to constantly re-narrate their
stories in an expectation of justice, but the testimony of the relatives of the
disappeared may be important in assessing the level and form of paramilitary
violence and the roles of perpetrators. In 2009, a case related to the unsolved
political murders and the disappearances committed in Cizre in the 1990s did
come to trial. The case began as a result of political conflicts between the state
elites in Turkey, and a verdict was finally reached in 2015. Eight defendants,
including Temizöz and Atağ, were sued in what became known as the 'JİTEM
case' in relation to the killings and disappearances of twenty-one people for the
crime of 'forming an entity with the intention of committing crimes, joining
this entity by becoming a member, killing individuals and instigating to kill'.[116]
The impunity policy was maintained in this 'cold case' with a complete acquit-
tal due to the lack of evidence.[117]

---

[114] Campbell, 'Death Squads', 1–26; Ron, 'Territoriality and Plausible Deniability', 287–312.

[115] Göral et al., The Unspoken Truth: Enforced Disappearances, 82.

[116] 'Suç: Cürüm işlemek için teşekkül oluşturmak ve bu teşekküle katılarak mensubu olmak,
adam öldürmeye azmettirmek, adam öldürmek'. Indictment filed at Diyarbkır High
Court, Investigation No. 2009/906 (14.7.2009), https://www.failibelli.org/wp-content/
uploads/2013/02/Temizoz_Iddianame.pdf.

[117] '. . . inandırıcı delil elde edilemediği ve yüklenen suçun sanık tarafından işlendiği sabit
olmadı. . .' Minutes of the Proceedings of Eskişehir 2nd High Court, Case No. 2015/47
(5.11.2015), https://www.failibelli.org/wp-content/uploads/2013/02/Temiz%C3%B6z_
Davasi_Beraat_Karari.pdf.

CONCLUSION: THE CONTINUITY OF THE RELIABLE AND DENIABLE PARAMILITARY HISTORY IN TURKEY

The Turkish state was built with the support of the continuity of an ideologically reliable, institutionally deniable paramilitary legacy. Although the government systems have changed, from the Empire to Republic and from a single-party regime to a multi-party system, for over a hundred years, Turkish state elites have regularly used paramilitary groups as a deterrent, as an intimidatory and punitive tool against opposition, especially the Kurds. Enjoying the monopoly on the use of violence that defines the modern state is incomplete for Turkey as well as for Middle Eastern states in general since the monopoly on violence is shared with subcontractor paramilitary groups. Therefore, these reliable paramilitaries, which are used against groups that the state encodes as opponents or enemies, are among the strongest yet at the same time most invisible pillars on which the country is built.

Paramilitary groups are used across the globe as a pro-state apparatus in internal conflicts and domestic problems. Although state elites use these groups mainly to suppress dissident voices within the country, they sometimes employ paramilitaries as part of state strategy abroad. Additionally, paramilitary groups have not only been exported abroad, but also imported, as seen in the conflicts that razed Kurdish cities in 2015–16. Some groups that fought alongside Turkish forces in the Syrian civil war were brought into the fighting in the Kurdish provinces. There was also testimony in my interviews that many people in the paramilitary groups used in the 2015–16 conflict were over the age of fifty. One of my interviewees, a politician who witnessed the conflicts both in the 1990s and in 2015–16, explained this situation as follows:

> In one of his speeches, just before [the destruction of] Cizre, Erdoğan said, 'We will utilise our experienced operation forces, our security forces who have worked in the region before, when we destroy these trenches.' Then we saw 50–55 year old men, with grey hair, with automatic weapons in their hands, shouting Allahu akbar. Those called experienced were people who had served in Kurdistan in the 1990s.[1]

This illustrates that the state elites have benefited from the experience of the paramilitaries of the 1990s. In other words, some groups that had been deactivated after the 1990s were reactivated when needed in 2015.

It should also be added that the paramilitaries used in internal conflicts sometimes have serious effects on the politics of the state due to their relations and influence. Such periods may be referred to as the *paramilitarisation of the state*. The main aspects of this can be explained in a few points, as involving (1) domination of state institutions (parliament, judiciary, army) and politics by paramilitary groups; (2) increasingly complex illegal relations between various government agencies, paramilitary groups and gangs; (3) the usage of these complex relationships for economic gain/motivation; (4) the use of paramilitary forces instead of legally defined official armed forces during the conflicts; (5) the use of paramilitary groups against dissidents who oppose state policy; and (6) the illegalisation and deformation of state institutions.

The 1990s as a Symbol of Violence

Regarding the emergence, development and functions of paramilitary groups in the 1990s, various characteristics distinguish this period from others – a topic that has been discussed throughout the book. With a history of rebellion and resistance led by different political groups with different leaders, the political and sometimes violent struggle of Kurds had been a recurrent feature in the history of the Republic prior to the 1980s and the subsequent

---

[1] Interview #12, conducted in Cologne, 13 February 2017.

war between the PKK and the Turkish state.[2] One feature that distinguished this period of the 1990s from other periods of struggle and conflict was the intensity of state violence over a long period of time, almost ten years. The violence of the 1990s was a result of the experience the state had gained from violence enacted in previous periods and stands as a reference point for the violence subsequently deployed.

The end of the twentieth century was a period of significant transformations, not only in Turkey but across the world. The 1990s saw the end of the Cold War, the (First) Gulf War and the resurgence of genocides. Such political transformations, particular the end of the Cold War and the Gulf War, had a direct impact on Turkey's experience of the 1990s. The end of the Cold War and the growing influence of the PKK at the start of the decade led to a structural transformation of the Turkish Armed Forces and a change to their strategies (as discussed in Chapter 3). During the decade, the position and strategy of the PKK and the Kurds changed as a result of a series of popular uprisings (*serhildan*), with the growing popularity of the PKK making claims related to Kurds and Kurdistan more visible in Kurdish society. The end of the decade, however, saw the arrest of Öcalan in 1999 and his own shift of focus (from ethno-national statehood to local, bottom-up democracy), after which the PKK began to implement a strategy prioritising a discourse of peace.

From the perspective of the Republic, there were two key points that determined the rise and then fall of the paramilitarisation of the state in the 1990s. The first was the strategic shift adopted in 1991, comprising a decision to refashion the definition of threat to Turkey to the internal, PKK/Kurdish-ethnic threat rather than the external, Soviet/communist threat. This decision determined the character of both the army and politics, and set in motion the paramilitarisation of the state. The change has paramilitarised the institutions

---

[2] Academic studies meant to understand the 1990s and the nature of war then are ever expanding. See Onur Günay, 'Geçmişin İşlenmesi Ne Demektir?,' *Toplum ve Kuram*, no. 9 (2014): 13–30; Jongerden, *The Settlement Issue in Turkey and the Kurds*; Ayhan Işık *et al.*, eds, *1990'larda Kürtler ve Kürdistan*, 1st edn (Istanbul: Istanbul Bilgi Üniversitesi Yayınları, 2015); Akkaya, 'The Kurdistan Workers' Party (PKK)'; Göral Birinci, 'Enforced Disappearance and Forced Migration in the Context of Kurdish Conflict'; Güneş, *The Kurdish National Movement in Turkey*; Ayşen Uysal, ed., *İsyan, Şiddet, Yas: 90'lar Türkiyesine Bakmak* (Ankara: Dipnot Yayınları, 2016); Çelik, 'Temps Et Espaces De La Violence Interne'.

of the state, fused or blurred the military and the political, such that political ends were sought to be achieved by military means (violence, at all costs, etc.) and military ends were sought to be achieved by political means (extreme nationalism, obedience to the judiciary, etc.). As the role of paramilitary groups became more prominent in northern Kurdistan, their numbers and the forms of their actions altered.

The end of the Cold War and the increase in the influence of the PKK resulted in a range of transformations in Turkey. The conventional army, positioned according to NATO's threat definition, was made more mobile, in order to wage asymmetric warfare with the guerrilla. In politics, radical politicians who believed that the Kurdish issue would be solved by violence gained power in the government, and a network of secret relations formed from the bureaucrats, politicians and leaders of the mafia and paramilitary groups emerged. This development links to the second key point that determined the paramilitarisation of the state in the 1990s, referring, after the rise, to its fall. This was triggered by the infamous car accident at Susurluk in 1996, the 'Susurluk scandal'.

The political and military transformation with the new war doctrine determined the nature of paramilitary groups active in the 1990s, as these became the principal perpetrators of the violence carried out against civilians as an integral although unstated part of that doctrine – a key method by which field domination and territorial control was gained and maintained. Thus, the violence carried out in the 1990s exhibited important differences compared to that of previous periods. The Kurdish rebellions during the early Republic and the massacres that ensued generally lasted for a short period of time and were spatially limited. For instance, in the 1980s, the violence carried out in Diyarbakır prison was predominantly limited to that prison alone (even if similar torture methods were employed in other prisons). Thus, it is possible to speak of a limited geography and duration of violence in previous periods. The violence of the 1990s, however, lasted throughout the decade and encompassed all of northern Kurdistan.

In both temporal and spatial terms and the violence employed, the 1990s was simply the most intense period of conflict of the past century. It was a time of extreme violence, with the most extrajudicial killings, the most enforced disappearances, and the most burnings and destruction of villages and their lands.

And it was paramilitary groups that defined the nature of the state violence carried out during this period.

Without putting too fine a point on it, there are certain taboos in Turkey that have largely delimited the public discourse in both academic and popular life: the Armenian genocide is one, most of Kurdish history is another, and the bloody history of paramilitarism is a third. State institutions have approached JİTEM in like fashion. Consequently, the denial of the existence and operations of JİTEM by state institutions and general avoidance of the subject (wilfully, voluntarily and/or under duress) has largely been determined by the state. In the academic, English-language literature, there are analyses of paramilitary groups from Colombia to Indonesia, from the UK to Mozambique, making the lack of discussion of paramilitary groups in Turkey (with perhaps the partial exception, as noted, of the Village Guards) actually rather striking. This is particularly so in the context of the significance of the case of Turkey in the field, from where the phrase 'deep state' originated, with an original meaning that very much included paramilitaries. If we add to this list the ongoing nature of the conflict, which continues to make research in the field very difficult, and the contemporary political (and judicial) climate in Turkey, where many people are jailed for a wide range of actions determined quite vaguely as 'crimes' – including academics signing a peace petition objecting to the state's brutal treatment of Kurdish cities but who were legally charged as 'terrorists' – then the limitations in the literature on paramilitarism are understandable and perhaps inevitable, at least at this juncture.[3]

Paramilitary groups can be approached in different ways, including by the degree and nature of the use of violence, variations in their relationship to state

---

[3] Northern Kurdistan witnessed an intense escalation of violent conflict in the Summer of 2015 following the failure of two-year-long peace negotiations between the Turkish state and the Kurdish movement. During the one-year-long episode of political violence that continued into the summer of 2016, more than two thousand people were killed in Kurdish towns and cities. Furthermore, thousands of Kurdish activists were imprisoned, and the possibility of any public talk on the Kurdish conflict was suppressed with a violent veil of securitisation. In this process, more than two thousand academics ('Academics for Peace') who signed a 'peace petition' asking the state to end the violence on Kurdish settlements and civilians were also purged and put on trial on 'terrorism' charges.

institutions, and different stances vis-à-vis the law.[4] The main criteria adopted here when defining paramilitary groups has been their legal ties with state institutions, hierarchical positions or obfuscation of hierarchical responsibilities, roles in military and political strategies, semi-formal and informal organisational structures, legal responsibilities and extra-legal actions and violence, plausible deniability and economic gain.

This broad definition is based on the variety of reasons for these groups' foundation, their functions and their relations with state institutions in general, which were quite fragmentary and unclear. Moreover, much of the literature on paramilitary groups is not based on sources focusing on the paramilitary groups themselves, but emerges as a by-product of various debates on paramilitaries. That is, the concepts of paramilitarism or pro-government militias (PGMs) are either insufficiently employed in the literature or used out of context.

Therefore, I suggest that paramilitary groups as studied both in the literature and in the case of Turkey can be defined on the basis of the following criteria: (1) their existence as armed groups working in some capacity with the state (whose membership may be more or less fixed and recognised within and without the group, which is thus itself more or less clearly defined, to the point of a group having or not having a formal or agreed name, operational centre, etc.); (2) their hierarchical and administrative flexibility (unlike the official security forces of the state); (3) their active role in the military and/or political execution of strategies (from auxiliary forces to death squads); (4) the presence of different structures relative to those of the state's formal armed units (such as the official accounting procedures of the army and police, with their multilevel mechanisms for oversight, etc.); (5) legal flexibility (being theoretically bound under the law but actually protected, given considerable immunity and thus practically quite free), which allows state institutions to deny their existence (and thus permit, sponsor and order acts, particularly of violence, that are illegal); and (6) the economic gains from the acts they carry out (which may run to organised crime as a highly lucrative business and from which state

---

[4] Romain Malejacq, 'Pro-Government Militias', *Oxford Bibliographies*, 2017, http://www.oxfordbibliographies.com/abstract/document/obo-9780199743292/obo-9780199743292-0213.xml?rskey=QUF8FZ&result=1&q=pro-government+militias#firstMatch.

actors also profit). This listing represents a paradigm of core characteristics of paramilitary groups, not a definitive detailing of necessary and sufficient conditions for a group to be counted as such – indeed, the very nature of paramilitaries as blurry, shifting, hidden and secretive mitigates against such a thing.

Focusing on north Kurdistan in the 1990s, this book has defined and discussed the Ottoman and Turkish history, formation and functions of state-sponsored paramilitary groups used against the social and political opposition movements and the civilians who support them. It has also argued that the paramilitary groups are not just a tool of the state elites but also more 'reliable' than the army and police institutions for those elites. They are not accidental elements of the state's toolbox, but integral to its range of options and thus determinative of its approaches to major issues and future programmes, as well as involved in more detailed levels of policy.

The Mutable Structure of Turkish Paramilitarism

The main concern of this research, then, is how the paramilitary groups emerged, developed, functioned and then deactivated in the context of the war in Turkey in the 1990s. I have investigated the sub-questions of the study within the analytical framework of these aspects, intended to shed light on paramilitary groups (i.e. emergence, development, function and aftermath).

Paramilitary groups are formed for various reasons. In addition to groups that states deploy against oppositional forces, other groups are formed with the permission of those in power to protect certain sections of society that side with the state (mercenaries in Latin America being a well-known example).[5] Also, the counterinsurgency groups formed by colonialist states against the societies rebelling against colonialism are one of the important factors that led to the formation and spread of paramilitary groups during the twentieth century.

Paramilitary groups may further exhibit both quantitative and qualitative differences. From vigilante groups organised like gangs (according to certain ideological and economic motivations), to countless numbers of entities established to assist formal armed forces (from extensive tribal militias to death squads made up of a few people), the concept of the paramilitary is remarkable

---

[5] Mazzei, *Death Squads or Self-Defense Forces?*

broad. I have employed it here to refer to armed units that support the state. In the example of Turkey, paramilitary groups have generally been formed as either semi-formal or informal organisations, and when the reasons for their foundation periodically wane, these groups are either dispersed or deactivated. Such groups existed in different forms in the early twentieth century, and again emerged in the second half of the twentieth century. I have discussed how such groups were established to eliminate oppositional forces thought to constitute a threat to the existence of the state in the various conflicts of the 1990s, how they played a role as auxiliary forces in certain situations where state security forces were found lacking, and how they functioned nominally as the state, yet could also be used to carry out legally problematic actions that the state could deny any knowledge of or ties to.

Additionally, the paramilitary groups considered here also display differences in terms of membership, their position vis-à-vis the law, the levels of violence they employed, their relations to state institutions and their hierarchies and functions.[6] While some groups occupied a semi-formal position (e.g. Village Guards), the existence of others, such as JİTEM, is still denied by the state. What I mean by semi-formal is that these groups possess an organisational structure outside the state's official security forces such as army and police. Yet this situation shifted. For instance, the Special Warfare Department, ÖHD, established in the 1950s and funded by the USA, occupied a semi-formal, quite controversial space and was cited as responsible for a number of unsolved killings. In the beginning of the 1990s, however, it was transformed into a formal unit of the army. By contrast, among the army's formal divisions, some commando units exhibited paramilitary characteristics during combat actions. The same is true of the Special Police Teams. One indication of this is that even if the latter appears to be a special division of the police, most members in the 1990s belonged to an extreme nationalist party, not to the party of government, and the processes by which they were hired were less than legal. Thus, the lines between legality, semi-legality, and illegality in the formation and use of paramilitary groups are quite blurry and mercurial. This is further reflected in the position of the leaders of paramilitary groups.

[6] Malejacq, 'Pro-Government Militias'.

The leaders of JİTEM, for instance, were at the same time and to varying degrees commanders in gendarmerie units (e.g. Cem Ersever and Cemal
Temizgöz), and some leaders of the Village Guards, the largest paramilitary
group, were also MPs (Sedat Bucak) or local mayors (Kamil Atağ). However,
the relations with paramilitary groups formed and supported by ruling elites
were conducted largely through individuals rather than institutional structures.
The aim of this was to ensure that a formal relationship between and hierarchy
involving government agencies and paramilitary groups could be denied. There
is a well-known expression in Turkish politics that explains this situation as being
'out of routine'. When paramilitary groups or official institutions of the state
carried out an extra-legal action, the state elites say it is an individual action that
is out of routine (so unsanctioned). The shady relationships that emerged in the
Susurluk scandal were also named and described in this way. Therefore, there
was no institutional trace of the thousands of unsolved murders and enforced
disappearances for which paramilitary groups were mainly responsible.

Since the late 1980s, there had been frequent debates in the press with
regards to forming a large paramilitary army, a territorial force working alongside the state's military and political bureaucracy to battle the PKK.[7] This idea
never came to fruition and instead, paramilitary units of a smaller scale were
formed, with characteristics varying according to the particularities of different
provinces and even different sub-provincial districts. These small-scale units
were granted either a broad or more limited autonomy, depending on the strategic importance of the varied geographies in which they operated. Groups in
spaces where support for the PKK was significant and the conflict was intense
played a role in serious violations of basic rights to life, from extrajudicial killings to forced disappearances. Thus, in spaces where the PKK's presence was
relatively light and civilian support less widespread, the level of violence carried
out by the paramilitaries tended to be lower. Consequently, the functions of
such units depended on the conditions of conflict in the particular geographies
where they were stationed, as well as to the intensity of local civilians' demands
and uprisings (serhildanlar). For instance, while JİTEM was used frequently
in Şırnak and Diyarbakır, in Urfa, Village Guards from the Bucak tribe were
prioritised, and in Batman, Hizbullah.

---

[7] 'Sivil Orduya İsviçre Modeli', *Milliyet Gazetesi*, 11 April 1988; Sirmen, 'Teritoryal Tartışması'.

The state's establishment and use of such small-scale groups with functions tailored to different regions was a model that suited the doctrine of low-intensity warfare in place after 1991 far more than that of a large paramilitary group. The fact that spaces of conflict were so different from one another meant that a large paramilitary unit that would act similarly everywhere, possessing the same characteristics, would serve little function for the state. The strength of paramilitary groups was precisely their ability, through semi-formal and informal means, to fill gaps in the state's abilities in conflict due to legal or other reasons – the establishment of a large paramilitary army would not have been significantly different from the extant, official state army. Any violations of rights carried out against civilians by a large paramilitary force would be more visible relative to small-scale units, whose activities were harder to trace. Thus, the formation of groups that were more flexible – and unaccountable – in the face of the law, that could be deactivated when necessary, whose activities could be covered up or denied as required and whose hierarchical links to power were ambiguous was a more acceptable method for ruling elites.

After the second half of the 1980s, such groups were founded and/or transformed and used extensively, with their imprint gradually waning after 1996. The latter date is important from two perspectives. The first and most significant was the infamous traffic accident in Susurluk, as noted above. The second reason had to do with a pause or stalemate of sorts in the conflict between the PKK and the state; neither side was able to declare victory. The expectation of ruling elites when establishing paramilitary forces was that they would sever the ties between the PKK and Kurdish civilians. Yet, by 1997, despite thousands of extrajudicial killings and enforced disappearances, this vision had clearly failed to materialise. As mentioned above, one of the main objectives of the LIC strategy was a rupturing of the ties between civilians and the PKK. The paramilitary groups were among the actors of this strategy. The ruling elite argued that this strategy had achieved its goal because it had ensured its dominance in the countryside. PKK leaders argued that the strategy had not achieved its goal because ties between the Kurds and the PKK had become stronger. Hence, after Susurluk, the ruling elites began to slowly abandon the LIC strategy, at the centre of which were paramilitary groups. In time, the functions of these groups decreased, and many were partially deactivated.

The Legacy and Continuity of Paramilitarism in Turkey

This book has argued for the continuity of paramilitary groups used in the 1990s and the long life of their violence, exploring their historical legacies and ties to previous periods from a number of perspectives. It has defended the claim that there is a continuity to paramilitary groups and their methods of violence in terms of ideologies, institutions and individuals that spans the Ottoman Empire and the Republican period into the 1990s.[8] This continuity is not linear in form, yet, even with all the disjunctures, fractures and shifts it contains, a certain degree of continuity can be perceived. The structures and methods have been and are frequently returned to and constitute one of the chief precautions mobilised by Ankara in the face of threats to the state. One can certainly see the traces and continuity of the paramilitary politics employed by the state in the 1990s in the military operations that razed more than ten Kurdish cities between 2015 and 2016.

Although possessing a sizable army and police force, the Turkish state has responded to perceived threats from the left and oppositions, including and especially Kurds, by forming and deploying paramilitary groups. One reason for this has been that the mass security forces – the regular army and the police – are made up of people from all backgrounds and every ideological wing of society. Military service is required of every male citizen in Turkey, while the police force recruits new members through public announcements, so the ideological perspectives of the individuals serving in these forces may not match that of the state elites or meet the hegemonic requirements of the state ideology.

Since the late Ottoman period, an extreme Turkish nationalism resting on an assumed Sunni Islam has defined the political and ethno-religious core of the Turkish state tradition. In order to combat oppositional movements, Turkish state elites have tended to trust small-scale paramilitary groups composed of extreme nationalists rather than military or police organisations. Against an administrative/military state structure that has ruled the country for nearly a century founded on an ideological stance of extreme Turkish

---

[8] And this could be extended to today, with the employment of Islamicist groups in 2015–16, when the conflict was reignited, again for political purposes (regarding the government party's election failure) – see below.

nationalism, even if of differing political shades, the demands for rights and equality by social groups of different identities have been continuously suppressed. Thus, the state has consistently made a point to keep alive an understanding of oppositional movements as internal threats, which in turn has led to the continued existence and use of paramilitary groups, if in different forms. I argue that this is the main reason why such paramilitary groups have been formed and made use of from time to time, since the late Ottoman era, in fact. This does not mean that the official security forces of the state are not affected by the Turkish nationalist ideology; on the contrary, the training of those forces has Turkish nationalism at its centre. However, these organisations could have caused problems for government agencies wishing to go a step further and carry out extra-legal acts through official powers.

The impact, across decades, of key individuals and staff, similarities in the organisation of different institutions and actions carried out within a shared ideological framework are important points for tracing the continuity of paramilitary groups. At the same time, this also reveals that state elites operated on a permanent culture of implicit violence, to be actualised and deployed in the face of any perceived internal threat, to all oppositions. Without veering into essentialism or reification, we can safely posit that from 1915 until 2015, similar paramilitary entities were formed and employed as a response to oppositional political groups defined as threats or enemies of the nation state. This may be largely explained by looking at the relationships between the state and paramilitaries, whose long-term foundations were established by the CUP, as well as by considering more recent institutional structures (such as the MHP) and influential staff members, the individuals in power who connected these institutions to one another across different periods.

Thus, the policy of using paramilitary groups in Anatolia and northern Kurdistan has clearly continued since the late Ottoman period. The ideological commitments of the ruling elite to use these groups have been generally similar – Sunni Turkishness – although they have differed in their organisational structure and their membership.[9] During the late Ottoman period, the paramilitary groups were organised in the form of Kurdish tribal units,

---

[9] Barış Ünlü, *Türklük Sözleşmesi: Oluşumu, İşleyişi ve Krizi*, 2. baskı (Ankara: Dipnot Yayınları, 2018).

intelligence groups and local criminal gangs. During the single-party dictatorship of the Republican period, the structure of these groups was predominantly tribal militias and nationalist youth organisations. From the 1950s to
the 1990s, intelligence groups, vigilante groups and assassins were primarily
used against oppositions. In the 1990s, the modernised tribal militias, various
intelligence organisations and death squads structured the paramilitary groups.
These groups have been usually semi-formal or informal, and the institutions
they were affiliated with could be different, ranging from military, police and
intelligence agencies through radical political parties and religious groups to
criminal gangs and organisations. Moreover, the members of these groups come
from very different social and political backgrounds: army and police recruits
and officers, intelligence agents, tribal members, youth members of the extreme
right-wing and Islamist parties, gang/mafia members, and so on.

Although the recent conflict of 2015–16 is the subject of a different study,
this was another important period in terms of demonstrating the continuity of
use of paramilitary groups against opposition groups and civilians and should
be emphasised briefly. During this period, an Islamist government of the AKP
led by Recep Tayyip Erdoğan was in power. This was the government also of
the period of the PKK ceasefire and negotiation known as the 'peace process'
that led to a series of organised meetings with PKK leaders and representatives.
However, the process ultimately remained grounded in its nationalist roots
and fixed to the old state tradition against the oppositions; thus, in the conflicts that started with the end of the peace process, the AKP government rapidly adopted strategies and tactics that were similar in terms of violence against
civilians and included the use of paramilitary groups.

Immediately after the final failure of the peace process in 2015–16, Turkish
military forces implemented very heavy attacks on youth groups of the Kurdish movement resisting state power in several Kurdish cities. Thousands of
civilians were killed in these attacks, which actively used paramilitary groups
as well as the regular army and police forces, resulting in massive and intended
destruction in many cities, neighbourhoods and houses.[10] Like JİTEM and the

---

[10] United Nations, *Report on the Human Rights Situation in South-East Turkey: July 2015 to
December 2016* (Geneva: Office of the United Nations High Commissioner for Human
Rights, February 2017); Harun Ercan, 'Is Hope More Precious than Victory? The Failed
Peace Process and Urban Warfare in the Kurdish Region of Turkey', *South Atlantic Quarterly*
118, no. 1 (1 January 2019): 111–27.

Special Police Teams active in the 1990s, paramilitary groups were used this time too, and with heightened capacities, operating under legal military units. During the interviews I carried out, it was pointed out that those leading such units tended to be older than fifty and dressed in civilian clothing, and some reportedly spoke Arabic with one another.[11] Among the names used for the teams that participated in the 2015 conflicts were 'JİTEM' and '*Esedullah*' (Lion of Allah).[12]

All of this indicates that a number of groups with experienced paramilitary members (experience from the 1990s), with ties to the Turkish state (possibly in the Syrian civil war), were employed for their experience in urban warfare.[13] Again, these groups had a capacity for irregular warfare that was far greater than that of the state, and they operated not as paramilitary units but under the army and the police. Thus, the state very quickly resorted to paramilitarism, once more, effectively building on its recent, living experience.

In fact, it may be stated that state elites operated with far more comfort in 2015–16 than in the 1990s in terms of accountability, feeling no need to conceal or deny violence carried out against citizens. While this type of situation had been specific to a few places before, like Cizre, now there was a generalised sense of impunity across the region (northern Kurdistan). State elites established that system of impunity with the laws and decrees issued in 2016.[14] Put differently, in the 1990s, state elites could ascribe forms of violence they denied to paramilitary groups, whose very existence they further denied; the existence of informal paramilitary groups was quite important in this regard. In particular, violence against civilians was ascribed to groups and individuals outside the control of state institutions. In any case, this was a reality that state elites were never willing to fully explain. The 2015–16 conflicts, however, represent a period when the state accepted the bare constraints of the geography

[11] Interview #12, conducted in Cologne, 13 February 2017.

[12] TİHV, 'Curfews Between August 16, 2015 – August 16, 2016 and Civilians Who Lost Their Lives', TİHV Ankara, 21 August 2016, http://en.tihv.org.tr/curfews-between-august-16-2015-august-16-2016-and-civilians-who-lost-their-lives/.

[13] 'Sur Raporu', Halkların Demokratik Partisi (HDP), September 2016, https://www.hdp.org.tr/tr/raporlar/hdp-raporlari/sur-raporu/8729.

[14] Hülya Dinçer, 'Kalıcı Olağanüstü Halin Yeni Cezasızlık Rejimi: Adaletin Yasa Eliyle İlgası', *Ayrıntı Dergi*, 1 August 2020, https://ayrintidergi.com.tr/kalici-olaganustu-halin-yeni-cezasizlik-rejimi-adaletin-yasa-eliyle-ilgasi/.

of northern Kurdistan as defining the sphere of operations within which it felt no need to hide in shadow any of the paramilitary violence. The paramilitary groups were, in a formal sense, operating within the army and the police, and from the images presented in a number of photos published in the press can be said to have sent things back to the 1990s regarding their use of names and symbols, which were reminiscent of JİTEM and Special Police Teams. Yet the attempt by state institutions in the 1990s to differentiate between the PKK and the Kurdish People (between 'terrorist' and civilian) was now implicitly recognised as having failed.

The main aim of paramilitary groups in the 1990s was to assume responsibility for severing the ties between the PKK and Kurdish society. Such, it can be said, was the division of labour between official armed groups and paramilitary groups in the 1990s. The state violence carried out in 2015–16, however, while much shorter in duration (for various reasons), targeted everyone, making no distinction between civilians and militants. 'According to the data of HRFT Documentation Center, since August 16, 2015 until August 16, 2016 at least 321 civilians lost their lives in regions and periods of time that curfews were officially declared. 79 are children, 71 are female and 30 are over the age 60 within these people.'[15] Various political and other dynamics were in place mitigating for this, of course, but it was certainly tied, we may assert, to the state having learnt that it was unable to draw a dividing line between the PKK and Kurdish society but no longer feeling the need to be very concerned with denial in order to act with impunity.

Map C.1 illustrates the provinces where curfews were imposed, cities destroyed, and the civilians affected in the recent (2015–16) violence. These areas are also the areas where violence was most intense in the 1990s. The similarities between this map and that of the mass graves (Map 3.1) clearly demonstrate, once again, the continuity of violence, in this case territorially, in the same area of northern Kurdistan.[16]

---

[15] TİHV-HRFT, 'Curfews Between August 16, 2015 – August 16, 2016 and Civilians Who Lost Their Lives According to the Data of Human Rights Foundation of Turkey Documentation Center', TİHV, 21 August 2016, 2, https://en.tihv.org.tr/curfews/16-august-2015-16-august-2016-fact-sheet/.

[16] 'Curfews in Turkey Between the Dates 16 August 2015 – 1 June 2017', Human Rights Foundation of Turkey, accessed 29 July 2019, http://en.tihv.org.tr/curfews-in-turkey-between-the-dates-16-august-2015-1-june-2017/.

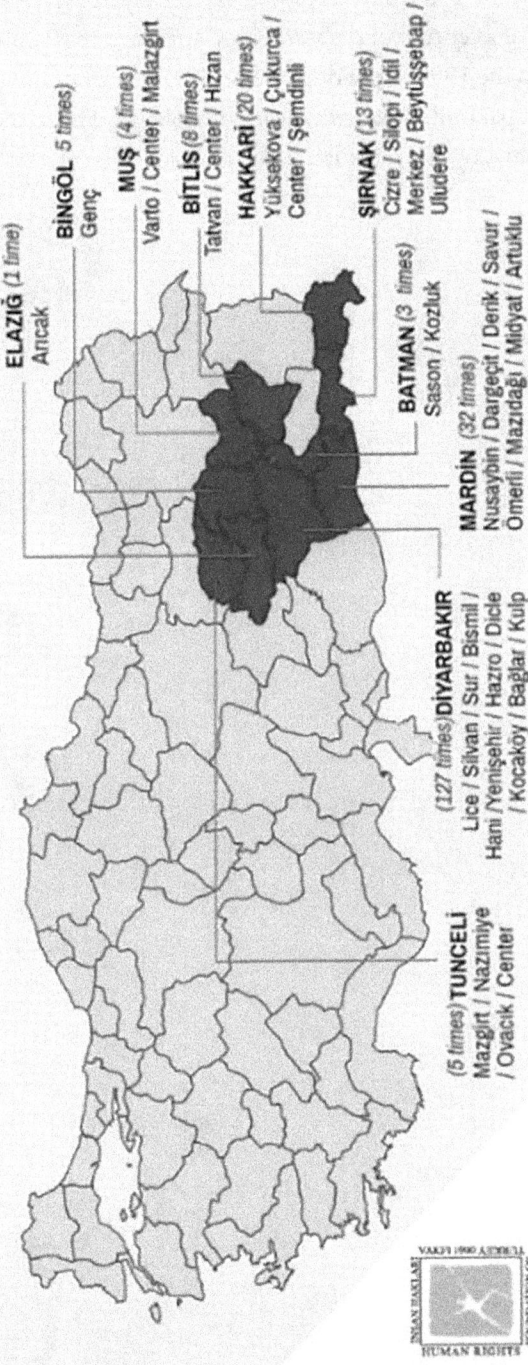

There has been at least 218 round-the-clock & open-ended curfews, in at least 43 districts of 10 cities in southeastern Turkey.

According to the 2014 population census made before the curfews, approximately 1 million 809 thousand people are affected.

ELAZIĞ (1 time)
Ancak

BİNGÖL 5 times)
Genç

MUŞ (4 times)
Varto / Center / Malazgirt

BİTLİS (8 times)
Tatvan / Center / Hizan

HAKKARİ (20 times)
Yüksekova / Çukurca / Center / Şemdinli

ŞIRNAK (13 times)
Cizre / Silopi / İdil / Merkez / Beytüşşebap / Uludere

BATMAN (3 times)
Sason / Kozluk

MARDİN (32 times)
Nusaybin / Dargeçit / Derik / Savur / Ömerli / Mazıdağı / Midyat / Artuklu

DİYARBAKIR (127 times)
Lice / Silvan / Sur / Bismil / Hani /Yenişehir / Hazro / Dicle / Kocaköy / Bağlar / Kulp

TUNCELİ (5 times)
Mazgirt / Nazımiye / Ovacik / Center

Map C.1 Curfews in Turkey between 16 August 2015 and 1 June 2017.

[Source: Human Rights Foundation of Turkey, accessed 29 July 2019, http://en.tihv.org.tr/curfews-in-turkey-between-the-dates-16-august-2015-1-june-2017/]

Formed in the 1980s and employed extensively in the 1990s, paramilitaries were a result of a century of the state elites' approach to Kurdish politics. What distinguished the 1990s from other periods was the centrality to the politics of the decade of paramilitarism as a means of violence. The effects of the violence of the 1990s are, by any measure, still very much present.

BIBLIOGRAPHY

Ağaşe, Çetin. *Cem Ersever ve JİTEM Gerçeği*. Istanbul: Pencere Yayınları, 1998.

Ahıska, Meltem, ed. *Sosyalizm ve Toplumsal Mücadeleler Ansiklopedisi*. Vol. 7. Istanbul: İletişim, 1988.

Ahram, Ariel I. 'Pro-Government Militias and the Repertoires of Illicit State Violence.' *Studies in Conflict & Terrorism* 39, no. 3 (3 March 2016): 207–26. http://dx.doi.org/10.1080/1057610X.2015.1104025.

Akay, Hale. 'Türk Silahlı Kuvvetleri: Kurumsal ve Askeri Boyut.' In *Güvenlik Sektörü ve Demokratik Gözetim: Almanak Türkiye 2006-2008*, edited by Ahmet İnsel and Ali Bayramoğlu, 117–71. Istanbul: TESEV Yayınları, 2009.

Akça, İsmet. '1960'lardan 2012'ye Türkiye'de Devlet: Hegemonya Krizleri, Sol Hareket Ve Kürt Meselesi.' *Toplum ve Kuram* 6–7 (2012): 83–105.

Akçura, Belma. *Derin Devlet Oldu Devlet*. 5. baskı. Istanbul: Belge Yayınları/Sınırötesi Yayınları, 2009.

Akçura, Yusuf. *Türk Yılı 1928*, 1928. http://212.174.157.46:8080/xmlui/handle/11543/508.

Akekmekçi, Tuba, and Muazzez Pervan, eds. *Dersim Harekâtı ve Cumhuriyet Bürokrasisi (1936-1950)*. Istanbul: Tarih Vakfı Yurt Yayınları, 2011.

Akfırat, Adnan. *Eşref Bitlis Suikastı: Belgelerle*. Istanbul: Kaynak Yayınları, 1997.

Akkaya, Ahmet Hamdi. 'The Kurdistan Workers' Party (PKK): National Liberation, Insurgency and Radical Democracy Beyond Borders.' PhD diss., Ghent University, 2016.

—. 'Ulusal Kurtuluş, Ayaklanma ve Sınırların Ötesi: 1970'lerden 1990'lara Kürt Hareketi'nin Değişim Dinamikleri.' *Toplum ve Kuram*, no. 9 (2014): 75–98.

Aktar, Ayhan. 'Trakya Yahudi Olaylarını "Doğru" Yorumlamak.' *Tarih ve Toplum* 155 (1996): 45–56. http://www.academia.edu/10986931/_Trakya_Yahudi_ Olaylar%C4%B1n%C4%B1_Do%C4%9Fru_Yorumlamak_Correct_Interpretation_of_the_Jewish_Pogrom_and_Jewish_Exodus_at_Eastern_Thrace_in_1934_.

Alaeddinoğlu, Faruk. 'Batman Şehri, Fonksiyonel Özellikleri ve Başlıca Sorunları.' *Doğu Coğrafya Dergisi* 15, no. 24 (14 September 2011): 19–42. http://dergipark.gov.tr/ataunidcd/31215.

Alış, Ahmet. 'The Kurdish Ethnoregional Movement in Turkey: From Class to Nation (1959–1974) and from Nation to "Revolution" (1974–1984).' PhD diss., Boğaziçi University, 2017.

Alpkaya, Gökçen. '"Kayıp"lar Sorunu Ve Türkiye.' *Ankara Üniversitesi SBF Dergisi* 50, no. 3 (1995): 31–63. http://www.politics.ankara.edu.tr/dergi/pdf/50/3/8_gokcen_alpkaya.pdf.

Altindag, Abdurrahman, Ozkan Mustafa and Oto Remzi. 'Suicide in Batman, Southeastern Turkey.' *Suicide and Life-Threatening Behavior* 35, no. 4 (7 January 2011): 478–82. https://doi.org/10.1521/suli.2005.35.4.478.

Alvarez, Alex. 'Militias and Genocide.' *War Crimes, Genocide, & Crimes Against Humanity* 2 (2006): 1–33.

ANF English. 'The First Bullet: Murder of Vedat Aydın.' July 2017. https://anfenglish.com/news/the-first-bullet-murder-of-vedat-aydin-20886.

Arcayürek, Cüneyt. *Derin Devlet: 1950–2007.* 13. baskı. Istanbul: Detay Yayınları, 2007.

Armağan, Haldun. 'Ordu Kontrolünde Yerel Savunma.' *Milliyet Gazetesi*, 31 October 1988.

Arslan, Ruşen. *Jandarma Genel Komutanlığının Raporu: Devletin İç Düşmanı Kürtler.* Istanbul: İsmail Beşikçi Vakfı, 2014.

Ateş, Kazım. 'Türk Milli-Kimliğinin İnşası ve Ulusal Cemaat İçinde Alevi-Yurttaşın Müphem Konumu.' *İnsan Hakları Yıllığı* 25, no. 1 (2007): 55–78.

Auyero, Javier. *Routine Politics and Violence in Argentina: The Gray Zone of State Power.* Cambridge: Cambridge University Press, 2007.

Avşar, Gülçin. *The Other Side of the Ergenekon: Extrajudicial Killings and Forced Disappearances.* Istanbul: TESEV Yayınları, 2013. http://tesev.org.tr/wp-content/uploads/2015/11/The_Other_Side_Of_The_Ergenekon_Extrajudicial_Killings_And_Forced_Disappearances.pdf.

Avşar, Gülçin, Levent Pişkin and Hande Özhabeş, *Ergenekon'un Öteki Yüzü: Faili Meçhuller ve Kayıplar: Ergenekon Dosyları İncelemesi.* Istanbul: TESEV Yayınları, 2013.

Aydin, Ayşegül, and Cem Emrence. *Zones of Rebellion: Kurdish Insurgents and the Turkish State*. New York: Cornell University Press, 2015.

Aydın, Suavi, and Yüksel Taşkın. *1960'tan Günümüze Türkiye Tarihi*. Istanbul: İletişim, 2014.

Aydınoğlu, Ergun. *Türkiye Solu, 1960–1980: Bir Amneziğin Anıları*. Istanbul: Versus Kitap, 2007.

Aytar, Osman. *Hamidiye Alaylarından Köy Koruculuğuna*. Istanbul: Medya Güneşi, 1992.

Bagasi, İ. 'Kendi Dilinden Hizbullah ve Mücadele Tarihinden Önemli Kesitler.' *Huseyni Sevda*, n.d. http://huseynisevda.biz/viewpage.php?page_id=33.

Balık, Uğur. *Kerberos: PKK'dan JİTEM'e Bir Tetikçinin Anatomisi*. 1. baskı. Istanbul: Timaş Yayınları, 2011.

Balta, Evren, Murat Yüksel and Yasemin Acar. *Geçici Köy Koruculuğu Sistemi ve 'Çözüm Süreci'*. Istanbul: SÜREÇ Araştırma Merkezi, 2015. http://aciktoplum-vakfi.org.tr/pdf/cozumsureci05052015.pdf.

Balta Paker, Evren. 'Dış Tehditten İç Tehdide: Türkiye'de Doksanlarda Ulusal Güvenliğin Yeniden İnşaası.' In *Türkiye'de Ordu, Devlet Ve Güvenlik Siyaseti*, edited by Evren Balta Paker and İsmet Akça, 407–32. Istanbul: İstanbul Bilgi Üniversitesi, 2010.

Balta Paker, Evren, and İsmet Akça. 'Askerler, Köylüler, Paramiliter Güçler: Türkiye'de Köy Koruculuğu Sistemi.' *Toplum ve Bilim*, no. 126 (2013): 7–34. https://www.academia.edu/10053030/ASKERLER_K%C3%96YL%C3%9CLER_VE_PAR AM%C4%B0L%C4%B0TER_G%C3%9C%C3%87LER_T%C3%9CRK%C4% B0YE_DE_K%C3%96Y_KORUCULU%C4%9EU_S%C4%B0STEM%C4%B0.

Barkey, Karen. *Eşkiyalar ve Devlet: Osmanlı Tarzı Devlet Merkezileşmesi*. Translated by Zeynep Altok. Istanbul: Tarih Vakfı Yurt Yayınları, 1999.

Başlangıç, Celal. 'Korucular Aday Oldu.' *Cumhuriyet Gazetesi*, 3 July 1994.

—. '90'ların İşaret Fişeği: Yeşilyurt Köylülerine Yedirilen Dışkı', *Bianet – Bağımsız İletisim Ağı*, Aralık 2014, https://www.bianet.org/bianet/medya/160934-90-la-rin-isaret-fisegi-yesilyurt-koylulerine-yedirilen-diski.

Batman Barosu Faili Meçhul Cinayet ve Kayıpları Araştırma Komisyonu 2011 Yılı Çalışma Raporu. Batman: Batman Barosu, 2011.

'Batman' Da Durum Nedir ?', *Xebat*, Kürdistan-1977/1979 Bildirileri (1980): 19–22.

'Batman'da Kayıp Silah Bilmecesi.' *Cumhuriyet Gazetesi*, 10 February 2000.

Batur Yamaner, Melike, Emre Öktem, Bleda Kurtdarcan and Mehmet C. Uzun. *12 Ağustos 1949 Tarihli Cenevre Sözleşmeleri Ve Ek Protokolleri*. Istanbul: Galatasaray Üniversitesi Hukuk Fakültesi Yayınları, n.d.

Bayrak, Mehmet, ed. *Kürtler ve Ulusal-Demokratik Mücadeleleri Üstüne: Gizli Belgeler – Araştırmalar – Notlar*. 2. baskı. Ankara: Öz-Ge Yayınları, 2013.

—. *Kürtler'e Vurulan Kelepçe: Şark Islahat Planı*. Ankara: Öz-Ge, 2009.

BBC. '90'larda Ne Olmuştu? Ismet Sezgin: Birtakım Öldürmeler, Hapsetmeler, Bir Mücadele.' 4 September 2015. http://www.bbc.com/turkce/haberler/2015/09/150903_90lar_3_ismet_sezgin_roportaj.

Belge, Murat. *Militarist Modernleşme: Almanya, Japonya ve Türkiye*. 2. baskı. Istanbul: İletişim yayınları, 2012.

Berkan, İsmet. 'Gladio'ya MGK Onayı.' *Radikal*, 6 December 1996.

Beşe, Ertan. 'Special Operations Unit.' In *Almanac Turkey 2005: Security Sector and Semocratic Oversight*, edited by Ümit Cizre, 1st edn, 118–27. Istanbul: TESEV Publications, 2006.

Beşikci, İsmail. *Devletlerarası Sömürge Kürdistan*. Istanbul: İsmail Beşikci Vakfı Yayınları, 2013.

—. *Doğu'da Değişim ve Yapısal Sorunlar Göçebe Alikan Aşireti*. Istanbul: İsmail Beşikçi Vakfı Yayınları, 2014.

—. *Orta Doğu'da Devlet Terörü*. Istanbul: İsmail Beşikci Vakfı Yayınları, 2013.

—. *Rejimin Niteliği ve Kürtler*. Istanbul: İsmail Beşikci Vakfı Yayınları, 2013.

Beşikçi, Mehmet. 'Militarizm, Topyekün Savaş ve Gençliğin Seferber Edilmesi: Birinci Dünya Savaşı'nda Osmanlı İmparatorluğu'nda Paramiliter Dernekler.' *Tarih ve Toplum Yeni Yaklaşımlar* 248, no. 8 (2009): 49–92.

Bezci, Egemen B., and Güven Gürkan Öztan. 'Anatomy of the Turkish Emergency State: A Continuous Reflection of Turkish *Raison d'état* between 1980 and 2002.' *Middle East Critique* 25, no. 2 (2 April 2016): 163–79. http://dx.doi.org/10.1080/19436149.2016.1148858.

Bezwan, Naif. 'Kuzey Kürdistan'da Devletin Değişen Savaş Stratejileri.' In *1990'larda Kürtler ve Kürdistan*, edited by Ayhan Işık, Bülent Bilmez, Ronayi Önen and Tahir Baykuşak, 1st edn, 43–8. Istanbul: İstanbul Bilgi Üniversitesi Yayınları, 2015.

—. 'The State and Violence in Kurdistan: A Conceptual Framework', *Kurdish Studies* 9, no. 1 (2021): 11–36.

Biçim, Hasan. 'Aşiretlerin Kente Eklemlenme Tarzı: Batman Örneği.' PhD diss., Ege Üniversitesi, 2018.

Bilâ, Fikret. *Komutanlar Cephesi*. 2. baskı. Istanbul: Detay Yayıncılık, 2007.

Biner, Zerrin Özlem. 'From Terrorist to Repentant: Who Is the Victim?' *History and Anthropology* 17, no. 4 (2006): 339–53. http://www.tandfonline.com/doi/pdf/10.1080/02757200600955519.

Bir Başkaldırı Destanı:Cizreli Berivan, 2010. http://archive.org/details/CIZRELR-BERVAN.

Blakeley, Ruth. 'Why Torture?' *Review of International Studies* 33, no. 3 (2007): 373–94.

Blum, William. *Killing Hope: US Military and CIA Interventions Since World War II.* London: Zed Books, 2003.

Bolkan, Aydın. *Faili Meçhul Bir Milletvekili Cinayetinin Öyküsü Mehmet Sincar.* Istanbul: Aram Yayınları, 2005.

'Bölücülere Karşı "Özel Polis".' *Milliyet Gazetesi*, 7 October 1986.

Bora, Tanıl, and Kemal Can. *Devlet, Ocak, Dergâh: 12 Eylül'den 1990'lara Ülkücü Hareket.* Istanbul: İletişim Yayınları, 1991.

Bovenkerk, Frank, and Yücel Yeşilgöz. 'The Turkish Mafia and the State.' In *Organised Crime in Europe: Concepts, Patterns and Control Policies in the European Union and Beyond,* edited by C. Fijnaut and L. Paoli, 585–602. Dordrecht: Springer Netherlands, 2004.

—. *Türkiye'nin Mafyası.* 2. baskı. Istanbul: İletişim, 2000.

Bozarslan, Hamit. *Akp'nin Artık Legalite Diye Bir Derdi Yok.* İnterview by İrfan Aktan, 13 April 2019. https://www.gazeteduvar.com.tr/yazarlar/2019/04/13/hamit-bozarslan-akpnin-artik-legalite-diye-bir-derdi-yok/.

—. 'Bir "Bölücü" ve "Birleştirici" Olarak Şiddet.' *Toplum ve Bilim*, no. 116 (2009): 6–20.

—. '"Neden Silahlı Mücadele?" Türkiye Kürdistan'ında Şiddeti Anlamak.' In *Türkiye'de Siyasal Şiddetin Boyutları,* edited by İbrahim Şirin and Güney Çeğin, 1. baskı, 149–63. Istanbul: İletişim Yayınları, 2014.

—. *Network-Building, Ethnicity and Violence in Turkey.* Abu Dhabi: ECSSR, 1999.

—. 'The Turkey of the 2010's: Conflict, Pluralism, and Spaces of Life in a Modern Anti-Democracy.' Keynote lecture presented at the *Societal Conflict and Cohabitation in Turkey and Beyond, CEST Conference 2018, Stockholm University, November 29, 2018.*

—. 'Why the Armed Struggle: Understanding the Violence in Kurdistan of Turkey.' In *The Kurdish Conflict in Turkey: Obstacles and Chances for Peace and Democracy,* edited by Ferhad Ibrahim and Gülistan Gürbey, 17–30. Münster: LIT Verlag, 2000.

Bozkurt, Serhat, Alişan Akpınar, eds. *Osmanlı Kürdistanı,* 1. baskı. Istanbul: bgst Yayınları, 2011.

Brubaker, Rogers, and David D. Laitin. 'Ethnic and Nationalist Violence.' *Annual Review of Sociology* 24 (1 January 1998): 423–52. http://www.jstor.org/stable/223488.

Bruinessen, Martin van. *Ağa, Şeyh Ve Devlet: Agha, Shaikh and State: the Social and Political Structures of Kurdistan*. 5. baskı. Istanbul: İletişim Yayınları, 2008.

—. *Agha, Shaikh, and State: The Social and Political Structures of Kurdistan*. London: Zed Books, 1992.

—. *Kürdistan Üzerine Yazılar*. 6. baskı. Istanbul: İletişim Yayınları, 2008.

—. 'Turkey's Death Squads.' *Middle East Report*, no. 199 (1996): 20–3. http://www.merip.org/mer/mer199/turkeys-death-squads.

Bulut, Engin Çağdaş. 'Devletin Taşradaki Eli: Umumi Müfettişlikler.' *CTAD: Cumhuriyet Tarihi Araştırmaları Dergisi* 11, no. 21 (2015): 83–110. http://www.ctad.hacettepe.edu.tr/11_21/4.pdf.

Bulut, Faik. *Dersim Raporları*. 2. baskı. Istanbul, 2013.

—. *İslamcı Örgütler 2*. 3. baskı. Doruk Yayımcılık, 1997.

—. *Kürt Sorununa Çözüm Arayışları: Devlet ve Parti Raporları, Yerli Ve Yabancı Öneriler (1920–1997)*. Istanbul: Ozan Yayıncılık, 1998.

Bulut, Faik, and Mehmet Faraç. *Kod Adı Hizbullah: Türkiye Hizbullahı'nın Anatomisi*. 2. baskı. Istanbul: Ozan Yayıncılık, 1999.

Çakır, Ruşen. *Ayet ve Slogan:Türkiye'de İslami Oluşumlar*. 1. baskı. Istanbul: Metis Yayınları, 1990.

—. *Derin Hizbullah: İslamcı Şiddetin Geleceği*. 2. baskı. Istanbul: Metis Yayınları, 2011.

Campbell, Bruce B. 'Death Squads: Definition, Problems and Historical Context.' In *Death Squads in Global Perspective: Murder with Deniability*, edited by Arthur D. Brenner and Bruce B. Campbell, 1–26. Basingstoke: Palgrave Macmillan, 2002.

Can, Başak. 'State-Making, Evidence-Making, and Claim-Making: The Cases of Torture and Enforced Disappearances in Post-1980 Turkey.' PhD diss., University of Pennsylvania, 2014.

Canefe, Nergis, and Tanıl Bora. 'The Intellectual Roots of Anti-European Sentiments in Turkish Politics: The Case of Radical Turkish Nationalism.' *Turkish Studies* 4, no. 1 (1 March 2003): 127–48. http://dx.doi.org/10.1080/714005725.

Carey, Sabine C., and Neil J. Mitchell. 'Progovernment Militias.' *Annual Review of Political Science* 20, no. 1 (2017): 127–47. https://doi.org/10.1146/annurev-polisci-051915-045433.

Carey, Sabine C., Neil J. Mitchell and Will Lowe, 'States, the Security Sector, and the Monopoly of Violence: A New Database on Pro-Government Militias', *Journal of Peace Research* 50, no. 2 (2013): 249–58.

Case of Cyprus v. Turkey. Council of Europe: European Court of Human Rights, 10 May 2001. http://www.refworld.org/docid/43de0e7a4.html.

Çelik, Adnan. '1990'lı Yılların Olağanüstü Hal Rejimi ve Savaş: Kürdistan Yerellerinde Şiddet ve Direniş.' *Toplum ve Kuram*, no. 9 (2014): 99–145.

—. 'Kürdistan Yerellerinde 90'ların Savaş Konfigürasyonu: Baskı, Şiddet ve Direniş.' In *İsyan, Şiddet, Yas 90'lar Türkiye'sine Bakmak*, edited by Ayşen Uysal, 71–113. Ankara: Dipnot Yayınları, 2016.

—. 'Temps Et Espaces De La Violence Interne: Revisiter Les Conflits Kurdes En Turquie À L'échelle Locale (Du Xixe Siècle À La Guerre Des Années 1990).' PhD diss., de l'École des hautes études en sciences sociales (EHESS), 2018.

Çelik, Adnan, and Namık Kemal Dinç. *Yüzyıllık Ah: Toplumsal Hafızanın İzinde 1915 Diyarbakır*. Istanbul: İsmail Beşikci Vakfı Yayınları, 2015.

Çelik, Serdar. *Türk Kontr-Gerillası*. 2nd edn. Köln: Ülkem Presse, 1995.

Çetin, Berfin Emre. *The Paramilitary Hero on Turkish Television: A Case Study on Valley of the Wolves*. Newcastle: Cambridge Scholars Publishing, 2015.

Çetinkaya, Hikmet. 'Yüzü Kapanmış Yara.' *Cumhuriyet Gazetesi*, 12 February 2000, 5.

Çiçek, Cuma. *The Kurds of Turkey: National, Religious and Economic Identities*. London: I. B. Tauris, 2017.

Çiçek, Nevzat. *İtirafçı*, 1. baskı. Istanbul: Timaş Yayınları, 2009.

'Çiller'den Özel Time Övgü.' *Milliyet Gazetesi*, 7 November 1993.

Cizre, Ümit. 'Ideology, Context and Interest: The Turkish Military.' In *The Cambridge History of Turkey, vol. 4: Turkey in the Modern World*, edited by Reşat Kasaba. Cambridge: Cambridge University Press, 2008.

Cizre Sakallıoğlu, Ümit. 'The Anatomy of the Turkish Military's Political Autonomy.' *Comparative Politics* 29, no. 2 (1997): 151–66. http://www.jstor.org/stable/422077.

Clark, Ramsey. 'İnsan Hakları ve "Low Intensity Conflict".' In *Düşük Yoğunluklu Çatışma: İlân Edilmemiş Savaş*, edited by Jochen Hippler, 43–5. Istanbul: Belge Yayınları, 1996.

Collins, John M., Frederick Hamerman and James P. Seevers. *U.S. Low-Intensity Conflicts 1899–1990*. Washington, DC: Committee on Armed Services House of Representatives, 1990.

Crenzel, Emilio. 'Argentina's National Commission on the Disappearance of Persons: Contributions to Transitional Justice.' *International Journal of Transitional Justice* 2, no. 2 (1 July 2008): 173–91. https://doi.org/10.1093/ijtj/ijn007.

Cûdî, Rênas. 'Kürdistan–Türkiye İlişkilerine Yönelik Eleştirel Bir Okuma.' *YeniOzgurPolitika.com*. Accessed 20 July 2022. https://www.ozgurpolitika.com/haberi-kurdistan-turkiye-iliskilerine-yonelik-elestirel-bir-okuma-156972.

Dadrian, Vahakn N. 'A Summary of the Conditions Surrounding the Trials.' In *Judgment at Istanbul: The Armenian Genocide Trials*, edited by Vahakn N. Dadrian and Taner Akçam, 1 edn, 154–76. New York: Berghahn Books, 2011.

Danışman, Funda, and Rojin Canan Akın. *Bildiğin Gibi Değil: 90'larda Güneydoğu'da Çocuk Olmak*. Istanbul: Metis Yayınları, 2011.

Demirel, Emin, and Ali Burak Ersemiz. *Ömrüm: Bir İstihbaratçı Askerin Anıları*. Istanbul: Lagin Yayınları, 2010.

Demirer, Hüseyin. *Ha Wer Delal Emine Perixane'nin Hayatı*. Istanbul: Avesta Yayınları, 2009.

Demirer, Temel, and Sibel Özbudun. *Derin Milliyetçiliğin Siyasal İktisadi*. Ankara: Ütopya Yayınevi, 2006.

Denker, Arif Cemil. *I. Dünya Savaşı'nda Teşkilat-ı Mahsusa*. Istanbul: Arba, 1997.

'Derin Vali'den Derin Açıklamalar.' *Hürriyet*, 11 December 2007. http://www. hurriyet.com.tr/gundem/derin-validen-derin-aciklamalar-7673014.

'"Devlet Hatırası" Albümü: Ulus-Devletin Portresini Çizmek.' *Toplum ve Kuram*, no. 6–7 (2012): 29–81.

'Devlet Menfaati Icabı.' *Hürriyet*, 13 February 2000. http://www.hurriyet.com.tr/ devlet-menfaati-icabi-39133096.

'Devletin Derebeyi: Korucu Kamil Atak.' *Birgün Gazetesi*, 19 March 2009. https:// www.birgun.net/haber-detay/devletin-derebeyi-korucu-kamil-atak-45222.html.

Dicle, Hatip, Ragıp Duran, Rıza Doğan and Selahattin Çelik. 'Hüseyin Baybaşin Ile Röportaj.' In *Çete Devlet – Susurluk Dosyasi*. Mezopotomya Yayinlari, 1997.

Dilsoz, Selman. 'İslami Değerler Çiğnetilmedi.' *Hira*, 1993.

Dinç, Namık Kemal, ed. *Stories of Migration 'One Who's Seen Pain Doesn't Inflict Pain Upon Others'*. Translated by Kolektif Atölye. Istanbul: Göç-Der Yayınları, 2008. http://www.gocder.com/sites/default/files/proje-photo/goc-hikayeleri-en.pdf.

Dinçer, Hülya. 'Kalıcı Olağanüstü Halin Yeni Cezasızlık Rejimi: Adaletin Yasa Eliyle İlgası.' *Ayrıntı Dergi*, 1 August 2020. https://ayrintidergi.com.tr/kalici-olaga-nustu-halin-yeni-cezasizlik-rejimi-adaletin-yasa-eliyle-ilgasi/.

Dirican, Ahmet. 'Eski Vali: Jitem'le Çalıştık.' *Sabah Gazetesi*, 17 April 2006. http:// arsiv.sabah.com.tr/2006/04/17/gnd106.html.

Doğan, Arif. *JİTEM'i Ben Kurdum*. 1. baskı. Istanbul: Timaş Yayınları, 2011.

Doğan, Mazlum. *Toplu Yazılar*. Weşanen Serxwebun, 1982.

Doğan, Sinan, ed. *Mit Raporu Olayı*. 1. baskı. Istanbul: Sistem Yayıncılık, 1988.

Dorronsoro, Gilles. 'La Torture Discrète: Capital Social, Radicalisation Et Désengage-ment Militant Dans Un Régime Sécuritaire.' *European Journal of Turkish Studies – Social Sciences on Contemporary Turkey*, no. 8 (31 December 2008), http://journals. openedition.org/ejts/2223.

Dündar, Can, and Celal Kazdağlı. *Ergenekon: Devlet İçinde Devlet*. 10. baskı. Ankara: Can Yayınları, 2013.

Dündar, Fuat. *İttihat ve Terakki'nin Müslümanları İskan Politikası (1913–1918)*. 1. baskı. Istanbul: İletişim, 2001.

—. *Modern Türkiye'nin Şifresi: İttihat ve Terakki'nin Etnisite Mühendisliği, 1913–1918*. 3. baskı. Istanbul: İletişim, 2008.

Durukan, Ayşe. 'Batmanda Kadınlar Hala İntihar Ediyor.' *Bianet – Bagimsiz Iletisim Agi*, 21 June 2005. http://www.bianet.org/bianet/kadin/62684-batmanda-kadinlar-hala-intihar-ediyor.

Durukan, Namık. 'MHP'li Aşiretler DYP'ye Transfer.' *Milliyet Gazetesi*, 10 November 1994.

Düzel, Neşe. 'JİTEM Itirafçısı Abdülkadir Aygan Anlatıyor.' *Taraf Gazetesi*, 29 January 2009.

Ebinç, Sait. 'Doğu Anadolu Düzeninde Aşiret-Cemaat-Devlet (1839–1950).' PhD diss., Ankara Üniversitesi, 2008.

Efe, Ahmet. *Kuşçubaşı Eşref*. Tarih Dizisi 4. Istanbul: Bengi Yayınları, 2007.

EGM. 'EGM – Özel Harekat Daire Başkanlığı.' Accessed 20 March 2017. https://www.egm.gov.tr/Sayfalar/%C3%96zel-Harekat-Daire-Ba%C5%9Fkanl%C4%B1%C4%9F%C4%B1.aspx.

Ekinci, Nihat. *Faili Meçhul Cinayetler: (Batman'ın 1990–2000 Tarihi) Akan Katran Değil Kandı*. Istanbul: Do, 2012.

Ekinci, Yılmaz. '"Rutin Dışı" Vali'den Özel Tim Gerçeği.' *haber7.com*, 13 November 2007. http://www.haber7.com/guncel/haber/280001-rutin-disi-validen-ozel-tim-gercegi.

Engin, Aydın. 'Devlet Hizbullah'a Göz Yumuyor.' *Cumhuriyet Gazetesi*, 19 February 1993.

—. 'Hizbullah'ı Devlet Kurdurdu.' *Cumhuriyet Gazetesi*, 20 February 1993.

Ercan, Harun. 'Dynamics of Mobilization and Radicalization of the Kurdish Movement in the 1970s in Turkey.' Masters thesis, Koç University, 2010.

—. 'Is Hope More Precious than Victory? The Failed Peace Process and Urban Warfare in the Kurdish Region of Turkey.' *South Atlantic Quarterly* 118, no. 1 (1 January 2019): 111–27.

Erdendoğdu, Feza. 'Türkiye Basınında 1978–1980 Yıllarında Yaşanan Alevi Katliamlarına Dair Manşet Haberlerinin Karşılaştırılması Üzerine Bir İnceleme.' Mimar Sinan Güzel Sanatlar Üniversitesi, 2014.

Ertan, Mehmet. 'The Circuitous Politicization of Alevism: The Affiliaton Between the Alevis and the Left Politics (1960–1980).' Masters thesis, Boğaziçi University, 2008.

'Esas Hakkında Mütalaa-Hizbullah Terör Örgütü.' Diyarbakır 6. Ağır Ceza Mahkemesi Esas No: /171 C. Sav. Es. No: 2000/559 2000.

Esmer, Selahattin. 'Uluslararası İnsancıl Hukukta Çatışma Kategorileri Ve Minimum Silahlı Şiddet Eşiği.' *İnsan Hakları Derneği*, 2 July 2016. http://www.ihd.org.tr/uluslararasi-insancil-hukukta-catisma-kategorileri-ve-minimum-silahli-siddet-esigi/.

European Court of Human Rights. *Case of Loizidou V. Turkey (Application No. 15318/89)*. Strasbourg, 18 December 1996. file:///Users/ayhanisik/Downloads/001-58007%20(2).pdf.

'Evinde Ölü Bulunan Hayri Kozakçıoğlu'nun Eşi İfade Verdi.' *t24.com.tr*, 23 May 2013. http://t24.com.tr/haber/turkiyenin-ilk-ohal-valisi-hayri-kozakcioglu-intihar-etti-iddiasi/230493.

Eymür, Mehmet. *Analiz: Bir Mit Mensubu'nun Anıları*. 9. baskı. Istanbul: Milenyum Yayınları, 2006.

'Faşist Hareket ve MC İktidarları.' In *Sosyalizm Ansiklopedisi*, 8:2216–31, 1988.

Ferman, Cumhur. 'Kuruluş Günümüzde.' *Mülkiyeliler Birliği Dergisi* 1, no. 1 (1965): 4, 36. http://mulkiyedergi.org/article/view/1003000073/1003000058.

Fraenkel, Ernst. *The Dual State: A Contribution to the Theory of Dictatorship*. New York: Oxford University Press, 1941.

Frunze, M. V. *Frunze'nin Türkiye Anıları Kasım 1921–Ocak 1922: Ukraynalı Devrimci Lider*. Translated by Ahmet Ekeş. İzmir: Cem, 1978.

Ganser, Daniele. *NATO's Secret Armies: Operation GLADIO and Terrorism in Western Europe*. Abingdon: Routledge, 2005.

Gaunt, David, Jan Beṯ-Şawoce and Racho Donef. *Massacres, Resistance, Protectors: Muslim–Christian Relations in Eastern Anatolia during World War I*. Piscataway: Gorgias Press, 2006.

Genelkurmay Belgelerinde Kürt İsyanları I. 1. baskı. Istanbul: Kaynak Yayınları, 1992.

'Genelkurmay'dan Açıklama: 'Jitem Diye Bir Birim Yok.' *Cumhuriyet Gazetesi*, 30 December 2009. https://www.cumhuriyetarsivi.com/oku/?clipId=3481941&home=%2Fmonitor%2Findex.xhtml.

Georgeon, François. *Sultan Abdülhamid*. Istanbul: Homer, 2006.

'Gerekçeli Karar-Hizbullah Davası.' Diyarbakır 6. Ağır Ceza Mahkemesi Esas No: /171, Karar No: 2009/727 2000.

Gingeras, Ryan. *Heroin, Organized Crime, and the Making of Modern Turkey*. Oxford: Oxford University Press, 2014.

—. 'Last Rites for a "Pure Bandit": Clandestine Service, Historiography and the Origins of the Turkish "Deep State".' *Past & Present* 206, no. 1 (1 February 2010): 151–74. http://past.oxfordjournals.org/content/206/1/151.

GÖÇ DER. *Türkiye'de Koruculuk Sistemi: Zorunlu Göç ve Geri Dönüşler*. Istanbul: GÖÇ DER, 2013.

Göç-Der Zorunlu Göç Raporu. Istanbul: Göç Der, 2001.

Gökçe, Dinçer, and Enis Tayman. 'Susurluk'un İtirafları İfade Verecek!' *Radikal*, 26 March 2011. http://www.radikal.com.tr/turkiye/susurlukun_itiraflari_ifade_verecek-1044155/.

Gökdemir, Orhan. *Pike: Bir Polis Şefinin Kısa Tarihi*. Istanbul: Chiviyazilari, 2001.

Göral Birinci, Özgür Sevgi. 'Enforced Disappearance and Forced Migration in the Context of Kurdish Conflict: Loss, Mourning and Politics at the Margin.' PhD diss., École des Hautes Études en Sciences Sociales Histoire et Civilizations, 2017.

Göral, Özgür Sevgi, Ayhan Işık and Özlem Kaya. *The Unspoken Truth: Enforced Disappearances*. Istanbul: Truth Justice Memory Center, 2013.

Günay, Onur. 'Geçmişin İşlenmesi Ne Demektir?' *Toplum ve Kuram*, no. 9 (2014): 13–30.

Güneş, Cengiz. *The Kurdish National Movement in Turkey: From Protest to Resistance*. New York: Routledge, 2012.

Gunter, Michael M. 'Susurluk: The Connection between Turkey's Intelligence Community and Organized Crime.' *International Journal of Intelligence and CounterIntelligence* 11, no. 2 (1 June 1998): 119–41. https://doi.org/10.1080/08850609808435368.

Gürbey, Gülistan. 'The Kurdish Nationalist Movement in Turkey Since the 1980s.' In *The Kurdish Nationalist Movement in the 1990s: Its Impact on Turkey and the Middle East*, edited by Robert W. Olson, 9–37. Lexington: University Press of Kentucky, 1996.

Gürcan, Metin. 'Arming Civilians as a Counterterror Strategy: The Case of the Village Guard System in Turkey.' *Dynamics of Asymmetric Conflict* 8, no. 1 (2 January 2015): 1–22. https://doi.org/10.1080/17467586.2014.948026.

Gurses, Mehmet. *Anatomy of a Civil War: Sociopolitical Impacts of the Kurdish Conflict in Turkey*. Illustrated edn. Ann Arbor: University of Michigan Press, 2018.

Güven, Dilek. *Cumhuriyet Dönemi Azınlık Politikaları Bağlamında 6-7 Eylül Olayları*. Istanbul: Tarih Vakfı Yurt Yayınları, 2005.

Haberturk. 'Atilla Kıyat'tan Şok Edici Açıklamalar.' 3 August 2010. http://www.haberturk.com/polemik/haber/538375-atilla-kiyattan-sok-edici-aciklamalar.

Halis, Müjgan. *Batman'da Kadınlar Ölüyor*. Istanbul: Metis Yayınları, 2001.

Hanioğlu, M. Şükrü. *Bir Siyasal Düşünür Olarak Doktor Abdullah Cevdet ve Dönemi*. Istanbul: Üçdal Neşriyat, 1981.

—. *Preparation for a Revolution: The Young Turks, 1902–1908*. Oxford: Oxford University Press, 2001.

—. *The Young Turks in Opposition*. Oxford: Oxford University Press, 1995.

Has, Özlem, 'Structured Agencies of Paramilitaries in the Kurdish-Turkish Conflict: The JİTEM Case.' PhD diss., University of Copenhagen, 2021.

'Hayri Kozakçıoğlu İntihar Etmedi, Öldürüldü.' *Radikal*, 19 November 2013. http:// www.radikal.com.tr/turkiye/eski_ohal_valisi_hayri_kozakcioglunun_olu-munde_kritik_gelisme-1161646/.

HDP. 'Sur Raporu.' Halkların Demokratik Partisi (Peoples' Democratic Party), September 2016. https://www.hdp.org.tr/tr/raporlar/hdp-raporlari/sur-raporu/8729.

'HEP İl Başkanı'nın Kuşkulu Ölümü.' *Cumhuriyet Gazetesi*, 9 July 1991, 5.

Hippler, Jochen, ed. *Düşük Yoğunluklu Çatışma: İlân Edilmemiş Savaş.* Istanbul: Belge Uluslararası Yayıncılık, 1996.

Hironaka, Ann. *Neverending Wars: The International Community, Weak States, and the Perpetuation of Civil War.* Cambridge, MA: Harvard University Press, 2009.

'Hizbullah'ı Koman ve Küçük Kurdu.' *Birgün Gazetesi*, 29 July 2008. https://www. birgun.net/haber-detay/hizbullah-i-koman-ve-kucuk-kurdu-41968.html.

'Hizbullah'ın Militan Deposu: Habizbin Aşireti.' *Sabah Gazetesi*, 23 January 2000.

HRW. 'The Kurds of Turkey: Killings, Disappearances and Torture.' Human Rights Watch-Helsinki Watch, March 1993, https://www.hrw.org/report/1993/03/01/ kurds-turkey/killings-disappearances-and-torture.

HRW. 'Weapons Transfers and Violations of the Laws of War in Turkey.' Human Rights Watch, November 1995. https://www.hrw.org/legacy/reports/1995/ Turkey.htm.

Human Rights Foundation of Turkey. 'Curfews in Turkey Between the Dates 16 August 2015 – 1 June 2017.' Accessed 29 July 2019. http://en.tihv.org.tr/ curfews-in-turkey-between-the-dates-16-august-2015-1-june-2017/.

Hür, Ayşe. 'Çağımızın Bir (Başka) Kahramanı: Topal Osman.' *Birikim*, 31 January 2006. http://www.birikimdergisi.com/guncel-yazilar/70/cagimizin-bir-baska-kahramani-topal-osman#.WB3--dxer_R.

ICRC. 'Protocols I and II Additional to the Geneva Conventions.' 1 January 2009. icrc.org/en/resources/documents/misc/additional-protocols-1977.htm.

İHD. 'Bilançolar-İnsan Hakları Derneği.' Accessed 2 August 2017. http://www.ihd. org.tr/sample-page-2/.

İHD. 'Ocak 1990–Mart 2009 Döneminde Köy Korucuları Tarafından Gerçekleştirilen İnsan Hakları İhlallerine İlişkin Özel Rapor.' 2009. http://www.ihd.org.tr/ images/pdf/ocak_1990_mart_2009_koy_koruculari_ozel_raporu.pdf.

'İnsan Hakları Derneği Diyarbakır Şubesi Toplu Mezar Haritası.' Diyarbakır: İHD Diyarbakır Şubesi, n.d. http://map.ihddiyarbakir.org/Map.aspx.

Interview #8, conducted in Diyarbakır, 25 July 2016.

Interview #11, conducted in Diyarbakır, 28 July 2016.

Interview #12, conducted in Cologne, 13 February 2017.

Interview #13, conducted in Cologne, 14 February 2017.

Interview #17, conducted in Istanbul, 10 May 2017.

Interview #22, conducted in Istanbul, 18 May 2017.

Interview #28, conducted in Spaubeek, 28 June 2017.

Interview #34, conducted in Den Haag, 28 February 2018.

Interview #38, conducted in Amsterdam, 25 May 2018.

Interview #42, conducted in Amsterdam, 21 October 2020.

Interview conducted with A.K. in Cizre, Archive of Truth Justice Memory Center – 2 September 2012, Hafıza Merkezi Arşivi.

Interview conducted with A.Ş. in Cizre, Archive of Truth Justice Memory Center – 3 September 2012, Hafıza Merkezi Arşivi.

Interview conducted with B.G. in Cizre, Archive of Truth Justice Memory Center – 4 September 2012, Hafıza Merkezi Arşivi.

Interview conducted with Ç.T. in Cizre, Archive of Truth Justice Memory Center – 4 December 2012, Hafıza Merkezi Arşivi.

Interview conducted with İ.B. and İ.İ. in Cizre, Archive of Truth Justice Memory Center – 12 October 2012, Hafıza Merkezi Arşivi.

Interview conducted with K.A. in Cizre, Archive of Truth Justice Memory Center – 2 September 2012, Hafıza Merkezi Arşivi.

Interview conducted with M.Ö. in Cizre, Archive of Truth Justice Memory Center – 12 October 2012, Hafıza Merkezi Arşivi.

Interview conducted with Ö.H. in Cizre, Archive of Truth Justice Memory Center – 1 September 2012, Hafıza Merkezi Arşivi.

Interview conducted with Ö.T. in Cizre, Archive of Truth Justice Memory Center – 2 September 2012, Hafıza Merkezi Arşivi.

Interview conducted with Ü.F. and Ü.A. in Cizre, Archive of Truth Justice Memory Center – 5 September 2012, Hafıza Merkezi Arşivi.

İpekçi, Ercan. 'Korucular ve İstikbaldeki Korucular.' *Cumhuriyet Gazetesi*, September 1989.

Işık, Ayhan. '1990'larda Devletin "Sivil Siyaseti" Olarak Zorla Kaybetmeler.' *Toplum ve Kuram*, no. 9 (2014): 43–52.

—. 'Kurdish and Armenian Relations in the Ottoman Kurdish Press (1898–1914).' MA thesis, İstanbul Bilgi University, 2014.

Işık, Ayhan, Bülent Bilmez, Ronayi Önen and Tahir Baykuşak, eds. *1990'larda Kürtler ve Kürdistan*. 1st edn. Istanbul: İstanbul Bilgi Üniversitesi Yayınları, 2015.

Işık, Serap. *Jitem Ana Dava Geniş Özeti*. Hakikat Adalet Hafıza Merkezi, 2014. http:// failibelli.org/wp-content/uploads/2013/01/Jitem_Ana_Dava_Genis_Ozet.pdf.

—. *Temizöz ve Diğerleri Davası Geniş Özeti*. Hakikat Adalet Hafıza Merkezi, 2013. http://failibelli.org/wp-content/uploads/2013/02/Temizoz_Genis_Ozet.pdf

İşleyen, Ercüment. 'Eşref Bitlis Zinciri.' *Milliyet Gazetesi*, 17 February 1994.

—. '"Valiye Özel" Tabur.' *Milliyet Gazetesi*, 11 February 2000. http://www.milliyet. com.tr/2000/02/11/haber/hab02.html.

Jacoby, Tim. 'Fascism, Civility and the Crisis of the Turkish State.' *Third World Quarterly* 32, no. 5 (1 June 2011): 905–24. http://dx.doi.org/10.1080/014365 97.2011.578965.

Jentzsch, Corinna, Stathis N. Kalyvas and Livia Isabella Schubiger. 'Militias in Civil Wars.' *Journal of Conflict Resolution* 59, no. 5 (1 August 2015): 755–69. https:// doi.org/10.1177/0022002715576753.

'Ji Tirkiye Teror û İşkence Ji Gel Berxwedan.' *Welat*, 29 Gulan 1992.

Jones, Adam. 'Parainstitutional Violence in Latin America.' *Latin American Politics and Society* 46, no. 4 (1 December 2004): 127–48. http://onlinelibrary.wiley.com/ doi/10.1111/j.1548-2456.2004.tb00295.x/abstract.

Jongerden, Joost. *The Settlement Issue in Turkey and the Kurds: An Analysis of Spatial Policies, Modernity and War*. Leiden: Brill, 2007.

—. 'Village Evacuation and Reconstruction in Kurdistan (1993–2002).' *Études rurales*, no. 186 (29 March 2010): 1–22 (77–100). http://etudesrurales.revues.org. proxy.library.uu.nl/9241.

'Kaçakçılık Yasası Çıktı.' *Milliyet Gazetesi*, 8 May 1985. http://gazetearsivi.milliyet. com.tr/Ara.aspx?araKelime=Pi%C5%9Fmanl%C4%B1k%20Yasas%C4%B1%20 %C3%A7%C4%B1kt%C4%B1&isAdv=false.

Kahraman, Ahmet. *Kürt Isyanları: Tedip Ve Tenkil*. Istanbul: Evrensel Basım Yayın, 2004.

—. *Kürt İsyanları: Tedip ve Tenkil*. Istanbul: Evrensel Basım Yayın, 2013.

Kaldor, Mary. *New and Old Wars*. Stanford: Stanford University Press, 2007.

Kalyvas, Stathis N. 'Ethnic Defection in Civil War.' *Comparative Political Studies* 41, no. 8 (1 August 2008): 1043–68. http://journals.sagepub.com/doi/ abs/10.1177/0010414008317949.

—. *The Logic of Violence in Civil War*. Cambridge: Cambridge University Press, 2006.

'Kanlı Nevruz: 38 Ölü.' *Cumhuriyet Gazetesi*, 22 March 1992.

Karayılan, Murat. *Bir Savaşın Anatomisi Kürdistan'da Askeri Çizgi*. Neuss: Mezopotamya Yayınları, 2011.

—. *Bir Savaşın Anatomisi Kürdistan'da Askeri Çizgi*. Diyarbakır: Aram Yayıncılık, 2014.

Karpat, Kemal H. *Turkey's Politics: The Transition to a Multi-Party System*. Princeton, NJ: Princeton University Press, 2015.

Kasaba, Reşat, ed. *Turkey in the Modern World*. The Cambridge History of Turkey, vol. 4. Cambridge: Cambridge University Press, 2008.

'Kayıp Silahlar Salih Şarman.' *Satranç Tahtası* – MPL TV, 25 November 2007. https://www.youtube.com/watch?v=IxaFqhb_Mj0.

Kieser, Hans-Lukas. 'Dr Mehmed Reshid (1873–1919): A Political Doctor.' In *Der Völkermord an Den Armeniern Und Die Shoah – the Armenian Genocide and the Shoa*, 3. Auflage mit neuem Vorwort, 245–80. Zürich: Chronos, 2014.

—. *Iskalanmış Barış: Doğu Vilayetleri'nde Misyonerlik, Etnik Kimlik ve Devlet 1839–1938 = Verpasste Friede: Mission, Ethnie Und Staat in Den Ostprovinzen Der Türkei 1839–1938*. 2. baskı. Istanbul: İletişim, 2005.

'Kimseyi Dinlemedi.' *Cumhuriyet Gazetesi*, 11 February 2000.

Kılıç, Ecevit. *JITEM: Türkiye'nin Faili Meçhul Tarihi*. 2. baskı. Istanbul: Timaş, 2009.

—. *Özel Harp Dairesi*. Istanbul: Timaş Yayınları, 2010.

Kırcı, Haluk. *Zaman Süzerken (Hatıralar)*. Istanbul: Burak Yayınevi, 1998.

Kışlalı, Mehmet Ali. *Güneydoğu: Düşük Yoğunluklu Çatışma*. Ümit Yayıncılık, 1996.

'Kitlesel Mücadeleler ve Dev-Genç.' In *Sosyalizm ve Toplumsal Mücadeleler Ansiklopedisi*, edited by Ertuğrul Kürkçü. 7:2134–65. Istanbul: İletişim Yayınları, 1988.

Kızıldağ Soileau, Dilek. *Koçgiri İsyanı: Sosyo Tarihsel Bir Analiz*. Istanbul: İletişim Yayınları, 2017.

Kızılyürek, Niyazi. 'Rauf Denktaş ve Kıbrıs Türk Milliyetçiliği.' In *Modern Türkiye'de Siyasi Düşünce 4: Milliyetçilik*, Kolektif, 335–44. Istanbul: İletişim Yayınevi, 2008.

Klein, Janet. 'Power in the Periphery: Hamidiye Light Cavalry and the Struggle Over Ottoman Kurdistan, 1890–1914.' PhD diss., Princeton University, 2002.

—. *The Margins of Empire: Kurdish Militias in the Ottoman Tribal Zone*. Stanford: Stanford University Press, 2011.

Koçak, Cemil. *Umumi Müfettişlikler (1927–1952)*. Istanbul: İletişim, 2003.

Kodaman, Bayram. *Sultan II. Abdülhamid Devri Doğu Anadolu Politikası*. Ankara: Türk Kültürünü Araştırma Enstitüsü, 1987.

Köker, Levent. 'Kemalizm/Atatürkçülük: Modernleşme Devlet ve Demokrasi.' In *Modern Türkiye'de Siyasi Düşünce Cilt 2 – Kemalizm*, edited by Ahmet İnsel, 97–112. Istanbul: Iletisim Yayincilik, 2009.

'Kontrgerilla Hizbullah Kılığında.' *Yeni Ülke*, 11 Ocak 1992.

Kowalewski, David. 'Counterinsurgent Vigilantism and Public Response: A Philippine Case Study.' *Sociological Perspectives* 34, no. 2 (1991): 127–44. http://www.jstor.org/stable/1388987.

'Köy Kanunu.' TBMM. 1924. http://www.mevzuat.gov.tr/MevzuatMetin/1.3.442. pdf.

'Kulp'u Asker İnceleyecek.' *Milliyet Gazetesi*, 24 December 2004.

Kundakçı, Hasan. *Güneydoğu'da Unutulmayanlar*. 4. baskı. Istanbul: Alfa Yayıncılık, 2004.

Kurban, Dilek, Deniz Yükseker, Ayşe Betül Çelik, Turgay Ünalan and A. Tamer Aker. *Coming to Terms with Forced Migration: Post-Displacement Restitution of Citizenship Rights in Turkey*. Istanbul: Tesev-Turkish Economic and Social Studies Foundation, 2007. http://tesev.org.tr/wp-content/uploads/2015/11/Coming_To_Terms_With_Forced_Migration_Post-Displacement_Restitution_Of_Citizenship_Rights_In_Turkey.pdf.

Kurban, Dilek, Deniz Yükseker, Ayşe Betül Çelik, Turgay Ünalan and A.Tamer Aker. *Zorunlu Göç Ile Yüzleşmek: Türkiye'de Yerinden Edilme Sonrası Vatandaşlığın İnşası*. Istanbul: TESEV, 2006.

Kurdish Human Rights Project: KHRP. *Turkey's Anti-Terror Laws: Threatening the Protection of Human Rights*. KHRP Briefing Paper 11 August. London: KHRP, 2008.

Kurt, Mehmet. *Din, Şiddet ve Aidiyet:Türkiye'de Hizbullah*. Istanbul: İletişim Yayıncılık, 2015.

Kurtcephe, İsrafil, and Mustafa Balcıoğlu. 'Birinci Dünya Savaşı Başlarında Romantik Bir Türk-Alman Projesi -Rauf Bey Müfrezesi-.' *OTAM (Ankara Üniversitesi Osmanlı Tarihi Araştırma ve Uygulama Merkezi Dergisi)*, no. 3 (1992): 247–69. http://dergiler.ankara.edu.tr/dergiler/19/835/10573.pdf.

'Kürtler Katledildi.' *Yeni Ülke*, 27 Haziran 1992.

Kutay, Cemal. *Beş Kıt'ada Bir Türk Paşası: Daniş Karabelen*. 2. baskı. Istanbul: Avcıol Basım Yayın, 2006.

'Laik Devlet Cihada Çağırıyor: Doğuda Dağıtılan Bildiri ve Afişler.' *İkibin'e Doğru* 1, no. 1 (10. Ocak 1987): 8–9.

Lessa, Francesca. 'Beyond Transitional Justice: Exploring Continuities in Human Rights Abuses in Argentina between 1976 and 2010.' *Journal of Human Rights Practice* 3, no. 1 (1 March 2011): 25–48.

'Mahkumiyet.' *Cumhuriyet Gazetesi*, 14 February 2004.

Malejacq, Romain. 'Pro-Government Militias.' *Oxford Bibliographies*, 2017. http://www.oxfordbibliographies.com/abstract/document/obo-9780199743292/obo-9780199743292-0213.xml?rskey=QUF8FZ&result=1&q=pro-government+militias#firstMatch.

Malmîsanij. *İlk Kürt Gazetesi Kurdıstan'ı Yayımlayan Abdurrahman Bedirhan, 1868–1936*. Araştırma Inceleme 5. Istanbul: Vate Yayınevi, 2009.

Mann, Michael. *Fascists*. Cambridge: Cambridge University Press, 2004.

—. 'The Autonomous Power of the State: Its Origins, Mechanisms and Results.' *European Journal of Sociology/Archives Européennes de Sociologie/Europäisches Archiv Für Soziologie* 25, no. 2 (1984): 185–213. http://www.jstor.org/stable/23999270.

—. *The Dark Side of Democracy: Explaining Ethnic Cleansing*. Cambridge: Cambridge University Press, 2005.

Mardin, Şerif. *Jön Türklerin Siyasi Fikirleri, 1895–1908*. 6. baskı. İst: İletişim Yayınları, 1999.

—. *The Genesis of Young Ottoman Thought: A Study in the Modernization of Turkish Political Ideas*. Princeton, NJ: Princeton University Press, 1962.

Mason, T. David, and Dale A. Krane. 'The Political Economy of Death Squads: Toward a Theory of the Impact of State-Sanctioned Terror.' *International Studies Quarterly* 33, no. 2 (1989): 175–98. http://www.jstor.org/stable/2600536.

Massicard, Elise. '"Gangs in Uniform" in Turkey: Politics at the Articulation between Security Institutions and the Criminal World.' In *Organized Crime and States: The Hidden Face of Politics*, by Jean-Louis Briquet, 41–71. Basingstoke: Palgrave Macmillan, 2010.

Mater, N. *Voices from the Front: Turkish Soldiers on the War with the Kurdish Guerrillas*. Basingstoke: Palgrave Macmillan, 2005.

Mazzei, Julie. *Death Squads or Self-Defense Forces?: How Paramilitary Groups Emerge and Challenge Democracy in Latin America*. Chapel Hill: University of North Carolina Press, 2009.

McDowall, David. *A Modern History of the Kurds*. London: I. B. Tauris, 2004.

'Mehmet Ağar: Devlete Doğmak ve Devletten Olmak.' *Toplum ve Kuram*, no. 6–7 (2012): 66–9.

Meşe, Ertuğrul. 'Türk Siyasal Yaşamında Komünizmle Mücadele Dernekleri.' Masters thesis, Selçuk Üniversitesi, 2013.

Morgenthau, Hans J. *Politics Among Nations: The Struggle for Power and Peace*. New York: Alfred A. Knopf, 1955.

Muller, Mark. 'Nationalism and the Rule of Law in Turkey: The Elimination of Kurdish Representation During the 1990s.' In *The Kurdish Nationalist Movement in the 1990s: Its Impact on Turkey and the Middle East*, edited by Robert W. Olson, 173–99. Lexington: University Press of Kentucky, 1996.

Murat İpek ve Murat Demir'in İtirafları. Interview by Şanar Yurdatapan. Istanbul, 1997.

NTV. '"Karakutu" Yine Ağzından Kaçırdı.' 23 September 2010. http://www.ntv.com.tr/turkiye/karakutu-yine-agzindan-kacirdi,3Q5dK4I350OStXhyyXNcJg.

Nur, Riza. *Mangal Yurekli Adam Topal Osman*. Istanbul: Orgun Yayınları, 2010.

'Öcalan: "Hizbullah", MHP'nin Kürdistanlılaştırılmış Biçimidir.' *Yeni Ülke*, Şubat 1993.

Öktem, Kerem. *Angry Nation: Turkey Since 1989*. London: Zed Books, 2011.

Okutan, M. Çağatay. *Bozkurt'tan Kuran'a Milli Türk Talebe Birliği (MTTB) 1916–1980*. Istanbul: İstanbul Bilgi Üniversitesi, 2004.

Olson, Robert W. *The Emergence of Kurdish Nationalism and the Sheikh Said Rebellion, 1880–1925*. 1st edn. Austin: University of Texas Press, 1989.

OMCT. 'Extrajudicial Killings.' Accessed 24 January 2023. https://www.omct.org/en/what-we-do/extrajudicial-killings.

Önder, Mehmet Seyman. *Devlet ve PKK İkileminde Korucular*. 1. baskı. Istanbul: İletişim Yayınları, 2015.

—. 'Geçici Köy Korucuları Üzerine Sosyolojik Bir Araştırma.' PhD diss., Fırat Üniversitesi, 2013.

Öndül, Hüsnü. 'Faili Meçhul Siyasal Cinayetler.' İnsan Hakları Derneği, 24 January 2000. http://www.ihd.org.tr/faili-mel-siyasal-cinayetler/.

—. 'İnsancıl Hukuka Giriş.' In *Her Zaman Yaşamak*, edited by Cennet Ayhan, 16–40. Ankara: SES Yayınları, 1998. http://www.ihd.org.tr/insancil-hukuka-g/.

Orak, Aydın. *Bir Başkaldırı Destanı: Cizreli Berivan* [documentary]. 2010. http://archive.org/details/CIZRELRBERVAN.

Örneklerle Türkiye İnsan Hakları Raporu 1991. Ankara: TİHV-Türkiye İnsan Hakları Vakfı, 1992.

'Özal'ın Ölümü İçin Araştırma Önergesi.' *Cumhuriyet Gazetesi*, 22 May 2002.

Özar, Şemsa, Nesrin Uçarlar, and Osman Aytar. *From Past to Present a Paramilitary Organization in Turkey: Village Guard System*. Diyarbakır: Disa Yayınları, 2013. http://disa.org.tr/pdf_media/SONKORUCULUKKTAPNG.pdf.

Özbay, Turan. *Eve Dönmeyeceğiz*. Istanbul: Manifesto, 2006.

Özcan, Ahmet. 'Son Kürt Eşkıyaları: Kürt Meselesinde "Adi" Şiddetin Olağanüstülüğü, =Siyasallığı ve Yasa Yapıcı Mirası.' In *Türkiye'de Siyasal Şiddetin Boyutları*, edited by Güney Çeğin and İbrahim Şirin, 165–206. Istanbul: İletişim Yayınları, 2014.

—. 'The Missing Link in the Chain of Oppression and Resistance: Last Era of Kurdish Banditry in Modern Turkey, 1950–1980.' PhD diss., Boğaziçi University, 2014.

Özdağ, Ümit. 'Faili Meçhuller.' Yüzyıl Türkiye Enstitüsü, 2013. https://stratejisite.files.wordpress.com/2015/10/faili-mehuller-tarihe-gre-sral-liste.pdf.

—. *Türkiye'de Düşük Yoğunluklu Çatışma ve PKK*. Ankara: Üç Ok Yayınları, 2005.

'Özel Time "Bozkurt" Referansı.' *Özgür Ülke*, September 1994.

Özgüden, Doğan. *File on Turkey, Democratic Resistance of Turkey*. France, 1972. http://www.info-turk.be/File%20on%20Turkey.pdf.

Özgür Açılım. *Unutturulanlar – 3 Maraş Katliamı*, 2011. https://www.youtube.com/watch?v=JZ7b9J-Q5jM.

Özkan, Tuncay. *MİT'in Gizli Tarihi*. 9. baskı. Istanbul: Alfa, 2003.

Özsoy, Hişyar. 'Between Gift and Taboo: Death and the Negotiation of National Identity and Sovereignty in the Kurdish Conflict in Turkey.' PhD diss., University of Texas at Austin, 2010.

Paker, Murat, and Burcu Buğu. 'Türkiye'de İşkence Mağdurlarının Psikolojisi Üzerine Yapılmış Araştırmaların Gözden Geçirilmesi.' *Türk Psikoloji Yazıları*, no. 19 [Özel Sayı] (Kasım 2016): 76–92.

Parlar, Suat. *Osmanlı'dan Günümüze Gizli Devlet*. 3rd edn. Istanbul: Mephisto, 2005.

Pekmezci, Necdet, and Nurşen Büyükyıldız. *Ülkücüler Öteki Devletin Şehitleri*. Istanbul: Kaynak Yayınları, 1999.

'PKK'yı 1 Yılda Kazırız.' *Milliyet Gazetesi*, 8 August 1993.

Polat, Göksel. 'Özel Time "Türk" Aranıyor.' *Cumhuriyet Gazetesi*, 3 November 1993.

Poyraz, Bedriye. 'Bellek, Hakikat, Yüzleşme ve Alevi Katliamları.' *Kültür ve İletişim* 16, no. 1 (2013): 9–39.

Rejali, Darius. *Torture and Democracy*. Princeton, NJ: Princeton University Press, 2009.

Reynolds, Michael A. 'What the Assassination of the Russian Ambassador May Be Telling Us About Erdoğan's Turkey.' *Foreign Policy Research Institute*. 23 December 2016. http://www.fpri.org/article/2016/12/assassination-russian-ambassador-may-telling-us-erdogans-turkey/.

Robben, Antonius C. G. M., and Jeffrey A. Sluka, eds. *Ethnographic Fieldwork: An Anthropological Reader*. 2nd edn. Chichester: Wiley-Blackwell, 2012.

Rogan, Eugene L., and Alişan Akpınar. *Aşiret Mektep Devlet Osmanlı Devleti'nde Aşiret Mektebi*. Istanbul: Aram Yayıncılık, 2001.

Ron, James. 'Territoriality and Plausible Deniability: Serbian Paramilitaries in the Bosnian War.' In *Death Squads in Global Perspective – Murder with Deniability*, edited by Bruce B. Campbell and Arthur D. Brenner, 287–312. Basingstoke: Palgrave Macmillan, 2002. //www.palgrave.com/us/book/9780312213657.

'"Rutin" Tartışma.' *Milliyet Gazetesi*. 15 February 2000.

Sabuktay, Ayşegül. 'Locating Susurluk Affair into the Context of Legal-Political Theory: A Case of Extra-Legal Activities of the Modern States.' PhD diss., Middle East Technical University, 2004.

Şahan, Timur, and Uğur Balık. *İtirafçı: Bir JİTEM'ci Anlattı . . .* Diyarbakır: Aram Yayınları, 2004.

Şahin Fırat, Bahar. 'Türkiye'de "Doksanlar": Devlet Şiddetinin Özgünlüğü ve Sürekliliği Üzerine Bir Deneme.' In *Türkiye'de Siyasal Şiddetin Boyutları*, by Güney Çeğin and İbrahim Şirin. Istanbul: İletişim Yayınları, 2014.

Sancar, Mithat. *'Devlet Aklı' Kıskacında Hukuk Devleti*. 4. baskı. Istanbul: İletişim, 2008.

Saraç, Necdet. 'Türkiye'deki Alevi Örgütlenmesi.' *Dersim News*, 22 July 2013. http://dersimnews.com/alevilik/alevileri-kim-temsil-ediyor.html.

Sarısaman, Sadık. 'Birinci Dünya Savaşı Sırasında Ihtiyat Kuvveti Olarak Kurulan Osmanlı Genç Dernekleri.' *OTAM (Ankara Üniversitesi Osmanlı Tarihi Araştırma ve Uygulama Merkezi Dergisi)*, no. 11 (2000): 439–501. http://dergipark.ulakbim.gov.tr/otam/article/view/5000085498/5000079585.

Sarkin, Jeremy, and Grażyna Baranowska. 'Why Enforced Disappearances are Perpetrated against Groups as State Policy: Overlaps and Interconnections between Disappearances and Genocide.' *Catholica Law Review*, 2018.

Şarlak, Zeynep. 'Atatürkçülükten Millî Güvenlik Rejimine: 1990'lar Türkiye'sine Bir Bakış.' In *Bir Zümre, Bir Parti: Türkiye'de Ordu*, edited by Ahmet İnsel and Ali Bayramoğlu, 283–93. Istanbul: Birikim Yayınları, 2004.

Şarman, Salih. *Rutin Dışı: Jitem-Kayıp Silahlar ve Harcanan Hayatlar*. Istanbul: Pozitif yayınları, 2007.

Savaş, Kutlu. *Susurluk Raporu*, 1997. https://tr.wikisource.org/wiki/Susurluk_Raporu_(Kutlu_Sava%C5%9F).

Şen, Serdar. *Türkiye'de Sıkıyönetimler: 1925–1980*. Propaganda Yayınları, 2016.

Şener, Cemal. *Topal Osman Olayı*. 10. baskı. Istanbul: Etik Yayınları, 2004.

Sevdiren, Öznur. 'The Recognition of Enforced Disappearance as a Crime Under Domestic Law and the Statute of Limitations: A Problematic of International Criminal Law.' In *Enforced Disappearances and the Conduct of the Judiciary*, edited by Gökçen Alpkaya, 66–107. Istanbul: Truth Justice Memory Center, 2014.

Sezgin, Enver. *Batman Bolşoy*. Istanbul: Vapur Yayınları, 2018.

Shaw, Stanford J., and Ezel Kural Shaw. *History of the Ottoman Empire and Modern Turkey*. Cambridge: Cambridge University Press, 2002.

Shultz, Richard H. 'The Low-Intensity Conflict Environment of the 1990s.' *Annals of the American Academy of Political and Social Science* 517 (1991): 120–34. http://www.jstor.org/stable/1047190.

Silopi, Zinar. *Doza Kürdistan. Kürt Milletini 60 Senden beri Esaretten Kurtuluş Savaşı Hatıratı*. Beirut: Stev Basımevi, 1969.

Sinclair-Webb, Emma. 'Sectarian Violence, the Alevi Minority and the Left: Kahramanmaraş 1978.' In *Turkey's Alevi Enigma: A Comprehensive Overview*, edited by Paul J. White and Joost Jongerden, 215–35. Leiden: Brill, 2003.

Sirmen, Ali. 'Teritoryal Tartışması.' *Cumhuriyet Gazetesi*, 13 November 1988.

'Sivil Orduya İsviçre Modeli.' *Milliyet Gazetesi*, 11 April 1988.

Smith, M. L. R. 'Guerrillas in the Mist: Reassessing Strategy and Low Intensity Warfare.' *Review of International Studies* 29, no. 1 (January 2003): 19–37. https://www.cambridge.org/core/journals/review-of-international-studies/article/guerrillas-in-the-mist-reassessing-strategy-and-low-intensity-warfare/E0D4B-B64883E51A05699498BBBF586B2.

Söyler, Mehtap. 'Informal Institutions, Forms of State and Democracy: The Turkish Deep State.' *Democratization* 20, no. 2 (2013): 310–34. http://dx.doi.org/10.10 80/13510347.2011.650915.

—. *The Turkish Deep State: State Consolidation, Civil–Military Relations and Democracy*. Abingdon: Routledge, 2015.

Sunkar, Murat, and Sadettin Tonbul. 'Batman Şehrinin Kuruluş ve Gelişmesi.' *Coğrafya Dergisi*, no. 21 (2010): 18–38. http://www.journals.istanbul.edu.tr/iucografya/article/view/1023010522.

Süphandağ, Kemal. *Hamidiye Alayları Ağrı Kürt Direnişi ve Zilan Katliamı*. İstanbul: Pêrî Yayınları, 2012.

Şur, Tuncay. 'Mehmet Sincar Cinayeti ve DEP'in Legal Siyasete Dâhil Olma Çabası: Anaakım Basın Üzerinden Bir İnceleme.' *Kültür ve İletişim* 19, no. 38 (2016): 42–63.

Tansu, Samih Nafiz. *Teşkilat-ı Mahsusa İki Devrin Perde Arkası*. İstanbul: Nokta Kitap, 2012.

'Tansu Çiller'den Özel Time: Ben Sizin Ananızım.' *Cumhuriyet Gazetesi*, 28 December 1996.

TBMM. *TBMM Darbe ve Muhtıraları Araştırma Komisyonu Raporu*. Ankara: Türkiye Büyük Millet Meclisi, 2012. https://www.tbmm.gov.tr/arastirma_komisyonlari/darbe_muhtira/.

TBMM. *TBMM Meclis Araştırma Komisyonu Başkanlığı*. T. C. Başbakanlık Milli İstihbarat Teşkilatı Müsteşarlığı, 25 December 2012.

TBMM. *TBMM Susurluk Komisyonu Raporu*. Ankara, 3 April 1997. https://www.tbmm.gov.tr/sirasayi/donem20/yil01/ss301.pdf.

TBMM. *Ülkemizin Çeşitli Yörelerinde İşlenmiş Faili Meçhul Siyasal Cinayetler Konusunda Meclis Araştırma Komisyonu*. Ankara: TBMM, 1995.

TBMM Göç Araştırma Raporu. Ankara: TBMM, 1998.

TBMM İnsan Haklarını İnceleme Komisyonu. *Terör ve Şiddet Olayları Kapsamında Yaşam Hakkı İhlallerini İnceleme Raporu*. Ankara: TBMM, 2013.

T. C. Başbakanlık MIT Müsteşarlığının Banker Bako Raporudur. Ankara, 1987.

Temel, Celal. *1984'ten Önceki 25 Yılda Kürtlerin Silahsız Mücadelesi*. 1. baskı. İstanbul: İsmail Beşikci Vakfı Yayınları, 2015.

'Temizöz ve Diğerleri Davası – İddiname' (indictment) [court documents], No. 2009/906-1040-972, https://www.failibelli.org/dava/temizoz-davasi/.

'Teröre Yeni Tanım.' *Cumhuriyet Gazetesi.* 13 April 1991.

'Terörle Mücadele Kanunu.' *T.C. Cumhurbaşkanlığı Resmi Gazete,* 12 April 1991. http://www.resmigazete.gov.tr/.

Thompson, Paul. *Voice of the Past: Oral History.* Oxford: Oxford University Press, 2000.

TİHV. 'Curfews Between August 16, 2015 – August 16, 2016 and Civilians Who Lost Their Lives.' TİHV Ankara. 21 August 2016. http://en.tihv.org.tr/curfews-between-august-16-2015-august-16-2016-and-civilians-who-lost-their-lives/.

TİHV-HRFT. 'Curfews Between August 16, 2015 – August 16, 2016 and Civilians Who Lost Their Lives According to the Data of Human Rights Foundation of Turkey Documentation Center.' TİHV, 21 August 2016. https://en.tihv.org.tr/curfews/16-august-2015-16-august-2016-fact-sheet/.

Toprak, Zafer. '1934 Trakya Olaylarında Hükümetin ve CHF'nin Sorumluluğu.' *Toplumsal Tarih* 34 (1996): 19–25. http://www.academia.edu/20797197/1934_Trakya_Olaylar%C4%B1nda_H%C3%BCk%C3%BCmetin_ve_CHF_nin_Sorumlulu%C4%9Fu.

—. 'İttihat ve Terakki'nin Paramiliter Gençlik Örgütleri.' *Boğaziçi Üniversitesi Dergisi: Hümaniter Bilimler* VII (1979): 95–114. http://www.dlir.org/archive/archive/files/bogazici_1979_vol-7_p95-114_a1c0c28906.pdf.

Tümerkan, Mete. *Emekli Albay'dan Şok Açıklamalar!* 21 January 2013. http://haberkibris.com/emekli-albaydan-sok-aciklamalar-2013-01-21.html.

Tunander, Ola. 'Democratic State vs. Deep State: Approaching the Dual State of the West.' In *Government of the Shadows: Parapolitics and Criminal Sovereignty,* edited by Eric Wilson and Tim Lindsey, 56–72. London: Pluto Press, 2009.

Tunaya, Tarık Zafer. *Türkiyede Siyasi Partiler: 1859–1952.* Vol. 1. 2nd edn. Istanbul: Hürriyet Vakfı Yayınları, 1988.

Tunçay, Mete. *Türkiye Cumhuriyeti'nde Tek-Parti Yönetimi'nin Kurulması (1923–1931).* Ankara: Tarih Vakfı Yurt Yayınları, 1999.

Türkiye Büyük Millet Meclisi 18. Dönem Tutanak Dergisi. TBMM, 23 May 1990.

Türkiye Göç ve Yerinden Olmuş Nüfus Araştırması. Ankara: Hacettepe Üniversitesi Nüfus Etütleri Enstitüsü, 2006. http://www.hips.hacettepe.edu.tr/TGYONA-AnaRapor.pdf.

Türkiye İnsan Hakları Raporu 1991. Ankara: TİHV-Türkiye İnsan Hakları Vakfı, 1992.

Türkiye İnsan Hakları Raporu 1992. Ankara: TİHV-Türkiye İnsan Hakları Vakfı, 1993.

Türkiye İnsan Hakları Raporu 1993. Ankara: THİV-Türkiye İnsan Hakları Vakfı, 1994.

Türkiye İnsan Hakları Raporu 1993. Ankara: TİHV-Türkiye İnsan Hakları Vakfı, 1994.

Türkiye İnsan Hakları Raporu 1994. Ankara: TİHV-Türkiye İnsan Hakları Vakfı, 1995.

Türkiye İnsan Hakları Raporu 1995. Ankara: TİHV-Türkiye İnsan Hakları Vakfı, 1997.

Türkiye İnsan Hakları Raporu 1996. Ankara: TİHV-Türkiye İnsan Hakları Vakfı, 1998.

Türkiye İnsan Hakları Raporu 1997. Ankara: TİHV-Türkiye İnsan Hakları Vakfı, 1999.

Türkiye İnsan Hakları Raporu 1998. Ankara: TİHV-Türkiye İnsan Hakları Vakfı, 2000.

Türkiye İnsan Hakları Raporu 1999. Ankara: TİHV-Türkiye İnsan Hakları Vakfı, 2002.

Türkiye İnsan Hakları Raporu 2000. Ankara: TİHV-Türkiye İnsan Hakları Vakfı, 2003.

Türkiye'de Toplu Mezarlar Raporu. Diyarbakır: İnsan Hakları Derneği Diyarbakır Şubesi, 2014.

Türkmen, Emir Ali, and Abdurrahman Özmen, eds. *Kürdistan Sosyalist Solu Kitabı.* Ankara: Dipnot Yayınları, 2013.

Tüysüz, Nur. 'Geçici Köy Koruculuğu Sisteminin Toplumda Yarattığı Dönüşüm ve Korucu Olmanın Kişisel Gerekçelendirmeleri.' *Toplum ve Kuram*, no. 9 (2014): 177–201.

Uğraş, Nejat. 'Unutulan Bir Özyönetim Deneyimi: Batman ve Edip Solmaz (1979).' *Gazete Karınca.* 15 November 2017. http://gazetekarinca.com/2017/11/unutulan-bir-ozyonetim-deneyimi-batman-ve-edip-solmaz-1979/.

Ülker, Erol. 'İşgal İstanbul'unda Müdafaa-i Milliye'nin Kuruluşu Üzerine Bir Değerlendirme: İttihatçılar, Komünistler, Sosyalistler' [An Assessment on the Establishment of the Committee of National Defense in Istanbul under Occupation: Unionists, Communists, Socialists]. *Kebikeç İnsan Bilimleri İçin Kaynak Araştırmaları Dergisi*, no. 41 (January 2016): 67–94.

Ülkücü Komando Kampları: AP Hükümetinin 1970'te Hazırlattığı MHP Raporu. Istanbul: Kaynak Yayınları, 1997.

Ulugana, Sedat. *Ağrı Kürt Direnişi ve Zilan Katliamı (1926–1931).* 2. baskı. Istanbul: Pêrî Yayınları, 2010.

Üngör, Uğur Ümit. *Paramilitarism: Mass Violence in the Shadow of the State.* Oxford: Oxford University Press, 2019.

—. 'Paramilitary Violence in the Collapsing Ottoman Empire.' In *War in Peace: Paramilitary Violence in Europe After the Great War*, edited by Robert Gerwarth and John Horne, 164–83. Oxford: Oxford University Press, 2013.

—. 'Rethinking the Violence of Pacification: State Formation and Bandits in Turkey, 1914–1937.' *Comparative Studies in Society and History* 54, no. 4 (October 2012): 746–69. https://www.cambridge.org/core/journals/comparative-studies-in-society-and-history/article/rethinking-the-violence-of-pacification-

state-formation-and-bandits-in-turkey-19141937/38B23A7C7236DD501EE4
677322076DBD.

—. *The Making of Modern Turkey: Nation and State in Eastern Anatolia, 1913–1950*.
Oxford: Oxford University Press, 2011.

Üngör, Ugur Ümit, and Mehmet Polatel. *Confiscation and Destruction: The Young
Turk Seizure of Armenian Property*. London: Continuum, 2011.

United Nations. *International Convention for the Protection of All Persons from Enforced
Disappearance*. Geneva: United Nations Human Rights Office of the High Commissioner, 1992. https://www.ohchr.org/EN/HRBodies/CED/Pages/Conven-
tionCED.aspx.

—. *Report on the Human Rights Situation in South-East Turkey: July 2015 to December 2016*. Geneva: Office of the United Nations High Commissioner for Human
Rights, February 2017.

Ünlü, Barış. 'Türklüğün Kısa Tarihi.' *Birikim Dergisi*, no. 274 (2012): 23–34.

—. *Türklük Sözleşmesi: Oluşumu, İşleyişi ve Krizi*. 2. baskı. Ankara: Dipnot Yayınları,
2018.

Ünver, Akın. 'Turkey's "Deep-State" and the Ergenekon Conundrum.' *Middle East
Institute*, 2009. Accessed 14 April 2015. http://www.mei.edu/content/turkeys-
deep-state-and-ergenekon-conundrum.

Ünver, Hamid Akin. *Turkey's Kurdish Question: Discourse & Politics Since 1990*.
Abingdon: Routledge, 2015.

Üskül, Zafer. 'Olağanüstü Hal Türkiye'nin Yazgısı Mı?' *Cumhuriyet Gazetesi*, 19 July 1992.

—. *Siyaset ve Asker*. Ankara: Imge Kitabevi, 1998.

Üstündağ, Nazan. *Dealing With the Past: Argentinean Experience*. Istanbul: Anadolu
Kültür-Truth, Justice and Memory Studies, 2011. https://hakikatadalethafiza.
org/wp-content/uploads/2015/02/ARG_Report_EN.pdf.

Uysal, Ayşen, ed. *İsyan, Şiddet, Yas: 90'lar Türkiyesine Bakmak*. Ankara: Dipnot
Yayınları, 2016.

Uzgel, İlhan. 'Ordu Dış Politikanın Neresinde?' In *Bir Zümre, Bir Parti: Türkiye'de
Ordu*, edited by Ahmet Insel, Ali Bayramoğlu and Ömer Laciner, 2. baskı,
311–34. Istanbul: Birikim Yayınları, 2004.

Valentino, Benjamin, Paul Huth and Dylan Balch-Lindsay. '"Draining the Sea": Mass
Killing and Guerrilla Warfare.' *International Organization* 58, no. 2 (2004):
375–407. http://www.jstor.org/stable/3877862.

Vanderlippe, John M. *The Politics of Turkish Democracy: Ismet Inonu and the Formation of the Multi-Party System, 1938–1950*. Albany: State University of New York
Press, 2006.

Vermeulen, Marthe Lot. *Enforced Disappearance: Determining State Responsibility under the International Convention for the Protection of All Persons from Enforced Disappearance.* Cambridge: Intersentia, 2012.

Warren, Kay B. 'Death Squads and Wider Complicities: Dilemmas for the Anthropology of Violence.' In *Death Squad: The Anthropology of State Terror*, edited by Jeffrey A. Sluka. Philadelphia: University of Pennsylvania Press, 2000.

Wolpin, Miles D. *State Terrorism and Death Squads in the New World Order.* Dundas: Peace Research Institute-Dundas, 1992. https://search.library.wisc.edu/catalog/999715854402121.

Yalçın, Nilüfer. 'Sivil Orduya Asker Komutan.' *Milliyet Gazetesi*, 11 May 1988.

Yalçın, Soner. *Behçet Cantürk'ün Anıları.* 7. baskı. Istanbul: Su Yayınları, 2000.

—. *Behçet Cantürk'ün Anıları – Beco.* 7. baskı. Istanbul: Su Yayınları, 2000.

—. *Binbaşı Ersever'in İtirafları.* 8. baskı. Istanbul: Kaynak Yayınları, 1994.

Yalçın, Soner, and Doğan Yurdakul. *Reis: Gladio'nun Türk Tetikçisi.* 25. baskı. Istanbul: Doğan Kitap, 2004.

Yamak, Kemal. *Gölgede Kalan İzler ve Gölgeleşen Bizler.* Istanbul: Doğan Kitap, 2009.

Yamak, Sanem. 'II. Meşrutiyet Döneminde Paramiliter Gençlik Örgütleri.' PhD diss., İstanbul Üniversitesi, 2009.

Yaprak Yıldız, Yeşim. '(Dis)Avowal of State Violence: Public Confessions of Perpetrators of State Violence Against Kurds in Turkey.' PhD diss., University of Cambridge, 2018.

Yarkın, Güllistan. 'İnkâr Edilen Hakikat: Sömürge Kuzey Kürdistan.' *Kürt Araştırmaları*, no. 1 (2019): 45–69.

Yasadışı Örgütlerin Devletle Olan Bağlantıları İle Susurluk'ta Meydana Gelen Kaza Olayının ve Arkasındaki İlişkilerin Aydınlığa Kavuşturulması Amacı İle Kurulan Meclis Araştırması Komisyonu (10/89, 110, 124, 125, 126) Tutanakları. Ankara: TBMM Basımevi, 1998.

Yavuz Ertürk (Kulp) Davası. Accessed 4 April 2017. https://www.failibelli.org/pec-events/yavuz-erturk-kulp-davasi-7/.

Yazıcı, Vasfi Can. 'Anti-Communism and the Making of Ülkücü Paramilitary Identity, 1974–1980.' Masters thesis, Boğaziçi University, 2012.

Yeğen, Mesut. 'The Kurdish Question in Turkish State Discourse.' *Journal of Contemporary History* 34, no. 4 (1999): 555–68. https://www.jstor.org/stable/261251.

—. 'Türkiye Solu ve Kürt Sorunu.' In *Modern Türkiye'de Siyasi Düşünce*, 2. baskı, 1208–36. Sol. Istanbul: İletişim Yayınları, 2008.

Yerasimos, Stefanos. *Milliyetler ve Sınırlar: Balkanlar, Kafkasya ve Orta-Doğu.* Translated by Tekeli Şirin. 6. baskı. Istanbul: İletişim, 2010.

Yıldız, Kerim. *Ülke İçinde Göç Ettirilen İnsanlar: Türkiye'de Kürtler.* Translated by Emin Soğancı. London: KHRP, Haziran 2002. file:///Users/ayhanisik/Downloads/ulkeincinde.pdf.

Yıldız, Vedat and Jihat Akşa, 'Ailesi, Çiçek Botan'ı anlattı.' *Yeni Özgür Politika.* 28 October 2011. http://www.yeniozgurpolitika.com/index.php?rupel=nuce&id=3212.

Yılmaz, Ali. *Karanlık Vardiya 90'lı Yılların Politik Arşivi.* Istanbul: Doğan Kitap, 2015.

Yurteri, Kemal. 'Polis Olmak İsteyen MHP'ye Başvuruyor.' *Cumhuriyet Gazetesi*, 21 September 1994.

Zayas, Alfred de. 'The Istanbul Pogrom of 6–7 September 1955 in the Light of International Law.' *Genocide Studies and Prevention: An International Journal* 2, no. 2 (1 August 2007): 137–54. http://scholarcommons.usf.edu/gsp/vol2/iss2/4.

Zorla Kaybedilenler, Faili Meçhul Cinayet-Yargısız İnfazlar, Toplu Mezarlar Raporu. Diyarbakır: İnsan Hakları Derneği, 2014.

Zürcher, Erik Jan. *Milli Mücadelede Ittihatçılık.* Translated by Nüzhet Salihoğlu. 1. baskı. İnceleme-Araştırma 3. Istanbul: Bağlam, 1987.

—. *Turkey A Modern History.* 3rd edn. London: I. B. Tauris, 2004.

INDEX

EU representative:
Easy Access System Europe
Mustamäe tee 50, 10621 Tallinn, Estonia
Gpsr.requests@easproject.com

www.ingramcontent.com/pod-product-compliance
Lightning Source LLC
Chambersburg PA
CBHW050646270326
41927CB00012B/2899

9 781399 505994